MAJOR PERCY BLACK, D.S.O., D.C.M. (F.).

DEDICATED TO THE MEMORY OF PERCY BLACK AND THOSE OTHER
GALLANT MEN OF THE 16TH BATTALION, A.I.F., WHO
GAVE THEIR LIVES FOR AUSTRALIA, 1914–1918.

THE OLD SIXTEENTH
BEING A RECORD OF THE 16TH BATTALION, A.I.F, DURING THE GREAT WAR, 1914-1918

By

CAPTAIN C. LONGMORE, (F.)
(AUTHOR OF "EGGS-A-COOK!")

WITH FOREWORD BY
LIEUTENANT-GENERAL SIR JOHN MONASH,
G.C.M.G., K.C.B., V.D.

The Naval & Military Press Ltd

Published by
The Naval & Military Press Ltd
5 Riverside, Brambleside, Bellbrook
Industrial Estate, Uckfield, East Sussex,
TN22 1QQ England
Tel: +44 (0) 1825 749494
Fax: +44 (0) 1825 765701
www.naval-military-press.com
www.military-genealogy.com
www.militarymaproom.com

In reprinting in facsimile from the original, any imperfections are inevitably reproduced and the quality may fall short of modern type and cartographic standards.

16th BATTALION, A.I.F.

BATTLE HONOURS.

LANDING AT ANZAC.

SARI BAIR.

POZIERES.

BULLECOURT.

MESSINES, 1917.

YPRES, 1917.

POLYGON WOOD.

HAMEL.

AMIENS.

HINDENBURG LINE.

CONTENTS.

	Page
Foreword	vii
Author's Note	ix
Introduction	1
Chapter 1.—Formation	7
,, 2.—Blackboy Hill	12
,, 3.—Broadmeadows	14
,, 4.—The Voyage	18
,, 5.—The " Honk "	22
,, 6.—Egypt	29
,, 7.—Lemnos	34
,, 8.—The Landing	39
,, 9.—The Bloody Angle	46
,, 10.—Reorganisation	50
,, 11.—" Quinn's ! "	54
,, 12.—The Turkish Offensives	61
,, 13.—Behind the Front	66
,, 14.—" 971 "	71
,, 15.—The Outposts	78
,, 16.—A Change of Scene	85
,, 17.—The Evacuation	89
,, 18.—Touring Egypt	102
,, 19.—" Somewhere in France "	111
,, 20.—Pozieres	115
,, 21.—Holding the Line	121
,, 22.—The German Retreat	131
,, 23.—Bullecourt	133
,, 24.—Messines	143
,, 25.—Paschendaele	148
,, 26.—Flanders Again	161
,, 27.—" Backs to the Wall "	166
,, 28.—Hamel	178
,, 29.—The Break Through	186
,, 30.—" The Super V.C."	190
,, 31.—The Last Fight	194
,, 32.—The Armistice	197
Prisoners of War Fund	201
Decorations Won	202
Battalion Casualties (Table)	207
A.I.F. Infantry Casualties (Table)	208
Officers' Casualties	211
Officers Captured by Enemy	212
Engagements and Casualties	213
Officers Promoted from Ranks	213
Athletic Cups Won by 16th	214
Nominal Roll	215

MAPS.

	Page
Lemnos, Imbros, Tenedos and the Dardanelles	36
Anzac Position on May 5, 1915	55
Attack on Hill 971	71
North of Anzac, August 7, 1915	74
Anzac-Suvla Position, August 12, 1915	78

ILLUSTRATIONS.

Major Percy Black, D.S.O., D.C.M., (F.)	Frontispiece

	Page
Lieut.-Col. H. Murray, V.C., C.M.G., D.S.O. (and bar), D.C.M., (F.) ...	2
Lieut-Col. H. Pope, C.B.	3
Lieut.-Col. E. L. Margolin, D.S.O.	5
Machine Gun Section, Blackboy Hill, 1914	9
Original Officers at Broadmeadows, 1914	15
Brigade Champions, 1914	16
Marching Through Streets, Melbourne, 1914	18
A Ceramic Souvenir	19
The Camp at Heliopolis	30
Pope's Hill	40
Lieut.-Col. L. E. Tilney, D.S.O.	43
The Trench at Quinn's	56
A Gallipoli Roll Call	58
Quinn's Post	59
The Armistice, May 24, 1915	64
A Summer Residence, Gallipoli	69
Private A. Carlson and a Souvenir	75
The Firing Line, Gallipoli, August, 1915	84

ILLUSTRATIONS—continued.

	Page
A Picquet at Lemnos, September, 1915	86
16th at Mudros, October, 1915	87
Sikh's Post, Gallipoli	90
Sandbag Trenches on Canal	108
Sergt. M. O'Meara, V.C.	113
Mouquet Farm—Pre-war	116
Mouquet Farm—As the 16th Knew It	118
A "Jack Johnson"	122
Switch Trench, 1916	126
The Road to Flers	127
Gird Trench, 1916	128
Group at 7th Brigade Headquarters, March, 1917	129
Bullecourt—From Road near Norcuil	134
A Party of Reinforcements	141
A Railway Line in France. 1917	143
The Men with Moving Jobs	148
A Platoon on its Way to the Line	149
Wounded on Menin Road	150
The Battalion "Baby"	151
Derelict Tanks near Zonnebeke	153
Three Sixteenth Officers	154
Zonnebeke!	155
Lieut. J. B. Minchin, D.S.O., M.C.	157
Captain W. J. Lynas, D.S.O., M.C.	169
A Bridge Across the Somme, 1918	173
Billets "Somewhere in France," 1918	174
Sergt. H. Axford and Corpl. T. L. Axford, V.C., M.M.	182
Lieut. L. D. McCarthy, V.C., (F.)	191

FOREWORD.

By Lieutenant-General Sir John Monash, G.C.M.G., K.C.B.,
V.D., D.C.L., L.L.D.

Although it fell to my lot, during the last year of the Great War, to assume the leadership of the whole of the Australian field army on the Western Front, and it therefore became my duty to make contact with upwards of three hundred separate units of the A.I.F., yet I was never able to divest myself of that close interest in and affection for the four battalions of the Fourth Australian Brigade which I had the honour to organise in the early days of the great conflict, and to command until the summer of 1916.

Of these battalions, the Sixteenth, recruited in Western and South Australia, shared with its comrade units of that brigade, for a period of nearly two years, my intimate comradeship, my daily and continuous responsibility, my acquaintance with their inner life and spirit, and my admiration for their devotion to duty and their battle prowess.

I esteem it an honour, therefore, to be accorded the privilege of penning these lines to commend to the reader this story of the Sixteenth Battalion, a story which fills a glorious page in the history of Australia, and which goes to the making of a great tradition. In the A.I.F. there was no ideal so lofty, no motive so potent as loyalty to the unit; and it was within the unit that bonds of comradeship were forged which no lapse of time can sunder, and in no unit was this spirit stronger than in the Sixteenth Battalion.

The Fourth Brigade, of which it formed a part, unconscious of its great destiny, entered upon methodical war training, first at Broadmeadows, in Victoria, and, later, on the sands of Egypt. Although not privileged to sail with the first convoy of Australian troops, it aspired to rank, as an equal, beside its three senior infantry brigades in all that the fortune of war might bring. It was not disappointed. By intense concentration upon the work of war training, the brigade was deemed fit to participate in that great adventure of the Gallipoli Landing. In the hectic days that followed the landing, the Fourth Brigade held the key position on the Peninsula, and valiantly defended it against many imperious assaults. It led the advance to Sari Bair of August, 1915, and it had the distinction of being the only Australian brigade which gained extensive ground during the Dardanelles campaign. Its subsequent services—in the defence of the Canal zone in Egypt; on the Sinai desert; in its successful occupation and active defence of the Armentières sector in France; in the first battle of the Somme; at Pozieres; at Bullecourt; at the operations of Messines and of Paschendaele; at the defence of Hebuterne; in the great victories of Hamel, Amiens and Hargicourt—are 'one long record of glorious and successful endeavour. No other infantry brigade of the A.I.F. dare challenge the reputation of the Fourth for its first rank soldierly prowess and performance, or for its brilliant record of battle honours.

The Sixteenth Battalion, which ranked second to none of the component units of this wonderful fighting force, was maintained, during four years of war, by reinforcements drawn from the areas of its first enlistment, to the number of several times its original complement. It bore, throughout its history, its full share of the labours, the hardships, the sacrifices, the fighting record and the honours which made up the story of the Fourth Brigade.

It is right and proper that the tale of this famous battalion should be written for posterity, and the tradition which it did so much to create will surely be an inspiration to the youth of Australia in all the days to come.

July 19, 1929.

AUTHOR'S NOTE.

I desire to acknowledge with thanks the help given me in the compilation of this record by Mr. R. C. Yeldon, the first secretary of the 16th Battalion History Committee, whose energy and resource were mainly instrumental in the work being commenced; Lieut. Vic. Ketterer, M.C., the present secretary, for much information and general assistance; Lieut.-Col. E. L. Margolin, D.S.O., for documents, information, and, particularly, the enthusiasm with which he entered into the project; Mr. C. P. Smith, managing editor of the "West Australian," for editing the manuscript and invaluable technical help; Colonel H. B. Collett, C.M.G., for statistical information and advice; Colonel H. Pope, C.B., for the loan of his splendid collection of records and photographs; Mr. Chas. Taylor, deputy commissioner for repatriation, for his kindly co-öperation at all times; Brigadier-General C. H. Brand, C.B., C.M.G., and Brigadier-General C. H. Jess, C.M.G., for perusing the proofs and checking facts; and to the Trustees of the Perth Public Library for the use of the 4th Brigade War Diaries. I referred extensively to Vols. 1 and 2 of the "Story of Anzac," by Captain C. E. W. Bean, and "Australian Victories in France," by Lieut.-Gen. Sir John Monash, G.C.M.G., and am indebted to them for a great deal of the data contained in this book. Lieut.-Cols. W. O. Mansbridge, D.S.O., and E. W. Parks, D.S.O., M.C.; Captains W. Lynas, D.S.O., M.C., R. T. Goldie and H. J. Sykes, and Messrs. Newick, J. Parker, C. Martin, J. Cutmore, H. S. Day, and G. L. Curlewis forwarded me documents and material which were useful. I trust that they will not be disappointed with the result of their co-operation as expressed in the following pages.

I would like to add that several attempts were made to obtain personal details relating to comrades in South Australia, unfortunately with very little success. Due publicity in both States was given by the History Committee to the fact that the history was being written and requests were made for 16th men to forward matter of interest. If this book is not as complete as it might be the fault does not lie with those who responded to the call.

C. LONGMORE.

May 4, 1929.

Brigadier-General E. Drake-Brockman, C.B., C.M.G., D.S.O., etc.,

who commanded the Battalion during the whole of its distinguished career in France, and who has obtained for the Unit more Decorations and Distinctions than any other Commander in the A.I.F.

THE OLD SIXTEENTH.

INTRODUCTION.

The deeds of many units of the A.I.F. have been immortalised by publication in book form. There are others whose exploits will be forgotten with the passing of their own generation. The trials and tribulations which were gone through with flying colours, the magnificent feats of arms which were achieved, and the glorious sacrifices which Australia's soldiers made in the cause of freedom deserve to be recorded accurately for future generations. For there can be no question that the Australian soldiers proved themselves worthy of the stock from which they sprung. As a nation Australia was practically unknown until that epic adventure of April, 1915, when her troops stormed the broken heights of Gallipoli. It was "The Landing" that proved to an astonished world that the untried men from "down under" were a force which had to be reckoned with in the stormy years to come. And Australia's representatives, during the following three and a-half years of continuous fighting on various fronts and under widely differing conditions of service, further enhanced the reputation which had been gained on April 25, 1915.

The 16th Battalion played a proud part in establishing and maintaining the reputation of the Australian Corps. On Gallipoli and in France and Belgium, for three years and a-half, the battalion was in action almost incessantly. Few other units in the British Army were so strenuously engaged or took part in so many separate engagements as the famous 4th Brigade, A.I.F.—and the 16th Battalion was part of the 4th Brigade throughout its career.

There is little that is glorious about war excepting individual examples of heroic endurance and courage. In this regard the 16th Battalion produced more than its share of super-men. The cold and official accounts of their personal records read almost like the improbable and impossible—the truth that is stranger than fiction. Men with no previous military training, they rose to the occasion and performed prodigies of valour and endurance that were in keeping with the very highest traditions of the British race. And these outstanding men came from no privileged class in the community of Western Australia. Military opportunity, when it came, was just as readily seized by the unskilled worker of civil life as by the man with the University degree.

Percy Black was one of these super-men. He was a miner and prospector at Southern Cross when he enlisted in the 16th.

With no previous experience of the profession of arms he brought with him into the army a wide knowledge of men and the initiative and energy which are always parts of the personal equipment of the pioneer. A lance-corporal in the machine-gun section when he left Australia, he was a rock to lean upon in those stirring first-days on Gallipoli. Mentioned in despatches at The Landing, wounded twice (without leaving his post), he was awarded the Distinguished Conduct Medal and promoted to a commission. At the Evacuation he was a captain and one of the last men to leave Gallipoli. In France he received his majority, a D.S.O. at Mouquet Farm, and a Croix de Guerre. When he fell across the German

LIEUT.-COL. H. MURRAY, V.C., C.M.G., D.S.O. AND BAR, D.C.M. (F.).

wire at Bullecourt in April, 1917, there was a wide-spread feeling of sorrow throughout the whole of the A.I.F. that was not often shown for any individual in those days when casualties were so numerous. Percy Black, after Bullecourt, was only an A.I.F. memory—but what a glorious memory!

Harry Murray was a timber-getter from the south-west of Western Australia when he joined the 16th at Blackboy Hill. He was in the machine-gun section with Percy Black, and distinguished

LIEUT.-COL. H. POPE, C.B.,
Original C.O. of the 16th Battalion.

himself during The Landing operations. Wounded twice, he was awarded the D.C.M. and a commission. He was then transferred to the 13th Battalion—and so goes out of the picture of the 16th. However, it is interesting to follow his later career. Promoted captain, he received in France a D.S.O. and bar and two more wounds. Hair-raising exploits brought him a Croix de Guerre, and then the V.C. Wounded again, he was promoted to major and later, when appointed to command the 4th M.G. Battalion, he was given the rank of Lieutenant-Colonel. His work in that capacity in the last 60 days of the war brought him the C.M.G. To Murray belongs the honour of rising within three and a-half years from a machine-gun private to the command of a M.G. battalion of 64 guns, and of receiving in the process more fighting decorations than any other infantry soldier in the British Army in the Great War—rewards and decorations every one of them richly deserved.

"Bill" Lynas when he enlisted was posted to the Signal Section of the 16th. He did splendid work on Gallipoli in the days when the signaller's job was one that incurred as many (if not more) chances of death than that of the purely fighting soldier. After the Evacuation he was granted a commission, and in France he was appointed Scout Officer for the battalion. In that capacity he was never happier than when he was out in No Man's Land patrolling along the enemy wire in search of scalps. While attached in England to a training battalion he heard of the Bullecourt disaster, and took "French" leave in order to rejoin the battalion in the line. It required considerable effort on the part of his C.O. and of General Brand to save Lynas from a courtmartial for being absent without leave from his training camp in England! As a captain and company commander, "Bill" Lynas was ever an inspiration to his men, and in the final stages of the war he commanded the battalion. This wonderful soldier and leader of men was popular with all who soldiered with him, and his services were rewarded by a D.S.O., M.C., and two bars.

E. L. Margolin, better known as "Margie," was a manufacturer at Collie and a lieutenant in the Citizen Forces when he was ap pointed to the 16th. He went through all the stirring operations on Gallipoli and for some time, as a major, commanded the battalion. He was born in central Russia in 1875, and when 17 years old left with his parents for Palestine, where he engaged in vineyard and orchard work. On the death of his parents he came to Australia in 1901, arriving without a knowledge of the English language. As a navvy and a teamster he sampled hard work, but drifted into business. With the 16th "Margie" served right through Gallipoli, and commanded the battalion at the Evacuation. On the voyage to France he was second in command to Lt.-Col. E. A. Drake-Brockman,

LIEUT.-COL. E. L. MARGOLIN, D.S.O.

and fought in most of the unit's engagements up to its first entry into the Paschendaele fighting, when the dislocation of a cartilage caused his evacuation to England. Operated on, he was officially declared P.U.G.S. (permanently unfit general service). Under private medical men, however, he recovered, and was found fit again for active service. Then he transferred to the Imperial Army, and was appointed to command the 39th Royal Fusiliers (Jewish). With that unit he took part in the last phase of the Palestine campaign. On the conclusion of the war he was engaged by the Palestine Government for the formation of the Palestine Defence Force, but resigned the appointment in 1921, when he returned to Australia. He was awarded the D.S.O.

"Fat" McCarthy was another whose deeds helped to make A.I.F. history. A happy-go-lucky nature and a splendid physique assisted him to make light of stresses which broke other men. Through Gallipoli from early in May to the Evacuation, he was awarded the Croix de Guerre and V.C. in France—the latter for an exploit in the final stages of the war which caused the English press to dub him "the Super V.C."

Colonel Pope should be mentioned here. To his personality can be attributed much of the magnificent spirit which characterised the battalion. Especially on Gallipoli, when he carried the worries and cares of a C.O. on his shoulders, his genial presence and confident bearing acted like a tonic on troops whose endurance was strained almost to breaking point. After the August fighting, when sickness and hardship had greatly reduced the morale of the 16th, he moved around the trenches, hiding his own physical disabilities, and talked and joked the spirit back into his weary men. For seven months he bore the heat and burden of a battalion command on Gallipoli. His services were recognised by the respect of the officers and men of the battalion, and gained for him the award of a C.B.

There are many others who stood out above their fellows. The 16th was fortunate in that respect—the occasion never failed to produce the man. In these pages it is intended to try and picture the life of the 16th as it actually was. For that purpose a committee of members of the battalion was "got together" to gather the necessary data and write its story. Some such effort was due to the memories of those comrades still left on foreign strands. Readers will appreciate the difficulties when they realise that the job was started nearly ten years after the armistice, when memories were dimmed and records lost. However, every effort has been made, and the committee, in publishing the result, trusts that it will win the approbation of those splendid men who, from 1914 to 1918, collectively formed the unit known as "The Old Sixteenth."

CHAPTER I.—FORMATION.

From two States of the Commonwealth—South and Western Australia—came the men who formed the original 16th Battalion, A.I.F. The Australian Government had already one Australian division in training when it was decided that another infantry unit should be formed—to be known as the 4th Brigade—and this was commanded from its inception by Sir John (then Colonel) Monash. To Western Australia was allotted the task of raising headquarters, M.G. section, signal section, and five companies of the 16th Battalion, while South Australia's share was the other three companies to complete the establishment. In the West the men were recruited from the metropolitan area, the goldfields, the south-west and the country districts generally—including a sprinkling from the far north. In South Australia three companies were raised from enlistment all over the State, and it can safely be said that the battalion as a whole represented men drawn from every section of the community and from every district of the two States concerned.

The battalion was born at Blackboy Hill on September 16, 1914. When the orders were received to organise the Western Australian quota of the 4th Brigade it was done by transferring the personnel from five depot companies already in camp and training as reinforcements for the 11th Battalion (which was also at Blackboy Hill), and giving them a name—the "16th Battalion, A.I.F."

As far as possible men from the same districts were allotted to the one company in order to give a community of interest, while the specialists were drawn from those whose civil occupations were thought to fit them for particular military work. Percy Black's introduction to a machine gun was more or less accidental. Major Mansbridge was allotting the men to their respective companies, and he had arranged that the goldfields men should form "A" Company. Before moving the men over to the tent lines he noticed Black standing alone, and inquired of him what district he came from. The reply was "The Goldfields," and it was followed by "Look here, Mister, I don't know anything about this soldiering game. What crowd would you recommend me to join up with?" The major asked if he had a mine. Yes, he had. Did he have a battery on it? Yes, he did. What motive power? A gas engine. Can you drive it? Yes, and I can drive a gas producer engine. "Very well," said Mansbridge, "Wait here, and I'll place you with the machine gunners." Thus was Black first introduced to the weapon with which he was destined to play such a prominent part in the life of the 16th Battalion.

Harry Murray, as it happened, wanted from the first to join the machine-gun section, but when the men were allotted he was overlooked and sent to the company formed of the men from the south-west. After parade that day he presented himself at the tent of the staff sergeant-major who was the instructor to the machine-gun section, and earnestly begged to be allotted to that section. He was a happy man when he was told to take his kit down to the section's tents. Luck was certainly with the 16th when those two men, and probably many others also, were from the start placed in roles for which they were so eminently suited.

For a few days at Blackboy the battalion was under the command of Lieut.-Colonel "Biltong" Vialls, C.B., an officer who had greatly distinguished himself in the South African War. The arduous duties associated with the organisation and training of the new unit, however, proved too strenuous for one who was well over military age, and Colonel Vialls relinquished the command on October 11, after having done some splendid ground work.

The command was then offered to and accepted by Lieut.-Colonel Harold Pope. This officer had a period of service with the Australian Citizen Forces, dating from the year 1900, to his credit. He was 41 years of age, and eminently suitable for his new position. Well versed in the technicalities associated with the command and training of men, perhaps the success which attended his efforts was due even more to his personality than to the military experience he brought with it. His happy nature reflected itself in those surrounding him, and while everyone thoroughly understood that the object of training was efficiency for war, and discipline was therefore strict, it was leavened with that spirit of humour which caused the maximum amount of benefit to be got out of work. Indeed it was the spirit of the A.I.F.; and the 16th was inculcated with it in the first week of Colonel Pope's command.

In those early days the establishment of a battalion consisted of headquarters, M.G. section of two guns, and eight companies—the whole totalling approximately one thousand men. To the second-in-command fell much of the administrative work in connection with the raising of the new unit. This was capably performed by Major L. E. Tilney, who was appointed to that position in the 16th. The adjutant, Captain R. T. A. McDonald, was, prior to his appointment, an officer on the Administrative and Instructional Staff. He was a zealous soldier, and his military knowledge was an immense help in the training of the battalion, and to him particularly were the younger officers indebted for the instruction which he made it his special duty to impart to them.

Major W. O. Mansbridge was the original O.C. of "A" Company. He had served for many years with the Citizen Forces on the goldfields. Always a keen soldier, his knowledge stood him in good stead when he took over his company of mostly raw recruits.

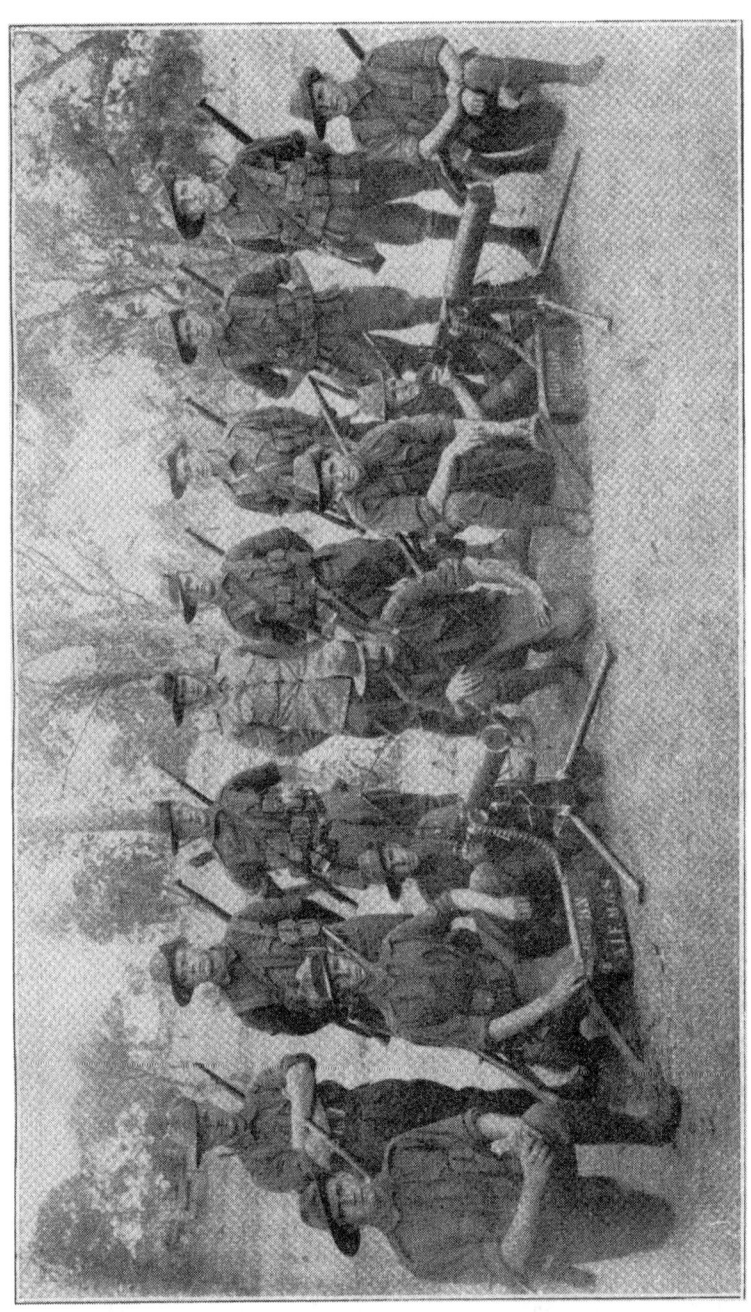

SOME OF THE ORIGINAL 16th BATTALION MACHINE GUN SECTION AT BLACKBOY HILL IN 1914.

"B" Company was originally commanded by Major Abrahall, an officer who had served previously in the Royal Marines. He was new to purely infantry training, and had not properly settled into his stride when he was recalled to the Imperial Army. (By a strange coincidence this officer, in command of a company of English marines, was killed alongside the 16th during the first few days of the Gallipoli campaign.) His place as O.C. was taken by Lieut. E. L. Margolin, whose previous military experience had been gained as an officer in the 86th Infantry at Collie.

The O.C. "C" Company was Captain Townshend, who was an officer on the staff of the Western Australian University prior to the war. He had also experience in the training of the Citizen Forces.

Major F. B. Carter was in charge of "D" Company, and he also had long service in the Citizen Forces to help him in the training of his new command.

"E" Company was under Captain J. Miller, an officer with long Citizen Force training to his credit. He was serving with the 86th Infantry (as were a big proportion of the other officers) when war was declared.

"F," "G" and "H" Companies were commanded by Major Baker, Captain Gladman and Captain Brittain respectively. They were South Australians, and had an extensive Citizen Force training behind them. These officers, while the major portion of the battalion was being raised and trained at Blackboy, attended to similar duties in connection with the three companies raised in South Australia.

The signal section was commanded by Lieut. E. A. Wilton, a Duntroon officer; the regimental transport by Lieut. E. McVickers-Smythe, and the Quartermaster was Lieut. T. Gorman. Lieut. A. E. Carse was the O.C. M.G. Section. He had for some years served as a machine-gun officer in the Citizen Forces. The machine-gun section was composed of one officer and seventeen other ranks. This little band afterwards achieved for itself and the battalion a splendid reputation of efficiency and daring. During the training days at Blackboy the gun section's record was unique. In a few weeks' time the men had mastered the intricacies of the guns, and were out after speed, and six weeks from the time they commenced training records were being broken. Most A.I.F. soldiers know what "action" means in Maxim machine gun drill. The 16th gun section could do "action" correctly five times out of six in 13 seconds, whereas 45 seconds was the standard time laid down for efficiency. It took three men to do "action," and a series of tests just before the section left Blackboy for Broadmeadows showed that with the men changing places in the teams the average time for the whole section for "action" was 16 seconds. This efficiency in drill was reflected on service. On Gallipoli the gun section of the 16th became famous, and earned the commendation of the troops from the G.O.C. downwards.

The personnel of the Australian Army Medical Corps attached to the 16th was under the command of Captain Roy McGregor, who also organised and trained the stretcher-bearers in their special work.

CHAPTER II.—BLACKBOY HILL.

Life at Blackboy in those early days was strenuous. A long and fast march or "physical jerks" before breakfast brought everyone to that meal ready to swallow anything the mess orderlies put before them. The long forenoons on squad drill, rifle exercises, signalling, gun drill and trench digging made one wonder what was on for dinner. The afternoons, with either a repetition of the morning or else some tactical work in the hills around Blackboy made thoughts wander again towards the cook-house. Stew and bread and jam was the staple diet. All ranks (or should it be "other ranks"?) seemed to thrive on it, but the issue was helped considerably by private purchases and extra meals bought at the "tuck shops" which sprang up on the outskirts of Blackboy Hill. Looked back on now the training days at Blackboy were wonderful days. The stiffness of the body of civil life was painfully changed to the suppleness of the trained athlete by long periods of drill and marching; the minor ills of digestion which were a worry in pre-war days were cured by wholesome food, fresh air and exercise; and the brain grown sluggish through its travels along the one civilian groove was transformed into activity by the unsympathetic tongue of the "Sar-major." The Staff-Sergeants-Major were a source of wonder to the troops at that stage. Members of the Instructional Staff of the C.M.F. and permanently on the job before the war, they were perfectly fitted for the task of moulding the raw material into the perfect soldier. Sometimes their methods were not pleasant, but always they were efficient. Each was a store of military knowledge to whom the aspiring private could go after parade for further information to assist him on the road to stripes. It was no uncommon thing to see these staff men (who with a few exceptions were not permitted to enlist because their services were required as instructors at home) after a hard day's work on the parade ground, voluntarily hold classes for N.C.O.'s during the evenings. Theirs was the most thankless task in the training of the A.I.F. Thankless, because the war which ordinarily would be the professional soldiers' opportunity for campaigning with consequent promotion, saw them condemned by official decree to remain in Australia and train the troops required for active service.

Training at Blackboy was indeed a strenuous business for all concerned. The results obtained were astonishing. This was probably due to the fact that practically every officer, N.C.O. and man was out to become efficient as soon as possible. Commencing with the elementary work laid down for recruits—such as squad drill and rifle exercises—it seemed no time before the unit was able to perform battalion drill with a fair amount of precision. Of course, there was exercised the usual "old soldier" privilege of grumbling at the monotony of the more elementary military training, but as each lesson was mastered the work became more interesting. The field days just prior to embarkation for Melbourne were thoroughly enjoyed by all ranks, who felt then that they were training for the real thing at last. During this period the exacting nature of the training found out the weaklings and these were replaced by men from the depot companies in camp at the same time. There was no difficulty in keeping the ranks up to full strength, for already it was the ambition of the men in the depot companies at Blackboy to belong to an original unit like the 11th or 16th, instead of joining them overseas later as reinforcements.

Towards the end of its two months of Blackboy Hill training the battalion had thoroughly settled down. Esprit-de-corps was very high and all ranks were happy in their relationship with one another. It had been decided that the 4th Brigade was to assemble at Broadmeadows, in Victoria, to complete its organisation and training before embarkation overseas. In November, therefore, all ranks were given final leave. The troops were practised in entraining and detraining, in embarkation and debarkation (the grandstand at Helena Vale was the "troopship") and kit inspections were rigidly carried out.

On November 21, 1915, the battalion entrained for Fremantle and embarked in two parties on the s.s. "Indarra" and the "Dimboola," respectively, which arrived, after uneventful voyages, at Port Melbourne about a week later. Entraining there, each party was transported to Broadmeadows, near Melbourne, where was situated the military training ground for the Victorian A.I.F. Here the 4th Brigade assembled prior to proceeding overseas.

CHAPTER 3.—BROADMEADOWS.

The camp site at Broadmeadows was a contrast to Blackboy Hill. The latter was an ideal camping ground on account of the undulating nature of the country. Broadmeadows was generally flat —in wet weather it was very muddy and in fine weather the dust was almost intolerable.

The battalion was now a complete unit of headquarters, M.G. section and eight companies, having been joined by the three companies formed in South Australia. With the whole of the 4th Brigade congregated more advanced training began. Battalion drill; outposts, day and night; protection on the march; battalion in attack; communications; field fortifications; the digging and occupation of trench systems; musketry and lectures to officers and N.C.O.'s were the main items on the syllabus. The tactical exercises were enjoyable and instructive. True, the instruction came in the main from the very mistakes committed. The instructors and umpires, who were senior officers, were merciless in pointing out to the officers responsible where the latter had erred in not applying some principle of warfare laid down in Field Service Regulations and had thereby succeeded in losing most of their men. The discussions at the officers' "pow-wows," as they were called, were always valuable, and the frank criticism quickly taught the officers more of the art of war than they would otherwise have learned in months of reading the regulations. The men, too, were taking an intelligent interest in tactical exercises and when each "stunt" was finished and "smoko" was the order while the officers attended the pow-wow prior to the march back to camp, some of the debates and criticisms by the "other ranks" were certainly to the point. Probably it is well that the officers concerned knew nothing about these discussions. otherwise their vanity and perhaps their very necessary self confidence would have suffered. The rank and file of the A.I.F. were keen critics.

A welcome interlude in the training operations was the championship sports meeting of the 4th Brigade, which was held on December 12, in ideal weather at Broadmeadows camp in the presence of several thousands of soldiers and civilians. The meeting, which was excellently managed by Captain C. H. Jess, of the brigade headquarters staff, was very successful. Everything was carried out with military precision and as several events were in progress at the same time interest was sustained throughout. The 15th (Queensland and Tasmania) Battalion won the championship and the silver cup given by Colonel Monash with an aggregate of 48 points. The 16th was second with 43 points and the 13th third with 28 points. The 14th Battalion scored 9 points and the Fourth Field Ambulance 3 points. Great interest was evinced in the cham-

ORIGINAL OFFICERS OF 16th BATTALION AT BROADMEADOWS, VICTORIA, 1914.

pionship races, the heats and also the finals providing exciting and close finishes. The best performer was Scouller of the 15th, who won several races and was placed in others. The final of the 220 yards championship was splendidly contested over the last 25 yards, Scouller just winning from Brackenbridge (16th). Gilbert (16th) won the final of the hurdles championship over 120 yards with Treasure (16th) and Sykes (16th) closest to him. The Tug-o'-war was won by the 13th Battalion. In the marching, turn-out

THE WINNING TEAM IN THE 4th BRIGADE CHAMPIONSHIP AT BROADMEADOWS IN 1914.
They are Pte. P. O'Brien (left, No. 2), Pte. C. Hatcher (centre, No. 1), Pte. A. McLeod (right, No. 3), of the 16th Battalion Machine Gun Section.

and drill championship splendid work was shown and the various units were cheered as they marched past the judges, who included Colonel Monash. The 15th won this event with 87 marks, the 16th next with 71, 14th third with 70 and the 13th gained 64 marks.

The machine gun competition proved an interesting feature of the programme and the marvellous rapidity with which the various teams came into action astounded the spectators. This event was won by the 16th team (Hatcher, O'Brien and McLeod) who recorded the astonishing time of 12½ seconds; the 13th Battalion was second and the 15th third. The comic side was not lost sight of. The best sustained character in the burlesque event was won by Tudley of the 14th Battalion. The 100 yards championship was won by Brackenbridge (16th), with Harris (15th) second, and Scouller (15th) third.

The V.C. race (one competitor to run 50 yards to wounded comrade and return carrying him to starting point) was won by Stephenson and Sandry (16th), with Smith and Hall (16th) second.

These sports provided a welcome diversion from the monotony of drill and training and the enthusiasm worked up by supporters for the success of their own battalion representatives proved that "esprit-de-battalion" was already a potent factor in the life of the 4th Brigade.

The next noteworthy event was the march, in fighting order, of the 4th Brigade from Broadmeadows through Melbourne and back to camp on Thursday, December 17, the occasion being a review by His Excellency the Governor-General, Sir Ronald Munro Ferguson. This was a trying day for the troops but the brigade presented a splendidly martial sight as it moved through the city streets, which were lined with cheering crowds. The salute was taken by His Excellency on the steps of Federal Parliament House at the top of Collins Street and he afterwards expressed his appreciation of the fine physique and soldier-like bearing of the troops on parade.

CHAPTER 4.—THE VOYAGE.

After the review by the Governor-General it was understood by all ranks that the date set down for embarkation was close at hand. This proved not to be a "furphy" (as persistent camp rumours were termed in the A.I.F.) and on the morning of December 17 an advance party, in charge of Lieut. Elston, boarded the "Ceramic," of which Captain John Stivey, R.N.R., was commander, to prepare for the rest of the troops who were to be her passengers.

On the 21st Colonel Pope and Capt. McDonald, who were to act as O.C. Troops and Ship's Adjutant respectively, went aboard at 5 p.m. The carpenters were still busy completing the work of fitting the vessel as a troopship and these men did not finish until the next morning. The 16th embarked on the "Ceramic" at the Railway Pier, Port Melbourne, on December 22. The embarkation was carried out from 10.30 a.m. until 12.30 p.m. prompt to time-table. The "Ceramic" was known officially as the A.40. She was a fine vessel of 18,500 tons burthen. The lower decks had been divided into areas and a certain number of tables and forms were placed in each. The troops had been organised into messes and when embarking each party was met by a guide from the advance party and taken direct to its quarters. Hammocks, blankets and eating utensils were issued forthwith and the men were shown where to stack their rifles and kits. The following is the list of officers of the 16th, who embarked on the "Ceramic":—

Lieut. Col. H. Pope,
Major L. E. Tilney,
„ W. O. Mansbridge,
„ F. B. Carter,
Capt. R. T. A. McDonald,
„ E. L. Margolin,
„ S. E. Townsend,
„ J. Miller,
„ F. B. Gladman,
„ H. P. Brittain,
„ R. S. McGregor,
Lieut. H. A. Southern,
„ E. W. Elston,
„ N. Durston,
„ E. A. Wilton,

THE 16th BATTALION ON THE MARCH IN MELBOURNE IN 1914.

A CERAMIC SOUVENIR.

Lieut. F. G. Chabrel,
„ L. D. Heming,
„ G. L. Curlewis,
„ T. Gorman,
„ J. K. Langsford,
„ E. O. Bruns,
„ A. T. Mountain
„ A. Imlay,
„ A. E. Carse,
„ R. Harwood,
„ E. H. Kretchmar,
„ C. A. Geddes,
„ J. H. Burton,
„ D. H. Kerr.

At 1.30 p.m. the Governor-General and Lady Munro Ferguson came aboard and bade the troops farewell. At 2.30 in the afternoon the "Ceramic" cast off from the wharf and another stage in the Great Adventure had begun.

On board the "Ceramic" were 72 officers and 2,632 other ranks. These were made up of 32 officers and 979 other ranks belonging to the 16th; about the same number of the 15th under Lieut.-Col. Cannan; and the remainder were composed of the Divisional Ammunition Park under Lieut.-Col. Tunbridge and Divisional Supply Column under Lieut.-Col. Moon. The first day was occupied in settling into quarters. After the excitement and enthusiasm which reigned when the ship cast off, it was surprising how soon each man found his own "niche" in the general scheme of things. The first few days, naturally, found the weak spot in many a landlubber and during this period a prevailing opinion was "Gimme the ground!"

By Christmas Day, however, all on board were feeling cheerful. They were old soldiers; now they felt they could justly claim the title of "old salts." A church parade was held in the morning. Then the messes were decorated and Christmas dinner was a vast improvement on the previous efforts of the cooks. For the evening a concert had been organised. This was well carried out and thoroughly appreciated by the troops. The programme was given by members of the 15th Battalion and the Divisional Ammunition Park and the concert was held on the forward deck. The printed programme was the work of the "D.A.P. Press."

On the 26th (Boxing Day) the two 4.7 inch guns, manned by naval reservists, with which the ship was equipped as a protection against hostile submarines, fired six rounds at a target at 5,000 yards. The 15th and 16th machine gun sections then each fired two belts (500 rounds) at the same target at 1,000 yards. In the evening a concert, organised by the 16th Battalion and the Divisional Supply

Column was held. The following is the programme which was printed and issued:—

H.M.A.T. "CERAMIC," (A.40.)

Programme of Concert to be held on the *After Deck*,

Boxing Night, 1914, at 8.15 p.m.

By 16th Batt. and Div. Supply Col. A.I.E.F.

Chairman: Lt. Col. H. Pope.
Committee:
    Capt. C. J. Goddard,
    Lieut. and Q. M. Craig,
    Lieut. W. E. Parry-Okeden,
    Lieut. G. K. Langsford, (Secretary).

1. Band Selection—D.S.C. Band.
2. Recitation (Humorous)—Driv. Mech. B. Scott.
3. Ragtime Quartet—D.S.C. Quartet.
4. Song (Humorous)—L/Corp Parker.
5. Song.—Lieut. Geddes.
6. Ragtime—Bandmaster Murison.
7. Song (Humorous)—Driv. Mech. A. R. Jones.
8. Band Selection—16th Batt. Band.
9. The Nightingale—Scanlon.
10. Elocution—Cutler.
11. Song—Sgt. Mitchell.
12. Song—Driv. Mech. Freeman.

God Save the King.

(Printed on board by the D.A.P. Press.)

About this time deck space for training was allotted and programmes for organised utilisation of the ship's spaces were prepared. The training of personnel continued actively throughout the voyage, the whole of the deck spaces allotted to units being in constant use from 9 a.m. until 5 p.m. The continued employment of officers and men in this manner had the effect of preventing discontent or grumbling, besides maintaining a high standard of discipline, keeping the troops fit and adding in some measure to their military knowledge. Training in rapid loading, firing, and snapshooting was thorough, a circumstance which was later to stand the 16th in good stead in the supreme test of battle. One lecture was given per day to each unit on its own troop deck.

THE OLD SIXTEENTH.

The system of training was on similar lines throughout the ship, and being very keenly watched by the O.C., no slackness or falling off was permitted. All officers paraded on the boat deck from 5 to 6 o'clock on three afternoons weekly and, divided into suitable squads, were exercised in physical training, semaphore signalling, bayonet fighting, sword exercises, revolver practice, etc.

The general syllabus embodied theoretical instruction in fire tactics, outposts, duties in camp, bivouacs, protection, semaphore, first aid and machine gun. In addition, the officers attended a school of instruction which embraced Field Service Regulations, map reading, rules of civilised warfare, lessons from military history, and supply of food and forage.

Albany was reached on December 28, at 6 a.m. At this port much remained to be done by the headquarters staff of the battalion in finalising and correcting returns of stores, pay and personnel, etc. Eight men of the 16th, who refused to be inoculated were put ashore. Lieut. E. T. H. Knight joined the battalion here in place of Lieut. E. K. McVickers-Smythe, who had been left in Melbourne with fever. A pleasing memory the troops had of Albany was Archbishop Riley's visit when he boarded the ship per medium of a swaying rope ladder and moved among the troops with his usual cheery words of comfort. No shore leave was granted, and the only people who were fortunate enough to visit the town were those officers whose official business necessitated the trip.

At 8 a.m. on the last day of the year 1914, the "Ceramic" sailed from King George's Sound. It was a magnificent sight to see sixteen transports moving majestically in three lines across the wide expanse of sea. As the shore faded away the thoughts of many a man of The Old Sixteenth were with the loved ones whom he was leaving behind and the idea would intrude that possibly he might never see them again.

The next day the programme of training was resumed and, practically without a break, was kept up until the ship arrived at Aden. The health of the troops was reasonably good throughout the voyage, although minor illnesses were prevalent. On January 20, a sick return showed that there were 10 cases of pneumonia, 13 of measles, 7 of influenza and 15 with other diseases in hospital, a total of 45 or 1.7 per cent. of the troops on board. During this period of the trip all hands were vaccinated and inoculated, to the obvious disgust and temporary discomfort of the troops. Sentries were posted at all the vital points on board the "Ceramic." There were twenty posts constantly manned, with detailed orders issued for each. A sharp look-out was kept, too, for enemy submarines or raiders. At night all lights were shaded so that from the sea nothing could be seen. A fact that was not generally known at this time was that the boats, rafts and life-belts were not nearly sufficient to accommodate the personnel on board.

CHAPTER 5.—THE "HONK."

Naturally time passed slowly and the routine became monotonous, as nothing eventful happened to awaken interest. The D.A.P. published a paper which was a creditable effort under the circumstances. Some news received by wireless was printed in its pages and contributions were welcomed even if they were not always published. Having time on their hands it was not surprising how many men forwarded "stuff" to "Honk," as the production was called. It ran for five issues, and extracts from its pages are reproduced. It was headed:—

"'HONK!'
"The Voice of the Benzine Lancers.
"Printed every sometimes for the D.A.P.
"Edited by P. L. Harris; printed by G. H. Vincent."

No. 1 copy was dated January 4, 1915, and its editorial opened the venture in this breezy manner:—

"The Organ of the Gear-box Musicians.

"The 'Honk' cheerfully blows into the scheme of things aboard A.40. Its object is to entertain and amuse those on board the troopship.

"Yes, boys, 'Honk' has started. And the Editor wants you to help to keep it going strong. Contributions are wanted. So get your idea factory working. But send the right kind of contributions. Personal pleasantries if you like, but no objectionable personalities. And no smut. The 'Honk' doesn't want to be a dirt receptacle. The Editor wants to make this little paper clean and unoffending, something that you will keep as a pleasant memento of this great adventure we have entered upon together, something of which you will all be proud. And he wants you to help him to do it.

"We want the 'Honk' to make its readers laugh. So if you've got any laughter about you, send it along. Amusing episodes that come under your notice, smart sayings you've heard, bright verse you know; bring 'em up; they're all wanted. You'll find the 'Honk' letter box on the promenade deck, next to the D.A.P. orderly room. The name of writer, his unit and section or company must appear on all matter sent in. If you can't write it, come and tell us about it.

"A leather medal made by the D.A.P. regimental bootmaker will be given for the wittiest paragraph sent in each issue. Everyone is wanted to write something for the 'Honk.' So buck up and bog in. Do a little honking. You're all in it.

"Do you Honk???"

Naturally a sergeant's personal idiosyncrasies got an early mention in despatches in a column captioned "Honks":—

"Notta—moooooove O'Loughlin was not to be heard when the ship started to roll just after clearing Queenscliffe Heads. When the 'Honk' saw him he was leaning enthusiastically over the side of the boat and seemed to have something on his mind. It is rumoured that when the men were paraded the first evening, a man in his section actually allowed his eyelid to slip and nobody heard the ruddy sergeant shout 'Notta—mooooove.' In fact he didn't even say 'Oi kno' yah!'"

These verses give an indication that the Ceramic was a dry ship:—

"*Anticipation.*
"Have you heard about the paper?
  I presume it's newly born.
The name, it sounds familiar
  'Cause it's like a motor horn.

"And it's coming very shortly,
  But I hope it don't go plonk,
And it's going to be a bonza
  'Cause it's entered as the 'Honk.'

"I wonder if it mentions anything
  About some beer.
Or if there's any prophecies
  About the coming year.

"We print this exactly as we received it.

"It is evidently the output of two master minds, because the M.S.S. bears two sets of initials—'A.H.' and 'T.B.P.' Although the metre is a bit 'out of timing' and the rhyme badly gone in the knees, it is published with all faults out of appreciation for the sentiments expressed, and with the regretful announcement that we don't know anything about beer. Also, we think that the writers should have been more respectful and spelt Beer with a capital B. —Ed. 'Honk.'"

From the 16th Battalion page, edited by Lieut. A. P. Imlay, are culled the following:—

"There is a fair leavening of veterans in the ranks of the 16th— not veterans in age, let it be understood, but men who have seen active service in different parts of the Empire; in Africa, India, China, Ashanti, Egypt, Burma, South America, Mexico, and wherever the flag has been under fire. The number as shown on the attestation paper is 76, being 7.5 per cent. of the strength of the battalion."

"New Year Greetings:—The C.O. and officers wish the men of the 16th Battalion a very happy new year, and trust they will have sufficient opportunities in 1915 to further prove that the best is always reserved for last."

In the next paragraph the 16th blew out its chest with:—

"The 16th is well represented on the staff of the A.40, most, if not all, of the responsible positions being filled by members of the 16th; O.C. Troops being Lieut.-Col. Pope; Ship's Adjutant, Capt. R. T. A. McDonald; Ship's Quartermaster, Lieut. Elston; Ship's Q.M.S., L./Sgt. Delacour; Ship's Orderly Room Sgt., Sgt. Orchard; while it is understood that the commander of the ship, the chief engineer and the surgeon are feeling miserable because they are not on the strength of the 16th. We might find room for them yet, however."

In the next issue the 15th replied:—

"To the 16th.
"Your recent claim to run the ship
  Does not our hearts with envy fill.
In fact, when we complete the trip,
  We'll let you do the running still."

On the D.A.P. page some verses expressed excellent sentiments:—

"BE MEN

"By Edward Vance Cooke.

"Did you tackle the trouble that came your way
  With a resolute heart and cheerful?
Or hide your face from the light of day
  With a craven soul and fearful?

"Or, a trouble's a ton, or a trouble's an ounce
  Or trouble is what you make it;
And it isn't the fact that you're hurt that counts
  But only, how did you take it?

"You are beaten to earth? Well, well, what's that?
  Come up with a smiling face.
It's nothing against you to fall down flat,
  But to lie there—that's the disgrace.

"The harder you're thrown, why the higher you'll bounce;
  Be proud of your blackened eye.
It isn't the fact that you're licked that counts,
  But how did you fight, and why?

THE OLD SIXTEENTH. 25

"And though you be done to the death, what then?
If you battled the best you could;
If you played your part in the world of men
Why the critic will call it good.

"Death comes with a crawl, or comes with a pounce;
And whether he's slow or spry,
It isn't the fact that you're dead that counts
But only—how did you die?"

The second issue of "Honk" was published on January 18. Some samples:—

"Overheard on the fore deck:—
'What's the matter with you?'
'There's nothing the matter with me.'
'Well, you gave me a nasty look!'
'You've got a nasty look alright, but I didn't give it to you!'"

This one indicates the trend of thought:—

"SPORTING.

"Destination Stakes.—Latest prices by 'The Old Firm.'

Aden (for service)	5 to 1
Cairo	6 to 4
Alexandria (to stay)	9 to 2
Joppa	5 to 1
Marseilles	4 to 1
Old Dart	3 to 1

Commissions Executed."

Out of the same issue are taken the accounts of the two occasions on which land was sighted after leaving Albany.

"LAND AHOY!

"On Thursday last a good deal of interest was created when land was sighted—the first seen for fourteen days. It was a small island called Minikoy. The big ship passed very close to the land and dozens of native boats put off, but kept well away from the vessel. The island is claimed by a woman named Ranee (or Bibi) of Kannamore, but is actually under the rule of the British authorities in Malabar. The island is a little over 6 miles long and very narrow. It has a village of about 300 huts and a population of 3,000. The inhabitants are coloured of the Molpal caste and they observe the Mahommedan religion. The island was discovered by Vasco de Gama on his first voyage. The P. and O. steamer "Colombo" was wrecked there in November, 1862. The products of the island are cocoanuts, coir, cowries, sugar and salt fish. Minikoy is the furthermost island of the Lacadive Group, which extends for 120 miles from Kanara. There are no horses, cattle or sheep, but ducks and fowls are plentiful."

"LAND AGAIN.

"Land was again sighted on Monday last, but it could only be dimly discerned on the horizon. It was the island of Socotra, a British possession in the Indian Ocean, South of Arabia and East of Cape Guardafui. It is 71 miles long and 22 miles broad. The products are aloes and dragon's blood tree, the gum from which is collected at all seasons. Sheep and goats abound in enormous numbers. In 1506 the island was occupied by the Portuguese and in 1834 by British troops. The latter afterwards evacuated it in order to fortify Aden, but it was again occupied by them in 1876, the Sultan of Keshun being allowed an annual subsidy from the British Government. There are several towns on the island. The population numbers 5,000, and is composed of Bedouins and Arabs who observe the Mahommedan creed."

The next two "Honks" seem to indicate that the weather was warming up!

"Things are so congested on the promenade deck these hot nights that a flea would feel that it was being overcrowded if it tried to force its way between the sleepers. This state of affairs leads to a good deal of bickering at times. But the limit was reached the other night when Driver J. B. Martin put his foot into Driver L. Robinson's mouth and then abused him for sleeping with his mouth open!"

"Judging by the amount of moisture that accumulates on Sgt. McSwain's forehead, it is quite obvious that drink goes to the head. Eh? No, we do not think that it goes there because that's where there's most room for it."

Of course "Honk" published its letters to the Editor:—

"CORRESPONDENCE.
"(To the Editor.)

"Sir,—After reading your valuable paper, especially the ladies' notes, I would venture to make this appeal. Can you advise me? I am a lady on board this ship, disguised as a bugler, and I wish to get married. Would you advise me to marry an officer of high rank, or only an adjutant? There is a colour-sergeant I am very fond of. I believe I could learn to love him in time, but he is cold and distant. He belongs to the 16th Infantry. His description is as follows:—Height, about 5 feet 9 inches, fair hair, worn short, blue eyes, fair and ruddy complexion, rather stout and well on the side of forty. I am told he is well known in Perth. I come of a very good family—being an officer's daughter. Papa was a general in the navy (submarine department). Consequently I move in the best society and usually stay when in Victoria at Ah Fo's restaurant in Little Bourke Street. I am considered by my friends to be handsome (when sober) and of a charming disposition. I am 23. We could be married at the first port of call. Failing the colour-sergeant I think I would like to marry an adjutant. Anxiously awaiting your next issue for your best advice. Believe me,

"Yours very sincerely,

"GERTRUDE ST. LEDGER."

And the Editorial answer:—

"(If you really love the colour-sergeant, Gertrude, then you should be able to make him yours. For what man can escape a woman once she makes up her mind to get him? Of course, there are a lot of material advantages to be secured by marrying an officer, but if your love for the colour-sergeant is as strong as you say, we should advise you to try your "charming disposition" on him. If you fail, you can always fall back on an adjutant. Let's know how you get on, Gerty, we're not married ourselves.—Ed.)"

The next two proved that the Ceramic was still dry:—

"THE PLAN OF CAMPAIGN.

"(As suggested by various conversations heard on board.)

    To visit Leicester Lounge.
    ,, climb the pyramids.
    ,, drink beer.
    ,, shoot the Kaiser.
    ,, drink more beer.
    ,, capture Constantinople.
    ,, raid the Sultan's harem.
    ,, drink more beer.
    ,, shave our moustaches (some of us).
    ,, drink more beer.
    ,, flirt with French girls.
    ,, return home covered with medals and
    ,, drink more beer."

"Examining Medical Officer to Stretcher Bearer:—

" 'Supposing Private Brown were to fall down in a faint, what would you do?'

"S.B.: 'Give him some rum, sir.'

"E.M.O.: 'But suppose that you had no rum?'

"S.B.: 'I'd promise him some, sir.' "

The last is one against the doc:

"A bandsman went sick one day with a sore throat. Doctor Luther, R.M.O., 15th Battalion, examined the throat carefully and said that perhaps it would be better if he did not use it for a while, and wrote on his sick report, 'Exempt for one week.' At the end of the week the doctor met the bandsman on the deck and recognising him, said: 'Well, my man, how's your throat?' 'Quite well, now, thank you, sir,' responded the bandsman. 'Oh, good! you're quite fit for duty then,' said the doctor. 'By the way,' he added, 'what instrument do you blow in the band?' 'I play the cymbals, sir,' said the bandsman. 'Whew. Wait till I vaccinate him,' thought the doctor."

"Honk" did its job. It amused and entertained the troops. It is interesting to know that its Editor, Philip L. Harris, was, as a lieutenant, the Editor of "Aussie" which did the same job so splendidly for the Australian Corps in 1918.

CHAPTER 6.—EGYPT.

The voyage was quite uneventful and the only two occasions on which land was sighted proved welcome breaks in the monotony. On January 20 the "Ceramic" anchored in the inner harbour at Aden at 1.30 p.m. No shore leave was given and the troops were not able to stretch limbs that were tired of cramped quarters in a crowded ship. The first death of a member of the battalion occurred on this day, when Private C. Robinson, of "F" Company (South Australia), died of pneumonia, following on measles. He was buried with military honours in Aden cemetery on January 21, members of his own company being taken ashore to act as the firing party.

On the 23rd the "Ceramic" sailed from Aden at 4.30 p.m. Soon after leaving a member of the 15th Battalion died from penumonia and the ship was stopped while his body was committed to the deep. Another member of the 15th died on January 27, while in the Gulf of Suez, from sunstroke, of which there were quite a number of cases at this time.

The "Ceramic" arrived off Suez at 6.30 a.m. on the 28th. News was received here of the fighting which had taken place at Kantara, on the Suez Canal. As a precautionary measure, the bridge of the ship was protected against rifle fire by bales of wool. Something of a shock was given those in authority, however, when an experiment proved that a bullet would penetrate those barricades very easily. The machine guns were mounted for use against aircraft and the ship's 4.7 guns were manned ready for instant use.

The next day the Suez Canal was entered at 9 a.m., passing the warships "Ocean," "Himalaya," "Minerva" and two French ships. These evidences of the Allied naval power were subjected to an intense scrutiny by the troops on board the "Ceramic." An interesting feature of this portion of the trip were the earthworks forming part of the defences of the canal. At 2.30 p.m. the transport anchored at Port Said, near a French mailboat, whose passengers displayed intense enthusiasm when the 16th's band struck up the "Marseillaise." The canal at this time was guarded by New Zealand and Indian troops. On the 30th many of the Australians saw their first aeroplane, when a reconnaissance machine passed high overhead returning from a scouting trip over the desert. The boys were now quite excited at the proofs they had that they were at last in a theatre of war.

Port Said was left at 9 a.m. on the 31st. The "Ceramic" anchored two miles out until 4.30 p.m., when the anchor was weighed and she proceeded slowly on her way. The next day, February 1, the ship reached Alexandria Harbour at 8.30 a.m., and anchored there until the morning of the 3rd, when she moved in and berthed at 44 Quay, at 11 o'clock. The troops disembarked and felt solid ground for the first time for nearly six weeks. One half of the 16th left Alexandria by train at 7 p.m. and the other half at 9.30 the next morning (February 4). Their destination was Zeitoun, Cairo, about 100 miles from Alexandria, and the journey took seven hours, when the battalion detrained and marched two miles to Heliopolis to camp in the desert, which was of a fine gravel and sand.

There the troops were settled into tents and the rest of the day was spent in overhauling gear, checking equipment, and all the other tasks which were found necessary on the completion of a long voyage overseas. The 4th Brigade was camped near the New Zealand Brigade and the Australian First Light Horse Brigade. The 4th Brigade was not attached to the 1st Australian Division, which was at Mena, but, with the 1st A.L.H. Brigade and the New Zealand Brigade, was under the command of Major-Gen. Godley.

On February 5 the battalion was organised under the new double company system of four companies each of four platoons. Under this scheme the officers and the old companies were distributed as follows:—

"A" Company—
    O.C., Major W. O. Mansbridge.
    2nd in C., Capt. S. E. Townsend.
    No. 1 Platoon, Lieut. E. W. Elston.
    „ 2 Platoon, Lieut. N. Durston.
    „ 3 Platoon, Lieut. E. H. Kretchmar.
    „ 4 Platoon, Lieut. R. B. Blythe.

"B" Company—
    O.C., Major F. B. Carter.
    2nd in C., Capt. E. L. Margolin.
    No. 5 Platoon, Lieut. G. L. Curlewis.
    „ 6 Platoon, Lieut. H. A. Southern.
    „ 7 Platoon, Lieut. A. T. Mountain.
    „ 8 Platoon, Lieut. C. A. Geddes.
    Spare—Lieut. T. Taylor.

"C" Company—
    O.C., Capt. J. Miller.
    2nd in C., Capt. H. P. Brittain.
    No. 9 Platoon, Lieut. F. G. Chabrel.
    „ 10 Platoon, Lieut. E. O. Bruns.
    „ 11 Platoon, Lieut. E. T. H. Knight.
    „ 12 Platoon, Lieut. A. Imlay.
    Spare—Lieut. J. A. Brayshaw.

THE CAMP AT HELIOPOLIS.

"D" Company—
    O.C., Capt. E. K. Baker.
    2nd in C., Capt. F. B. Gladman.
    No. 13 Platoon, Lieut. L. D. Heming.
    „ 14 Platoon, Lieut. J. K. Langsford.
    „ 15 Platoon, Lieut. D. H. Kerr.
    „ 16 Platoon, Lieut. J. H. Burton.
    Spare—Lieut. K. L. Anderson.

The troops found Heliopolis an interesting and beautiful city. The name means "City of the Sun," to which title a brave attempt had been made by the residents to do justice. The architecture was very fine and the manner in which this city had been laid out was indeed a credit to those responsible, while the roads and thoroughfares were kept in remarkably good condition. On the outskirts of the city was a beautiful building, known as Baron's Castle, the ornamentation of which was magnificent. Heliopolis was well furnished with means of transport to Cairo, which was connected by electric and steam trains, electric tram and all varieties of road vehicles. The Palace Hotel was a magnificent building. Constructed originally for a casino at immense cost, the authorities had refused the license. Prior to 1914 it was used as a palace for the Sultan's relations. It had 1,300 rooms, and a wonderful ball room. When the 16th arrived the building was being used as a general base hospital.

In Cairo the troops found much to interest them. Essentially, the whole show was so different to anything Australians had ever experienced that the days of leave could be spent in one long neverending exploration. The people, their manners, their habits, their language, their methods of doing business and of working, were a source of ceaseless inquiry by the visitors from Australia. The styles of architecture, the methods (or lack of methods) of sanitation, the old and the new monuments were all subjects for keen discussion. In Cairo, the European quarter was voted fairly good, but the native quarter was reckoned to be the absolute limit in filthy conditions of living. There were no sanitary arrangements whatever, and refuse was got rid of by throwing it into the narrow streets. The smell pervading the whole quarter was vile and the wonder was that human beings could possibly exist at all in such obnoxious surroundings. Familiarity must certainly have bred immunity from disease amongst Egyptians. The Gyppo newsboys caused great amusement with their quaint sayings, some of them obviously inspired by previous contact with Australians. Their methods of selling their wares were the reverse of complimentary to rival newspapers—"Egyptian Mail! English paper no———— good!" or "Daily Telegraph! The Colonel is a German————!" The Gyppo was an indefatigable vendor. Whether he was met in Cairo or miles out in some remote spot in the desert, he always had something to sell. His artlessness was delightful. Beginning by asking a fabulous sum for his goods, he would be quite pleased in the end if he got the equivalent of a penny.

Throughout the behaviour of the 16th had been excellent. The men had taken in a philosophic spirit such restrictions as had been imposed upon them since the formation of the unit, and in Egypt their conduct compared very favourably with that of other battalions. Naturally, military "crimes" were committed, but they were all of a minor character and nothing of a nature calculated to seriously harm the good name of the battalion. This was something for which all ranks were to be congratulated, for in Cairo there seemed to be no control of the drink traffic. Every shop apparently was allowed to retail it and, worse still, to make it. Some of the stuff which was sold as liquor was the limit in deadly poison and, sometimes, after one drink the unfortunate soldier would remember nothing of the (perhaps) exciting incidents which followed.

The native ladies of Egypt were rather interesting—what could be seen of them! They wore a coarse netted veil from the nose down and it was aggravating to see a pair of fine eyebrows and eyes, a dainty nose, and then have to leave the rest to the imagination.

While at Heliopolis the battalion was issued with rations on the British Army Egyptian scale. This was not equal, by a long way, to the Australian scale. In order to make up the difference, battalion commanders were granted (on demand) sixpence per day per man to purchase extra food to make up the deficiency. It was not a good system. There was no proper organisation in existence for buying and being new to the customs of the country, the buying officers were at a disadvantage when pitting their commercial knowledge against the bargaining instincts of the native trader. The sixpence per day per man did not buy much.

Training at Heliopolis continued along strenuous lines. To the troops, impatient to get into the real thing, it was rather uninteresting, especially when the operations embraced divisional exercise over Egyptian sand. These latter stunts, of course, were necessary to give the higher commands and staffs some experience involving the actual movement and manœuvring of large bodies of men and transport. Night operations were also practised and plenty of musketry and machine gun fire was given on the rifle range and in the desert. Route marches, entrenchments, bivouacs, outposts, and field firing filled in the time. By the end of March the battalion could be classed as a very efficient instrument of war. The officers and men were physically fit and all ranks had behind them six solid months of intelligent study and preparation which had resulted in the knowledge of what they were expected to do and how to do it under the various circumstances which might arise.

On March 22 the battalion paraded east of Zeitoun, when the division was inspected by His Excellency the High Commissioner, Sir Henry McMahon. General Sir Ian Hamilton, General Sir William Birdwood and some French officers were also present. Something in the air at this parade told the troops they were due to move at any time. This rumour was confirmed when specially urgent orders were received on April 2 that no further training programmes would be issued for the time being and that C.O's were to take steps to keep the rank and file well in hand and usefully employed in, or at no great distance from the camp lines. Ordinary leave was stopped and special efforts were made to adjust outstanding matters of personnel, equipment, clothing, etc.

On April 2 there was a disturbance in Cairo in which soldiers from probably every Australian and New Zealand unit in Egypt were concerned. It started in a small way, but developed into a serious riot, which was not quelled until some of the houses in the "Wazza" had been burnt to the ground.

On the 4th the New Zealand and Australian Division received orders to hold itself in readiness to leave Egypt at short notice. The 16th was notified that it would probably move on April 11, and on that date the battalion, divided into three parties, left Cairo by train for Alexandria.

CHAPTER 7.—LEMNOS.

At Alexandria "C" Company, under Captain Miller, consisting of 224 personnel all ranks, with one cooker, embarked on the transport "Seeangbee," and came under the orders of the O.C. Troops on that vessel. The remainder of the 16th (headquarters "A," "B" and "C" Companies), marched from Heliopolis to Cairo railway station and entrained in two trains, leaving respectively at 12.30 and 3.30 a.m. on Sunday, April 11. These trains reached Alexandria at 5.30 and 8.30 a.m. respectively, and were run on to the wharf at which the transport A28, "Haida Pascha," was berthed. The total embarked represented 821 all ranks, 89 horses, 9 limbered wagons, 1 maltese cart, 2 water carts, 4 G.S. wagons and 2 cookers.

The unfinished condition of the transport was apparent at first glance. The conveniences and cooking accommodation required had not even been put on board and carpenters were at work completing officers' cabins under the bridge. The loading of horses and vehicles was proceeded with, but the personnel would have congested the whole ship in its then unfinished condition and they were, therefore, bivouaced until the afternoon on the wharf.

The following officers of the battalion embarked at Alexandria on the "Haida Pascha":—

C.O., Lt. Col. H. Pope.
2nd in C., Major L. E. Tilney.
Adj., Capt. R. T. A. McDonald.
Q.M., Hon. Lt. T. Gorman.
T.O., Lieut. R. Harwood.
Sig. O., Lieut. E. A. Wilton.
M.G.O., Lieut. A. E. Carse
Med. Off., Capt. Roy S. McGregor, A.A.M.C.

"A" Company—
Major W. O. Mansbridge.
Captain S. E. Townsend.
Lieut. W. E. Elston.
Lieut. N. E. Durston.
Lieut. H. Kretchmar.
Lieut. R. B. Blythe.

"B" Company—
Major F. B. Carter.
Capt. E. L. Margolin.
Lieut. G. L. Curlewis.
Lieut. C. A. Geddes.
Lieut. A. T. H. Mountain.

"D" Company—
    Major E. K. Baker.
    Lieut. L. D. Heming.
    Lieut. J. K. Langsford.
    Lieut. H. J. Burston.
    Lieut. K. L. Anderson.
    Lieut. W. B. Kerr.

"C" Company (on "Seeangbee")—
    Capt. J. Miller.
    Lieut. H. A. Southern.
    Lieut. F. G. Chabrel.
    Lieut. A. P. Imlay.
    Lieut. E. O. A. Bruns.
    Lieut. E. T. H. Knight.

Capt. F. B. Gladman (medically unfit), and Capt. H. P. Brittain (in hospital), were left behind at Heliopolis.

During the day it was noticed that 277,000 rounds of S.A.A. put on board were not supplied with chargers. Attention was drawn to this and 23 boxes of chargers were supplied about half an hour before leaving the wharf. At 6 p.m. the ship cast off the wharf and anchored in the harbour. Certain deficiencies in ship's equipment and horse slings having been adjusted, the "Haida Pascha" weighed anchor at 4.10 p.m. on April 12 and put to sea. The next day a breakdown in the engine room caused a delay of about five hours. At 7.30 a.m. on the 14th, in the passage between Rhode's Island and Scarpanto, it was reported that an object had been passed about half an hour previously having resemblance to a lighter or something of that sort. On investigation, it was found to be an empty steel lighter of about 200 tons capacity. As this was likely to be of use the "Haida Pascha" took it in tow and it was eventually handed over to the navy.

The 23 boxes of chargers when opened for issue were found to contain only 600 chargers apiece, 13,800 in all against 50,800 required. It was decided to issue ammunition as far as it would go and to make special representation on arrival at Mudros.

The "Haida Pascha" was a German prize, a cargo ship with excellent holds, the iron upper decks making fairly good troop decks. Deck space had been almost entirely utilised for horse stalls, conveniences, wash houses or ship's gear, so that no space at all was available for training. The crowded nature of the ship resulted in everyone experiencing the utmost discomfort which was increased by the activities of the vermin which swarmed everywhere in the vessel.

The voyage through such a classic sea proved of great interest to all ranks. No casualties were incurred, nor were any men reported unfit for duty. In fact, the health and spirits of the troops on board were excellent.

On the transport the final touches were given to equipment by the issue of ball ammunition to all ranks. Pay was distributed on April 14, and for some it was the last pay they ever received. On the 15th, at 6.30 p.m., the ship arrived at Lemnos and anchored outside the boom across Mudros Harbour. The next morning she moved inside and anchored about 400 yards from the boom entrance. The scene in the harbour baffled description. In its capacious waters were hundreds of ships of all shapes and sizes—trans-

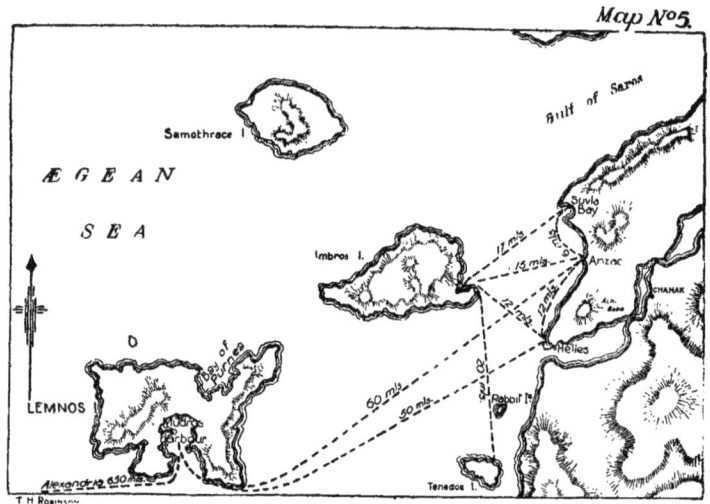

LEMNOS, IMBROS, TENEDOS, AND THE DARDANELLES.

ports and men-o'-war (both British and French). The first warship seen by the 16th at close quarters was the "Agamemnon," which showed signs of having received some hard knocks in the effort to force the Straits of Gallipoli. Her deck, from the bow to the bridge, was one mass of twisted iron and wreckage. One funnel was hanging over the side and only part of the mast remained standing. As the "Haida Pascha" passed, her crew gave a rousing cheer which the 16th heartily reciprocated.

For the next three days the 17th, 18th and 19th, the troops were practised in landing from the ship's boats—an operation which demands much repetition before the requisite speed and lack of confusion in completing the operation are obtained. This training was carried out in marching order, but only the men were disembarked for the reason that no lighters were available for horses, wagons, etc. The 20th and 21st found a strong wind with rain and the water in the harbour too rough for a continuance of this work.

On April 22 the weather moderated and by this time all ranks were anxiously awaiting the orders which would set them travelling a further stage to the real thing. That active service was close ahead was realised when, on the 23rd, the following order was received and the King's message read to the battalion:—

GENERAL ROUTINE ORDER.

(*Special.*)

General Headquarters,
22nd April, 1915.

The following gracious Message has been received to-day by the General Commanding and is published for information:—

"The King wishes you and your army every success, and you are all constantly in His Majesty's thoughts and prayers."

E. M. WOODWARD,
Brig. Gen.
Deputy Adjutant General,
Mediterranean Expeditionary Force.

This was followed by one from the Corps Commander, General Sir Wm. Birdwood, as follows:—

"Officers and Men,

"In conjunction with the navy, we are about to undertake one of the most difficult tasks any soldier can be called upon to perform, and a problem which has puzzled many soldiers for years past. That we will succeed I have no doubt, simply because I know your full determination to do so. Lord Kitchener has told us that he lays special stress on the role the army has to play in this particular operation, the success of which will be a very severe blow to the enemy—indeed, as severe as any he could receive in France. It will go down to history to the glory of the soldiers of Australia and New Zealand. Before we start, there are one or two points which I must impress on all, and I most earnestly beg every single man to listen attentively and take them to heart.

"We are going to have a real hard and rough time of it until, at all events, we have turned the enemy out of our first objective. Hard, rough times none of us mind, but to get through them successfully we must always keep before us the following facts. Every possible endeavour will be made to bring up transport as often as possible; but the country whither we are bound is very difficult, and we may not be able to get our wagons anywhere near us for days; so men must not think their wants have been neglected if they do not get all they want. On landing, it will be necessary for every individual to carry with him all his requirements in food and clothing for three days, as we may not see our transports until then. Remember then that it is essential for everyone to take the very greatest care, not only of his food but also of his ammunition, the replenishment of which will be very difficult. Men are liable to throw away their food the first day out and to finish their water bottles as soon as they start marching. If you do this now, we can hardly hope for success, as unfed men cannot fight, and you must make an effort to try and refrain from starting on your water bottles until quite late in the day. Once you begin drinking you cannot stop and a water bottle is very soon emptied.

"Also, as regards ammunition, you need not waste it by firing away indiscriminately at no target. The time will come when we shall find the enemy in well entrenched positions from which we shall have to turn him out, when all our ammunition will be required; and remember—

"Concealment wherever possible,
"Covering fire always,
"Control of fire and control of your men,
"Communications never to be neglected.

"W. R. BIRDWOOD."

The next day, 24th, the companies were issued with the last of their field service equipment—one pick or one shovel per man. These tools were then looked upon chiefly as an extra and unnecessary burden for the "P.B.I.," but the time was coming when they would be thought just as comforting a companion in a tight corner as was the rifle.

CHAPTER 8.—"THE LANDING."

About noon on April 25, the "Haida Pascha" weighed anchor and put to sea. During the morning distant firing was heard, which announced that the Australians were in action at last.

Approaching the shore of Gallipoli about 4 o'clock in the afternoon, all that could be seen from the "Haida Pascha" was a thick haze of blue smoke and flashes of guns ahead. Battleships and destroyers were numerous and very busy bombarding the shore where the 3rd Australian Brigade had landed at daybreak. The scene from the deck of the "Haida Pascha" was a memorable one. From right to left the ships of the navy were spread like the ribs of a fan, each battleship and cruiser having an allotted section of the coast to attend to with its enormous guns. The work of disembarking the rest of the 1st Australian Division was actively in progress and destroyers were fussing about between transports and the shore, towing long lines of boats, laden to the gunwales with Australian soldiers.

The covering force, the 3rd Brigade, had succeeded in effecting a landing at daybreak on the 25th and during the day the rest of the 1st Division had disembarked and been absorbed into heavy fighting in the tangle of hills and gullies that skirted the coast of Anzac.

By far the most critical position in the front on the evening of the 25th was the gap then known to exist at the head of what was later called Monash Valley. How narrow or how wide this gap might be was unknown. All that was clear was that touch had not been gained between the 3rd Brigade's left at the spur, known afterwards as Pope's Hill, and the New Zealanders on Walker's Ridge. Between them came Russell's Top—unknown and unexplored—and looking into the back of Pope's Hill. Who held Russell's Top, none was certain. The Turks were threatening to appear on it and the commander of the 3rd Brigade at dusk asked urgently for reinforcements of the 4th Brigade, which was then due to land.

The first party of the 16th to land were its first reinforcements, 98 men under Lieuts. Brashaw and Taylor. They landed at 5.45 a.m. and were detailed as a beach fatigue party, occupied in unloading ammunition and stores from the boats, and later carrying ammunition to the front line of the 1st Division. They were returned to the battalion on May 2.

At about 5.30 p.m. the 16th came ashore from the "Haida Pascha." The destroyer "Ribble" and the open boats from which the landing was made were heavily shelled, but with only half a dozen casualties. Colonel Pope, Capt. McDonald, Lieut. Wilton, R.S.M. Emmett, with headquarters,

"A" Coy., under Major Mansbridge, "B" Coy., under Capt. Margolin, and the M.G. section were in the first landing party. The C.O. was taken to General Godley and was ordered to move to the top of Monash Valley with a mixed column of all the troops available—two companies and M.G.S., 16th, one company 15th and half company of New Zealanders —about 400 rifles all told. A staff officer, Major Villiers Stuart, was sent with Colonel Pope as guide. The light was failing and the pace was slow. As they filed into Shrapnel Gully, the mules of the 26th Indian Mountain Battery, which was landing at the time, moved across the track and cut the column in two. Major

POPE'S HILL.
As seen on April 26, 1915, by the artist, Signaller Ellis Silas, of the 16th Battalion. Note Russell's Top on the left occupied by concealed Turks.

Villiers Stuart went to find its tail and eventually put it into the line between Courtney's and Steele's Posts. Colonel Pope, with "A" and "B" Companies and M.G.S. of the 16th and half company New Zealanders, went forward in the direction of the head of the gully.

In the dark, the column filed up the muddy channel of Monash Valley and reached the fork at the valley's end. Between the two branches rose the dark mass of Pope's Hill. The Colonel reconnoitred the vicinity. The roar of rifle fire came from the heights around, but this hill and Russell's Top, on its left, were found to be empty except for a few men on Pope's from various units of the 1st Division, under Captain Jacobs. Then the column occupied the sharp edge of the spur, which ever afterwards bore Pope's name.

As to the position at the valley's head, the C.O. was entirely in the dark. All that he knew was that the 3rd Brigade had been driven back with heavy losses. Captain McDonald found on the left of Pope's Hill, in charge of a small party there, a sergeant of the 11th. The sergeant said that his men formed the extreme left flank; that no officers near them were left alive and that their losses in the retirement had been very heavy. He added that Indian troops had been fighting on their left ever since the retirement began and were still on their left rear. McDonald, not suspecting any mistake in this information, reported it to the C.O., who sent Lieut. Elston, of "A" Company, and Private Lushington to the left to obtain communication—the latter understanding Hindustanee. They moved for 150 yards through the low scrub and shouted back that they had obtained touch with Indian soldiers—and that a senior officer was required to discuss matters with their officer. Captain McDonald was, therefore, sent forward and he called back through the night that they wished to deal with the C.O. Accordingly, Colonel Pope went forward and about 150 yards along the northern ridge of the gully found McDonald, Elston and Lushington in parley with six soldiers who had rifles and bayonets fixed. A suspicious movement among them made the Colonel think that these men were Turks and not Indians. He warned the others, whereon the strangers pressed around the party. The C.O. burst through and jumped over the edge of the ridge into the gully and so escaped, although several shots were fired at him. Captain McDonald, Lieut. Elston and Private Lushington were less fortunate and became prisoners of war.

On getting back to his own party, and it being evident that the information received as to Indian troops on the left was false, the C.O. decided to occupy the position on the summit of the spur (Pope's Hill) covering about 300 yards of front, and to entrench at once. This was done and the defences were improved and organised from time to time as opportunity allowed. All night long the fighting for this portion of the line was very fierce, for as soon as the Turks located the new line, they poured in an incessant rifle and machine gun fire. It was found that the position was not only open to fire from the front, but was subsequently much harassed by the fire of snipers who had penetrated Russell's Top, and were actually in rear of the 16th trenches. This sniping fire caused many casualties.

On the morning of the 26th, the trenches were down to a depth of 3 or 4 feet. It was found that 450 men were necessary for the proper defence of the position. The problem at this time was to link up the left of the 16th line on Pope's Hill with the right of the Australians and New Zealanders, on Walker's Ridge. The warships had shelled Russell's Top at dawn and broken up the organised bodies of Turks who occupied it, but there were still many snipers left, who kept up an extremely accurate and destructive fire. Later in the evening more Turks came across the head of Monash Valley, past The Nek and on to Russell's Top. From there they commenced to make the position on Pope's Hill untenable, picking off the men at the back of the hill like flies. At 8 o'clock Colonel Pope reported the position to headquarters. The men in the trenches on Pope's Hill were better protected than the supports at the back of the hill, who were entirely without cover from the fire coming from Russell's Top. Both the 16th machine guns were placed in position with the supports and all day long these guns sniped the snipers and the Turks creeping about on Russell's Top. The gun crews did magnificent work. Both guns were hit often with Turkish bullets. Percy Black, shot through the hand and later through the ear, refused to leave his gun during any of the heavy fighting of this and the following week. The barrel casings, shot through in many places, had to be plugged with pieces of ammunition boxes in order to hold the water necessary to keep the barrels cool. Murray was wounded during the morning, but remained on duty. Indeed, it was necessary that he should do so, for by this time many of the original gun crews had been killed or wounded. The work of the guns, while it kept down organised movement of Turks along Russell's Top, could not prevent various small parties of two or three from becoming established.

This was the situation all through the day of April 26. As opportunity offered, the men belonging to other units in the 16th's trenches were weeded out and instructed to report to their battalions, while during the day various parties of 16th men reported who, when they had landed the night before, had been thrown into the line at other points. Towards nightfall both machine guns were disabled by hostile fire and the gun crews commenced a diligent salvage hunt for others, without success. However, two naval machine guns were sent up at daybreak the next morning and, when mounted, they lifted at least one load off the mind of that sorely tried officer, Colonel Pope.

In the meantime, on the morning of the 26th, the 13th Battalion was brought up and in the face of a desultory fire, the men climbed Russell's Top and effected a junction with the composite force of Australians and New Zealanders who were holding Walker's Ridge. Unfortunately, they could not advance sufficiently far along the Top to relieve the 16th of the fire from its rear. During the afternoon the 13th was heavily attacked and forced to withdraw into Monash Gully, and this left the whole length of Russell's Top still open to the Turks. On the morning of the 27th it was found that the Turks had dug themselves in there and a company of the 2nd Battalion was sent forward to take the trench. A desperate struggle then began for the much prized possession of Russell's Top. The 2nd Battalion took it. It was driven out, but

LIEUT.-COL. L. E. TILNEY, D.S.O.

rallied and took the trench again. This time it was held and with a reinforcement of New Zealanders it was strongly manned.

At about 2.30 in the afternoon, the Turks delivered an attack in six lines across the whole face of Battleship Hill, advancing on Walker's Ridge, Russell's Top, and Pope's Hill. The navy's guns opened on them and the first shell fell on Pope's Hill; the second beyond and the third, a huge shrapnel shell, which passed overhead with a heavy rumble, burst fairly over the Turks. As the dust of the explosion cleared, they could be seen running around, dazed, like ants on a disturbed nest. They then took cover in the scrub and commenced to snipe. The organised attack had completely failed.

But the snipers on Russell's Top were still doing considerable damage to the 16th. The 13th was not far enough along the ridge to relieve Pope's Hill from this harassing fire, which made communication very difficult. The slightest indiscretion of movement was met by a very well-aimed bullet.

Later in the afternoon a determined local assault was made upon Pope's Hill. A line of about 300 Turks emerged from a gully and charged across the Chessboard. An officer led them with his sword flashing and others, revolver in hand, were encouraging their men. This party was practically annihilated by an intense rifle and machine gun fire which the 16th brought to bear.

The night of the 27th was full of tension following a series of attacks. Signs of Turkish activity could be heard in bugle calls, shouts of officers rallying their men and the men calling on Allah— in between times opening up a furious fusilade on the Australian trenches. Some of the 16th, worried by the continual bugle calls. climbed over the parapet and reconnoitred in front of the trenches. When daylight came, however, on the 28th, it was evident that no Turkish attack was imminent. It was probable that they were just as exhausted as were the Australians. So far as the 16th was concerned, the one thing that worried the troops was the fact that the snipers on Russell's Top were still active—and invisible.

The 28th was a day of digging with intervals of rest and some fighting. The whole situation was still obscure, although as the men got their holes dug and connected them up, matters in this connection improved. The runners and stretcher bearers, whose jobs necessitated movement, suffered heavily during the day, but there was never a lack of volunteers to fill the places of casualties. As the messages were pieced together at the various headquarters in rear and the whereabouts and numbers of the front line troops were made known, so, gradually, was order and system brought into the business of supplying them with ammunition and food. The rear slope of Pope's Hill was so steep that access to the firing line on top was a task of no small difficulty even to an unencumbered man; to those with water, ammunition and rations, it was almost impossible to surmount. A stout rope was therefore secured from the navy and, fastened securely to a bush on the top of the hill, it formed a useful help in scaling the slope.

The situation did not change to any marked degree during the 29th. The rifle and machine gun fire during the period was intense, but both sides had got below ground and the casualties were not so severe as previously. Pope's Hill trench was continuous and afforded a safer position than the slope in rear, which was still covered by the fire of snipers.

On the evening of Friday, April 30, after having been in action on Pope's Hill for five days, the 16th was relieved by the 15th Battalion. As the various sectors of trench were relieved, the weary occupants moved down the slope in rear and congregated at a spot in one of the gullies, called Rest Camp. Here they rested until Sunday, May 2. The rest was by no means a peaceful one, and the spot could only be called a rest camp in comparison with the greater activity of the front line. During its two days "residence," the 16th lost 50 men through snipers, so that much of the time that should have been devoted to rest was occupied in digging a "possy" which would be proof against the efforts of the wily Turk.

CHAPTER 9.—THE BLOODY ANGLE.

On Sunday, May 2, orders were received that the 16th Battalion, as part of a left-flank forward movement, would assault and entrench on the ridge covering the south-easterly front of the general position, to the left of the ground then occupied by Captain Quinn—Quinn's Post. The plan was that the 16th should file up the eastern branch of the valley past the foot of Quinn's until its head had reached the end of the "Bloody Angle." The 13th Battalion was to follow the 16th and prolong its line to the left, joining with the Otago Battalion (N.Z.) reaching out from Knoll 224 D5. The 15th Battalion was to move out from Pope's Hill and co-operate.

Reconnaissance of the ground during the day was made and at 7 p.m. the battalion entered the gully below the ridge referred to. It was the first time the battalion had been in an assault and the men were very keen. In defence of Pope's Hill, with Turks firing at them from front and rear, they had held on until nearly worn out. Withdrawn into Monash Valley "to rest," they had still suffered heavily from snipers. The "rest camp" had become a place where enemy snipers made it almost compulsory to keep quite out of the open and the idleness was tiresome. Consequently the prospect of being on the offensive for the first time after a week's irksome defensive and getting at the enemy in earnest gave grim pleasure to the 16th.

The attack was covered by a bombardment from the guns and this in itself was inspiring. At 7.15 p.m., when the guns eased and lengthened, the 16th did a right turn and climbed the steep side of the valley head. Not a shot was fired while the men were in the gully, but when they reached the top of the ridge connecting Quinn's Post with the Chessboard, a heavy fire was opened on them. The extreme right of the 16th clambered over the northernmost trenches of Quinn's Post, which were held by a weak company of the 13th. The rest of the 16th advanced a few yards over the level scrub and began to dig a trench line in prolongation to Quinn's. Then a fierce fire was turned upon them from the Turks in position on The Nek and the Chessboard in their left rear. The supports were digging on the rear slope of the hill and some of the men on the left drew back into the gully of the Bloody Angle. At the foot of Dead Man's Ridge they rallied and climbed the hill again. Throughout the night the 16th continued to fight and dig by turns. Part of the line found a Turkish trench five yards in from the crest of the Bloody Angle and occupied it. On the left, where there was no trench, the men dug rifle pits in the scrub.

The fire which poured in upon the rear slope of the ridge occupied by the 16th made the task of carrying ammunition to it a most dangerous one. As the supply began to fail, Private Fink, runner to Major Mansbridge, and other brave men volunteered to bring the boxes up the hill. Again and again the volunteers were shot as they scrambled up with heavy cases; others took their places only to fall dead across the boxes they were dragging, or to roll down the steep side of the hill. Communication with the line of the 16th digging on the crest of the Bloody Angle became, towards morning, almost impossible.

The 13th Battalion, in the meantime, had worked into position astride the high land with the fork of the gully between its right and the left of the 16th. No touch was gained between the two battalions and throughout the whole action the 16th was unaware of the position of the 13th. But the plans of the New Zealanders who had the attack on the left of the 13th had gone wrong and consequently the 13th's left flank was completely in the air. The New Zealanders had been delayed in their approach march and when they finally made attempts to advance beyond the crest they lost very heavily and their objective, Baby 700, was never reached. They dug in somewhere near The Nek and the 13th towards midnight discovered their position and made arrangements to have the gap between the two lines filled. The situation then was: The 16th was in very nearly the position assigned as its objective; the 13th was separated from it by a gully and neither knew the other's exact position; the left of the 13th was in touch with the Otago Battalion which was dug in on a line 500 yards short of its objective. This all meant that the 16th line was enfiladed by a heavy fire from the left flank.

At dawn the intense fire on the extreme left of the New Zealand line caused an order for it to withdraw. This left the flank of the 13th again in the air with Turks occupying the line vacated by the New Zealanders. Towards morning a body of Turks on the right, in front of the 16th, advanced to take its trenches but they were soon driven back. Rifle fire from a Turkish position about 80 yards away was very intense and eventually the 16th clambered out of its trenches to attack it. But something had fired the scrub and the rush was seen. Machine guns from Baby 700 on the left raked the line. The Turks threw bombs and met the attack with a murderous fire. The attempt failed and when dawn came the dead of the 16th lay thickly on the slopes between the two positions.

As the light grew the Turks came creeping through the scrub and heavy casualties were inflicted on them by the rifles and machine guns of the 16th.

During the night a battalion of marines had been sent to reinforce the attacking troops. These marines, hampered by the crowds of wounded men in the valley, did not reach the head of it until the dawn was breaking. At 4 a.m. the C.O. Portsmouth Battalion, R.M.L.I., reported to Colonel Pope that he had been ordered to support the 16th Battalion. He was instructed to proceed to the head of the gully and from there send 50 to 100 men to support the right of the 16th line—the ba'ance to reinforce and prolong the firing line on the left. Major Tilney was sent forward to indicate the ground and positions to which the Portsmouth Battalion was allotted. After half an hour he returned and reported that the C.O. Portsmouth Battalion had not conformed to instructions, arguing that his orders were merely to form a support—not a firing line; that there was in fact no accommodation for additional troops in the firing line and that to carry out the instructions would involve breaking up his platoon formations.

Colonel Pope at once proceeded to the head of the gully and there repeated the instructions that 50 or 100 men should be sent to the right of the line and the balance to the left and in prolongation of the left flank. The C.O. Portsmouth Battalion further hesitated. The situation was rapidly becoming critical. Finally he agreed, "under the special conditions and accepting no responsibility," to do as requested, but at this moment several shells from the right rear burst over and in the trenches constructed and occupied by the 16th at the head of the gully, blowing their occupants out and causing a general stampede among the rank and file of the Portsmouth Battalion, who were congregated in the gully approaches. This stampede was checked and stemmed by the presence of mind and personal efforts of Major Tilney and Major Festing (Brigade Major, R.M.L.I.). Considering that the shells were from Turkish guns Colonel Pope immediately telephoned headquarters 4th Brigade with the object of getting naval and artillery fire to reply and to shell the position, so as to prevent its occupation by the enemy.

Confusion prevailed and many men of the Portsmouth Battalion occupied the ridge to the left of the gully where they were caught by Turkish fire from the flanks. Some time later, in full daylight, the marines strove to climb the hills and reinforce the 16th men who were still in the trenches. As they neared the top they came under view of Turkish machine guns on The Nek and Baby 700. They were killed in scores, and were forced to retire to the foot of the gully. It was in this attempt that Major Abrahall, who had been with the 16th at Blackboy, was killed while leading his men to its assistance. Captain Jess accompanied the marines and after the latter had been wiped out he and a private in the 16th were pinned in a shallow hole by a Turkish machine gun which fired at their slightest movement. Over an hour elapsed before they were able to get back.

Communication with the 16th over the open hilltop was thus clearly impossible. The only chance was to sap a communication trench through to it. Captain Jess and an officer of the marines endeavoured to start the marines upon this work but the fire of the machine guns followed them and defeated the attempt. The men of the 16th who were still in the trenches on the crest had watched the marines striving vainly to reach them and realised that the effort had failed. Throughout the morning the 16th gradually fell back in twos and threes, the men jumping over the top and rolling down the hill. A few still stayed in their trenches. Lance-Corporal Percy Black, twice wounded earlier in the week, hung on with his machine gun until he had fired all his ammunition into the advancing Turks and then brought his gun back safely. Sgt.-Major Harvey lay in the trench until the Turks reached it. They bayoneted him and flung him on the parapet for dead. He eventually rolled down the hillside and three days later reached the lines of the battalion, dazed and mortally wounded. Another man, Private M. J. Troy, when the Turks attacked, was knocked senseless by a bomb. He woke to find his mates, Private J. W. White and M. W. Grey, dead beside him and all others in the trench dead or wounded. He attempted to crawl away after dark but was captured.

While the 16th was thus gradually falling back the scene at the foot of the gully baffled description. It was crowded with troops, Australians, marines, wounded men, fighting men and stretcher bearers. Some of the trenches were held by 16th men until 10 a.m. on Monday, May 3, but, the left flank being exposed to frontal and enfilade rifle and machine gun fire, their resistance was gradually subdued and by 1 p.m. on that day the gully and trenches were practically abandoned. The trenches were then occupied by the Turks, and, as they joined at Quinn's Post, both Turks and Australians were in occupation of the same trench line with only a block between. At 6 p.m. the remnants of the 16th were collected and moved back to Rest Camp. During the night, the 13th, which had hung on to its trenches throughout a trying day, being deprived of support on both flanks, was also withdrawn.

CHAPTER 10.—RE-ORGANISATION.

On May 3 the effective strength of the 16th was found to be:—

Officers	9
Other Ranks	298
Total	307

It went into action on May 2, at the Bloody Angle, with 17 officers and 628 other ranks, so that the losses there in killed, wounded and missing totalled 8 officers and about 330 other ranks.

Re-organisation of the Battalion to meet temporary requirements was arranged as follows:—

Headquarters and M.G. Section	3 off.	55 O.R.
"A" Coy. (formed from old "A" and "B" Coys.)	4 ,,	126 ,,
"D" Coy. (formed from old "C" and "D" Coys.)	2 ,,	117 ,,
Total	9 ,,	298 ,,

On this re-organisation "A" and "D" Companies were sent that evening (Tuesday, May 4), to relieve the garrison of the trenches at Quinn's Post. The enthusiasm of the survivors was in no way diminished. All were still buoyed up by the spirit of the "Old Sixteenth," and more than proud of their share in its fighting. It was obvious, however, that a complete re-organisation and filling up of men and material would be necessary before the battalion could move forward again. Both the machine guns had been put out of action twice. The machine gun section was reduced to less than half its proper strength. The signallers of headquarters and of the companies were reduced to almost an unworkable proposition. Two half-size companies only remained. Nominal rolls, returns and records, many of which were in the adjutant's haversack at the time of his capture by the Turks, had been lost irretrievably. The records of "A" Coy. were in possession of Major Mansbridge when on Sunday morning his equipment was destroyed by shell fire and many men were lying dead on Bloody Angle with pay books on them, whose bodies could not be recovered. To fill gaps in the establishment of officers, the C.O. recommended many of the men who had distinguished themselves in the recent fighting and had shown the necessary qualities of leadership therein. Many deeds of courage and resource—both spontaneous and sustained for periods—occurred during these few strenuous days. The first recommendations by the C.O. for special recognition were as follow:—

"Lieut. A. E. Carse and Sergt. George Demel—the former mortally wounded on Pope's Hill, and the latter killed on Sunday night (May 2), deserve special mention for their work in the machine gune section. The very highest form of commendation is due to No. 170, L/Corp. Percy Black, who, although shot through the hand the day after landing and later through the ear, has continued on duty without cessation. During the action on the night of May 2/3 he, in company with Sgt. Demel, mounted a gun beyond the Gully Ridge. Demel was shot dead, but Black, surrounded by Turks and without other assistance—fired all available ammunition into them and eventually brought the gun safely back with him.

"Major W. O. Mansbridge commanded the left section of Pope's Hill position from Sunday night until relieved on the following Friday (25th to 30th April) with conspicuous resource and gallantry. He was for these five days constantly under fire and continually pressed by Turkish attacks. During the action on May 2/3 also, Major Mansbridge performed service beyond description throughout.

"Lieut. E. H. Kretchmar, who was with Major Mansbridge, gave him most valuable support and assistance. Lieut. Kretchmar was killed in the trenches on Quinn's Post on May 5.

"Major E. K. Baker, in command of the leading company during the assault on Gully Ridge on May 2, carried out his duty with the utmost skill and vigor.

"Major L. E. Tilney, V.D., in the early morning of May 3, when the shelling of our trenches seemed almost certain to produce a stampede among the supporting Portsmouth Battalion, R.M.L.I., stemmed the streams of retiring men with coolness and vigor, his own personal example having an effect which could be obtained in no other way. He did this although himself struck and slightly hurt by shrapnel.

"Capt. R. S. McGregor, A.A.M.C., R.M.O., has been indefatigable in his attention to wounded men and in the organisation of stretcher-bearers. He was shot through the arm on April 30, but continued on duty until compelled to desist.

"No. 291, Pte. W. A. Pullin, who has acted as orderly and given meritorious service—carrying messages quickly and effectively under hot fire ever since the landing. He has been hit on the hand once, but has not left duty. His attention to wounded comrades and his unfailing cheerfulness in the face of all difficulty have had a very useful effect wherever he has been.

"H. POPE,

"Lt.-Col.,

"Com. 16th Batn. 7/5/15."

THE OLD SIXTEENTH.

The following was the casualty return up to 9 a.m. on May 4:

	Off.	O.R.
Landed from Transport 25/4/15 ..	28	898
1st Reinforcement joined 27/4/15 ..	1	68
Total	29	966

Casualty Reports to date:

	Off.	O.R.
Killed in action	7	82
Wounded	9	282
Missing	3	15
Invalided	1	1
Unaccounted for	—	288
Total Casualties	20	668
Actual strength 6 p.m., 4/5/15 ..	9	298
Total	29	960

The first Gallipoli promotions were:—

Lieut. George Leveson Curlewis to be Capt. and Adjutant.
Lieut. Robert B. Blythe to be Capt.
346 Sgt. H. C. Parker to be 2nd Lt.
612 C.Q.M. Sgt. W. E. Collins to be 2nd Lt.
170 L/Cpl. Percy Black to be 2nd Lt.
344 Sgt. P. R. Paull to be 2nd Lt.
5 Corp. G. C. Curlewis to be 2nd Lt.
541 Sgt. H. T. Crouch to be 2nd Lt.

The baptism of fire to which the battalion had been subjected caused most of the survivors to view life in general from a new angle. Particularly was this so in regard to each other, for the events of those first seven days on Gallipoli had brought to light qualities of manhood which had never been suspected before the supreme test came. "Scotty" Thorpe was one of the "hard doers" of the 16th. It can be said that during the training days of the battalion he was a decided nuisance and all the harder to deal with because he had served in the navy and was, therefore, an "old soldier." Short of stature, tough as nails, he was continually in trouble in Blackboy Hill. He drank Capt. Margolin's whisky and the resultant "bender" kept him "A.W.L." for over a week. He was the refractory spirit on the "Dimboola," when "D" Company travelled to Broadmeadows, for that vessel was not a troopship and the bar was open. At Broadmeadows he "carried on" as usual, and on the "Ceramic" he was the only man of the ship's company who broke ashore at Port Said. His seafaring experience there came to his aid in climbing down an anchor chain to the "bum-boat," and then ashore. He was duly returned by the military police and arrived at Alexandria in detention. At Heliopolis he spent a good deal of his time in the guard tent, but happened to be "out" when the move was made to Lemnos. Once aboard the "Seeangbee," "Scotty's" sinews began to stiffen—he smelt War. Then came the events of The Landing, and the real man in him came to the surface. On Pope's Hill he fought like one possessed, cheering on the younger men, sharing his water with the less seasoned, and generally behaving like a real hero. When the Bloody Angle attack took place on May 2, "Scotty" was well to the fore. He carried Lieut. Curlewis to safety after he was wounded and then went back and met a glorious death in the firing line. "Scotty" Thorpe may have been no credit to the 16th as a parade ground soldier, but when the real test came, he set the example of duty well performed.

The ten days—April 25 to May 4—was a hectic period in the life of the battalion. Its introduction was a terrible ordeal and the number of casualties sustained was something in the nature of a record—even for the landing operations. Although cut to pieces and disorganised at times through losing their leaders, the survivors battled through the most trying situations and hung on to ground so long as there was a prospect of success. Up to this period Gallipoli was almost entirely a soldiers' battle. The higher commanders could do little to influence the course of each operation once the troops were launched until the ground on which they fought had been captured and consolidated. By May 4 this ground was held, stock was being taken and the reorganisation of units, staffs, and trench sectors was being rapidly accomplished in preparation for further rough work which lay ahead.

It is rather interesting to realise that the Turkish unit which put up such a stout resistance to the Australians at Anzac was the 19th Turkish Division, commanded by that brilliant soldier (and later President of Turkey), Mustafa Kemal Bey. One regiment (corresponding to an Australian brigade), was in trenches and camps as a coast defence; the other two regiments of the division were in reserve and camped near Maidos. On the morning of the 25th Kemal had ordered these reserve regiments to parade at 5.30 o'clock for field exercises in the direction of Hill 971. They were on parade when firing broke out and news was reported to them of the landing. Kemel handled the situation with coolness and judgment and it was due to his sound appreciation of the position that the evening of the 25th saw the Australians at a standstill and their line completely enveloped by Turks.

CHAPTER 11.—"QUINN'S!"

The situation at the beginning of May was that while the Australians and New Zealanders had secured a precarious foothold on Gallipoli they had nowhere succeeded in reaching their objectives. The Third Ridge was the first objective which had been allotted to the covering force, the 3rd Brigade, but the position on which the whole attacking force—the 1st Australian Division and the Australian and New Zealand Division—was eventually forced to dig and consolidate was known as the Second Ridge, whereon the Turks were also entrenching. With the Anzac line dominated by the enemy (on Baby 700 and in the network of trenches at the Chessboard) the position gained by the Australian was tactically very unsound.

On May 1 the 4th Brigade was allotted the sector which was admitted to be the most difficult part of the front—the disconnected posts at Courtney's and Quinn's and Pope's Hill. The trenches at Quinn's were so close that voices of men in the opposing trenches could be heard. Only twenty yards separated them at their furthest point (the length of a cricket pitch), and this proximity meant an unceasing struggle by both sides to maintain their foothold. It therefore resolved itself into an active trench warfare; each side holding the front line trench strongly while sapping, tunnelling and digging in every possible direction behind in order to improve communications to it and thus give supporting troops quick access to danger points. This involved great strain on all ranks responsible for holding the line.

The system adopted was for the front and support trenches to be manned by different companies of the same battalions, the reserve companies being employed as carrying and digging parties during the day. These reserve companies at night slept close behind the support lines in their great coats and with their arms. At all times of special anxiety—which were frequent—any troops which happened to be in "rest" were liable to be moved up night after night to positions in rear of, or between important points. With all the uncertainty of the situation, however, it was surprising how soon the troops settled down to routine, with headquarters, regimental aid posts and Quartermasters' stores in fixed locations.

In the front line the trench was deepened to such an extent that firing steps had to be cut to enable men to shoot over the parapet when necessary. At Quinn's, commanded as it was by Turkish snipers and machine guns, it was not possible to show a head over the parapet by day. A few periscopes, improvised from mirrors on warships and transports, were obtained early in May, but these were almost immediately smashed by aimed rifle fire from the Chessboard.

In addition to the superiority of fire and position which the Turks had at this stage they possessed a weapon with which the Australians were not equipped and of which they, as yet, knew nothing. This was the hand bomb, an ideal accessory for trench fighting. From the beginning the closeness of the trenches at Quinn's subjected that post to incessant enemy bombing. At first this method of offence could not be replied to; later some genius invented the

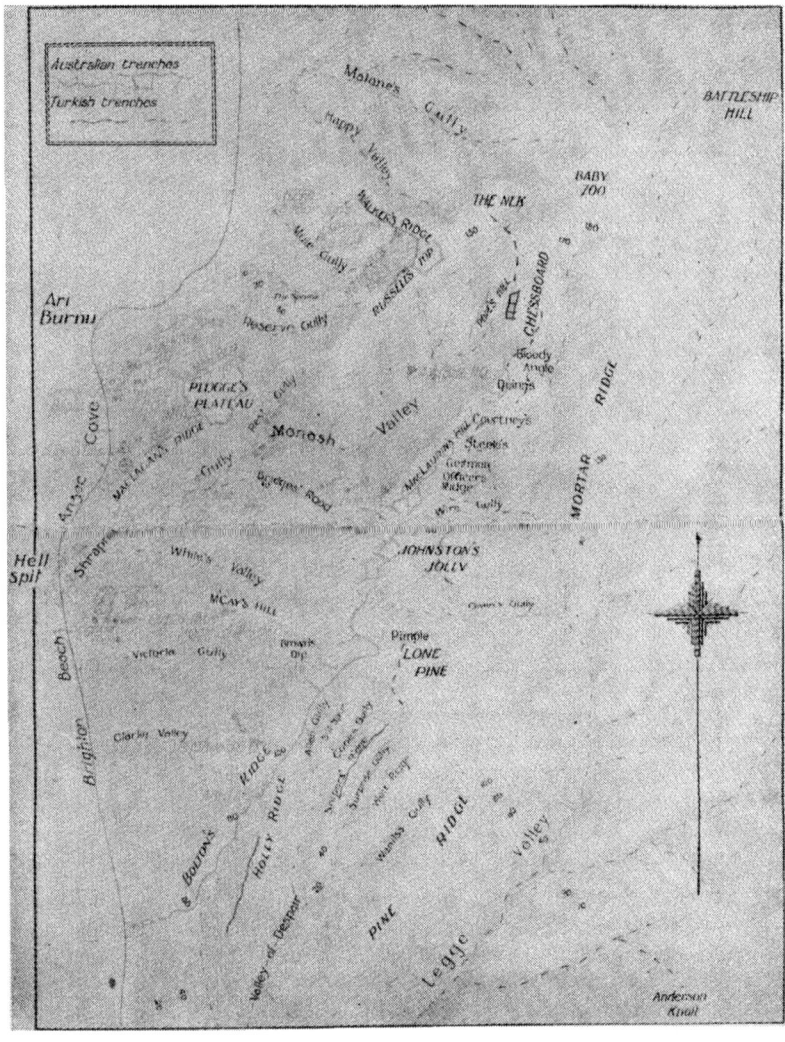

THE ANZAC POSITION ON MAY 5.

"jam tin" bomb—crude but effective—with which the Quinn's Post garrison retaliated with the few that were issued to them. Later the "Garland" grenade thrower was first used at Quinn's by the 16th.

The mere holding of Quinn's Post involved more strain on the troops than did other parts of the line and it was arranged that instead of being the responsibility of one unit it should be held alternately by the 15th and 16th Battalions, each having a tour of duty of 48 hours. This routine was followed during May with the exception of a short period when 200 men of the 16th were detailed as a beach fatigue party. On the evening of May 4, the 16th took over Quinn's, with Major Tilney in command of the post and battalion headquarters at the Rest Camp. It was a tragic introduction.

IN THE TRENCHES AT QUINN'S POST.
Drawn by Signaller Ellis Silas, who was one of the garrison.

The next day several men were killed and wounded, Lieut. Kretchmar was shot through the head and killed, while Major Baker was seriously wounded through the lung.

On May 9 the 16th Battalion was in support to the 15th, which was holding the line. It had been arranged that the 15th should deliver a night attack with 200 men on the Turkish trenches immediately in front of Quinn's. The object, primarily, was reconnaissance, but it was ordered that, if possible, the Turkish trenches were to be held permanently. Parties were therefore organised whose duties were to dig three communication trenches across No

Man's Land between the two front lines. These trenches were to be commenced as soon as the Turkish line was entered. Just prior to the hour set for the attack a terrific fire was opened from the enemy trenches and the assault was delayed until it lessened.

In the first stage the attack by the 15th was successful. The Turkish front line was taken and the digging parties commenced the joining of the two fronts across No Man's Land. A change in the situation took place when the Turks counter-attacked with bombs up two communication trenches and re-entered their own front line in both places, thus cutting the 15th into three parts, none of which was in touch with the others. At the same time machine guns from the flanks commenced to sweep No Man's Land with a devastating fire.

Messages came back for reinforcements and Capt. Margolin with 30 men of the 16th charged and supported the 15th centre party. The portion of trench which this party held was so crowded that Margolin's men were forced to lie on the parapet, where they suffered from the machine gun fire sweeping the whole area. Lieut. Harwood and 30 men of the 16th were then sent to reinforce the digging parties, which at this stage were in a parlous condition, having suffered heavy casualties from the bombs of the counter-attacking Turks and the machine gun fire from the flanks. Lieut. Curlewis and 20 men volunteered to go forward and Curlewis was killed almost immediately. As Margolin's party was unable to be used effectively and in its exposed position men were being needlessly hit, its situation was reported to Colonel Cannan, the commanding officer of the 15th, who ordered the withdrawal of all 16th men. Both parties were then brought in after having lost 20 men killed and wounded. Captain Margolin was hit in the chest by a rifle bullet, but a thick pocket book, which the bullet just failed to penetrate, saved his life.

The whole situation at this time appears to have become confused. The night was dark and the Turks were vigorously bombing the parties of the 15th (who had no bombs with which to reply) along the captured trenches, while the machine gun fire across No Man's Land had practically wiped out the digging parties. At this stage, Capt. Townshend, with 40 men of the 16th, was ordered to charge one of the sections re-occupied by the Turks.

This was a very gallant effort. The party was met with a murderous fire and only a few men reached the Turkish parapet, where they threw the pitifully few jam tin bombs they had and then found themselves powerless. Capt. Townshend and Lieut. Durston were killed in the charge and the attack completely failed. During the remainder of the night and at dawn the few survivors moved about No Man's Land attending to wounded and carrying them back to Quinn's Post. L/Corp. L. D. McCarthy ("Fat"), who acted as runner to Capt. Townshend, brought that officer's body in during the night. The Turks counter-attacked early in the morning and one party entered the trench but all were killed.

May 10 was a day spent in cleaning up the debris of war in Quinn's Post trenches—and various working parties were detailed for unpleasant jobs. One party of six men, under L/Corp. "Fat" McCarthy was instructed by an officer to clear a certain section of trench of dead Turks and bury them, reporting the number for submission to headquarters. The job was completed and

THE ROLL CALL.

The roll call revealed to the actors the grim significance of every fight. This sketch was drawn by Signaller Ellis Silas and depicts a company of the 16th Battalion the morning after the heavy fighting at Quinn's Post on May 9, 1915.

McCarthy reported the number of enemy dead as thirteen and a half. The officer queried the half but was assured that the number was literally correct—thirteen corpses and half a one—so that number was officially forwarded to headquarters. McCarthy then requested a special issue of rum for his party in view of the gruesome task just accomplished. As the 16th quartermaster was deficient in that commodity McCarthy was given a note to the brigade Q.M. informing him of the circumstances. Armed with that note the cheerful "Fat" set off and returned soon after with the smile that betokened his successful efforts to "work the oracle."

With the failure of this "reconnaissance" the conviction grew that Quinn's position was so dominated by the spurs on either side that no local attack from it could be successful. The communication trenches which had been partially dug during the attack were found to have added a further danger to the garrison at Quinn's. They enabled the Turks to creep upon them at night and throw bombs accurately into the Australian front line. To overcome this a party of 60 of the 2nd Light Horse on May 15 attempted to attack and hold the Turks' front line while other parties filled in the communication trenches. This attack was a failure and the Light Horse lost 25 men killed and 21 wounded.

QUINN'S POST FROM ITS EXTREME LEFT,
showing the bomb-stop which separated the Australian and Turkish trenches.

Owing to the number of casualties in the 4th Brigade the Light Horse and Royal Marine Light Infantry were used for a time in the occupation of Quinn's in conjunction with the 15th and 16th Battalions. With them and the assistance of engineers a comprehensive system of support trenches and bomb proof dugouts was commenced, but Quinn's was still recognised by the troops as the worst "possy" on Anzac.

On May 12 the 16th, on relief by the 15th, proceeded to Rest Camp. It was a red letter day by reason of the fact that a tot of rum was issued to all ranks. The casualty report submitted up to May 13 was as follows:—

	Off.	O.R.
Landed from transport 25th and 26th April 1915	28	898
Reinforcements joined 27/4/15	1	68
,, ,, 6/5/15	—	51
,, ,, 7/5/15	1	98
Landed ex "Haida Pascha" 8/5/15	2	60
	32	1,175
Casualties reported by name to 13/5/15	25	441
Unaccounted for (missing)	—	291
Actual strength 13/5/15	7	443
	32	1,175

The weather was fairly hot at this period and lice and vermin were making their presence felt. It was impossible to combat them owing to the absence of conveniences, but right to the end of Gallipoli "chatting" parades were one of the most regular occupations of the troops. The presence of many hundreds of rotting human bodies in inaccessible places between the lines was also a matter which the tainted air brought forcibly home to all ranks, and the medical authorities began to fear that an epidemic of disease would be the result. The one bright gleam in life on Anzac at this period was organised bathing at the beach.

CHAPTER 12.—THE TURKISH OFFENSIVES.

On May 18 certain signs reported by observers on various parts of the Anzac front led the higher commanders to expect an attack. "Dreary Dan," a Turkish gun, registered carefully on Courtney's, Steele's and Monash Valley. An unusual quietness in many localities where the Turks were normally active was one of the most suspicious indications and this, with other information, led to an instruction being issued that the troops were to stand to arms on May 19 at 3 a.m. instead of the usual hour. The front and support lines were reinforced and all necessary preparations were made to meet a general attack.

About midnight the Turks opened an intense rifle and machine gun fire along the whole of the Anzac defences and at 2 a.m. "C" and "D" Companies of the 16th were moved into the front line at Quinn's to reinforce the 15th, while "A" and "B" Companies were kept ready in close support. The machine guns of the four battalions had been previously brigaded and placed in positions which would enable them to fire obliquely across the whole front of the 4th Brigade.

Towards daylight the enemy left his trenches along the whole of his line. At Quinn's the Turks nowhere reached the front trench, being met as soon as they showed themselves with an intense rifle and machine gun fire. Just before the attack a shower of bombs was thrown from the old communication trenches into Quinn's, but these were countered by bombs thrown by the garrison. Everywhere the attack failed and the Turks were mown down in hundreds in their attempt to sweep the Anzacs into the sea. During the attack places on the Australian parapet were much sought after by many men for whom there was no room. It was here that the value of the rapid loading and firing instruction given on board ship and in Egypt was exemplified. Practically the only casualties were caused through the excitement of the occasion making men reckless and exposing themselves in an endeavour to secure better shooting.

By 5 o'clock in the morning the attack had definitely failed. The only enemy activity to be observed was the convulsive movement of many of the unfortunate Turkish wounded or the cautious wriggling of an unwounded soldier taking advantage of the sparse cover in order to regain his own lines. During the afternoon "A" and "B" Companies of the 16th relieved the remainder of the 15th in Quinn's and soon after they had taken over the enemy launched another attack. This and two or three other local attacks were easily beaten back and the situation, except for the number of Turkish casualties in front, again became normal. The night following was quiet and the enemy was obviously taking advantage of the hours of darkness to re-organise his badly shattered forces and prepare for a possible counter-attack.

This action had a strong moral effect on the 16th as it did on the whole Anzac force. Since The Landing on April 25 the 16th had frequently been in action against a mostly unseen enemy and its losses at the hands of Turkish snipers had engendered a very bitter feeling. After May 19, however, personal prejudice went by the board. The Turk had come out into the open and the 16th had hit back and repaid with interest the hard knocks previously incurred. The Turkish attack had been launched by 42,000 men of 4 divisions, of which two were composed of fresh troops, while the other two had been engaged since The Landing. The Turkish losses in killed and wounded along the Anzac front on that day totalled over 10,000; against which the casualties of the defenders did not exceed 600.

The next few days and nights were uneventful but anxious for Quinn's. At 5.30 in the evening of May 20 a white flag was shown by the Turks and there was an unofficial armistice during which some of the Turkish wounded of the day before were brought in. At 7.20 p.m., however, fire was resumed again with great activity until 11 o'clock, after which the night was quiet.

It was recognised by both armies that the presence of so many Turkish dead constituted a danger which must be coped with. After preliminary negotiations an official armistice was approved by General Birdwood from 7.30 a.m. to 4.30 p.m. on May 24 for the purpose of burying the dead. At Quinn's, during the cessation of hostilities, the narrow strip of No Man's Land was crowded and the Turkish dead were buried in the communication trenches dug during the 15th's attack on May 9, and which later assisted the Turks in their bombing of Quinn's. When the burial party had nearly completed this work a Turkish officer objected to the trench being made use of for that purpose. However, his objection, even if valid, was too late. It was said afterwards on doubtful authority that Mustafa Kemal, commander of the division occupying the sector which faced that of the Anzac Divisions, reconnoitred the whole of No Man's Land during the armistice dressed in the uniform of a sergeant. At the appointed time the burial parties withdrew and active warfare was resumed.

Both sides about this time appear to have settled down to trench conditions. The sinking of the "Triumph" on May 25 and the "Majestic" on May 27—the former in full view of the troops—were two events which cast a gloom over Anzac. The "Triumph" was an old and intimate friend and the loss was felt as such. On May 27 it was discovered that the enemy was mining towards Quinn's front line. Counter-mining was at once commenced, and this inaugurated another phase of warfare—underground.

That night the 13th Battalion relieved the 16th at Quinn's and in the evening of the next day, May 28, the Turks exploded their mine under Quinn's Post. Expecting an attack, Major Mansbridge, with "A" Company of the 16th, was sent a short distance up the Bloody Angle to make a demonstration against the Turks on its crest. Captain Margolin, with another company, was moved up the slope immediately in rear of Quinn's. After the mine explosion the attack took place as was expected. The Turks were armed with quantities of bombs and under cover of showers of these, which forced the 13th back, the enemy entered Quinn's front line. Considerable confusion prevailed in the darkness, which was increased when Colonel Burnage, the commanding officer of the 13th, was wounded. Colonel Pope then took over the command and after a series of stirring bayonet and bomb fights the front line was retaken by the 13th assisted by "B" Company of the 16th. Many Turks were found dead in the recaptured trenches and a number of the survivors surrendered to Major Tilney. One adverse result of this attack was that the mine crater was seized and held by the Turks, who afterwards used it to bombard Quinn's more effectively than ever with bombs.

On May 31, the 4th Brigade, which for five weeks had fought continuously in the key positions of Anzac, at the head of Monash Valley, and was much reduced in strength thereby, was withdrawn to a sheltered reserve position. Quinn's, the storm centre of Anzac, was handed over with no regrets to the New Zealanders.

Just before the 16th handed over, a copy of an order was taken from the body of a Turkish soldier. The enemy's opinion of Quinn's was exemplified by the fact that in the order was a paragraph stating that every Turkish soldier put into the fight against Quinn's Post would be promoted corporal. It was certainly an unsolicited testimonial to the fighting qualities of the men of the 13th, 15th and 16th who had garrisoned the post. The 16th's opinion of Quinn's can

THE ARMISTICE ON GALLIPOLI, MAY 24, 1915, showing burial parties at work near Quinn's Post.

be left to the imagination of the reader. The ground in front was almost literally covered with decomposing dead. The weather was warm. The almost appalling stench in the trenches was indescribable. It was one of those features of war which delicacy usually prevents from mention, but which was none the less real.

CHAPTER 13.—BEHIND THE FRONT.

From June 1 to August 6 the 16th Battalion was camped in the reserve area, near the Sphinx, and employed almost continuously on fatigues. During this period reinforcements joined up and men wounded in the early fighting returned from hospital. It was noticeable the effect which wounds had on men's nerves and daring. Usually men recovered from wounds were cautious. There were exceptions, of course, but they were so noticeable as to prove the rule.

During June some of the 16th took the opportunity to visit Pope's Hill, and were shown around by the troops then in garrison. As Colonel Pope remarked, "It was like re-visiting one's birthplace!"

The hot weather experienced at this time was not without its effect on the health of the troops, particularly as the flies were exceptionally bad and the whole area swarmed with body vermin. All ranks began to suffer from diarrhœa and dysentry. The number of troops sent away through these distressing complaints threatened to keep pace with the reinforcements arriving and thus prevent the battalion building up its strength to a total necessary for it to become an efficient fighting unit again.

There was plenty to do on fatigues but some time was made available for instructional purposes in sheltered positions in the gully. Here men were trained as reserve machine gunners and reinforcements were given musketry instruction which they urgently required.

Letters began to pour in at this time to the officers from the relatives and friends of those who had been killed or reported missing asking for information. Some of these letters were very distressing and often were quite impossible to answer on account of the difficulty of keeping records during the early stages of Gallipoli. The 16th had landed about 900 men on April 25, had later drawn 60 men from the ship who had been left on board to land stores, etc., and 200 odd reinforcements had joined the battalion. Yet on May 13 the strength was only about 450. The first batch of reinforcements was under the command of Lieut. Brashaw. This party, numbering 98, travelled on a different transport to that which carried the 16th and landed on Gallipoli on Sunday, April 25. It was used for beach work and did not report to the battalion until the following Friday night when the 16th was in bivouac in Rest Gully. In spite of every precaution during the next two days (Saturday and Sunday) 50 men were hit in that position by snipers and it was impossible to form up and distribute Brashaw's men to different companies. It was therefore decided that they should temporarily act as a separate unit of the battalion under Lieut.

Brashaw. On the Sunday evening (May 2) the 16th was engaged in the Bloody Angle fight. It did everything it was asked to do but, through lack of support and its own losses, it was not strong enough to hold the ground it had won. Therefore the men were ordered to withdraw. They had marched in 650 strong on Sunday evening and on the following afternoon were just about 300. Brashaw had gone into the fight with his party of 98 and had the roll containing the names of his men in his pocket. He was wounded and taken away with that information still in his possession. There was no other record of his men, consequently the difficulty of making up a correct casualty return of that party can be imagined.

Sergeant Bolton landed on May 8 with 26 reinforcements for the 16th, and the next night was killed in front of Quinn's Post. His body was right in the Turkish trenches at a point where it could not be recovered and on it was the only roll of the men he had brought with him.

In April and May the fighting was so intense that some trouble was inevitable in the matter of records. It is a matter for wonderment really that any records were kept at all. The casualties, as reported by platoon and company commanders, were almost illegible owing to the rain, the dust, the extreme fatigue of the writers and the general discomfort. When the lists did come into battalion headquarters it still required a great deal of ingenuity and initiative to get the regimental numbers and initials to complete the details. After that it was necessary to check and verify each name as far as possible and finally send the list down to the comparative security of brigade headquarters in Monash Valley.

After May several rolls of reinforcements which arrived were compiled as soon as they reported to battalion headquarters. It will be seen, however, that whatever regrets the officers of the 16th may have had at this time on the matter of the defects in their records and their sometimes inability to supply information to the relatives of men missing, their failure to do so was unavoidable. The question was never overlooked and the utmost pains were taken to obtain correct information as to casualties, and while the people in Australia may have thought in some cases that there was an unreasonable delay in supplying details, the delay was quite beyond the control of the company and battalion staffs. The entire blame lay with the enemy.

On June 2 the commander of the Australian and New Zealand Division, Major-General Sir Alexander Godley, K.C.M.G., delivered an address to the 4th Brigade, which was congregated for that purpose in a sheltered position in Reserve Gully. Sergeant C. Taylor took the speech down in shorthand. It was as follows:—

"Colonel Monash, officers, N.C.O.'s and men of the 4th Brigade. I have come here to-day to tell you all with what great pride and satisfaction I have watched your performances during the last five weeks. I wish to tell you all of the 4th Australian Infantry Brigade that the whole Army Corps has looked with the greatest admiration on your doings on the Peninsula.

"You have been for five weeks in the trenches fighting particularly hard the whole time. Never before have troops been subjected to such heavy shell and rifle fire and very often you have been met with bombs. You have been always in such a din and turmoil as would have tried a great many men indeed.

"You started on your arrival, pitchforked, I may say, into the middle of the battle. You were in the firing line under the heaviest fire until the 29th—three days with nothing but what you carried on you. It took us some time to get the battalions sorted out and the respective units together. There were many acts of heroism and gallantry performed. There were a great many killed and wounded and in many cases, perhaps, no records of the gallant deeds performed were kept.

"On the 2nd and 3rd of May your brigade (Note a.) took part in a sortie from your lines which was far-reaching in its effects —operations on your part which staved off an advance by the enemy most successfully. On the 9th (Note b.) the brigade took part in another sortie and a few days ago on the 18th and 19th (Note c.) of May you bore the brunt of a very severe Turkish attack, which fell on your section of the defence at Quinn's.

"Yours is a fine record and one which you yourselves and Australia should be proud of. You are making military history for Australia—history equal to the former histories of any other brigades and troops of the Empire and of the world; deeds the Commonwealth has every reason to be proud of.

"At Pope's Hill, named after the gallant commander of the 16th Battalion; Courtney's Post, called after the officer commanding the 14th Battalion and which has been occupied by it since The Landing; also the post, the most difficult of all, Quinn's, named after Major Quinn, who, I am sorry to say, died bravely at his post while in the service of his country and who I am sure, if he had to meet his death during the campaign, would have preferred to have died on the post named after him. All these points have been taken and held against odds most gallantly. Colonel Cannan of the 15th and Major Tilney of the 16th must ever be associated with Quinn's, no less than the 14th at Courtney's. The 13th, under Lt.-Col. Burnage, and the 16th Battalion, for their valiant efforts on the 2nd and 3rd of May and again the 16th Battalion for its magnificent conduct at Pope's Hill, towards the direction of the enemy's trenches and the 13th Battalion throughout the whole of the day that followed, although their withdrawal was necessary in view of subsequent operations, are worthy of the highest admiration.

"With the names of all those deserving it is hard to single out anyone particularly, but as G.O.C. the Division I have had pleasure in sending twenty names for special mention in despatches, as you have seen in brigade orders. It has pleased His Majesty the King to confer upon this brigade two (Note d.) D.S.O's and two Military Crosses for officers and seven D.C.M.'s to N.C.O.'s and men.

These rewards between the landing of the brigade on the 25th April and the 5th May form indeed a grand and enviable record."

(Note a) : 16th and 13th Battalions.
(„ b) : 15th and 16th „
(„ c) : 15th and 16th „
(„ d) : One D.S.O. to Major W. O. Mansbridge.

About the beginning of July the battalion was informed that it would be taken off the Peninsula for a few days' spell. On July 5, with the exception of the machine guns and their crews, it left

A SUMMER RESIDENCE ON THE PENINSULAR.

Anzac at 6.45 p.m., being towed out from the jetty in barges to the "El Kahira," which sailed for the harbour of Kephalos in the island of Imbros. It was a wet night and Imbros was reached early the next morning, when the battalion landed and marched to camp. The next day, July 7, marked another red letter day in the career of the 16th. All hands received another issue of rum and it was also a pay-day! There were no roads—only mule tracks—on

Imbros, but on the 9th the battalion tried a route march which afforded an opportunity for all ranks to see the country. The next day, July 10, the boat was again boarded and at 7 p.m. she left Imbros, arriving at Anzac at 10 p.m. The troops landed and moved back to Reserve Gully after a much appreciated few days' rest from the trials and tribulations that were incidental to Anzac.

On July 14 the following despatch was received from corps headquarters:—

"The Army Corps Commander has much pleasure in publishing the names of the officers, N.C.O.'s and men of the 16th Battalion whose names have been brought to his notice for having performed various acts of gallantry and valuable services during the period May 6 to June 28, 1915. He cordially thanks them for the good work performed, which more than ever testifies to their devotion to duty and to King and country. His regret is that they cannot all be rewarded.

"Capt. Curlewis, G. L.
"677 Corp. Hummerston, S. H.
"366 ,, McLeod, A.
"241 ,, Briand, L. D.
"315 L/C Murray, H. (D.C.M.)
" 77 Pte. Mack, W.
"513 Sgt. Carr, T. J.
"1150 L/C Davis, H. D.
"Capt. R. S. McGregor, A.A.M.C."

The remainder of July was a quiet period and all ranks were inoculated against cholera. The heat, the flies and the incessant labour were having their effect on the battalion and its original members were by this time a gaunt and haggard band, showing obvious signs of the trying experiences through which they had passed. They afforded a striking contrast in appearance to the sturdy reinforcements arriving every week to make good the enormous wastage of war.

CHAPTER 14.—"971."

Early in August arrangements were made for a resumption of the offensive by the troops at Anzac. The general scheme was for a series of demonstrations to be made along the Anzac front to pin the enemy to his present line and, if possible, draw his reserves into action. The main operation, in which the 4th Brigade and some English and Indian troops were employed, was to consist of a night march northwards along the beach from Anzac and an advance up to the Abdel Rahman Spur; to be followed by an attack on Hill 971, a commanding position which overlooked the whole of the Anzac area. North of this again, new English divisions were to land at Suvla Bay and capture the high ground to the east of Salt Lake and join up with the troops from Anzac.

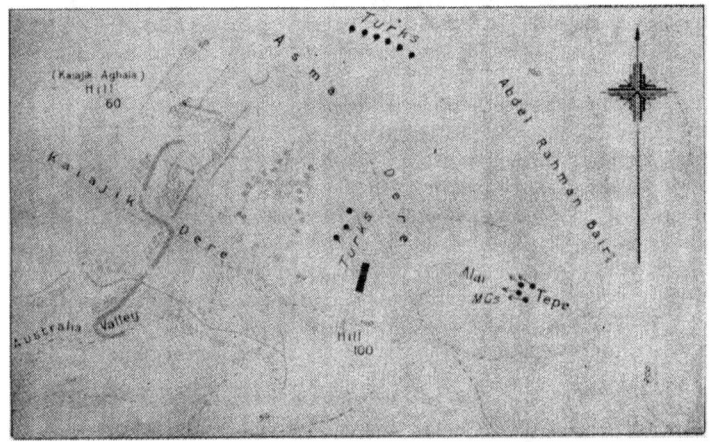

THE ATTACK ON HILL 971.
Showing the disposition of the 4th Brigade on August 8, 1915.

The only reconnaissance which could be made was from the sea, and officers were taken in daylight on a destroyer which steamed slowly along the coast and enabled them to get a vague idea of the country over which they were to attack. Incidentally, the position of the Anzac trenches, viewed from the sea, seemed very precarious, dominated as they were by higher hills occupied by the Turks.

For the approach march by night from Anzac to the jumping off point for the attack, a time-table was prepared to minimise confusion among the troops using the beach road. The head of each unit was ordered to pass the starting point at Anzac at a given time. In the case of the 4th Brigade, the starting point was No. 5 Supply Depôt, Reserve Gully, and the time 9.35 p.m. on August 6. Badges consisting of white patches 8 inches square on the right shoulder blade and white armlets 6 inches wide on each arm were worn by the troops participating in order to distinguish them to the supporting lines in rear. An instruction given was that rifles were not to be loaded except by the direct order of an officer. The intention was that the night attack should consist of surprise so far as possible and all work was to be accomplished with the bayonet. All ranks were warned that they could expect no sleep for two nights and that economy in the use of water, rations and ammunition was essential. The force with which the 16th was associated was called the Northern Assaulting Column and comprised the 29th (Indian) Brigade, Engineers and Mountain Artillery and the 4th Australian Infantry Brigade.

The Turkish outposts on the left of Anzac having been previously driven in or captured by the New Zealanders, at 10 p.m. on August 6 the 4th Brigade moved from Reserve Gully on a slow night march of four miles along the beach and thence into the valley of the Aghyl Dere to its forming-up position. Notwithstanding the care with which the arrangements had been made, unexpected obstacles caused vexatious delays. There was a disjointed start, owing to the necessity of keeping the road clear for a British brigade, which was to attack north of the 4th Brigade. Marching along the beach was rather a novel experience for the 16th after having been cooped up in trenches or the narrow back areas of Anzac for months. Many checks were felt in the column during which the man lay down; some casualties being incurred from unaimed fire from inland. Shells from the warships went rumbling overhead and the rattle of musketry was incessant in the hills inland.

There was a further delay in the march of the 4th Brigade, caused by the guide taking a short cut to the gully, called Aghyl Dere, up which it was to advance. The short cut was very narrow and rough, permitting only movement in single file, and the head of the column was fired upon from the right before it reached the Aghyl Dere. The flank had to be cleared with the bayonet before the column could proceed. In the Aghyl Dere, when it was reached, fire was opened on the 13th and 14th Battalions, which were leading the column, and they were both employed in action on the right and left clearing the opposition to enable the rest of the brigade to advance.

The 15th, followed by the 16th, at 3 a.m., set out on the final portion of the march to the Abdel Rahman Spur, the forming up point for the attack on Hill 971. The two battalions soon found themselves working over rough, broken, stoney ridges, densely covered with low prickly undergrowth, in which the Turks had taken cover and were obstinately disputing every yard of the advance. As dawn approached and each side could see its targets more clearly progress became more rapid. During this movement, the 16th kept to the southern flank and routed the enemy from position after position. Many dashing bayonet charges were made and in one attack on a commanding knoll Captain Chabrel was killed. During these charges Colonel Pope was with the leading companies and fired several shots at Turks with his revolver. The enemy was obviously surprised and his early resistance was comparatively ineffective. From the top of the knoll it could be seen that there was a fairly connected line of men extending seawards to the left, but although 971 was in sight, it was still a long way in front, with difficult country intervening. The men, weak through continued sickness, although they had been sustained through the night by excitement, were by this time showing signs of excessive weariness, and at 5 a.m. Colonel Pope ordered the 16th to dig in and hold its ground. The fire, at first, was not very heavy, but the men were too exhausted to dig vigorously and casualties were incurred from the desultory shots which concealed Turks opened upon the line. Captain Brashaw at this time was shot through the heart while kneeling up to study the ground in front. As the morning advanced the enemy snipers, having gained breathing space, established themselves on commanding ground and digging and movement of any sort became almost impossible.

It was obvious by 7 a.m. that the 4th Brigade could not carry out the task assigned to it of capturing Hill 971. The three attacking battalions, 14th, 15th and 16th, were on the lower slope of a ridge running westward from Hill 971. The enemy was very strong in machine guns and commenced to use artillery to which no effective answer was available. Casualties had been very heavy and the whole line was at a standstill and preparing to hold the ground it had gained. In view of the precarious position, instructions were issued to company commanders to get all wounded back in preparation for expected orders for a withdrawal. However, a further attempt was made that night to reach the coveted objective. The casualties of the 16th to 6 p.m. on August 7 were 2 officers and 22 other ranks killed and 3 officers 42 other ranks wounded.

At 7 p.m. Colonel Pope was called to Colonel Monash's headquarters, and received orders to the following effect. The 13th Battalion was to take over and hold the present line of the 4th Brigade with some of the King's Own. The 15th, 14th and 16th Battalions were to move forward in column in that order at 3 a.m. on August 8, the 15th guided by Captain Locke, who had made a careful reconnaissance during the day. The column was to move up Abdel Rahman Spur and then north to the objective, Hill 971. No serious opposition up Abdel Rahman Spur was expected.

A fatal obstacle to the success of this plan, however, was the fact that it was based on the supposition that the 4th Brigade was then on a spur further inland, and, therefore, closer to Hill 971 than the spur on which it actually was in position.

At 2 a.m. on August 8 the leading troops of the 15th were led by Captain Locke over the front line and down the steep valley-side to the bed of the gully. With flank guards out, it reached the next ridge, moved across the crest and then turned to the right and worked up the spur. The navy was bombarding Hill 971 and other high positions, but owing to the mistake in the location of the jumping off position, the head of the column, instead of being at dawn on the spur leading to Hill 971, was actually on another and lower spur not even connected with the objective. At 4.15 a.m., when the bombardment was to cease, the column, according to orders, should have

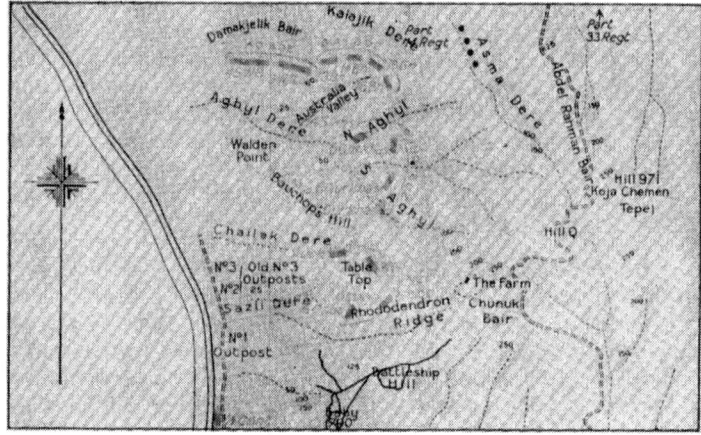

BRITISH POSITION NORTH OF ANZAC, DAYBREAK, AUGUST 7, 1915.

been ready to reach Hill 971. At that time, however, while the head of the 15th was clearing the ridge, and the 14th was in the gully, the 16th was not fully clear of the front line of the day before. The 15th Battalion, moving along the spur of the ridge, found itself under heavy machine gun fire and also that of a field gun firing direct. By platoons at a time the advance continued. The 14th was also involved and a few platoons were directed northwards to guard against an enemy force which had appeared on the left. The 16th moved north across the spur and was then turned to the east. The fire from several machine guns and heavy shrapnel fire caused many casualties and eventually the line was forced to come to a halt. The mistake in the location of the position of the night before had caused the whole situation to become very obscure. On the crest of the spur movement became absolutely impossible and the 15th, which by then had lost nearly 400 men, was ordered to withdraw. The 14th had lost over 250 men, but was in a fairly sheltered position and was in touch on its right with Indian troops. The 16th was protecting the left flank. Its position was desperate as the enemy was estab-

No. 31, PTE. A. CARLSON,
of the 16th Battalion, and the clip of cartridges hit by a Turkish bullet on August 8, 1915.

lishing himself on the northern edge of the spur. In a fold of the ground, behind the firing line, the medical officer had his dressing station and was attending to numbers of wounded, who were carried in or who found their way there after being hit. At 7 a.m. the telephone wire to brigade headquarters, which had been cut by shell fire, was repaired and Colonel Pope informed Colonel Monash that the task could not possibly be accomplished by the 4th Brigade and that hanging on where they were was only incurring needless loss. The order then came to withdraw the troops. Over the spur, the fire was extraordinarily heavy and the Turks could be seen moving into favourable positions for a counter-attack. At this stage, the machine guns of the 4th Brigade, with the 16th Section, under Lieut. P. Black and L/C. (acting Sgt.) H. Murray, came up and the guns were placed in suitable positions to sweep the crest. From that moment there was no anxiety regarding the withdrawal. Every attempt by the enemy to move brought heavy losses and the guns pinned him to his ground. A rear-guard of 50 men under Captain Harwood and Lieut. Day was ordered by Colonel Pope to cover the machine guns. The 16th, together with the remnants of the 14th and 15th Battalions, then withdrew to the lines held by the 13th and the King's Own and later to a bivouac in a gully in rear.

In this disastrous fight, the 16th Battalion lost 4 officers and 114 other ranks killed and wounded. The country was very difficult, but the whole operation was rendered impossible of fulfilment on account of the mistake made in the location of the line from which the start was made. The hostile fire met with during the operation was at times intense and many men were hit on two or three different occasions. Captain Heming was shot in the leg, then in the thigh, and while having these wounds dressed was killed by a bullet through the head. Another factor contributing to the failure was the physical weakness of the troops. A big percentage of the men had suffered, more or less, for weeks from diarrhœa and dysentry and conditions at Anzac had sapped the strength and vitality of the majority. When it came to a day's fighting, digging and climbing over the rough country on the Peninsula, they were not so fitted for it in August as they had been in April.

The following recommendations were made by Colonel Pope on August 8 in connection with the two days' fighting:—

"To Headquarters,

"4th Brigade.

"In connection with the fighting of yesterday and this morning, may I draw attention to:—

"Captain Rose, Brigade Machine Gun Officer, for the masterly way in which he organised the machine guns and escort which covered the withdrawal of the brigade.

"A man, name and battalion at present unknown, who although having five bullet wounds in one arm, carried Lieut. Benporath, when shot in the leg, to the nearest place of safety, about 500 yards distant. Lieut. Benporath reported this to me.

"The brigade signaller who, when telephone communication with brigade headquarters was interrupted, went back along the line under heavy fire and repaired same, necessitating his stopping several times under ordinary and sniping fire.

"Captain Heming, who was wounded while leading his company and was subsequently shot dead while a field dressing was being applied. He also did excellent work yesterday morning during the process of seizing our present position and organising lines of trenches. He spared no fatigue in that work and was consequently very tired this morning.

"Certain machine gunners, who acting under Captain Rose, went forward under fire while troops were being withdrawn, to bring in wounded. Captain Rose could probably give their names.

"H. POPE, Lt-Col.
"Com. 16th Batt."

No. 16, Pte. A. B. Foster, was also recommended to notice by Lieut. T. V. Taylor, for conspicuous bravery.

CHAPTER 15.—THE OUTPOSTS.

On August 9 the battalion took over No. 1 Outpost from the Sikh Battalion. During the night a sap was dug to connect the left and right sections of the post. Communication trenches were started and the foreground was cleared of scrub for some distance in front of the line. The next day the New Zealanders fought a strenuous battle to capture Hill 971. From their position the 16th obtained a splendid view of the fight put up by the gallant New Zealanders in an attempt which, like that of the 4th Brigade, was a costly failure.

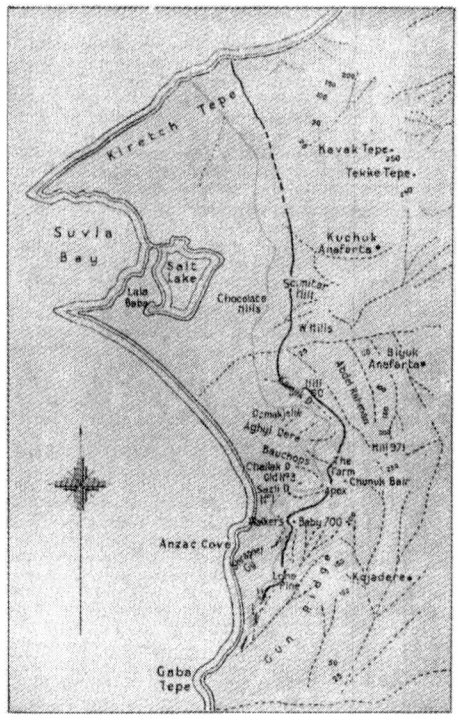

ANZAC-SULVA POSITION, AUGUST 12, 1915.

No. 1 Outpost was divided into a left section manned by 100 men under Lieuts. Taylor, McPherson and McLeod; a right section with 50 men and two machine guns under Major Margolin, Lieuts. Black, Day, Edge, Harwood and Jeffrey; and a detached post with 50 men under Lieuts. Ahearn and Adams. Post headquarters was in the centre of the left section. All ranks were enjoined to use the utmost energy in the defence of the outpost, not only by stubborn fighting in accordance with the traditions of the 16th but also by constant spade work for the strengthening of the post. On the 10th 6 men were killed and Lieut. Ahearn and 15 men were wounded in the trenches, which were still far from safe from enemy fire. For the next few days the improvement of trenches was the main task of the weary men of the 16th. Water and rations at this period were difficult to get and the general spirit of the men was at its lowest ebb. Realising this, Colonel Pope went the rounds, gathered them into parties in sheltered positions, and succeeded in infusing the sorely tried troops with a share of his indomitable spirit. His methods were typical of the man. He drew the men's attention to the beautiful view to be obtained from that part of the line—the sea and Suvla Bay where British troops could be seen moving on the shore; inland, where Turks could be seen moving in the gullies, was provided a shooting gallery for their amusement. Delivered in his own inimitable style, Colonel Pope's remarks certainly left the men "bucked up."

The following letter sent by Colonel Pope to the 4th Brigade is interesting in view of Murray's later record. It concerned the latter's transfer and promotion to the position of Machine Gun Officer in the 13th Battalion:—

"13th Aug., 1915.

"H. Qrs., 4th Inf. Bde.

"Herewith No. 315, L/C H. W. Murray, D.C.M. as requested.

"I have no objection (beyond the natural objection to losing a most excellent man) to his being transferred to the 13th Battalion.

"H. POPE, Lt.-Col.
"Com. 16th Batt."

Another letter written by Colonel Pope gives an idea of the risks which the Australian soldier would take in order to save life—and enemy life at that:—

"13/8/15.

"H. Qrs., 4th Inf. Bde.

"The following incident is brought under notice. About 11.30 to-day it was reported that a wounded and maimed Turk was making signs of distress about 60 yards in front of my detached post. I gave orders that if he were able to crawl in he was to be allowed to do so and that signs should be made to indicate this to him. Otherwise he should be brought in at night. It turned out that he was unable to crawl in.

"No. 1887, Pte. C. Howland and No. 1787, Pte. G. V. Brown, both of "B" Coy., 16th Battalion, volunteered to bring the man in in daylight. They crept out through the scrub to the man and alternately the one carrying and the other guiding, brought him in. They were about an hour and a half carrying out the task and from the time they left our trench until they returned to us with the wounded prisoner they were on ground which they knew to be subject to constant machine gun fire.

"As a feat of skill in crawling through bush; of physical strength in carrying the wounded Turk back under the midday sun; and as an exhibition of cool, cold-blooded courage extending over an hour and a half, this action of these two men appeals to me as the best thing it yet has been my privilege to see. The Turk, whose right leg was broken above the ankle, apparently a day or two ago, was medically attended to and is being sent down. He was utterly famished and thirsty.

"H. POPE, Lt.-Col.
"O/C No. 1 Post, 4th Inf. Bde Sector."

It was one of those feats which stands out—a blazing jewel—in the mullock heap of war. One of the men was killed later in the month on Hill 60.

Private R. A. Annear, of "A" Coy., Sgt. F. R. Howard, of "C" Coy., and L/C. F. H. Benporath, of "C" Coy., were also recommended for official recognition for their bravery in rescuing wounded men.

During the fighting on August 7 eighty men of the 16th, under Lieut. G. C. Curlewis, who took command after Lieut. Parker was wounded, became mixed up with the 6th Ghurkas, under Colonel Firth. As they were doing good work there were no special efforts made to bring them back to the battalion. On August 13, when the 16th had to take over a part of the Ghurkas' line, Colonel Pope went over to their headquarters and arranged in detail how the handing over should be carried out. After finalising this matter, Colonel Firth said to Colonel Pope: "Look here, Colonel, I have been very hardly pressed these last few days and I want to thank you for not pressing for the return of your men. They have done magnificent work while with me—work beyond all praise; but it is not only the work they have done, *it is the example they have shown my Ghurkas, which has been invaluable.*" This eulogy from an officer of a regiment renowned in history for its fighting qualities was much appreciated by the battalion when it was made known.

During this week of close association the 16th men and the Ghurkas learned a great deal of each other and the intimacy fostered a mutual respect. Many incidents occurred to cement this regard.

On the morning of August 7 one of the 16th received a terrible wound in the face. His comrades dressed the wound and made him as comfortable as possible under the circumstances and placed him in a little depression just behind the ridge on which they were trying to dig in. Stretcher bearers were busy and the poor fellow was left to lie there for some hours with a large khaki handkerchief over his face to protect him from the heat and flies. During a lull in the fighting in the afternoon Lieut. Curlewis seized the opportunity of attending to him and on reaching him discovered a little Ghurka kneeling by his side with his water bottle to his lips. At that particular stage water was worth pounds a drop and the Ghurka was quite exposed to enemy fire. During the evening the wounded man died but his end was made the more easy by the little Ghurka's ministrations.

On August 15, when the post was extended and the party under Lieut. Curlewis had rejoined, No. 1 Outpost was organised into four sections. No. 1 Section was manned by 110 men of "A" Coy. under Lieut. Curlewis; No. 2, by 80 men of "B" Coy. under Lieut. Hummerston; No. 3, by 100 men of "D" Coy. under Lieut. Harwood; and No. 4 by 140 men of "C" and "B" Coys. under Lieut. Taylor. Major Tilney had previously been transferred to the 13th Battalion, which he commanded in all its August fighting. Major Mansbridge had been evacuated sick, and consequently Major Margolin was second-in-command of the 16th.

The Turks at this time were working hard and strong positions were being dug opposite the whole line. The health of the troops was bad and most of the men were affected with some form or other of intestinal complaint.

On August 21 the front of the battalion was again extended by its having to take over the 14th Battalion trenches on the left. The 13th and 14th Battalions on this day made a local attack, which the 16th supported with very effective covering fire on to Turkish reserves which were being brought up to help quell the attack. The next day the 18th Battalion (of the 2nd Australian Division) attacked and the 16th covered it also. The 18th's introduction to active service was a particularly hot one and it lost very heavily in its maiden effort.

On the nights of August 22 and 23 the 16th was relieved by the newly arrived 17th Battalion, a unit from the 2nd Australian Division.

On No. 1 Outpost, Colonel Pope, with 90 men and three machine guns, stayed with the 17th to work them in. The instruction of new troops in the front line was a ticklish and anxious business. It is fairly certain that the Turks, had they known that inexperienced men were in occupation, would have tried their powers of resistance. The accession of strength for digging purposes was from the first acceptable and the new men proved apt pupils in the various artifices which made up trench warfare.

While the Colonel and part of the 16th held No. 1 Outpost with the 17th., Major Margolin, with the remainder, about 300 men, relieved No. 5 Outpost, taking over from Major Herring of the 13th Battalion on the night of August 23.

On August 27 an attack was projected on Hill 60 and the trenches south of it by 1,200 men under Brigadier-General Russell, commanding the New Zealand Infantry Brigade. The attacking party included 350 men from the 13th, 14th and 15th Battalions and 100 men from the 17th. Major Margolin's party of 300 was to man the trenches and assist wherever possible by fire, as were the men under Colonel Pope on No. 1 Outpost. It was not expected that these latter could do very much, but as a fact they did more damage to the enemy than did all the rest of the attacking troops. It was found that from a certain point a machine gun could fire into about 200 yards of a main Turkish communication sap down which reinforcements were being moved two abreast during the Anzac attack. With this machine gun, fired by Sgt. H. J. Sykes, sighted at 800 to 850 yards, the length of trench was completely filled with dead and wounded Turks, and when it was thus blocked, a large circular patch on either side was covered with dead Turks who had climbed out of the trench to get past the obstruction. This gun continued in action until darkness fell and commenced again at daylight. Contrary to the usual procedure there was not a single shot fired at it in reply. As a means of demonstrating the power of the machine gun to the 17th Battalion it was an unique opportunity.

On August 28 Colonel Pope handed over No. 1 Outpost to the officer commanding the 17th and withdrew all 16th men except those manning the machine guns. With the others he reinforced Major Margolin's men (now down to 185) at No. 5 Outpost. The plight of the men at this period was most distressing. Many of them could hardly walk, and their physical condition was the subject of many anxious conferences between battalion and brigade headquarters. By August 29 both officers and men were very nearly at the limit of human endurance. Colonel Pope asked that their relief should be expedited as, if a determined attack was delivered on his post, he expressed doubts that his men would have sufficient vitality left to resist it.

There was not sufficient variety in the food issued to help the men overcome their physical disabilities. The hot weather caused the "Fray Bentos" tinned meat to become a greasy, salty, melted liquid when opened; the jam was usually so thin that it could, if required, be taken as a beverage. Desiccated vegetables, with the Fray Bentos, generally formed the sole ingredients of the stew which was made, and this had to be eaten with the aid of three Army biscuits as hard as cast iron.

About this time arrangements were made with the British Expeditionary Forces Canteen to land a supply of stores and a certain quantity was allotted to the 4th Brigade. The cases were packed on 22 mules driven by Indians and taken to brigade headquarters, where they were opened up and found to contain tinned fruits, chocolates, Cambridge sausages, biscuits, etc. A fatigue party, under Sgt.-Major J. Ozanne and Sgt. C. Taylor, was detailed to draw the 16th portion for approximately 240 officers and men. The stores were taken to battalion headquarters, just in rear of the front line, to be distributed. The idea was for each man to receive goods up to the value of 20/-, the amount to be debited against him in his pay book.

While the stores were being issued, the observant Turks on Hill 971 located the scene of unusual activity and landed a shell among the men and stores which inflicted much damage. Among the casualties were R.S.M. Goldie and Sgt. C. Taylor, who were both wounded by flying fragments.

On August 30 six men were killed and 22 wounded, mostly by an enemy 75 m.m. gun enfilading the line from the right. There were also 26 men evacuated sick. Orders were then received for the relief of all but the fittest men, who were to hang on as instructors to the relieving troops—the 161st British Brigade. This "relief" meant that practically the whole of the tired and work-sick men of the 16th were kept at No. 5 Outpost until September 16. About that time, however, all hands were finally relieved and wended a weary way back to bivouac at Reserve Gully, Anzac.

A casualty return rendered on September 12 gave the following information:—

	Killed.	Died Wounds.	Missing.	Wounded.	Died Disease.	Prisoners.	Total.
Officers	15	2	1	18	...	2	38
Other Ranks	154	75	88	833	12	2	1,164
Totals	169	77	89	857	12	4	1,202

The officers killed were Captains Carter, Miller, Townshend, Curlewis, Southern; Lieuts. Geddes, Kretchmar, Durston, Mountain, Bruns, Kerr, Anderson, Burton, Carse, Chabrel, Heming, Brashaw, Thyer. The officers on duty with the battalion were Lt.-Col Pope, C.O., Major Margolin, Second in Command, Lieut. Paull, Adjutant, Lieut. Edge, Q.M., Lieut. Slater, Transport Officer, Lieuts. Adams, Harwood, Cumming, Parks, Black, Imlay, Wilton, Parker, Hamersley, McLeod, Cooke, Morris, Evans and Tucker.

The 16th, after its heavy losses on Pope's and Quinn's in April and May, had gradually built up its strength so that at the beginning of the August offensives it was about 900 strong. When the time came to leave Gallipoli to rest the troops, the battalion's strength was only about 200. Its casualties had been exceptionally severe. The 16th at all times on Gallipoli bore a prominent part in the heavy fighting and none of the casualties was needless, unnecessary or avoidable. The battalion had its orders. It carried them out. The loss in going forward or holding on was always great, but

A POST HELD BY THE 16th ON GALLIPOLI, AUGUST, 1915.

retirement at any of the critical periods in April and May or August would have meant annihilation. If the 16th suffered it is certain that for every casualty it lost at the hands of the Turks it caused five casualties to the enemy.

Such bravery as was shown by officers and men in these engagements could hardly be conceived as being possible in human nature. It was that bravery which saved the troops at Anzac from disaster.

CHAPTER 16.—A CHANGE OF SCENE.

On September 13 the battalion, less the machine gun officer, Lieut. Black, and 12 machine gunners, and 1 officer and 40 of the fittest men, marched out of Anzac at 11.20 p.m. and embarked on the "Abassieh" and the "Osmanleh." Six officers and 198 other ranks were shown on the parade state and the intention was to give the 4th Brigade a few weeks' spell at Mudros. The men were landed at 5 p.m. on September 14 and marched to Sarpi Camp. There was a shortage of tents, and as it rained heavily, the first night was a miserable one, for most of the troops were quite without shelter. Until all the camp equipment was issued, the men were not given the comfort that was their due, but after a few days, matters in this respect underwent a desirable change.

The 16th on arrival at Lemnos presented rather a weird spectacle. Some of the men had Australian tunics much the worse for wear; many had "Tommy" tunics; others wore "shorts" and "converted" Tommy slacks. Australian hats in various stages of age and dilapidation and many caps with the wire stiffening removed were worn. Scarves, cardigans, and cap comforters and other miscellaneous articles completed a motley parade.

On September 16 the battalion was inspected by Admiral Guefratti, of the French navy.

At Lemnos, the Old Sixteenth rested and recuperated in peace and quietness. Food supplies after the first few days were good and luxuries could be bought in the Greek villages or from the warships in the bay. One enterprising member of the battalion purchased a quantity of stores from the navy and retailed them at a small profit, to the satisfaction of all concerned in the deal. A welcome addition to the daily rations was a pint bottle of English ale or half a bottle of stout. Eggs were evidently at a premium, one per man twice weekly being the issue. The main town, Castro, was out of bounds to all troops and this fact made it all the more popular as a holiday resort. Needless to say, most of the 16th visited Castro during their sojourn on the island.

Castro, the capital of Lemnos, is a very ancient town, with narrow, cobbled streets. Its inhabitants were chiefly Greeks and Armenians, who carried on trade consisting of fishing and the distilling of wine in a very old-fashioned manner. The fort which gave it military protection was quite out of date and the brass muzzle loading guns with their solid iron shot were useless under conditions of modern warfare. The ramparts, however, were in good order. Between the town and the camp was an inn, which provided good meals, and natural thermal springs, which were said to have wonderful medicinal properties.

A PICQUET AT A VILLAGE IN LEMNOS IN SEPTEMBER, 1915.

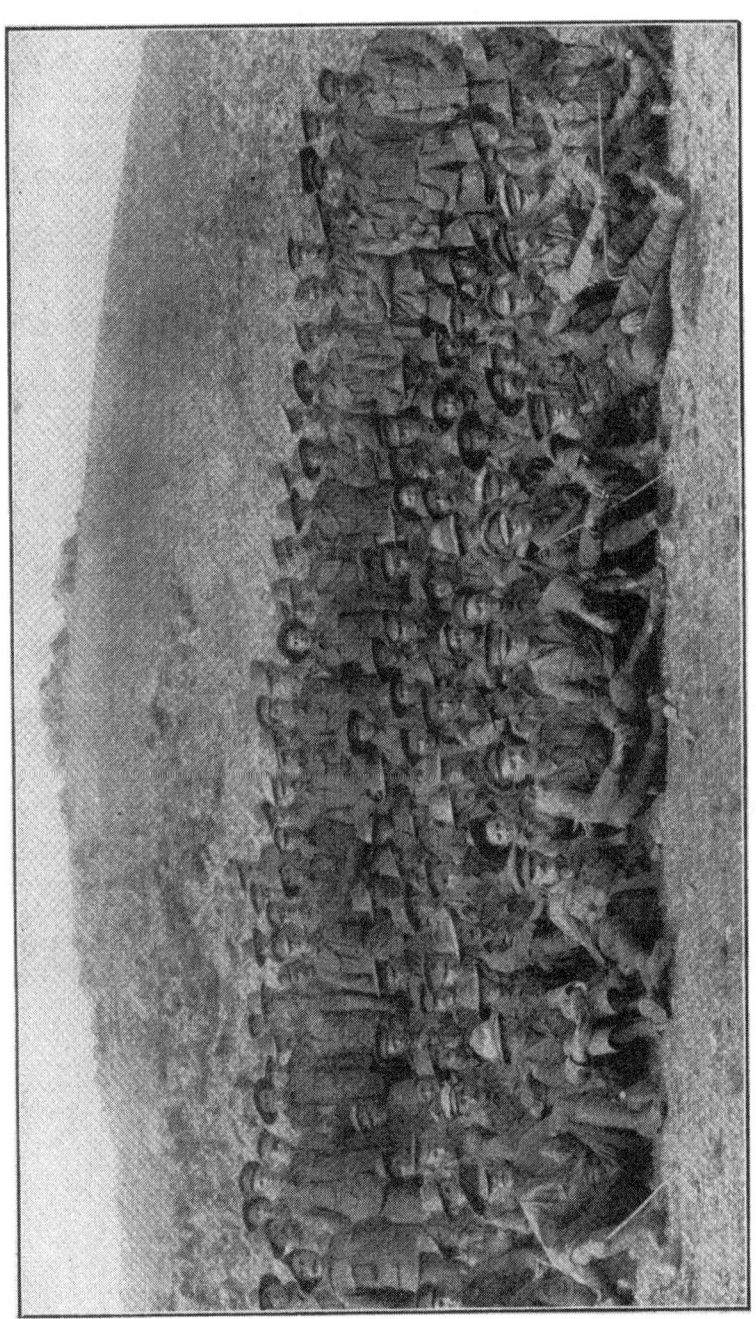

THE 16th BATTALION AT MUDROS IN OCTOBER, 1915.

Colonel Pope went to Egypt on regimental business on September 18 and Major Margolin took over the temporary command of the battalion. Two days later training commenced. This was of a light nature for a start, the object being to build the men up progressively to their former standard of physical fitness—a standard which the hardships of the past few months on Gallipoli had considerably impaired.

Major-General Godley inspected the brigade on the 21st and passed a word of praise on the hard fighting record of the four battalions and the magnificent work they had accomplished.

With the exception of the machine gunners, the men who had been left at Anzac rejoined the battalion at Lemnos on October 1. Soon afterwards Colonel Pope returned from Egypt, but was obviously a very sick man. He carried on for a short while and was then forced to enter a military hospital on the island.

The brigade was again inspected on October 27, this time by the new Commander-in-Chief, General Sir C. C. Munro.

With the regular food, rest and exercise, the men quickly regained a good measure of physical fitness. It looked a different battalion to what it had been on arrival from Anzac when it paraded for the return trip on October 31. Seven weeks had worked wonders and, with its band playing, the 16th marched again with a jaunty swing to the wharf, *en route* for Anzac.

The voyage back was not without incident. It was very dark when the transport left Mudros Harbour. On nearing Anzac the wind changed and came up from the south-east. Landing was delayed and the ship turned and ran for Imbros, where the men were taken ashore. They were marched to a camping ground, then back to the wharf, where they embarked on a barge which set out to locate the transport. In the darkness this was a thrilling feat, occomplished only after much cruising and cursing, after which the trip to Anzac was completed without further excitement on November 2.

On landing the battalion moved to a bivouac in Watercourse Gully, with the remainder of the 4th Brigade. Colonel Pope was still in hospital and the command of the battalion reverted to Major Margolin. Soon afterwards Major Margolin was sent to Egypt on temporary duty and during his absence Captain Wilton took over the duties of C.O.

CHAPTER 17.—THE EVACUATION.

The 16th was immediately sent in to garrison No. 2 sub-section of the line on the Aghyl Dere. This was divided into four sectors —Franklin's Post, Warwick Castle, Beck's Bluff and Newbury's Post.

The work of improving the trenches was at once embarked upon and, in addition, strenuous preparations were made to provide underground winter quarters which the nip in the air warned everyone would soon be necessary. On November 29 it was found that the machine guns were out of action through the water in the barrel casings freezing, and this caused considerable anxiety until the difficulty was overcome by the issue of non-freezable oil. When the 16th took over this sector, the Turks commanded No Man's Land, but active patrolling along the front became a recognised feature of the work of the garrison, and the position was soon reversed. On more than one occasion exciting encounters took place with Turkish patrols. The 16th's work in this connection earned commendation from the divisional commander for the thoroughness and enterprise shown by the patrols in carrying out their hazardous duties.

The Turks were at this time being prepared by periods of silence to enable the evacuation of Gallipoli to be carried out. Orders were given that no firing of any description should be indulged in for 48 hours from a given time. This ruse commenced in November and the command was rigidly observed. At the end of 48 hours, a further order was received extending the period of silence for a similar time.

By this time the Turks were walking about in front of the 16th as though they owned the place, strolling along trenches and exposing heads and shoulders in what was practically an invitation to shoot. Orders were orders, however, and the 16th obeyed them. At the end of the second 48 hours every man was itching for the word to recommence firing, and when the time did expire most of them had a Turk balanced on the foresight for the first shot.

A few days afterwards a further period of 24 hours' silence was ordered and later extended to 96 hours.

These silences were for the purpose of lulling the enemy into the belief that a period of quietness was the normal procedure. However, it was also ordered that if the Turks should be tempted out of cover in any strength, or should the position be in any danger from attack, the silence should be automatically broken. The only disobedience occurred when a flock of geese flew over the 16th position and a machine gunner could not withstand the temptation. He loosed a few bursts at the birds. This set other machine guns going and the silence was indeed broken for the next half hour.

One of those funny incidents which, fortunately, kept cropping up occasionally and thus helped to lighten the tragic side of war, happened on December 9. Reg. Sgt.-Major Goldie returned to Anzac on that day from hospital and on the way up to the battalion passed brigade headquarters where he met Colonel Monash, who smiled when he told Goldie that he would be sure of a welcome at

SIKH'S POST ON GALLIPOLI.

battalion headquarters. On arriving Goldie found C.S.M. Fraser, of "D" Company, who had been acting as R.S.M. during his (Goldie's) absence, looking rather sheepish and the C.O., Major Margolin, in a very bad temper. It appeared that the Anzac Tramway unit was being formed and each battalion on Gallipoli had to supply one man. The day before, Private Crook had been detailed for this job from the 16th Battalion. Major Margolin had been up all night and the adjutant, Lieut. Parker, had forgotten to tell him about it. Somewhere about dawn Acting R.S.M. Fraser paraded the man before the C.O., and the following conversation took place:—

Fraser: "This man is CROOK, sir."

C.O.: "Very well, take him to the medical officer."

Fraser: "But he is Crook, sir, for the tramway."

C.O.: "Go away and don't bother me. I am not a doctor. Take him to the tramway M.O. if you want to."

So Fraser went away and sent the following telegram—

'Mr. Birdwood, O.C., Australians—

'I have the man Crook for you when you want him.

"R.S.M. Fraser, 16th Battalion."

The "strafe" that came back from General Godley, at divisional headquarters, may well be imagined. The wire actually got past brigade headquarters, where there happened to be a 16th Battalion signaller on duty at the time. Both this man and the signaller at battalion headquarters were so sure of Fraser that they did not even refer the telegram to an officer. Fraser had served with the Seaforth Highlanders in the Soudan campaign and was most "regimental." When Goldie arrived back, he was just in time to relieve Fraser and allow him to retire to the comparative oblivion of his company until the joke had become stale.

On December 13 it commenced to snow. The next day the 16th extended its front by taking over No. 5 sub-section from the 14th Battalion. About this time a rumour began to go the rounds that the Peninsula was to be evacuated. Not much credence was given to it at first. No one was prepared to believe that the ground that was won at such a heavy cost would be given up. Rumour soon gave way to fact when each night saw a few men leaving Anzac. The "old hands" were left to the last for the purpose of giving them any honour associated with being in the last garrison.

Automatic rifles were arranged in the trenches so that a desultory fire could be continued for some 20 minutes or so after the last troops had departed. The 16th arranged some by leaving tins of water each with a small hole in the bottom, standing over the tops of empty tins, each of the latter being attached to the trigger of a loaded rifle. The bottom tin, when it filled with sufficient weight of water, would automatically release the trigger and fire the rifle.

The periods of silence had been continued on and off up to the evacuation. They prepared the way effectively for that very risky operation. It was essential, if heavy casualties were to be avoided, that the rear-guard should not be pressed by an attacking force. As it turned out, the final night of evacuation was thought by the enemy to be one of the periodic silences to which he had become accustomed. He only learned of his error when the mines at Walker's Ridge went up and killed a number of Turks in their front line. Some Turkish reinforcements coming up to resist an expected attack wandered into the empty Australian trenches by mistake. This led to the evacuation being discovered much earlier than would otherwise have been the case.

The following is a copy of the orders issued by Major Margolin in connection with the evacuation. The nominal rolls of the various parties are attached:—

BATTALION ORDERS.

By

Major E. L. MARGOLIN, 16th Battalion, A.I.F.

18th December, 1915.

1. The Battalion will proceed to Lemnos. The move will take place on two successive nights, commencing to-night, 18th December, 1915—

    (a) On the first night, the party leaving will be under the command of Lieut. Hartley and will consist of:
        3 officers
        106 other ranks.

    (b) The 14th Battalion will be relieved at No. 5 Sub-Post by the following personnel at 1800:
        B Coy.—21 N.C.O.s and men as per Nominal Roll, "C" Echelon 2nd day.
        D Coy.—10 N.C.O.s and men as per Nominal Roll, "B" Echelon 2nd day.
        D Coy.—35 N.C.O.s and men as per Nominal Roll, "B" Echelon 2nd day.
    The Post will be commanded by Lieut. Adams, who will be assisted by Lieuts. Hamersley and Cook.

    (c) On the second night the remainder of the Battalion will move off in three echelons as follows:—

A Echelon—

			Time of Departure (probable).
H.Q.	1 Officer	9 men	Under Lieut. Parker.
A Coy.	2 Officers	41 ,,	Leave 1720 (5·20 p.m.)
B Coy.	...	17 ,,	To be at starting point 1735
C Coy.	1 Officer	71 ,,	(5·35 p.m.)
D Coy.	1 ,,	85 ,,	

Total 5 Officers 223 men

B Echelon—

			Time of Departure
H.Q.	1 Officer	3 men	
		35 machine gunners*	Under Capt. Wilton.
A Coy.	...	20 men	Leave 2115 (9·15 p.m.)
B Coy.	1 Officer	20 ,,	To be at starting point 2130
C Coy.	1 ,,	20 ,,	(9·30 p.m.)
D Coy.	1 ,,	30 ,,	

Total 4 Officers 128 men

* Machine Gunners will leave 15 minutes before remainder of echelon.

THE OLD SIXTEENTH.

C Echelon—

H.Q.	2 Officers	5	men
M.G.	1 ,,	16	,,
A Coy.	...	19	,,
B Coy.	1 Officer	22	,,
C Coy.	...	15	,,
D Coy.	...	10	,,
Total	4 Officers	87	men

Under Major Margolin.
Time to be specified later.

The 5 attached A.M.C. details will go with " B " Echelon 2nd night.

2. ROUTE.—All echelons with the exception of " A " and " C " (2nd night) will march from starting point at Junction of Hotchkiss Valley and Chailak Dere to Divisional place of assembly at Supply Depot, No. 2 Outpost.

"A." and "C." (2nd night) will march from starting point to gap entering Mule Gully.

3. MARCHING.—(a) Echelons will march in an orderly manner, and as rapidly as possible without noise or lights, and it must be particularly impressed on all ranks that everything depends on perfect co-ordination and discipline. Men must obey without question or hesitation all Orders.

(b) On arrival at beach men will be loaded on barges on orders of M.L.O., and first on must go to furthest end of barge to enable loading to take place with utmost possible celerity. Senior Officer on each barge to act as Staff Embarkation Officer.

(c) Troops will carry two days rations, filled water bottles and all echelons except "C. " (2nd night) will have unloaded rifles ; 150 rounds will be carried per man.

4. GENERAL.—(a) " C " Echelon (last night) will hand one blanket per man to first night echelon, and on leaving No. 2 Subsection will travel light without blankets. Other echelons will carry one blanket per man.

(b) This programme will be adhered to even if the enemy should attack. If men are wounded they will be left behind unless so lightly wounded as not to impede progress of echelon.

(c) Up to the last, work will be carried on as usual and work in the firing line and gaps continued to create a normal appearance.

(d) Men of " C " Echelon (2nd night) are to be relieved as much as possible of work until to-morrow night.

(e) All dugouts and bivouacs will be left, but everything of value is to be rendered useless if such can be done without drawing attention. No demolitions by explosion. All mills bombs and pitcher grenades are to be carried away or destroyed.

No sign boards or papers are to be left which might give information to the enemy.

E. ARUNDEL WILTON, Capt.
Acting Adjt., 16th Btn.
18th December, 1915.

16TH BATTALION NOMINAL ROLL—EVACUATION OF GALLIPOLI.

18th, 19th and 20th December, 1915.

FIRST DAY "C" ECHELON.

(Leaving 10·40 p.m. on December 18th, 1915.)

Officers—Lieut. Hartley
,,   Morris
,,   Edge

HEADQUARTERS.

289	Pte.	Plater, G. B.	1626	Pte.	Knight, R.
1018	Cpl.	Clarke, A. F.	1148	,,	Croger, —
1512	Pte.	Phillips, H.	1232	,,	Allan, A. R.
1796	,,	Collins, W. J.	2720	,,	Alcom C. C.
1682	,,	Snowden, T.	1400	,,	Breen, A.
565	,,	Tindal, W. L.	2472	,,	Davies, T. O.
380	,,	Hutchins, H. W.	2202	,,	Dennie, —
2660	,,	Gee, F. W.	2553	,,	Green, —
1037	,,	George, T. F.	1471	,,	Gibson, T. G.
1143	,,	Cameron, W. S.	1183	,,	Jenkins, P.
1090	,,	Shervin, H.	2658	,,	Fox, —
2103	L./Cpl.	Baldock, H. B.	610	,,	Morgan F. W.
1815	Pte.	Pollard, D.	2722	,,	Scott, D.
2128	,,	Madigan, J.	273	,,	Job, J.
1391	,,	Wicker, A.	2078	,,	Redway, J.
814	,,	Warner, W. G.	1717	,,	Francis, A.
496	Sergt.	Smith, —	1485	,,	Irving, H.
1473	Pte.	Ganfield, R. T.	609	Sergt.	Ramming, C. W.
1513	,,	Pollard, A. A.	4749	Pte.	McMahon, —
1790	,,	Caudler, —	4754	,,	O'Callaghan, —
1498	,,	Matthews, W.	4746	,,	Marshall, —

"A" Coy.

2629	L./Cpl.	Twining, D. A.	2680	Pte.	Martin, H. M.
1542	Pte.	Dunn, D.	212	,,	Morton, T.
2655	,,	Ehrlick, V.	1845	,,	McPhee, W.
1994	,,	Evans, W. E.	1595	,,	Boswell, E. T.
2389	,,	England, E.	2358	,,	Nicol, J. R. C.
1808	,,	Glasson, E.	198	,,	Rowe, J. H.
1416	,,	Hayes, L.	2705	,,	Simpson, J.
776	,,	Hawes, R.	1889	,,	Parkin, A.
1623	,,	Johnson, F. H.	1874	,,	Wise, C. K.
358	,,	Minchin, J. B.			

"B" Coy.

2282	Pte.	Austin, B. W.	1839	Pte.	Mills, J. S.
2436	,,	Angel, V. H.	2696	,,	Roberts, B.
2628	,,	Bull, V.	394	,,	Salter, R.
2639	,,	Bruce, A. E.	2051	,,	Williams, J. F.
1805	,,	Tereday, J.	2714	,,	Wadeson, S. J.
2667	,,	Howlett, J. W.	1751	,,	Walton, W. P.
475	,,	Kelly, C. H.	2719	,,	Wynne, W.

THE OLD SIXTEENTH. 95

"C" Coy.

2250	Pte.	Phillips, —	1862	Pte.	Spouse, S. G.
445	,,	Matthews, —	2828	,,	Ware, C. C.
2087	Corpl.	Jorganson, W.	2797	,,	Gottlieb, H. A.
2007	,,	Jones, B. A.	1264	,,	Fechner, H. A.
2803	Pte.	Knight, —	1239	,,	Bilney, H.
1457	,,	Blinman, H. G.	1325	,,	Ryan, J.
1413	,,	Barker, H. G.	3064	,,	McMaster, S. G.
1386	,,	Harvey, L. F.	3019	,,	McMurray, L. W.
2298	,,	Garth, F.	2668	,,	Ick, H. G.
2682	,,	Meller, J. J.	2724	,,	Roberts, —
779	,,	Hutton, A.			

"D" Coy.

2818	Pte.	Patten, G. F.	2574	Pte.	Pelegrins, P.
2816	,,	Poole, J.	1359	,,	Cockington, J.
2607	,,	Shinn, S. W.	1213	,,	Saunders, H. W.
2612	,,	Grant, F. K.	2596	,,	Clark, A. C.
2661	,,	Grant, L.	2810	,,	McFarlane, W. J.
2546	,,	Howard, A.			

SECOND DAY "A" ECHELON.

(Leaving 5·20 p.m. on December 19th, 1915.)

Officers—2nd Lieut. Parker
           Lieut. Somerville
              ,, Hamersley
              ,, Cook
           Capt. McGregor

R.Q.M.S. Timewell, S.
R. Sg. Mjr. Goldie

Signallers :

331	Pte.	Hatcher, —	1511	Pte.	Pascoe —
606	,,	Ellis —	1550	,,	Yeldon R. C.
1052	,,	Jennings, —	2448	,,	Ivy, A. G.

"A" Coy.

708	Sgt.	Hough —	2689	Pte.	Nock —
216	L./Cpl.	Peacock, A. R.	2248	,,	O'Connor, J.
642	Q.M.S.	Braithwaite	2690	,,	Pekin, J.
1983	Pte.	Beverley, B.	1889	,,	Parkin, A.
2634	,,	Alger, F.	2305	,,	Rowe, S.
2444	,,	Brown, E. F.	2699	,,	Rodgers, W. R.
2046	,,	Thomas, W.	2695	,,	Randell, J.
2641	,,	Carter, G. G.	2069	,,	Sibley, C.
2658	,,	Compasse, L.	2709	,,	Smith, H. W. B.
2647	,,	Crawford, S. A.	1520	,,	Sanquay, H.
2465	,,	Cowling, A. E.	1711	,,	Thomson, F. C.
2652	,,	Kay	670	,,	Underwood, R.
2205	,,	Eggleston	2717	,,	Wilson, G. H.
2209	,,	Farrell, W. E.	157	,,	Wilson, H. P.
712	,,	Inglis, A.	1673	,,	Wood, A. H.
2403	,,	Kerr, E. A.	2637	,,	Armstrong, F.
2671	,,	Callow, F. G.	603	,,	Beckett, R.
2674	,,	Lewis, D.	2640	,,	Butler, H. J. R.
2679	,,	Marshall, W. J.	204	,,	Futcher, —
2919	,,	Marshall, H.	1555	,,	Wheeler, Roy
1734	,,	Nelson, J. J.			

"B" Coy.

981	Pte.	Baldwin —	1104	Q.M.S.	Turner —
1430	,,	Hill —	1463	Cpl.	Cowain —
627	,,	Johns —	2642	Pte.	Carter, T. B.
2633	,,	Acton —	743	,,	McQuade —
2438	,,	Brennan, J. A.	1295	,,	Robertson —
2462	,,	Collins, E. F.	121	,,	Scott, F. W.
2067	,,	Hoddy, L. P.	1459	,,	Burnette, G. E.
1632	,,	Lindsay, H. D.	1802	,,	Dawson, G. F.
272	,,	Innis, J. A.			

"C" Coy.

3026	Pte.	Olsen, P. R.	2524	Pte.	Stockton, W. A.
3041	,,	Willing, S. L.	3023	,,	Opie, J. B.
3048	,,	Chapple, D. L.	3001	,,	Backen, H. E.
3033	,,	Pearse, F. C.	1716	,,	Foden, A.
3032	,,	Pearson, F. S.	3031	,,	Peterson, G. O.
3040	,,	Talbot, H. A.	3021	,,	Nankivell —
3030	,,	Plummer, A.	3046	,,	Desland, C. M.
3044	,,	Emmius, A. O.	2811	,,	O'Neil, J. P.
2783	,,	Bampton, E. W. D.	2028	,,	Newton, I. R.
2809	,,	Marshall, A.	2233	,,	Allen, H. R.
2550	,,	Brewer, F. W.	2064	,,	Yates, A. V.
2713	,,	Truran, N. H.	1616	,,	Hall, S. C.
2665	,,	Holloway, E. C.	2646	,,	Cook, N. H.
2681	,,	Meikle, B.	2726	,,	Peake, J.
2635	,,	Anderson, W. J.	1281	,,	Hill, T. H.
3060	,,	McLean, E. E.	1316	,,	Mudie, D. V.
3034	,,	Pickering, G.	3038	,,	Reeson, A. T.
3010	,,	Hughes, B. J.	3061	,,	Park, J. H.
3028	,,	Old, R. H.	2004	,,	Hunter, W.
3012	,,	Hutton, E. N.	1327	,,	Marshall, T. E.
3009	,,	Gill, R. P.	2790	,,	Cronin, D. T.
3014	,,	Loton, V.	3051	,,	Johnson, A.
3063	,,	Cooper, J. C.	3024	,,	Rzejzkowske, L. E.
3057	,,	Strong, A. J.	1406	,,	Currie, A.
2636	,,	Archibald, M.	2047	,,	Calf, H. C.
2032	,,	Peebles, P. C.	2701	,,	Scott, J. A.
2456	,,	Connor, F.	1640	,,	Marhennet, P. J.
2708	,,	Smith, H. C. S.	1671	,,	Webb, A.
3059	,,	Noltage, R. W.	2488	,,	Jenkins, H. G.
3045	,,	Charles, F. A.	2552	,,	Donaldson, —
3047	,,	McGinnis, C.	2688	,,	McGarry, F. S.
139	,,	Sharp, G.	2706	,,	Sinden, F. C.
213	,,	Newell, B. E.	1305	,,	McLeod, N.
2692	,,	Purdy, T.	1366	,,	Ford, R. A.
2710	,,	Spry, W. H.	240	Q.M.S.	Burnette, —

"D" Coy.

1188	Sgt.	Liddy, J.	2583	Pte.	Staker, H. E. L.
2107	Q.M.S.	Court, —	2275	,,	Waters, M. H.
2610	Pte.	Drever, —	1106	Sgt.	Walsh, J.
2619	,,	Edgewood, J.	2132	L./Sgt.	Colebatch, H. E.
2611	,,	Emery, H.	2784	Pte.	Bowker, J. N.
2345	,,	Gray, J. C.	1006	,,	Beck, A. H.
1727	,,	Hann, B.	2329	,,	Campbell, H. L.
2120	,,	Harris, J. E.	2123	,,	Holton, A. G.
2124	,,	Howard, J.	2156	,,	Lovick, R. S.
2804	,,	Lawson, —	1345	,,	Marsh, J. C.
2134	,,	O'Brien, J. J.	2807	,,	McMahon, J. J.

"D" Coy.—continued.

2581	Pte.	Skinner, R. J.	2815	Pte.	Pitman, H.
3034	,,	Sowten, C. C. B.	2365	,,	Schmidt, H. E.
2826	A/Sgt.	O'Neil, F. M.	1338	,,	Spoils, T. H.
2379	Pte.	Beck, C.	2587	,,	Savage, A. A.
1904	,,	Birmingham, W. J.	2820	,,	Seef, L.
2788	,,	Croston, W. H. B.	2366	,,	Sharpe, H.
2631	,,	Crisp, .D. B.	2368	,,	Stone, J.
2621	,,	Hill, J.	2582	,,	Sparshott, R. H.
2633	,,	Hoare, S. J.	2592	,,	Thorye, D. W.
2350	,,	Kilmartin, F. T. J.	2370	,,	Tomlin, E. W.
2563	,,	Clemich, W. O.	2140	,,	Todd, E. J. J.
1926	,,	Lellis, J.	2372	,,	Twinning, P.
2572	,,	Maronan, F. H.	2627	,,	West, F. H.
2808	,,	Medlin, C.	2594	,,	Trudgeon, H. O.
2355	,,	Mundy, A.	2591	,,	Stevens, F. H.
2352	,,	McKim, W. J.	2812	,,	Okley, P.
3061	,,	O'Neil, J. C.	2597	,,	White, F. G
2360	,,	Pepal, C.	1720	,,	Gray, A. H.
2823	,,	Whitfield, W.	1732	,,	Murdock, H. E.
1024	,,	Craig, W. H.	2357	,,	Mutton, A.
1309	,,	Bowly, S.	1331	,,	Nourse, F. E.
1372	,,	Cooper, F. E.	1384	,,	Taylor, G.
2792	,,	Cole, H.	1740	,,	Tucker, J. R. H.
2787	,,	Clernow, E. B.	1115	,,	Bardett, —
2796	,,	Fitzgerald, T. V.	2778	,,	Beaumont, H. L.
1725	,,	Green, C. J. C.	2553	,,	Burrows, A. W.
2798	,,	Hall, H. A.	1394	,,	Williams, E. T.
2351	,,	Long, H.	2326	,,	Appleton, W. S.
2381	,,	McNeil, A. J.	1126	,,	Bates, H. L.
2353	,,	McNeil, T. B.	2789	,,	Cox, J.
2027	,,	Roeszler, —	1914	,,	Edwards, P.
2579	,,	Rowley, F. A.	1058	,,	Lodge, G.
1085	,,	Richards, F. P.			

SECOND DAY "B" ECHELON.

(Leaving 9·15 p.m. on December 19th, 1915.)

Officers—Capt. Wilton
,, Harwood
Lieut. Imlay
,, Parks

Machine Gunners:

1785	Pte.	Brady, D.	1592	Pte.	Brown, L. St. J.
1015	,,	Carter, J. E.	1657	,,	Shepherdson, H. M.
2556	,,	Kidgell, W. G.	2443	,,	Barnes, C. E.
1888	,,	Prater, W.	1313	,,	Codling, R.
2310	,,	Thompson, H. C.	622	,,	Collins, F.
514	,,	Window, A.	1468	,,	Fraser, A.
2011	,,	Knight, W. J.	2505	,,	McEntoe, C.
1193	,,	McMaster, J. C.	2614	,,	Neaylon, R. E. M.
1295	,,	Law, S.	2526	,,	Smith, J. A.
2328	,,	Breen, L.	2373	,,	Walstead, T.
2544	,,	Lacey, F.	2559	,,	Farley, T. F.
371	,,	McInerney, J. F. L.	1531	,,	Wallis, W. T.
2020	,,	Morrow, G. W.	1931	,,	Morgan, P.
1605	,,	Dunn, J. R.	1472	,,	Godfrey, L. J.
2554	,,	Carruthers, J. H.	2201	,,	Daniels, W. D.
2458	,,	Clarke, J.	1582	,,	Barnes, P. G.
2557	,,	Anderson, D. J. G.	617	,,	O'Brien, P.

THE OLD SIXTEENTH.

Grenadiers:

2657	Pte.	Emery, C.
2041	,,	Spencer, H.
1200	,,	O'Gorman, A.

"A" Coy.

2653	Pte.	Duffy, M.	161	Cpl.	Leake, —
2686	,,	Murphy, M.	21	,,	Courtney, G. E.
2700	,,	Saunders, W.	1719	Pte.	Austin, J.
2676	,,	Lockhard, J.	1396	,,	Addison, J. S.
1992	,,	Delaport, A.	1596	,,	Blunt, H. E.
2651	,,	Davies, L. F.	750	,,	Barker, W.
222	Sgt. Mjr.	Tegredine	1827	,,	Kelly, R. J.
220	Sgt.	Grant	393	,,	Kent. W. C.
419	,,	Walton	711	,,	McFarlane, T. S.
125	L./Cpl.	Phillips, D. C.	1684	,,	Morgan, L. G.

"B" Coy.

792	Pte.	Rice, A. E.	2253	Pte.	Smith, H.
234	,,	Afflock, W. T.	2528	,,	Steadman, W. T.
650	,,	Ball, G.	302	,,	Thompson, T.
2704	,,	Stremfield, —	1875	,,	Wrighton, P.
1600	,,	Carr, A.	2307	,,	Wheeler, H.
2193	,,	Chisholm, J.	662	,,	McClusky, C. L.
1995	,,	Elverd, W. A.	2675	,,	Lind, A.
2308	,,	Johns, D.	2670	,,	Johns, S. A.
2632	,,	Clopper, H. F.	2723	,,	Johns, S. J.
494	,,	O'Shea, P. W.	2293	,,	Gould, J.

"C" Coy.

2470	L./Cpl.	Doran —		Sgt.	Potts, W. A.
2656	Pte.	Elliott —	1343	,,	Whiting, G. A.
2250	,,	Phillips, R. T.	1252	Pte.	Cousins, B. E.
2240	,,	Strathan, W. T.	2176	L./Cpl.	Buckenara, C. L.
2296	,,	McCreery —	1373	Pte.	Newman, F. C.
1861	,,	Parks, R.	1395	,,	White, F.
1790	L./Cpl.	Carter —	1310	,,	Brown, F.
2025	Pte.	Rose, —	773	,,	Elliott, C.
2029	,,	O'Donoghue —	1336	,,	Shannon, R.
1750	,,	Whiting —	2727	,,	Harding, R. G.

"D" Coy.

1269	C.S.M.	Fraser, R.	1343a	L./Cpl.	Williams, P. E.
2125	Sgt.	Johnson, J. E.	1391	Cpl.	McCabe, H.
1362	Cpl.	Watts, N. R.	1915	L./Cpl.	Garratt, C. C.
2632	Pte.	Garland, H G.	1103	Pte.	Trowbridge, F.
1202	,,	Peters, R.	2105	,,	Budge, R. G.
1074	L./Cpl.	O'Neill, J. J.	2609	,,	Clark, C.
2617	Pte.	Bowden, A. J.	1378	,,	Coulthard, T.
2160	,,	Best, F. G.	1351	,,	Dowling, A. J.
2362	,,	Powell, F. W.	2343	,,	Foster, C. E.
1109	,,	Williams, A. T.	1719	,,	Fish, S.
2104	,,	Best, G. H.	1418	,,	Hyrons, J.
1121	Sgt.	Anderson, F.	1369	,,	Kerrtkye, A. C.
1130	,,	Bitmead, J.	2372	,,	Tyler, A. H.
3087	Cpl.	Cumming, D. G.	1386	,,	Simpson, W. J.
2338	,,	Chamberlain, J.			

THE OLD SIXTEENTH.

SECOND DAY "C" ECHELON.

(Leaving from 1·35 a.m. to 2·5 a.m. on December 20, 1915.)

Officers—Major Margolin
        Capt. Black
        2nd Lieut. McLeod.
        Adams.

"B" Coy.

52	Sg. Mjr.	Burrows	796	L/Cpl.	Thomas
300	Sgt.	Smith	2531	,,	Satinover
689	,,	Allan	611	,,	Beattie
123	,,	Smith	2454	,,	Cosson
686	,,	Jewell	1887	,,	Howland
656	Cpl.	Hart	1708	Pte.	Bennett
1494	,,	Lambus		Sgt. Mjr.	Jillie, O.
1438	,,	Walker	255	Pte.	Elliott
630	,,	Police	2486	,,	Harrison
1629	,,	Longson	1838	,,	Middleton
652	L./Cpl.	Clues	2262	,,	Thomson

"A" Coy.

422	Sgt.	McCarthy, L.		Sgt. Mjr.	Bush
361	,,	McKenzie, J. P.	2673	Pte.	Lenton, J.
564	Cpl.	Reid, T.	2685	,,	Moxham, J.
1610	,,	Graham, R. W. D.	566	,,	Lewis, A. G.
465	,,	McQueeny, J.	1656	,,	Scott, T. H. R.
138	,,	Shaw, W. R.	1684	,,	Caldwell, T. C.
1414	Pte.	Higgins, F.	480	,,	Adams, J.
1469	,,	Fay, T.	2654	,,	Edgar, E.
2694	,,	Rafferty, B. B.	90	,,	Marshall, V. H.
345	,,	Broad, T. L. C.			

"C" Coy.

1347	Sgt. Mjr	Woods	1279	Pte.	Hill
2479	Sgt.	Hulton	1938	,,	Speck
1777	,,	Benporath	2703	,,	Sharp, S. C.
18	Cpl.	Giles	1316	,,	Boyland, T.
1822	,,	Iffla	2363	,,	Quigley, A.
3	L./Cpl.	Burton	515	,,	Gordon, W. J.
1414	Pte.	Loar	1150	,,	Davies, H.
1348	,,	Connolly			

SECOND DAY "C" ECHELON.

Machine Gunners and Signallers.

Signallers :

	L./Cpl.	Lynas	1212	Pte.	Stokel
749	Sgt.	McGrath	1654	,,	Sansom
207	Cpl.	Mace			

"D" Coy.

1267	Sgt.	Foster	2356	Pte.	Mundy, J. W.
1039	Cpl.	Goldie	2361	,,	Puikkula
2598	L./Cpl.	Whittle	1162	,,	Fuller
2395	,,	Noland, T. H.	1721	L./Cpl.	Giles, F.
1715	Sgt.	Ey, A. L. P.			

Machine Gunners:

1680	Pte.	Touzel, J. C.	1859	Pte.	Simpson, J. C.
2464	,,	Coulter, W. L.	1824	,,	Jones, H. C.
1427	,,	Sparig, H. H.	503	Sgt.	Hicks, T.
1837	,,	Measures, J.	1918	Pte.	Gregory, S.
2149	,,	Gilbert, J.	411	,,	Dovey, R. W.
1353	,,	Millor, E. W.	2514	,,	Malone, J.
375	Sgt.	Grieveson, P.	1107	,,	Webling, D.
1538	L./Cpl.	Sullivan, D. J.	34	,,	Cadwallader
766	Pte.	Coulthard, R. W.			

The following farewell letter was left on behalf of the 4th Brigade.

"20th December, 1915, 2.30 a.m.

"To Commander,
    "Turkish Forces,
        "Gallipoli, Turkey.

"The Brigadier presents his compliments to our worthy Turkish opponents and offers those who first honour his quarters with their presence such poor hospitality as is in his power to give, regretting that he is unable personally to welcome them.

"After a sojourn of seven months in Gallipoli, we propose to take some little relaxation at that period in which we are instructed by a Higher Power to observe 'Goodwill towards all men' and in bidding 'au revoir' to our honourable foes, we Australians desire to express appreciation of the fine soldierly qualities of our Turkish opponents and of the sportsmanlike manner in which they have participated in a very interesting contest, honourable, we trust, to both sides.

"For a little while we have been with you, yet a little while and you will see us not. For us it is a matter of deep regret that the ancient friendship so long existing between the British and Turkish Empires should have been thus disturbed and broken by the insidious machinations of the arch enemy of humanity.

"We have left this area and trenches in which we have taken considerable trouble and pride, clean and in good order, and we shall be grateful if they may be so maintained until our return, particular care being taken in regard to matters of sanitation, so vital to the health and well-being of an army.

"We hope that you will find the wine, coffee, tobacco, cigarettes, and food to your taste and a supply of fuel has been left in the cupboard to ameliorate in some measure the discomfort during the cold watches of the winter.

"Our only request is that no member of the nation which was guilty of the inhuman murder of that noble woman, Miss Edith Cavell, to whose portrait this message is attached, will be permitted to pollute with his presence the quarters of soldiers who have not yet descended to such barbarous and ruthless methods."

On the night of December 18, the first party of the 16th to leave the Peninsula—107 men under Lieut. Hartley, moved off to the beach and embarked for Lemnos. On the next night, in three parties, the remainder of the battalion left their respective positions in the front line. The first consisted of 5 officers and 223 other ranks. It was commanded by Lieut. Parker. Capt. Wilton took the next party of 4 officers and 128 other ranks. The front was actively patrolled during the night by members who were leaving in the last party, and the Turks were reported to be working normally on their trenches. At 5 minutes past 2 on the morning of December 20, the rear party, consisting of Major Margolin, Captain Black, Lieut. McLeod, Lieut. Adams and 87 other ranks, marched silently through the deserted trenches, across the beach and on to the tiny jetty. There was little conversation. Each man was wrapped in his own thoughts during this grand finale of the Gallipoli campaign. Many were thinking of the splendid comrades they were leaving behind; others were bitter at this open confession of failure. They embarked on the lighter and were conveyed to H:M.S. "Mars," which was riding far out on the dark waters like a grim sentinel of the sea waiting to receive that gallant rear-guard of the Immortal Failure that was Anzac.

The evacuation was splendidly planned and must ever remain a magnificent tribute to the organising powers of those responsible. The time-table prepared, by which the troops left the trenches, worked to a nicety, and resulted, at the various jetties, in a complete lack of confusion or delay in loading the lighters and the transports with their living freight. On the beach everything was a marvel of quiet and efficient organisation. Shortly after the last troops left the jetty in a motor-lighter, the Walker's Ridge mine blew up. Then the stores on the beach began to blaze and gave the troops their last glimpse of Anzac.

The 16th landed at Lemnos the next day and with the rest of the 4th Brigade marched into camp and found tents erected at Mudros East. Food was not very plentiful even now. Very light training was the rule for the next few days and with camp-fire concerts and diversions of a like nature, a pleasant time was spent. Christmas Day was a holiday on which the Christmas Billies from Australia were distributed. Their contents were thoroughly appreciated by men long unused to the luxuries they contained.

On the 26th the Old Sixteenth, headed by its band, marched to the wharf and once more embarked on a transport—this time the "Ascanius." The next day that vessel left Mudros and after an uneventful voyage arrived at Alexandria at 10.30 a.m. on December 29, 1915.

CHAPTER 18.—TOURING EGYPT.

The 16th Battalion landed at Alexandria on January 1, 1916, and entrained at 6.30 a.m. for Moascar, from which station it marched to Ismalia. Tents were collected and pitched on the desert N.W. of the town and the next day was spent in settling down. Training was not commenced immediately. Indeed, a rest was an urgent necessity. However, after about a week, general training began. The officers and N.C.O.'s had been almost without exception promoted to their present ranks in the field, and while fully competent to fulfil their field duties, lacked the theoretical knowledge which was essential in carrying out the duties of leadership in camp. Therefore classes for officers and N.C.O.'s were established and as many as could be spared were released from ordinary duties to attend them. Specialist training was also a feature. Gallipoli had taught the necessity of having a plentiful supply of trained men to take the places of machine gunners and signallers who were rendered casualties, and the higher command was determined that men should be trained as reserves to the permanent personnel of those two important units in each battalion. Training was carried out in the morning while the afternoons were, as a rule, left free for battalion sports and recreational exercises. During its three weeks at Ismalia reinforcements joined up, and the depleted ranks of the Old Sixteenth began gradually to take once again the appearance of an effective fighting unit.

On one occasion the 16th was carrying out battalion and brigade drill formations. It was the custom of the company markers to bring out "parade states" at the "Fall In" and for the R.S.M. to make up his battalion return between the "Advance" and the actual assembly of the companies on their markers for the battalion parade. This day the return appeared to be quite wrong and the C.O. (Major Margolin) duly "strafed" R.S.M. Goldie for his carelessness. Not one of the sets of figures or totals would tally with the actual strength. The apparent error was not detected until about an hour after moving off the parade ground. Some few moments later the R.S.M. approached the C.O. and pointed out that the incorrect figures quoted appeared to him to be those of the previous day. The Major searched his pocket and, sure enough, found the correct return. The battalion was at the moment moving along in column of route and he gave the command "At the Halt—Form Mass," and thus addressed the men.

"16th Battalion, you just heard me call the R.S.M. a ——fool. The mistake was mine. I am the ——fool. His parade state was correct; I put it in the wrong pocket." Then the 16th continued its route march.

On January 21, the battalion, with the rest of the 4th Brigade, struck camp and moved to Moascar, where the now familiar routine was entered upon of erecting tents and laying out the lines of a new camp. During its five weeks in this location, advanced training and field operations were practised. Route marches over the desert, battalion and brigade tactical schemes, and divisional manœuvres, extending over three days, and which included night operations, were conducted. By the end of the five weeks all ranks were feeling fit again; the regular food and exercise had had their effect. All the vacant positions in the ranks of officers and N.C.O.'s were filled by promotions, and towards the end of February the organisation and routine of the battalion were running smoothly. Colonel Pope, who had been sent from Lemnos to England to hospital, rejoined the 16th about this time and was given a warm welcome by all ranks.

On February 26 the 16th entrained for Tel-el-Kebir, at which historic spot it arrived the same day. Advanced parties had previously prepared the camp and the 16th marched into its new quarters and at once settled down to the more or less hum-drum routine of military camp life.

March was a month of reorganisation. Machine guns were taken from battalions and formed into brigade companies, Lewis guns taking their place in the battalions. It had been decided to organise two more Australian divisions from the troops already in Egypt. Consequently a big proportion of each of the old battalions was detached from the parent unit and organised as the nucleus of the new battalion. Many officers were needed for the various staffs of the new divisions and brigades, and so, while it was a wrench to leave the old unit, the promotion involved in the transfer compensated those affected to a great extent. On March 2 the detached personnel from the 16th was organised into the 48th Battalion of the 12th Brigade and once more the 16th was left a skeleton unit. The 4th, 12th, and 13th Brigades were then constituted as the 4th Australian Division under Major-General Sir H. V. Cox, K.C.M.G. Reinforcements during the next fortnight filled the ranks, and by the middle of March it was almost up to full strength again. These changes necessitated a return to elementary training.

March 17 (St. Patrick's Day) was a holiday celebrated by a battalion sports gathering which gave the following results:—

> Hurdle Race: Pte. Skinner, "D" Coy. 1; Pte. Klopper, "B" Coy. 2.
> 100 Yards Champ.: Pte Brackenbridge (Transp.) 1; Pte. Griffiths "C" Coy. 2.
> High Jump: Pte. Lee "A" Coy. 1; Pte. Higgins "C" Coy. 2.
> Long Jump: Pte. Clark (Vickers M.G. Sec.) 1; Pte. Lee "A" Coy. 2.
> Siamese Race: Ptes. McGillivray and Higgins "C" Coy. 1.
> Sack Race: Pte. Peake (Transport).
> Throwing Bomb: Pte. Munday.

On the 22nd the 4th Brigade was inspected by H.R.H. the Prince of Wales. Afterwards the G.O.C. expressed satisfaction with the general turn-out of the brigade. The next day was a brigade sports day on which an advance party from the battalion was sent to Serapeum, to which place the brigade had been ordered to move.

On March 26 the battalion entrained at Tel-el-Kebir en route to Serapeum which was reached that afternoon. The next day saw the men engaged on the now familiar task of laying out the camp on the east bank of the canal. The next day training commenced, the hours laid down being from 6 to 8 a.m., 9 to 10.30 a.m. and 4 to 8 p.m., this schedule allowing the troops to rest during the heat of the day.

It was part of the battalion's duty at Serapeum to build sandbag trenches and patrol a sector of the canal at night. This sector was near where the Turks had reached the canal in January, 1915, and, close by, a German officer and several Turks had been buried. At dusk a camel led by a "Gyppo" would drag a large bush along the bank of the canal, sweeping a clean path, and it was the patrol's duty to promenade along the side of the path at dawn looking for hostile footprints, as it was thought possible that the Turk might still have designs on the canal.

The only other departure from the previous syllabus of training was the special instruction of 40 men per battalion as grenadiers with advanced training in bayonet work. Officers and N.C.O.s' schools were carried on as before.

A brigade sports was held on April 12 when the representatives of all units in the brigade competed in athletic events. The Brigadier's Cup was won by the 13th Battalion and the other results were as follow:—

Champion Athlete: Pte. Skinner, 16th.

100 Yards Championship: Pte. Griffiths, 16th, 1, Pte. Brackenbridge, 16th, 2.

Hurdle Race: Pte. Skinner, 16th, 1, Pte. Gunn, 13th, 2.

High Jump: Pte. Lee, 16th, 1, Pte. McArthur, 15th, 2, Pte. Anderson, 14th, 3.

Long Jump: Pte. Dullarty, 14th, 1, Pte. Williams, 16th, 2.

Sack Race: Pte. Peake, 16th, 1, Pte. Evans, 16th, 2.

Donkey Race: Pte. Coleman, 13th, 1, Pte. Wynn, 13th, 2.

Siamese Race: Ptes. McGillivray and Griffiths, 16th, 1.

Grenade Throwing: Pte. Bates, 13th, 1, Pte. Pearse, 13th, 2.

Tug of War: 13th Battalion.

Flag Race: 13th Battalion.

Platoon Competition: 13th Battalion.

Officers' Flag Race: Major E. Twynam.

On April 20 the brigade was inspected by General Sir A. Murray, who rode around and saw the various units engaged in their ordinary training.

April 25 was the first anniversary of Anzac Day. A church parade was held in the morning and in the afternoon a programme of athletic and swimming events, organised by the 4th Australian Division, was decided. The following is the official programme as printed:—

A.N.Z.A.C.

— ANZAC DAY —
First Anniversary
FOURTH AUSTRALIAN DIVISION
Serapeum, Egypt.
APRIL 25th, 1916.

PROGRAM
Divisional Championship Events.
Commencing 1500

JUDGES:

Maj.-Gen. Sir H. V. Cox, K.C.M.G., C.B., C.S.I., G.O.C. 4th Aus. Div.
Brig.-Gen. J. Monash, C.B., V.D., Commanding 4th Inf. Brigade.
Brig.-Gen. Duncan Glasfurd, Commanding 12th Inf. Brigade.
Brig.-Gen. T. W. Glasgow, D.S.O., Commanding 13th Inf. Brigade.
Lieut.-Col. G. C. E. Elliott, Commanding Divisional Engineers.
Lieut.-Col. G. H. M. King, C.M.G., Commanding 10th F.A. Brigade.

COMMITTEE:

Brig.-Gen. C. Rosenthal, C.B., Commanding 4th Div. Art. (President).
Major E. Twynam, 4th Infantry Brigade.
Major A. P. Imlay, 12th Infantry Brigade.
Capt. E. D. Hordern, Div. Artillery.
Lieut. M. M. Jeakes, R.E., Div. Engineers.
Capt. L. W. Jeffries, Divisional A.M.C.

REFEREE:
Capt. Henderson, 4th Infantry Brigade.

HON. SECRETARY:
Major R. B. Jacob, 13th Infantry Brigade.

PROGRAM.

		To Start
1.	Short Distance Sprint (across Canal, about 120 yards) N.C.O.'s and men	1500 (*i.e.,* 3 p.m.)
2.	Short Distance Sprint (across Canal, about 120 yards), Officers	1510
3.	Plunge and Swim under water, N.C.O.'s and men	1520
4.	Plunge and Swim under water, Officers	1525
5.	The Bellman, N.C.O.'s and men	1530
6.	Diving Championship (High dive, Fancy dive, Straight dive), N.C.O.'s and men	1540
7.	Diving Championship (High dive, Fancy dive Straight dive), Officers	1610
8.	The Anzac Derby (440 yards), N.C.O.'s and men (Improvised boats or rafts. No requisition on Engineers permitted. 10 Crews consisting each of 2 men, must have been present at first day of landing at Gallipoli.)	1640
9.	Long Distance Race (440 yards), Officers	1650
10.	Long Distance Race (440 yards), N.C.O.'s and men	1710
	(Trophies presented by Australian Comforts Funds per Commissioner H. E. Budden, J.P.)	
11.	Greasy Pole, N.C.O.'s and men (12 entrants, 2 per unit.)	1730
12.	Relay Race (4 times across Canal and return) N.C.O.'s and men (Teams of 8 men each.)	1745

Presentation of Prizes by Maj-Gen. SIR H. V. COX, K.C.M.G. C.B., C.S.I.

That Anzac Day at Serapeum offered opportunities other than sports for diversion was proved by the following note received the next day by the adjutant:

"Unofficial.

"Adjutant 16th Infantry.

"Private ―――― of your unit was discovered at 6 p.m. wandering about among the sand hills east of your post, wearing nothing in the way of clothes and *well blithered*. He was taken to the Casualty Clearing Station where he quoted Hamlet fluently and cheeked the officers. *On account of his language* he was put in the officers' ward, and afterwards, when we found he was a private, under arrest. He is now returned to his own unit.

"L. A. JEFFRIES,
"Capt.
"4th Field Ambulance."

THE OLD SIXTEENTH.

Towards the end of April divisional training was again resumed and on the 28th an "Encounter Battle" was fought which afforded all concerned in it much interest. May 2 saw another inspection, this time by the Corps Commander, Lt.-Gen. Sir A. J. Godley, K.C.B., after which for the rest of the month advanced training, with plenty of night operations, was the rule. An interesting demonstration given to all units during this month was the work of a Stokes Mortar Battery. Those who saw this simple but effective weapon regretted that it had not been available for Gallipoli. It would have solved many problems for the Anzacs.

Some interesting details were compiled on May 1 in connection with the officers of the battalion. They are given below.

Officers of the 16th Battalion who have been on duty since the battalion left Australia on December 22, 1914—

Killed in action	18
Died of disease	1
Absent through wounds	6
Prisoners of War	2
Absent through sickness	13
Transferred to other units	11
On duty with battalion on 1/5/16	30
Total	81

Original establishment of officers on leaving Australia	32
Reinforcement officers joined who were appointed in Australia	19
Officers promoted from the ranks of the battalion in the field	30
Total	81

Two of the officers had gone to the 13th Battalion—Colonel Tilney and Capt. Murray. Major Wilton and two others had transferred to the 4th Machine Gun Company and seven had been allotted to the 48th Battalion when it was organised in Egypt. In the 16th the thirty officers on duty were in the following positions:

      C.O.: Lt.-Col. H. Pope.
      Senior Major: Major Margolin.
      Adjutant: Capt. Parks.
      Q.M.: Lieut. Edge.
      M.G.O.: Lieut. Cook.
      Med. Officer: Capt. Steele.

"A" Coy., O.C. Capt. Harwood.
   Lieut. Slater.
    „ Lynas.
   2nd. Lt. Wadge.
    „ „ Whiting.
    „ „ Wilton.

"B" Coy., O.C. Capt. Black.
   Lieut. Ahern.
    „ Hummerston.
   2nd Lt. Stephenson.
    „ „ Smith.
    „ „ Goldie.

"C" Coy., O.C. Capt. McLeod.
   Lieut. McPherson
    „ Potts.
   2nd Lt. Wilson.
    „ „ Woods.
    „ „ Hutton.

"D" Coy., O.C. Capt. Parker.
   Lieut. Tucker.
    „ Somerville.
   2nd Lt. Robin.
    „ „ Penny.
    „ „ Johnson.

SANDBAG TRENCHES ON THE CANAL.

Colonel Pope had been awarded the C.B. for his distinguished services on Gallipoli and towards the end of April further honour came his way when he was appointed to command the 14th Brigade of the A.I.F. While all ranks in the 16th were glad to see him receive such a well-deserved promotion, there was genuine sorrow in the thought that it involved separation. Colonel Pope had guided the destinies of the 16th from its military infancy through a strenuous youth on the training ground, and finally had led it in lusty manhood to do the work for which it was raised. And during the whole of that stressful period of eighteen months' close intimacy he had enjoyed the confidence and respect of all ranks in the highest degree. Needless to say Colonel Pope felt the parting, and his farewell letter was evidently written with sincere emotion.

"Serapeum.

"May 1, 1916.

"To all the Members, past and present of the 16th Battalion.

"Having been ordered for duty with the Fifth Division to command the 14th Brigade, I want to bid good-bye to all those comrades of mine who have so splendidly helped me and stood by me in the 16th during my period of command.

"In the original training in Australia and at Heliopolis; in the dark days of Pope's Hill and Quinn's Post in April and May last year; in the period of weary preparation and digging and beach fatigues of June and July and then through the fighting of August and September on Sikh's Hill and Hill 60 on the left at Anzac; then afterwards in November and December (when I was away sick) at No. 2 Subsection the 16th Battalion has gained the highest of reputations, and latterly in Egypt in training, in reorganisation, in forming the 48th Battalion and the 112th Battery and in supplying officers and men to assist the formation of all sorts of other units the battalion has, I believe, been of real and material help to tne A.I.F. And so my dear old comrades all of Gallipoli, and those who have joined more recently and who will no doubt continue the old traditions of the battalion, I wish you all farewell. No one could have hoped to have seen greater bravery and endurance in human nature than I have seen in the officers and men of the 16th, and many times that bravery saved us and many others from disaster. We have never been turned out from any position on which we had got a hold; we have never had a live Turk come into any position which we have held; and I hope in the future you never will.

"Good-bye, dear old 16th, and may your reputation as a fighting unit in war and a well disciplined battalion in peace never grow less.

"H. POPE, Lieut.-Col."

Major E. A. Drake-Brockman, who had served on Gallipoli with another Western Australian battalion, the 11th, was transferred in May to the 16th and to command.

On May 28 orders were issued that the 4th Brigade would proceed to Alexandria and from there embark for active service "somewhere in France." The men were not sorry at the prospect of leaving Egypt, for coupled with the discomforts of life spent in the heat and sand of the desert, tormented by every wind that blew, was the disappointment of waiting for an enemy who, although several times promised, had never appeared.

CHAPTER 19.—"SOMEWHERE IN FRANCE."

On June 1 the 16th Battalion, with the rest of the 4th Brigade, embarked at Alexandria. The voyage through the Mediterranean in the s.s. "Canada" was uneventful. The weather was fine, the sea calm and the usual troopship routine was adopted on board with special precautions in the way of look-outs for hostile submarines. All ranks were told off to boats and practice was held in falling in on alarm stations.

The ship passed the historic Chateau d'If and arrived at Marseilles on June 7. A short march through cobbled streets from the wharf, and the battalion entrained for northern France. The train trip was intensely interesting. The green countryside of southern France was a welcome change to men long familiar with the neutral tints and sandy glare of Egypt. The scenery was delightful—olive groves, vineyards and orchards making for a general rural picturesqueness. The quaint mannerisms of the French people seen at the various stopping places and the obvious friendliness of their greeting were pleasing to the men, who all voted their first experience of France "trés bon." All along the line the French people waved a hearty welcome. With short halts for meals at places where hot water was provided, the train rolled northwards night and day. The second day of the journey was through beautiful country, grassy slopes and wooded chateaux along the valleys of the Rhône and Saône. The quaint architecture was exclusively French and the delicate tints of the surrounding trees and meadows were a pleasing sight indeed. Progress in Flanders was painfully slow, as the overburdened railways with their trainloads of men, guns and material could hardly cope with the traffic. The country up north was not picturesque, and generally its appearance was far less interesting than the southern and central portions. The surface was flat, and the farms and houses had a meaner appearance. Before the 16th arrived at its destination, the men had plenty of evidence that they were nearing the scene of fierce fighting. Trains passed them laden with battered guns for the repair shops, with wounded men for the hospitals, and with muddy French and English soldiers *en route* for the rest areas. On June 10 Bailleul was reached and the various companies detrained and were led by guides to their first billets in France.

The next few days were spent in sorting out and inspecting equipment, constructing cook-houses and conveniences, and in generally settling down to the new environment.

Billets might convey to the uninitiated the comforts of home. To the soldier in France they meant barns and stables, and in lucky circumstances, a supply of straw. There were always "good billets" and "billets." The former kept the weather out; the latter allowed it to come in through openings which the rest of the billet did not provide material to repair. In general the farm houses which provided the billets were well built and comfortably furnished, with all sheds and outhouses attached to the main building in the form of a square. The centre of this square was a large cess-pit, which was the dumping ground for all the refuse of the farm. Pig-stye, stables, cow-sheds, and kitchen all added their quota and the smell in summer time was indescribable. A peculiar feature was that invariably the drinking water was drawn from a well dug near the edge of the cess-pit. Yet the peasantry seemed to be immune indeed they appeared to be a healthy and vigorous type.

On the 13th General Sir Wm. Birdwood inspected the battalion in its billets and was evidently pleased with what he saw. About this time steel helmets and gas respirators were issued and instruction in the use of the latter was given. To keep up-to-date with the lessons taught by previous fighting in France, scouts, observers, and snipers—1 officer and 30 men—were detached from the companies and specially trained in their duties as they applied to trench warfare. During this period the bulk of the battalion was detailed to provide working parties. Indeed, the war, from now on, so far as the 16th was concerned, seemed to resolve itself into a war of work with occasional thrilling interludes in the shape of "stunts."

On June 20 parties of officers and men were detailed to proceed to the front line for experience in trench warfare as it applied in France. A raiding party also commenced training for a raid which it was intended the battalion should make during its first tour of front line duty. (As it happened, this raid did not come off.) This training was carried out over a full size replica of the enemy trenches at the intended point of entry, the information on which the model trenches were based being gained from aerial photographs.

The 13th and 14th Battalions of the 4th Brigade took over the front line at Bois Grenier on June 27 with the 16th Battalion as a brigade reserve at Canteen Farm. Its duties consisted mainly of supplying working parties—carrying material and digging trenches—and the officers and N.C.O's. familiarising themselves with routes to the front line. These duties occupied the battalion until July 10, when it was relieved by the 32nd Battalion and marched back to l'Hallobeau for the night and then next morning to billets just outside Bailleul. On this date Brigadier-General C. H. Brand took over the command of the 4th Brigade. On July 13 the battalion entrained at 4.30 a.m. for a move down south, where the "Big Push" had started on July 1.

SGT. M. O'MEARA. V.C.

It detrained at Doullens and marched by road to St. Ouen, a distance of 14½ miles. The destination was reached at 11.30 p.m. and although no men straggled it was a hard march on account of the bad condition of the men's feet. During the next two days route marches were the order in an endeavour to harden all ranks.

On July 16, with only 35 minutes' notice, the battalion moved by road to Naours. Here general training was resumed with special attention given to physical training and attack practices. A route march on the 22nd, when the battalion, with its first line transport, was inspected by General Sir H. Cox, led all ranks to expect that they were destined for "some dirty work at the crossroads" in, the very near future. On the 25th a further move was made to Toutencourt. Twenty-four hours' rest with some gas drill and the next day saw the 16th on the road to Warloy, where a battalion dump for extra baggage and packs was established. The next week was spent in specialist and attack training. Instruction was given in forming up at night in "jump off" trenches; in advancing in "waves"; in assaulting under a barrage; in taking two different objectives; and in the action of scouts, wire cutters, wiring parties, Lewis gunners, bombers, stretcher bearers, signallers, and runners during an attack. On August 4 the battalion left Warloy and arrived at Brickfields near Albert about midnight. The next day it moved to Tara Gully and came under the shellfire of the first phase of the Battle of Pozieres. On August 7 it moved up to Wire Trench, where it remained for the next two days.

CHAPTER 20.—POZIERES.

At 7 p.m. on August 9 the battalion moved up into the front line and relieved part of the 15th Battalion, and part of the 7th Suffolks. Arrangements were also completed for the continuation of the Pozieres attack by the 16th which was allotted as its objective, Circular Trench, north of Pozieres and south of Mouquet Farm. Pozieres was a small village on the main road, running in a straight line from Albert to Bapaume. It was situate 3½ miles from Albert and had extended for nearly half-a-mile along the road to a point about 300 feet higher than Albert, about 4 miles from that town. It will be easily seen then that the position it occupied was of great tactical importance. Under cover of an artillery and trench mortar barrage the attack was launched at midnight. The assault was everywhere successful and the 16th captured the whole of its objective against a fierce resistance by the German machine gunners. Seventy prisoners and three machine guns were taken and the battalion commenced the consolidation of the position won. Touch was obtained with the 15th on the right and the Suffolks on the left. Posts in advance of the main line were occupied with Lewis guns and their crews. The enemy was heavily shelling the whole of the captured position, evidently with a view to launching a counter-attack, but none followed.

During the next day, the 10th, the enemy bombardment of front and rear lines was intense and caused many casualties. At 1 a.m. the 16th made a further advance and captured some trenches which had been set as its further objective. The construction of a communication trench was at once commenced. The enemy then placed a heavy barrage in rear of the ground gained and rendered communication between the firing line and headquarters exceptionally difficult. At 1.40 p.m. on the afternoon of August 11 the Germans counter-attacked, advancing from Mouquet Farm in small groups and spreading fanwise. Preparations were made to meet this attack and when it developed at 2.45 p.m., the advancing Germans were opposed by a storm of rifle and Lewis gun-fire from the 16th's trenches. At 3.5 p.m. the enemy was completely demoralised and scattered. Ten prisoners were captured in this operation. During the night the Australian artillery played upon the ground in front of the 16th and so prevented any further possibility of a fresh counter-attack developing. Towards morning the enemy bombarded the left of the line, causing heavy casualties.

The men now were showing the effects of their strenuous tour of duty; and when information was promulgated that the day would bring relief, it was received thankfully. At 1.30 p.m. the leading company of the 50th Battalion arrived to take over. It was evidently seen by the enemy observers, for the whole area was bombarded with every calibre of shell. The relief, therefore, was not without plenty of incident and was not completed until 4 p.m. The route out was by Centre Way and Chalk Pit to Brickfields. Through Kay Trench and Pozieres and down Centre Way the 16th was chased by a vindictive bombardment of the enemy's "heavies."

MOUQUET FARM—PRE-WAR.

For conspicuous bravery during this period Private Martin O'Meara was awarded the Victoria Cross. He carried ammunition to the front line under a heavy barrage and, as a stretcher-bearer, he brought in many wounded officers and men from No Man's Land. Throughout a trying time he displayed the utmost coolness and was undoubtedly responsible for saving many lives.

. The casualties in this, the first action of the 16th in France, were as follow:—

	Killed.	Wounded.	Missing.	Total.
Officers	0	3	0	3
Other Ranks	39	345	19	403
Total	39	348	19	406

The next day the battalion moved from Brickfields to Warloy. The condition of the men, after their night's spell, was very good, considering the hardships they had just undergone. The next few days were spent resting and reorganising. On August 16, General Sir Wm. Birdwood addressed the men of the 4th Brigade and thanked them for their great work in the Pozieres fighting. On that day the 16th moved to La Vicogne by road, a distance of 12 miles. The next day was wet and the battalion moved to Halloy-Les-Pernois, where a few days were spent in reorganisation and specialist training.

The spell was not of long duration and on August 22, with the rest of the 4th Brigade, the 16th marched to Talmas and the next day to Vadencourt, where it bivouaced in a wood. On the following day it arrived, via Warloy, at the Brickfields, where it resumed training, while the 14th and 15th Battalions went into the line near Albert. On August 26 it rained heavily and the move on the 27th from Brickfields into Wire Trench as reserve to the 2nd Australian Division was full of discomfort owing to the muddy conditions experienced.

On the night of August 28, the 16th marched via Albert-Bapaume Road and Kay Trench into the front line, where it relieved the 14th Battalion. The relief was not completed until dawn on the morning of the 29th, owing to the difficulty of moving in the muddy trenches. It rained all that day and night. During the day there was a conference at headquarters of company commanders and specialist officers, in connection with the proposed attack on Mouquet Farm in front of the 16th's line that night. The farm was a large building, in ruins, surrounded by stone walls, and its defences consisted of extensive cellars and dug-outs leading to a main trench eight feet deep and strongly held. The enemy troops were sheltered from the barrage by the dug-outs from which, when it lifted to allow the infantry to attack, they emerged to man their trenches and machine guns. It was nothing less than a fortress. It could be taken, but the difficulty was to mop it up. This strong position had proved a veritable thorn in the side of the British, having been taken and re-taken several times.

The various tasks allotted were: "A" Coy. under Capt. Harwood, to take trenches to the south of farm; "B" Coy. under Major Black, with the bombing platoon under Lieut. Wilton, to capture and hold Mouquet Farm; "C" Coy. under Capt. McLeod, to take trenches north of Mouquet Farm; "D" Coy. under Capt. Ahearn, to capture and consolidate various enemy strong points. Tapes were placed in No Man's Land by the scouts to mark the jumping off position. During the night, the four companies were assembled along this line without casualties. At 10.56 p.m., the barrage came down like a clap of thunder and the troops moved as close as possible to it. When it lifted the various objectives were rushed with all possible speed. In every case the objective was taken. However, the worst was yet to come. Immediately after the 16th reached the German lines a very severe enemy barrage was placed on it. Then a fresh danger cropped up. Many dug-outs had been missed in the advance and their occupants left unharmed. These parties were in considerable strength and were reinforced by men who came through the labryinth of underground tunnels around Mouquet Farm. The enemy barrage lifted off the captured trenches and from the front and rear of the 16th, covered by machine guns and bombs, the enemy counter-attacked. Fighting every yard of the way and hard pushed at that to even find a way back, the four companies eventually managed to fight through the enemy to their original front line.

A factor in the non-success of the operation was the mud through which the attackers had to plough their way. This had rendered a big proportion of their rifles and Lewis guns useless, and under the prevailing conditions, very little opportunity was given to remedy the defects by cleaning.

The losses of the battalion in this disastrous fight were considerable. Even in the confusion of the forced withdrawal, most of the wounded were brought in. Some were taken prisoners. The difficulties of the whole operation may be gauged by the fact that some of the communication trenches had as much as 3 feet of mud in them. When morning dawned, Lieut. Lynas showed a Red Cross flag and went out in No Man's Land, where a German officer met him and gave

MOUQUET FARM AS THE 16th KNEW IT.

him half-an-hour to recover casualties. The 16th stretcher bearers then left their trenches and collected many of the wounded who had been missed during the night. They were not molested by the enemy who honourably observed the verbal conditions of this unofficial armistice. In this noble work the stretcher bearers went to within fifteen yards of Mouquet Farm and picked up three men of the 21st Battalion who had been lying there for five days.

On August 30 the weary 16th was relieved by the 47th Battalion. The relief was slow, due to the extremely muddy state of the trenches, and was not complete until dawn on the 31st. A tired battalion it was that moved back to the Brickfields and later to billets at Warloy.

THE OLD SIXTEENTH.

The casualties in the second entry into the Battle of Pozieres were as follow:—

	Killed.	Wounded.	Missing.	Total.
Officers ..	3	6	0	9
Other Ranks ..	27	144	51	222
Total ..	30	150	51	231

From August 6 to 31 the losses of the battalion were 3 officers killed, 9 wounded; 66 other ranks killed, 489 wounded and 70 missing—a total casualty list of 637.

The next day, September 1, the 16th marched to Rubempre. The men were very tired on arriving at their billets, but a wash and a very necessary issue of new underclothing revived them considerably. The battalion remained at this village for three days, and General Sir Wm. Birdwood took the opportunity to present military medal ribbons to the following men for conspicuous service during the first stage of the Pozieres fighting, August 6 to 14:—

    No. 34—L/Cpl. W. G. Cadwallader.
    „ 1400—L/Cpl. Alex. Breen.
    „ 2696—Pte. Benj. Roberts.
    „ 1822—Sgt. H. A. Iffla.
    „ 2389—Pte. Ernest England.
    „ 3413 Pte. Samuel Barrow.
    „ 534—Pte. P. H. Williams.
    „ 3848—Pte. H. Arundel.

During the month congratulatory cards were distributed by General Cox for conspicuous service during the battalion's second tour at Pozieres—August 27 to 31:—

    Capt. R. Harwood.
    Lieut. W. J. Lynas.
    2nd. Lt. V. B. Wilton.
    Capt. D. Steele (Med. Off.)
    Capt. C. Ahearn.
    No. 140—Sgt. H. J. Bradley.
    „ 2467—Sgt. G. C. Dow.
    „ 3446—L/Corp. F. Drew.
    „ 2797—Pte. H. A. Gottlieb.
    „ 2365—Pte. H. Schmidt.
    „ 350—Pte. L. H. White.
    „ 1943—Pte. L. Thornby.

No. 1468—Corp. A. Fraser.
 ,, 2053—L/C. J. Williamson.
 ,,   422—Sgt. L. D. McCarthy.
 ,,   494—Corp. P. W. O'Shea.
 ,, 3521—Pte. W. McGilvray.
 ,,   358—Sgt. J. B. Minchin.
 ,,   139—Corp. G. Sharpe.
 ,, 4599—Pte. T. A. T. Eldridge.
 ,,   209—L/Sgt. A. Mackie.
 ,, 2711—Pte. T. C. Thompson.
 ,,   416—L/C. T. Wootton.
 ,,   136—Pte. G. Richards.
 ,, 2788—Pte. H. R. Beaumont.
 ,,   458—Pte. R. Baker.
 ,, 3461—Pte. P. F. Fox.
 ,, 3532—Pte. P. Jenkins.
 ,, 1185—Sgt. A. Heasman.
 ,, 2107—L/Sgt. A. Towers.

The weather was still wet and miserable and after a hasty reorganisation, the battalion, with the rest of the 4th Brigade, moved to Fieffes, *en route* to Doullens. On September 6 it arrived at Gezaincourt and left for Doullens on September 8, when it entrained for its second visit to the northern sector.

CHAPTER 21.—HOLDING THE LINE.

The 16th detrained at Hopoutre in Belgium at 11 p.m. on September 8 and moved into huts near La Clytte at 2 o'clock the next morning. For a week or so training was continued, with special instruction in gas defensive measures. It was also notified that in future occupations of the line the greatest care should be exercised by all officers and men using the telephone as the German listening apparatus had reached such a degree of sensitiveness that it was possible for them to overhear telephone conversation in the opposing lines. During this period the usual method was adopted of sending officers, N.C.O.'s and specialists to look over the front line which the 16th was soon to take over.

The battalion commenced the relief of the 87th Canadian Infantry Battalion at 8.30 a.m. on September 17. "C" Company left the camp and proceeded to Scottish wood, via Dickebusch. Arriving there the men were dribbled through the wood and Convent Lane into Old French Trench. Soon after midday "B" Company left camp and followed the same method of arriving at Old French Trench. At dusk these two companies moved in and the Canadians came back in support where they remained until word was received that the remainder of the 16th, which left camp at 6 p.m. had occupied its allotted position at Spoilbank. "D" Company then went into the support line near Lock House. "A" Company occupied the reserve line with two platoons in Old French Trench and two in Arundel House. The frontage held by the battalion was about 850 yards.

The relief was completed at 11.30 p.m. at which time Lt.-Col. E. A. Drake-Brockman took charge of the sector. The enemy was very quiet. Patrolling at night by the scouts was the principal activity of the 16th. Listening posts were established each night, under company arrangements, and every precaution was taken to ensure that on this sector at least No Man's Land belonged to the battalion. Machine and Lewis guns were allotted S.O.S. lines of fire in case of an attack, which ensured that an advancing enemy would necessarily have to pass through at least one stream of bullets before he reached the 16th's trenches. Sniping and observation posts were also manned by day, and a close watch was kept for anything unusual happening in the enemy lines.

Rain set in steadily and the task of improving the trenches was actively entered upon. They were taken over in bad order as regards drainage and sleeping accommodation, and the wet weather rendered it imperative that these defects should be remedied as far as possible. Gum boots were issued and approved by the troops. They were water-tight and reached to the thighs, and had attachments to the belt to prevent the uppers sagging. They kept the feet dry and warm. Their only defect was that, if worn for long periods, they made the feet soft and unfitted for marching.

In this sector the war developed into a routine which became very monotonous. The trench stage of warfare has been correctly described as "weeks of monotony, punctuated by moments of intense fear."

Some of the "moments of intense fear" were created by trench mortar sections. The members of those units had a penchant for coming into a quiet section of the front line, mounting their imple-

A "JACK JOHNSON" SOUVENIRED SOMEWHERE IN FRANCE.

ments of destruction and firing a dozen or so shells on to a selected point in the enemy's trench. Then before he had time to reply, they would pick up their gear and make off, leaving the infantry, who had to remain there, to bear the brunt of the retaliation which always came over. On one occasion in this sector a "Plum Pudding" bomb section decided to place its mortars in the support trenches, about 150 yards behind the front line, to bomb the enemy front line! The first "pudding" fell half-way between supports and front line, the second fell just in front of the trench held by "A" Company and the third about 20 yards in the rear of it. That section fired no more, for Capt. Hummerston, the O.C. "A" Company, rushed down a communication trench from the front line and threatened the "mortar" men with a violent end if they did not pick up their "drain pipes" and practice on some other company or battalion front.

General Brand on one of his tours came across two 16th men in the front line. One was looking up, across No Man's Land; the other was intently gazing the opposite way, down Kent Road, a communication trench from the front line to Old French Trench. "What's the game?" asked the Brigadier. One of them replied as follows: "It's like this! I'm watching those ——— over there and my cobber is watching those ——— back there!" The "——— over there" were coming from a German minnewerfa; the "——— back there" were from an Australian 6in. mortar (plum pudding), a new addition to trench weapons. Both missiles could be seen coming over and there was always time for a watchful man to duck out of the way of splinters if one landed in the trench.

The garrisons of the front and support lines worked, lived and slept in their web equipment, which was never taken off while they were in the line. By night sentry groups, each of 1 N.C.O. and 6 men, manned every second or third bay of the front trench, with two men observing over the parapet and the remainder resting. This was in addition to the patrols and listening posts in No Man's Land already mentioned. Every day from 6.30 to 7.30 p.m. and from 4.45 to 5.45 a.m. the garrison "stood to," which meant that every individual in the line was at his allotted post prepared to resist an enemy attack.

Gas was an ever present foe. Gas guards were mounted in suitable places, whose duties were to give warning by gongs and wake all men in the vicinity of their posts as soon as the presence of gas was discovered. No officer, N.C.O. or man was allowed to be without his box respirator (*i.e.*, gas helmet) worn in the "alert" position, at any time, sleeping or waking, working or resting. Respirators were inspected daily and tests of them were continually being made. The trenches were cleaned daily by 10 a.m. and rifles, bombs and cartridges were inspected every morning by the platoon or company officer. An important task of the platoon commander was the inspection of the feet of his men which had to be rubbed daily with the whale oil which was issued as a preventative to that distressing affliction—trench feet.

The general principle followed in holding the front and support lines at this time was to man the front line as lightly as possible with machine and Lewis guns and sentry groups; the support line to be thinly held with as many dug-outs for the garrison as possible and the bulk of the men in the reserve line, in strong points, etc., which could be manned in case of an attack overwhelming the front and support lines, or from which the men could issue forth as a counter-attacking force should the enemy enter and try to hold the forward area.

Most of the work was done at night. During the hours of darkness the enemy machine guns showed great activity and this caused many casualties among the working parties, even in those at a distance from the front line. The problem of the 16th moving about their own trenches in the night time was solved by the Germans, who used an unlimited quantity of flares which lit the hours of night almost like daylight. He relied on his flares for protection against surprise. The 16th relied on the vigilance and the activity of its patrols. At this time British aeroplanes were active in this sector, while German 'planes very seldom appeared over the 16th's lines.

On September 25 a party of 1 officer and 12 other ranks raided the German trenches opposite the 16th's sector. The party was to bring back one prisoner if possible, in order to establish the identity of the unit opposite. The password was "Cobber." It left the parapet at 10 p.m. with artillery co-operation and reached the enemy wire, which had not been cut by shellfire, as expected. The wire cutters with which the raiders were issued were tried but found "not big enough in the bite" to take the wires. There was nothing else for it than to throw their bombs into the enemy trench and return. In this operation one man was slightly wounded. The enemy used flares plentifully during the whole course of the raid and it was only a very skilful use of cover and a knowledge of the value of shell-holes—"the better 'ole"—that enabled the party to escape the storm of machine gun fire which swept No Man's Land from the front and flanks. One thing the raid did establish and that was the fact that the enemy front line was strongly held.

A trench parade state of the 16th on September 30 gave the strength as 26 officers and 642 other ranks. The casualties incurred at Pozieres had not been made up at this time.

On October 4 the 16th trenches were heavily shelled for an hour and a half, following which a German raiding party made its appearance. Although the front line had been almost obliterated by the shell-fire the raiders were beaten off. Four or five Germans who entered the line got out in such a hurry as to leave behind their rifles and bombs. Several of the raiders were killed and wounded and in the bombardment the 16th lost 6 men killed and 8 wounded.

On October 7 the 16th was relieved by the 52nd Battalion and moved out of its trenches to Dickebusch. From there it marched to Chippewa Camp, Reninghelst, along the route to which it was inspected by General Sir Herbert Plumer, G.O.C. 2nd Army, who congratulated the C.O. on the apparent fitness of the men after a three weeks' tour of duty in the front line.

THE OLD SIXTEENTH. 125

From October 7 to 11 the battalion rested and performed light training. On the 12th it relieved the 2nd Battalion in the Bluff Sector in the reserve line of the Ypres salient. Battalion headquarters, "B" Company and details were situated at Woodcote Farm; "A" Coy. in Canal dugouts; "C" Coy. in Bedford House and "D" Coy. at Segard Chateau. For the next week the work consisted of carrying rations, munitions, engineering and trench stores up to the line at night.

On the 19th the 15th Battalion London Regiment relieved the 16th, which marched back to Chippewa Camp, Reninghelst. The weather at this time was bitterly cold. October 21 saw a move back to the 1st Anzac Rest Area, where the battalion went into billets at Godeswaersvelde. A week later, on October 26, it marched to Caestre, where it entrained for Pont Remy, a village on the Somme, about 10 miles from Amiens, where it occupied billets. Here the training programme continued until the 31st.

The battalion seemed no sooner to settle down and get comfortable in one billet when it was shifted to another. November 1 saw it moved from Pont Remy to L'Etoile; the next day to Picquigny, where it remained until the 8th. On that day a further move was made by motor 'bus to Ribemont and two days later Mametz Huts were occupied. A comparatively long stay was made here during which period, from November 11 to 26, the battalion was exclusively employed on railway maintenance work. The cold at this time was intense with heavy frosts at night which did not add to the comfort of men whose work necessitated their being in the open air after sundown.

On November 27, the battalion relieved the 47th Battalion in Switch and Gap Trench, as support battalion to the brigade. These were notorious trenches, even for France. The move was made by train from Mametz to Quarry Siding—thence by road *via* Longueval and Delville Wood.

The only road to Longueval had been badly damaged by shellfire in the summer fighting but had since been made passable for traffic by the laying of a corduroy track. As the 16th traversed this road it was a sea of mud and water varying in depth from two to fifteen inches, while the logs which had worked loose did not add to its usefulness as a pathway. One never knew whether the next step would land on solid track or in a gap or shell hole, knee deep in water.

Delville Wood, with its duckboard track winding its way round trees and between shell holes, was a depressing place. The wet, bare tree-trunks, most of which were mangled and hanging in unnatural positions as a result of shell fire, gave the place a weird, uncanny look. Most of the battle debris had been salvaged, but the multitudinous shell-holes and the hopelessly twisted tangle of barbed wire gave ample evidence of the tremendous artillery duel which had taken place in this vicinity.

Switch and Gap Trenches were merely canals with two to three feet of liquid mud underfoot. There were no shelters or "possies" of any kind and the wet conditions afforded little prospect of sleep for the unfortunate occupants, while the scarcity of R.E. materials made it impossible to do much in the way of improvements. The parados was infinitely preferable to the trench and the men preferred at night to leave its "shelter" in order to try and gain a short

SWITCH TRENCH, NOVEMBER, 1916.

respite in sleep. There was no place whatever during daylight where the men could even sit down, and the days were spent in this thick viscous mud up to and over the knees. The conditions in this sector caused one man to remark, "If we are winning, God help Fritz!"

On December 2 the 16th relieved the 14th at Flers with two companies in the front line and two in support. These trenches were also in such a shocking condition that the relief had to be carried out in the darkness over the top. The next morning all hands set to work to try and make the trenches as habitable as possible. Casualties were slight as the enemy was evidently thinking more of making himself comfortable for the coming winter than of offensive action.

It is well to record that hot meals were sent up to the front line twice every night—soon after dusk and just before dawn. The evening meal generally consisted of hot stew or curry and tea, while the morning meal was usually bacon (and sometimes porridge) with tea. The dry rations (*i.e.*, bread) were sent up in sand-bags containing five men's rations for 24 hours, while the hot meal was conveyed in a hot food container. This latter receptacle was a tin about 2 feet 6 inches high, with an outer covering. The intervening space was packed with a non-conductive material which gave to the container some of the properties of a thermos flask and kept the food hot for a number of hours. The containers were fitted with straps and were shaped to fit on to a man's back and usually held one meal for about forty men.

The life of the transport drivers at this time was not to be envied, and they must look back on it as a kind of nightmare. Long hours, heavy work, irregular meals, comfortless surroundings, with

THE ROAD TO FLERS.
Note how shell fire has splintered the trees.

little sleep and an element of danger at all times comprised their cheerless existence. They had to be up long before daylight grooming and feeding their animals after which they took them to water. Then to railhead with wagons and draw rations for the battalion. After loading the pack mules they started early for the line in order to cover as much ground in daylight as possible. The rest of the journey was in the dark and at a selected point the rations were handed over to the infantry carrying parties. Then the transport drivers and their four-footed comrades could wend their weary way back to their lines, which were usually reached in the early hours of the morning.

No. 2 Platoon of "A" Company was treated to a little excitement in this sector. It was manning at night a secret post which was about 100 yards in front of the main line. Sgt. T. Wootten and a party of 4 men were detailed to occupy this post and one evening, just as darkness set in, the men on nearing it were greeted with machine-gun fire, the enemy having occupied it just ahead of them. Sergeant Wootten and Corporal Benbow were wounded by the fire and the remaining three carried them back to the front line. The

THE 16th DIGGING GIRD TRENCH. NOV. 23, 1916.

next evening it was a race to see who would reach the post first. A 16th party led by Lieut. F. Wadge crept forward and took possession. The Germans did not attempt to occupy it again.

It was while holding this sector of the front that orders were issued for an attack by the 4th Brigade. The prospect was not looked forward to with any confidence for the bodies of the men of the 7th Brigade, which had previously attacked here, could still be

AT 7th BRIGADE HEADQUARTERS, MARCH 25, 1917.
Left to right: Colonel H. Pope, Colonel E. A. Drake-Brockman, Major Colpitts, Brigadier-General E. Wisdom, Brigadier-General C. H. Brand, Lieut.-Col. J. H. Peck, Major Reid.

seen on No Man's Land and hung in the German wire. However, owing to a runner belonging to another battalion losing his way and walking into the German lines with the orders for the proposed attack, it was cancelled. The 16th diggers when they heard of the circumstances congratulated themselves on the fact that their luck was in.

On the night of December 6 the 6th Battalion relieved the 16th which moved to hutments at Montauban for the remainder of the night. The next day it entrained for Meaulte from whence it marched to Ribemont. This village was several times occupied by the 16th. The billets were the usual type—old barns, sheds, etc.—but fortunately a good supply of clean straw could always be obtained. The estaminets were first favourites there, selling cheap, washy beer with no life in it and various kinds of vin blanc and vin rouge. "Champagne" could be obtained from five francs per bottle. One establishment usually had a supply of English Bass Ale in bottles. Its only drawback was that it was always crowded out as soldiers from far and near patronised its bar. A few of the shops stocked English biscuits and chocolates and did a thriving business in bread and eggs. In the winter the streets were very muddy and German prisoners were employed to sweep and keep the roads passable. The most notable character in the village was known as "Incinerator Kate." At all times of the day she could be located at the incinerator salvaging old clothes, boots, etc., and usually was well supplied with bully beef and biscuits by the good-natured Australians. A week or so here in rainy weather, with inspections of equipment and clothing and the policy of shift was again reverted to. The battalion moved to Cardonette on December 16 where short route marches and general training were the rule for the remaining days of the year. On the 21st General Sir Wm. Birdwood and the Chaplain General, Archbishop Riley, visited the 16th. Dr. Riley's visit was appreciated especially as, with his usual thoughtfulness, he saw to it that it entailed no formal parade. Perth's grand old man went the rounds of the billets and had a cheery greeting which was heartily reciprocated by all ranks and all creeds.

Xmas Day, 1916, was fortunately fine. A brigade church parade was held in the morning and in the afternoon battalion sports were run off. The following week was uneventful and the 16th saw the old year out and the new one in from their comparatively comfortable billets in Cardonette.

CHAPTER 22.—THE GERMAN RETREAT.

At Cardonette, on January 1, General Sir Wm. Birdwood presented the ribbon of the V.C. to Pte. M. O'Meara, the D.C.M. (medal) and the D.S.O. (ribbon) to Major P. Black, the D.S.O. (ribbon) to Capt. R. Harwood, and the M.C. (ribbon) to Lieut. F. Wadge. Military Medal ribbons were also presented to No. 1332, Sgt. A. A. Iffla, 212, Corp. T. Moreton and 317, L/Cpl A. McKinnon. He also presented Lt.-Col. E. A. Drake-Brockman with the Order of Danilo (4th Class).

The next day, January 2, the battalion marched to Ribemont and camped there until the 7th when a move was made to Mametz. Here the work consisted of improving the camp, draining, duck-boarding and building cook-houses and shelters. The 16th remained at Mametz until January 24 and sandwiched in with fatigues was training in drill, musketry, bombing and wiring. During this period the weather was very cold with heavy snow-falls. On the 24th a move was made to Townsville Camp at Bernafay where the 16th relieved the 48th Battalion as brigade reserve. Working parties around the camp and at Quarry Siding took up the time of all ranks and a hard frost did not add to their comfort.

The battalion relieved the 14th in the front line at Flers during the night of February 2. Two companies were in the firing line and two in support at Bull's Road, Flers Alley and Smoke Trench. The relief was carried out over the top as there were no communication trenches in this particular sector. Two of the posts—Fritz's Folly and Goodwin's—were completely cut off from communication by day except by telephone. All hands were at once set to work improving the position, which sadly needed it. On February 4 the right company suffered heavily from an artillery barrage and it was relieved by one of the support companies, while the other was lent temporarily to the 13th Battalion which attacked Stormy Trench during the night. The casualties in this company were very severe.

The attack by the 13th Battalion was a splendid success. It was launched against a strong position and encountered stubborn resistance. When the objective was taken incessant counter-attacks were made by the Germans throughout an eventful night. The 13th captured 600 yards of trench and the tenacity with which the companies held on to their objectives was nothing short of amazing. A heavy barrage was dropped on their new line as soon as it was captured, and, when this barrage lifted, it was followed up by waves of attacking Germans against the front and both flanks. It was only the extraordinary courage of the men, coupled with the fact that the bomb supply was plentiful, that enabled the position to be held. It is interesting to know that "A" Company of the 13th was commanded by Capt. H. W. Murray. It went over the top 140 strong and in the 24 hours lost 92 officers and men. The remnants, however, were full of fight, although the trench was nothing less than a shambles when they were relieved the next night by "D" Company of the 16th under Captain Ahearn. For his ability and courage on this occasion Murray was awarded the coveted V.C. The 13th Battalion during the night lost 2 officers and 41 other ranks killed, and 5 officers and 167 other ranks wounded and 18 other ranks missing. A platoon of the 16th under Lieut. J. Courtney supported the attack and carried bombs and ammunition to the front line during the engagement. Its losses during the night were considerable. The fact that the ground was frozen to a depth of three feet made the work of consolidation exceptionally difficult. Patrol work, too, was not easy on account of the snow. White suits which were issued assisted considerably in solving the problem of concealment in No Man's Land. On February 9 the 16th was relieved by the 47th Battalion and moved back to huts at Mametz. The casualties sustained from February 1 to 9 were 9 killed, 41 wounded, 1 missing and 16 sick.

A move was made to Albury Camp near Bazentin on February 11 and here the battalion stayed until March 17. Railway work, road repairs, and the training of specialists was the routine. On March 11 General Sir William Birdwood presented No. 34, Pte. W. G. Cadwallader and No. 2389, Pte. E. England with Military Medals. March 17 saw another move to Ribemont where for a few days open warfare training was given as the enemy was in retreat to the Hindenberg Line. On the 21st a football match between teams from the 16th and 14th Battalions was won by the 16th team. The next day the battalion marched to Crucifix Camp, Fricourt, and after three days here, marched on the 25th to Bazentin-le-Petit, where a dump was established for surplus gear while the unit was in the forward area. March 27 saw a move to Biefvillers and for two or three days the men were busy on the job of digging out those officers and men buried in the Town Hall, Bapaume, when it was blown up by a delayed action mine.

The Germans were carrying out a systematic retirement. All churches were blown up to prevent the towers being used as observation points. Houses were destroyed so that they could not be used as billets. Farmhouses were burnt, fruit trees cut down and even the trees had been sawn off close to the ground and felled across the roads they had lined, as an obstruction to traffic. All cross roads were mined and huge craters soon marked most of the intersections. In addition most of the wells in the evacuated territory had been destroyed.

CHAPTER 23.—BULLECOURT.

On April 1 the 16th marched to Beugnatre and relieved the 49th Battalion in the first defensive system, "A" and "C" Companies moving next day into close support of the 13th Brigade. Sleet, rain and snow alternated during the next few days till the 7th when the battalion moved into the sunken road east of Noreuil. "A" Company, under Captain Somerville, M.C., relieved a company of the 52nd Battalion on outpost duty in the railway cutting.

On April 9 orders were issued for an attack on a sector of the famous Hindenberg Line between Bullecourt and Queant. The reason for this attack was to take the fullest advantage of the recent British successes near Arras and to do this necessitated an advance on the sector opposite the Australians. The Hindenberg Line was defended by wire entanglements of enormous width while of the strength of the line the whole world had heard. It was recognised by military authorities as a scheme of defence hitherto unparalleled in the whole history of fortification. An officers' patrol sent out on the night of April 9 to ascertain if it was strongly held was commanded by Captain A. Jacka V.C., M.C., (14th Battalion) who had with him Lieuts. F. Wadge, M.C., and H. J. Bradley of the 16th. This patrol found the enemy's wire smashed by shell fire in places but it was generally unbroken. The garrison was holding it in strength and was very wide awake. German patrols were also active in front of their own wire. Jacka's patrol met an enemy patrol and a sharp fight resulted in the capture of a German officer and a soldier of the 123rd Wurtemburgers.

On the night of April 9 the 16th formed up in a sunken road for the attack timed to take place next morning. However on account of the tanks which had been detailed to co-operate with the infantry not being able to get up in time, the attack was postponed. "C" and "D" Coys. withdrew to a position near Noreuil; "A" Coy. was placed in the shelter of a railway cutting and "B" Coy. in a sunken road just south of the cutting.

During the night final conferences of company commanders with the C.O. were held and arrangements completed. The disposition of the companies in the attack was to be "B" Coy., under Major P. Black, D.S.O., on right, "A" Coy., Capt. R. Somerville, M.C., "D" Coy., Capt. V. Tucker, and "C" Coy., Capt. H. S. Hummerston on left. Battalion headquarters and the regimental aid post were to be located in the railway cutting.

The battalion moved into its jumping off position in the sunken road and reported all correct at 3.30 a.m. on the morning of the 11th. Six tanks had been allotted to cover the brigade front

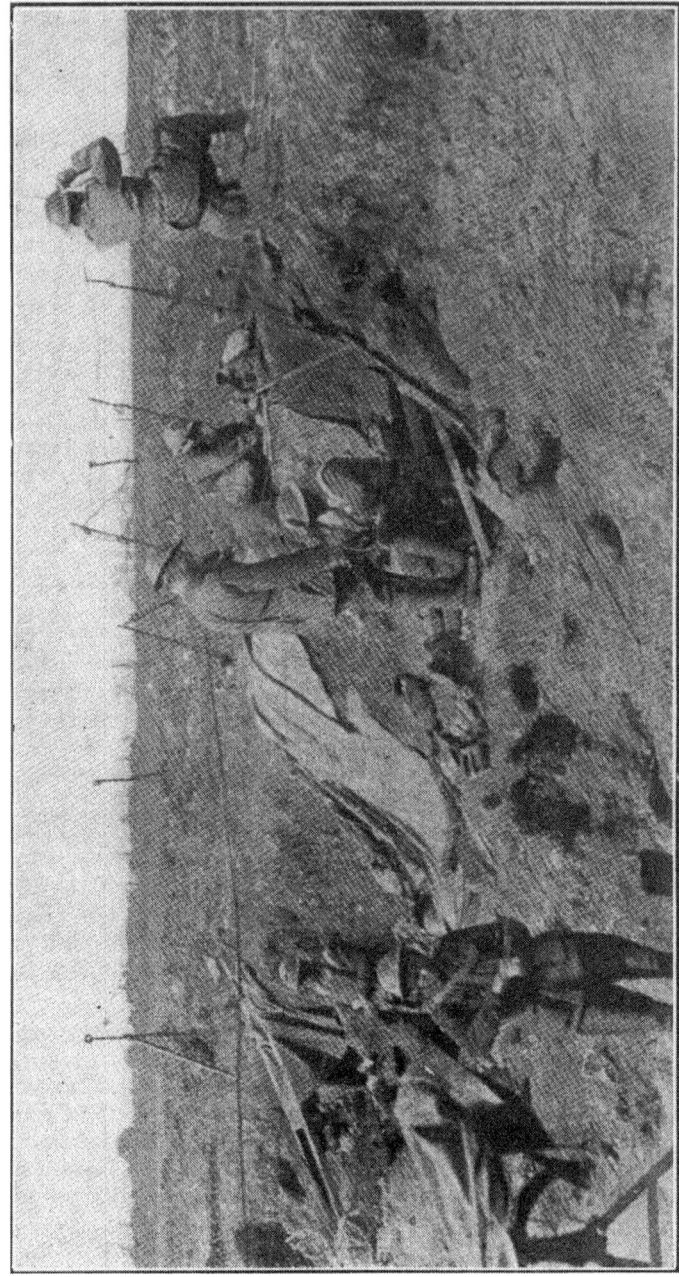

BULLECOURT, FROM THE SUNKEN ROAD NEAR NOREUIL.

and it was arranged that their first function would be to cruise along the wire and break it down sufficiently for the infantry to cross it without difficulty. The first hitch arose when only three tanks arrived at the jumping off position, the others having broken down or been bogged on the way up.

However at 4.45 a.m. the 16th went "over the top." The barrage originally provided for had been cancelled as it was intended that the tanks should adopt the role of the artillery by crashing the enemy wire and clearing the way generally for the infantry. The 4th Brigade was disposed with the 16th on right, 14th on left, moving in four successive waves, followed by the 13th behind the 16th and the 15th in rear of the 14th. Halfway to the first objective two of the tanks stopped. The 16th pushed on ahead. The advancing lines of men soon came under a fierce machine gun fire. The irresistible infantry fought their way through gaps here and there in the wire and after a strenuous struggle for possession the 16th took their brigade's first objective half an hour after the advance started. The battalion suffered very heavily in attaining this position and in the bomb fighting which immediately followed it. At 5.16 a.m. Major Black sent a runner back to headquarters with a message stating that the first objective was captured and he was pushing on to the second. Here the 16th was in very great difficulties. The wire in front of this second line of trench was found to be uncut and it was while moving along it to try to find a gap to lead his company through that the very gallant Major Percy Black was shot through the head and killed instantly. The losses were extraordinarily heavy but with the assistance of the 13th (the supporting battalion) the second objective was at last taken, and the communication trenches which led into it were entered and bombing parties pushed along them. Capt. Harry Murray, an old comrade of Percy Black in the original 16th Machine Gun Section, led his company through the wire at this point and saw the body of the latter hanging on the German wire. At 6.50 a.m. the second objective had been taken all along the line of the 4th Brigade front.

The position, however, was very precarious. Machine guns from enfilade positions were sweeping the parapet and movement above ground became absolutely impossible. Many prisoners had been taken but many of them were killed by their own machine guns when moving back. The carrying parties organised to take bombs and ammunition to the attacking infantry came under such heavy machine gun fire from Queant, Riencourt and Bullecourt that it was impossible for them to carry out their job. As both bombs and S.A.A. were running short this breakdown was fraught with serious consequences.

At 8 a.m. the S.O.S. signal went up several times in the second objective but there was no response by the artillery, owing, it was stated, to the artillery commander not being sure that Australian infantry were not in advance of the line on which fire was requested. A heavy counter-attack was developing. The first wave advanced over the top and was mown down by the rifle and machine gun fire of the 16th and 13th. Then from Riencourt, where communication trenches led to the Australians' position, a strong bombing attack was made by the Germans. This was beaten off by a combined party of the 16th and 13th bombers who drove the enemy back along the trench to within 100 yards of Riencourt, where a bombing block was put in. Another bombing attack on the right was also beaten back with heavy loss. At 9 o'clock a battalion of German infantry moved from Quéant to the north of Riencourt and was dispersed by machine gun fire. During this strenuous period visual signalling with headquarters in rear was impossible owing to the fierce machine gun fire sweeping the parapets. Very few of the runners sent back with messages got through with them.

At 10.45 the Germans attacked heavily with bombs from the front and flanks. Owing to the failure of the bomb supply it was impossible for the defenders to reply to this and while they could keep the enemy in front at a distance with rifle and machine gun fire it was found that the flanks where the attack was along the trenches were gradually being driven in. At 11.20 Lieut. Aarons of the 16th ran the gauntlet through the machine gun barrage in order to give first hand information of the position and to try and get reinforcements and bombs. At that time all the bombs were expended, about 75 per cent. of the battalion were casualties and the Germans were gradually closing in on three sides. Nothing could be done, however, and finally at 11.45 a.m. the left gave way and eventually the whole of the survivors withdrew, as best they could, to their original line, after one of the most gallant and hopeless efforts in the history of warfare. At nightfall the remnants of the Old Sixteenth were gathered together and marched, a weary and dispirited band, to Noreuil and thence to shelters near Favreuil. The 16th went into the fight with 20 officers and 797 other ranks. Of these the battalion lost in this one day's disastrous fighting 17 officers and 623 other ranks, while the 4th Brigade lost 79 officers and 2,260 other ranks. The officers' casualty list was as follows:—

Killed:
    Major P. Black, D.S.O., D.C.M.;
    Capt. V. Tucker;
    2nd Lt. L. G. Glowrey.

Missing:
    2nd Lt. F. M. Culverwell;
    „ „ M. Walton.

Wounded and Missing:
- Capt. H. S. Hummerston;
- Lieut. J. P. Courtney, M.C.;
- „ R. H. O. Cummings;
- 2nd Lt. J. H. Watson;
- „ „ S. B. Smith.

Wounded and Prisoners of War:
- Lieut. G. D. McLean;
- 2nd Lt. K. L. Johnston.

Wounded:
- Capt. R. S. Somerville, M.C.;
- Lieut. J. S. Kerr;
- 2nd Lt. W. Jorgensen;
- „ „ L. D. McCarthy;
- „ „ H. W. Leake.

The following is a nominal roll of those who actually took part in the attack and came back:—

"A." Company.

No.				No.		
5978	Pte.	Andrews, H. R.		209	Sgt.	Mackie, A.
5658	„	Adkins, A.		6319	Pte.	Pound, G. T.
6330	„	Anderson, J. N.		5164	„	Powell, G. S. (S.B.)
1984	Sgt.	Boully, L.		4046	„	Plummer, W. H.
750	L/Cpl.	Barker, W.		2690	„	Pekin, J.
5674	Pte.	Bowers, H.		6568	„	Ruthven, S. W.
1595	„	Buswell, E.		2600	„	Rodgers, W. R.
5691	„	Collins, A. J.		1860	„	Single, W.
1684	„	Caldwell, T. C.		6096	„	Smith, J.
5084	„	Dickens, A.		6598	„	Whitten, J.
2389	„	England, E. (S.B.)		6109	„	Wireford, R.
4599	„	Eldridge, T. (S.B.)		4960	„	Walsh, J.
5717	„	Ford, E. J.		5223	„	Whettem, A. R.
5503	„	Mansfield, A.		128	Sgt.	Phillips, D. C.

"B" Company.

No.				No.		
1454	Cpl.	Battison, R.		629	Pte.	Lovelock J. (S.B.)
6481	Pte.	Buckingham, A. R.		6060	„	Moore, A. F.
5520	„	Bent, E. T.		3530	„	Merchant, J.
5336	„	Boulton, C. P.		6066	„	Miles, E. G. (S.B.)
1783	„	Bolton, B. C.		5141	„	McDonald, R.
4568	„	Broadhurst, W. F.		6165	„	Nunan, P. (S.B.)
3413	„	Barrow, S. (S.B.)		6248	„	Oliver, L.
6610	„	Cooper, E. G		1888	„	Prater, W.
1995	„	Elverd, W.A. (S.B.)		6219	„	Packham, F
4808	„	Farmer, A. P.		120	„	Reed, W. E.
6019	„	Fair, A.		3545	Cpl.	Reed, A. A.
3461	„	Fox, P. F. (S.B.)		5423	Pte.	Spratley, W. N.
4030	„	Hulkes, J. E.		6338	„	Swindlehurst, A.
5723	„	Jennings, J. E.		6589	„	Taylor, A. E.
6049	„	King, A. H.		6205	„	Thorn, C. W. (Btn. H.Q. Runner)
3500	„	Kendrick, R. J. (Btn. H.Q. Runner)		5456	„	Wright, H. (S.B.)

"C" Company.

Lieut.		Kerr, J. S.		No. 6552	Pte.	Martin, R. B.
,,		Burrows, W.		,, 3137	,,	McNee, R.
No. 4543	Pte.	Brown, R. P.		,, 6349	,,	Noble, J.
,, 3854	,,	Bergstrom, P.		,, 317	,,	Palmer, E. G.
,, 1591	,,	Brett, J.		,, 3542	,,	Partlon, C.
,, 1794	L/Sgt.	Choules, H. L.		,, 5779	,,	Robin, C. H. J.
,, 3427	Pte.	Chalmers, W. R.		,, 6340	,,	Reid, J.
,, 5687	,,	Carter, C. F.		,, 4700	,,	Reardon, W. A.
,, 3890	,,	Douglas, J.		,, 6145	,,	Sadlier, J.
,, 3248	L/C.	Daw, R.		,, 6202	,,	Sermon, J. C.
,, 4805	Pte.	Fuhrmann, H.		,, 2524	L/Cpl.	Stockton, W. N.
,, 1281	L/C.	Hill, T. H.		,, 6349	Pte.	Walker, C. W.
,, 576	Pte.	Geggie, W.		,, 5937	,,	Weir, J. B.
,, 1295	Sgt.	Law, S.		,, 3037	,,	Rseszowski, L. J.

"D" Company.

Lieut.		Aarons, D. S.		No. 1042	Pte.	Halliday, W. J.
No. 2105	L/Sgt.	Bridges, R. G.		,, 768	,,	Jeffrey, J. G.
,, 1130	Sgt.	Bitmead, J.		,, 5370	,,	Kelman, W.
,, 650	Pte.	Ball, G.		,, 5371	,,	Longbottom, H, C.
,, 5337	,,	Bercovitch, M.		,, 1753	,,	Langford, A.
,, 6235	,,	Bonzer, G. E.		,, 5737	,,	Larrett, P.
,, 5670	,,	Benari, R. L.		,, 1196	,,	McDonald, A. D.
,, 2631	L/C.	Crisp, D. B.		,, 6072	,,	Riseley, A .E.
,, 6005	Pte.	Clarke, T. A.		,, 6573	,,	Payne, G.
,, 1713	,,	Dyer, C.		,, 294	,,	Riscci, J.
,, 5358	,,	Eve, F.		,, 2310	Sgt.	Thompson, H. C.
,, 6016	,,	Forrest, L.		,, 6111	Pte.	Woodland, C. A.
,, 1915	Sgt.	Garrett, C. G.		,, 1848	,,	Wilcox, W.
,, 4609	Pte.	Gladstone, F.		,, 1114	,,	Young, G.
,, 3704	,,	Holden, A. (S.B.)				

There was much bitterness over the failure. The tanks were allotted their share of blame. Of the 4th Brigade tanks only one got to the wire. It was said that their crews knew little about the methods of infantry and not much about this particular operation. They were late at the rendezvous and late at the jumping off point, where only three arrived. In the advance it was stated that one of them opened fire on the Australians at the jumping off line killing 4 and wounding others. Their organisation seemed to be hopelessly bad. One tank only reached its objective and did good work until put out of action by a direct hit from a gun at Riencourt. Other tanks seemed to make no effort to reach their objective although the machines were in no way damaged. The help of the tanks even after the attack had got well under way would have been of the greatest assistance but instead of going forward they wandered back. Other tanks which had apparently made no effort to reach their objectives were found in various places; on fire although not hit by shells. According to the general opinion in the 4th Brigade, from the highest to the lowest, the whole tank outfit showed inefficiency and a lack of that determination to go forward which is naturally looked for in a British unit. As we look back now it is easy to realise that the tanks had been brought into the war long before their time; before the tanks mechanically or their crews technically were in fit condition to undertake the exacting demands of modern warfare.

In the Australian War Museum to-day is a model, measuring 40 feet by 30 feet, illustrating the Battle of Bullecourt on April 11. Though it is impossible to indicate the bravery and self-sacrifice of those engaged in it, it is surely some satisfaction to know that the authorities regard Bullecourt as one of the memorable engagements of the A.I.F.; one which it is desired to hand down to future generations as a symbol of the valour displayed on that occasion— an occasion when the 16th Battalion's magnificent fighting reputation reached its highest point.

The following messages of appreciation were received relative to the Bullecourt fighting:—

"April 12, 1917.

"Message from G.O.C., 4th Australian Division, to G.O.C., 4th Infantry Brigade.

"Will you please accept yourself and convey to the officers, N.C.O's., and men under your command my sincere thanks for the gallant services rendered by them yesterday and my congratulations on the success achieved in breaking the formidable Hindenburg Line, notwithstanding the failure of the tanks of which so much was expected. The fact that we could not 'stick it' in the line was due to bad luck, and cannot be regarded in any way as a reflection on the brigade, which fought magnificently and in my opinion performed, under all circumstances, a herculean task in getting there at all, and staying as long as it did.

"Of course we all sincerely regret the loss of so many brave and gallant officers and men but in war this cannot be avoided.

"The brigade has well maintained the high reputation as a fighting unit it has had ever since its formation."

"April 25, 1917.

"Message from General Birdwood to Major-General Holmes, G.O.C., 4th Australian Division.

"You know what my feelings are as regards the magnificent work done by your division in the attack on the Hindenburg Line on the 11th inst. I have already endeavoured to express these in the messages which you sent out for me to the brigades. Having heard, however, so many more details on the subject since then, I feel I must send you a line to again let you know my feelings of intense admiration for and pride in, the officers and men in their really magnificent and gallant work that morning. No words can, I think, describe the reckless bravery with which they tackled the wire before them and went through everything in going in—in the desperate fighting they had while in the enemy's trenches, and again in the necessary retirement, which in the hands of inferior and less determined troops might well have led to panic and disaster.

"We can none of us ever sufficiently regret the losses which we sustained, but we, of course, every one of us, recognise that such are inevitable when we are playing a part in the huge battlefield from Arras to Champagne.

"I have been particularly struck with the way in which all company and platoon commanders conducted the most difficult retirement, seeing their men quietly through the wire as they did and then following after they had seen all safely through. It is through doing their duty nobly like this that I'm afraid we have lost so many valuable officers. That officers should have thus willingly sacrificed themselves for their men speaks for itself, and no episode in the annals of the A.I.F. will ever stand higher than the behaviour of the officers and all others on this occasion."

On April 12 the battalion moved back to Bapaume, and entrained for Albert, *en route* for a brigade camp at Mametz. At this latter place the unit was reorganised and re-equipped as far as possible while the men were rested. On the 19th a move was made to Ribemont where it remained until April 15. Here reinforcements joined up and the oft-shattered ranks of the 16th began to fill out. The new arrivals were not always up to standard, but they soon picked up, and a month or two usually found them as proud as the old hands of the reputation of the unit. Riding into Ribemont one day before the battalion returned from training near Buire, the Brigadier, General Brand, saw a 16th man sitting down near an estaminet, tired looking and smoking a cigarette. Judging him to be dodging parade, he pulled up his horse in front of the man, who took no notice. "Come here!" ordered the Brigadier. The man came over, hands in pockets, and cigarette in mouth, and was met by the inquiry "Who are you?" The reply came. "I'm a ——— reinforcement. I lobbed here last night." "Why didn't you salute when I called you up?" asked the General. "If you don't know your Brigadier now, I can assure you you soon will." "Oh!" answered the new arrival, "I thought you was one of those ——— A.P.M's!" A few words of advice as to the reputation of the 16th in and out of the line, and a wiser reinforcement watched the General ride away. Training was entered into thoroughly with special attention to the instruction of specialists. The second anniversary of Anzac Day was commemorated by a church service in the morning

THE OLD SIXTEENTH. 141

A PARTY OF REINFORCEMENTS.

and a sports meeting in the afternoon. The 16th won the cup for the highest aggregate number of points. On the 30th a poll was held in connection with the Federal elections. Not a great deal of interest was taken in this although most of the men exercised their franchise. On May 6 General Sir William Birdwood presented bars to their Military Medals to No. 2389, Pte. E. England, and No. 3461, Pte. P. F. Fox, and Military Medals to:—

No.	207	Sgt.	Mace, G.	No.	1959	Pte.	Buswell, E.
,,	650	L./Cpl.	Ball, G.	,,	500	,,	Turner, J. R. H. E.
,,	5473	Pte.	Spratley, W. M.	,,	2699	,,	Rogers, W. R.
,,	4960	,,	Walsh, J.	,,	234	,,	Affleck, W. T.
,,	1684	,,	Caldwell, T. C.	,,	768	,,	Jeffrey, F. J. V.
,,	5337	,,	Bercovitch, M.	,,	3037	,,	Rzeszkowski, L. I.
,,	5737	,,	Larratt, P. W.	,,	3427	,,	Chalmers, W. T.
,,	3854	,,	Bergstrom, P. E.	,,	1794	Sgt.	Choules, H. L.

At an inspection on May 7 of the transport belonging to the brigade the 16th won the first prize. The points were 16th, 308; 13th, 281; M.G. Coy., 281; 15th, 271; 14th, 268. A divisional rifle meeting was held on the 9th and "D" Coy. of the 16th came third in the divisional company match and the battalion team tied for third in the battalion match. On the 12th came an inspection by General Sir William Birdwood which preceded a move up North.

It is interesting to record here that two members of the 16th (Privates H. Parsons and G. Stewart), who were taken prisoners at Bullecourt, escaped a few days later. After many thrilling adventures they approached the front line held by the 32nd Battalion, and were challenged and shot at. Stewart was wounded in the shoulder, but both got in and explained matters.

CHAPTER 24—MESSINES.

The 16th entrained at Edgehill at 5.30 a.m. on May 15 and arrived at 6 p.m. at Bailleul, from which station it marched to billets outside Doulieu. Here it remained until May 31, and during this period training was energetically proceeded with. On the 23rd the final of the brigade football championship cup was played and won by the 16th team, to whom the cup was presented after the match.

On May 31 the battalion moved to Matuhonga Camp, at Neuve Eglise, and for the next week was engaged on working parties near Petit Douve Farm and constructing light railways in preparation

A RAILWAY LINE IN FRANCE, 1917.

for the attack which had been planned to take place on the Messines Ridge, the barrage preceding which was then in progress. On June 7, when Messines was captured, a move was made to La Plus Douve Farm as reserve. Not being wanted, the battalion marched back next day to Matuhonga Camp. On the 9th the 16th relieved a New Zealand battalion in the support line at the back of Messines, in which position it remained until the evening of June 11. While there the men were engaged on cable burying and working parties. At intervals the support line was heavily shelled and the 16th suffered casualties.

An instance happened here of betting on a certainty. Lieut. Webster bet Captain Lynas that he could not put a bullet through a steel helmet at 20 paces. Lynas, who was a good revolver shot, accepted the wager of 20 francs. The distance was paced off and a helmet fixed in position. He fired three shots and, making no impression, concluded he had missed and paid over the 20 francs. On receiving the money Webster said that he had tested the possibilities beforehand and had discovered that the lead bullet from the service Webley would not penetrate but glanced off the rounded surface of the "tin hat"!

Part of the battalion's duty while in this position was to erect wire entanglements. In one instance the support line near Gapaard Farm, opposite the Dolls' House, had to be wired, and each company was allotted a sector. "D" Company had the left flank, and owing to the big shell holes, for which Messines was noted, and the dark nights, the task was very difficult. The officer in charge of the wiring party therefore decided that at dusk, before the darkness became intense, he and a sergeant would screw in the iron pickets, which would make the job more easy when the main party arrived during the night. The two obtained their load of screw pickets and had hardly reached their wiring locality when they were greeted with a salvo of "whiz-bangs." Fortunately they were able to take shelter in rear of a near-by German concrete block-house. Scores of shells were fired and the pair wondered what had stirred up a German "hate" at this inopportune time. During a lull they attempted to bolt out of the "strafed" area, but no sooner had they started than down came the storm again, and they rushed back to the friendly wall of the old dug-out. When the company arrived during the night they were still there, and owing to the attraction, for some unexplained reason, of the locality for German shell-fire, very little wiring was done on it during that night at least.

The 44th Battalion of the 3rd Division was relieved by the 16th on the night of June 11 in the front line (the Green Line or second objective of the Battle of Messines), and in the secondary or Black Line, which was the first objective taken in the Messines advance. The position occupied by the 16th extended from La Douve River on the right to Bethlehem Farm on the left. During the night patrols were sent out, and, meeting with no opposition, a full company of the 16th was pushed out and a new forward line established. During the next night the battalion was relieved by the 2nd Battalion of the Lancashire Regiment and moved back to billets at Red Lodge. Here it remained, with the exception of various companies shifted temporarily to other localities for special jobs, until June 28. The work was mainly salvage operations during this time, with a little training of specialists. On the 26th H.R.H. the Duke of Connaught inspected a representative squad from each battalion, the 16th representatives being Capt. F. Wadge, M.C., 1130, Sgt. J. Bitmead, 1915, Sgt. Garratt, C.C., 431, Corp. H. L. Terry, and 3970, Pte. M. O'Meara, V.C.

On June 28 the battalion moved to Hill 63 *en route* for the front line, where, on the next night, it relieved the New Zealanders in the Ploegsteert sector. The frontage occupied ran from Truie Farm to the Warnave River, with battalion headquarters at the Convent. The weather at this period was very wet; the trenches were full of water, and the mud was as bad as had been experienced on the Somme. The difficulty lay in the fact that the country was so flat that no amount of draining could relieve the trenches of water, which consequently caused great discomfort. From July 1 to 7 this sector was occupied. The situation was comparatively quiet, with the enemy artillery not heavy, although consistent. The men worked hard in improving the trenches as far as possible and in constructing new posts. On the 6th, owing to a shell wounding most of the brigade staff, including the Brigadier, General Brand, Lt.-Col. Drake-Brockman temporarily took over the command of the 4th Brigade.

The next day, the 7th, the 13th Battalion relieved, and the 16th took over the support line, where it remained until July 12. Here "A" Coy was located from Maison 1875 to Touquet Berthe, "B" Coy. in Hunter's Avenue, "C" Coy. in Bunhill Row, and "D" Coy. lay between Lancashire Support and Laurence Farm. On the 13th a relief took place and the battalion moved back to Canteen Corner, where, until July 18th, it was engaged re-equipping, re-organising, and training. During this tour of the line from July 1 to 14 the casualties of the battalion were 8 killed and 40 wounded.

On the 17th a cricket match was played between the 16th and the 4th Machine Gun Company which was won by the Gunners.

In the evening a good show by the brigade Pierrot troupe, "The Blue Dandies," of which "Dinks" Patterson, of Kalgoorlie, was the comedian, was much appreciated. In passing it may be stated here that these shows were now recognised as a necessity in the preservation of the morale of the troops.

On July 19 the battalion marched to billets at Bleu Tour, where it settled down to a fortnight of steady training. Route marches, in full marching order, of ten miles each, were held three times weekly in order to harden the men's feet. The cobble-stoned roads of France were excellent for heavy wheeled traffic, but for the soldier doing long distances with a heavy pack they were quite unsuitable. At the end of the day's march every stone gave a feeling that it was needle-pointed. Sore feet, bad language and cobbled roads went always together. Under shell fire, too, these roads were particularly dangerous on account of the flying splinters of stone. Training of all descriptions was carried out with the men wearing gas helmets, and the rapid adjustment of the mask in the dark every night was made a special feature. Towards the end of this fortnight there was a noticeable improvement in the appearance and smartness of the battalion. At an inspection by General Sir Herbert Plumer, G.O.C., 2nd Army, he spoke to the senior officers, and asked that his words should be promulgated among all ranks, on the increasing prevalence of desertion, and desired that everything in the power of commanders should be done to decrease the figures in the 2nd Army. On July 31 Lieut.-Col. Drake-Brockman resumed the command of the 16th on the return to duty of Brig.-Gen. Brand.

On August 3 the battalion moved in motor lorries to Neuve Eglise and from there marched to the front line in front of Messines, again relieving the 44th Battalion, which had been in the line under shocking conditions for six days and which had lost very heavily. The 16th occupied this sector until August 9 and suffered severe casualties from several heavy bombardments. It rained heavily most of the time and the trenches were drains full of water in which the men had to live, eat, and sleep. It was impossible to build or dig dry positions. Imagine days and nights of these conditions with periods of bombardment by high explosives! The men of the 16th were very glad indeed when they were relieved on the night of the 9th by the 14th Battalion, and the filthy morass of drains called trenches was handed over without regret. In the six days' tour of duty the battalion lost one officer (2nd Lt. L. Boully) and 15 other ranks killed and one officer and 48 other ranks wounded.

After occupying billets at Neuve Eglise for a couple of days a move was made on August 11 to Locrehof Farm, near Dranoutre, where re-organisation and training was the routine until the 14th, when the battalion relieved the 13th Battalion in the support line, via Neuve Eglise. Here it remained until the 26th engaged on fatigues, salvaging, and general working parties. Slight casualties only were sustained. On the 26th the 15th Battalion took over and the 16th returned to billets in Neuve Eglise, where it remained for a few days engaged in light training. On August 31 it moved back to billets in Arrewage, near Merville. On the march the column was inspected by the divisional commander near Bailleul. Two days later the men were taken in motor 'buses to Crepy, where the battalion billeted until September 18. A cricket match on September 6 between the 16th and the 4th Field Ambulance was won by the 16th.

The 16th Battalion up to this period had had its share of hardships and seen much that was tragic. Let it be understood however that the spirit of the 16th digger was never quenched for long, and even in the most distressing stunts, probably that incident which is most easily remembered was the humorous one which usually occurred.

Every unit had its "hard doers" and the 16th had its full quota, among whom could be named Tom Caldwell, "Red" O'Shea, Napper Hall, "Old" Campbell and J. O'Neil, just to mention a few.

Probably Sgt. Thomas Campbell Caldwell holds pride of place. Joining up early, he was noted for his good work in the forward area, both on Gallipoli and in France. He growled most of the time but always did his own work and part of another man's. Behind the line he was hail fellow well met; was never happier than when close to bad beer, vin blanc, or vin rouge; was always broke, and never missed an opportunity of "subbing" any officer he might meet, General Sir Wm. Birdwood and Lt.-Colonel Drake-Brockman being numbered among his victims.

Caldwell was in the Bullecourt tragedy and was one of the few to get back. When, finally, the situation was hopeless and they were nearly surrounded, a German officer called on Caldwell and party to surrender. There was a rush to the rear, and in getting through the wire in rear of the German trench Caldwell and big "Digger" Smith collided heavily. Although there was a hail of machine gun bullets swishing through the air, the pair of them rolled into a shell hole and argued the point as to who was responsible for the collision!

At Neuve Eglise, on Anzac Day, Caldwell won the "Bullecourt" Cup, a prize given to the winner of a race over trenches and through wire entanglements. In a later stunt he was badly wounded in the neck, and after discharge from hospital was invalided to Australia.

"Red" O'Shea in the front line could generally be found doing a "four man job." In billets he was not too careful of himself. On many occasions he won promotion to corporal and sergeant by his good work in the forward area, but invariably succumbed to the temptation of the estaminet and had to relinquish his stripes when back in the areas of rest.

CHAPTER 25.—PASCHENDAELE.

September 18 saw another move towards the line. Ypres was the scene of furious fighting and the 16th on this day was taken in 'buses to billets near Staples. Two days later it marched to Steenvoorde. The strength of the battalion at this time was 22 officers and 575 other ranks. On the 22nd it marched through Ypres and bivouaced in an open field for the night. The next evening it relieved the 22nd Battalion in the support line.

THE MEN WITH MOVING JOBS.
The difficulties of evacuating wounded from the Paschendaele area were immense. This shows the Regimental Aid Post during the operations in October, 1917.

The 4th Brigade was to take part in a further offensive having as its ultimate objective the village of Paschendaele. The brigade's part was to capture two objectives near Zonnebeke. The 16th Battalion was allotted the capture of the first objective, the Red Line, where it was to construct three or four strong points. The 15th and 14th Battalions were allotted the second objective, the Blue Line, while the 13th Battalion was in reserve. The attack was to be accompanied by an intense artillery barrage which was to be put down 150 yards in front of the forming-up line at Zero hour and was then to move forward at the rate of 100 yards in four minutes for 200 yards and thereafter, up to the Red Line, at the rate of 100 yards every six minutes. The assaulting troops were to be in position one hour before Zero time.

On September 24 officers, N.C.O.'s and specialists made forward reconnaissances of the sector through which the 16th had to attack. The next night final preparations were made. These were very complete. Tapes were laid as a guide for the troops forming up on the jump-off line and also to denote the flanks of the units taking part. The duties of the various participants were denoted by scouts wearing a green band, 1½ inches wide, on the arm, runners red and signallers a blue patch on shoulder strap. Carrying parties wore a yellow band on the arm, moppers-up white, while men equipped with wire cutters wore white tape on their right shoulder straps.

A PLATOON MOVING UP AT DUSK TO THE FRONT LINE.

During the night of September 25 the 16th moved silently into its jumping off position in No Man's Land. The assembly was carried out without a hitch, and the men lay in shell holes along the line of tape waiting for the barrage which was to signal them to advance. Before the attack commenced the enemy opened a heavy bombardment on the back areas. At 5.50 a.m. (Zero time) the barrage came down with a thundering roar, the men moved as close to it as possible, and when it crept forward they followed. Each company was advancing in four platoon waves, the second platoon in each company acting as moppers-up and the last platoon as a carrying party. The Intelligence Officer of the 16th, equipped with a prismatic compass, directed the left flank in order that the battalion would keep in its allotted sector. One officer per company was also told off with a prismatic compass for use in case of fog or smoke causing doubt as to the correctness of the line of advance.

The attack was completely successful. The men kept close to the barrage and the objective was captured without trouble. The 16th took about 200 prisoners, while the enemy losses in killed and wounded were very heavy. The 16th's casualties were not very great. At 7.30 a.m. the 14th and 15th Battalions went through the Red Line on their way to the second objective. During the day the captured positions were strengthened and consolidated, and during this process many men were hit by snipers and machine gun fire from a distance. The 13th Battalion dug a communication trench from the old front line to the Red Line and on all parts of the route which crossed ridges, where the ground was under enemy observation. This

WOUNDED ON THE MENIN ROAD, 1917.

trench rendered communication to the Red Line possible by day. Two or three times during the day the Germans counter-attacked but each time were beaten back by the 15th and 14th Battalions on the Blue Line. Except for artillery fire there were no developments during the night, and after strengthening its position on the Red Line the 16th was relieved by the 48th Battalion on the night of September 28, when it moved back to billets in the Canal area in rear of Ypres. The next day it marched to Vancouver Camp, where all members of the battalion thoroughly enjoyed the hot baths which were provided at that place. On September 30 'buses conveyed the 16th to Steenvoorde. The losses sustained by the 4th Brigade in this most successful action were very light considering the importance and magnitude of the operation. The casualties of the whole four battalions were as follow:—

	Off.	O.R.	Ttl.
Killed	7	104	111
Wounded	17	448	465
Died of Wounds	3	6	9
Missing	0	9	9
	27	567	594

PTE. G. COBBIE, "BABY" OF THE BATTALION.

At Steenvoorde the 16th was located for twelve days. The weather was wet and cold, but training was attempted on all possible occasions. On October 11 the battalion marched to Halifax Camp and next day took up its position in the dug-outs on the Ypres Canal. The surplus gear was left at Halifax. The weather all this time was miserably wet, and mud everywhere hampered movement. On the 14th the battalion moved up to Westhoek Ridge, a position south of the railway, near Zonnebeke. Here for a few days the men were engaged as burying parties, salvaging stores and carrying material.

Near the 16th position and behind Westhoek Ridge dozens of batteries of 9in. and 6in. guns were dug in along the roadside, and their activities caused them to be raided by a flight of 14 German aeroplanes, which rained bombs on to the gun positions for over an hour. On the 18th a move was made to a position near Zonnebeke, where heavy shelling was encountered which included a big proportion of gas. This necessitated the wearing of gas masks for one period of 2½ hours.

"B" Company, under Captain Lynas, and "D" Company, under Captain Aarons, were to occupy a sunken road. "B" Company moved in without a great deal of trouble, but "D" Company's unlucky star was in the ascendant. At dusk, Captain Aarons decided to proceed with his runner to the sunken road and arrange the relief with the outgoing company commander, leaving Lieuts. V. Ketterer and H. Grieve to lead the company of about 60 men to the position. When nearing Zonnebeke, on the duck-board track, a shell wounded Lieut. Grieve and a few of the men. On reaching the sunken road, which was a support position, the men were allotted to dug-outs and they proceeded to make themselves as comfortable as the mud and slush would allow. Aarons and Ketterer occupied a dugout in about the centre of the company sector. During the night the area was subjected to a severe gas bombardment. Captain Aarons, on a tour of the position to see how the men were faring, got a few whiffs of "mustard gas" and was temporarily incapacitated. Ketterer decided to notify Capt. Lynas of his plight and that officer came over with four stretcher bearers, but when he saw them Aarons decided he could "carry on." However, the dug-out in which he and Ketterer were quartered reeked with gas and a good portion of the night was spent with gas masks on.

The next morning the two companies were detailed to dig a cable trench to forward headquarters, and under the guidance of engineers commenced that interesting operation. It was here that a fine soldier in Sgt. McMurray was killed. One of his platoon had a presentiment that something was going to happen and asked permission to leave the party for a few minutes. Sgt. McMurray took his place in the trench and the next moment a "whizz-bang" landed in it, killing McMurray and wounding two other men.

During his company's absence on the cable-burying Captain Aarons had decided to enlarge the company headquarters dugout in which they had spent such an uncomfortable night. While pulling off the old timber which formed the roof he found a small paper bag, which, when opened, proved to be full of curry powder. This had become wet and had given off the "mustard" gas, the smell of which had caused the two officers to wear their masks for some hours the night before!

The weather was still wet and the whole area around Zonnebeke was almost an impassable marsh. On October 21 two companies of the 16th relieved half the 13th Battalion in the front line from Daisy Wood to Broodseinde Road, the other two companies being in support. Heavy shelling accompanied this relief which caused 20 casualties, including Capt. D. S. Aarons, M.C., who was wounded.

The front line was only a series of outposts and "D" Company was to occupy two, with its right flank linking up with the 32nd Battalion. On moving up Captain Aarons took two platoons and Lieut. Ketterer the others. The latter completed his relief and some time later received word that Captain Aarons and his party had not

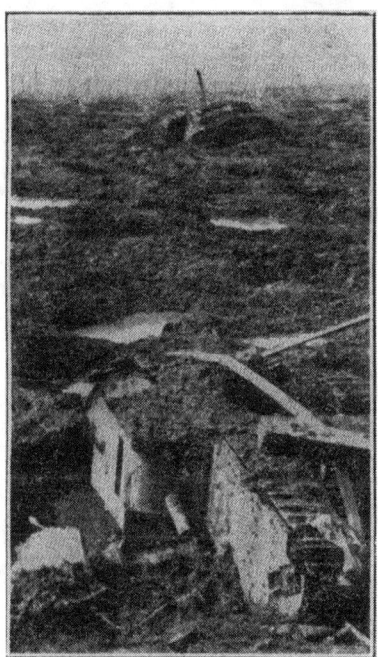

DERELICT TANKS EMBEDDED IN THE MUD NEAR ZONNEBEKE.

reached their destination. It turned out that a shell had severely wounded Aarons and a number of his men on the Broodseinde Road. However, the relief was completed during the night.

One of those incidents which demonstrated the democratic characteristics which were peculiar to the Australian officer occurred during this relief. Lieut. Ketterer sent a sergeant to get in touch with the 32nd Battalion. He was absent about two hours and came back in the early hours of the morning gloriously "tight." Having no use for a drunken N.C.O. in the front line, Ketterer sent him

CAPTAIN J. S. KERR, M.C., LIEUT V. KETTERER, M.C.,
and LIEUT. H. KLOPPER, M.C.

in charge of a runner to Captain Lynas. A little while afterwards the sergeant reported back to Ketterer and said that he had had a row with Lynas, who threatened to shoot him. The sergeant further stated that he had then pulled off his tunic, opened his shirt, and told Lynas to carry on. Being a good soldier, other than this one lapse, the matter dropped until the battalion was relieved and arrived back in billets. As soon as everyone had settled down, Lynas decided that the affair was one of honour and had to be settled. Taking off his tunic he proceeded to the sergeant's tent and offered to fight it out in the good old style. However, the sergeant was now sober. He frankly admitted he had been in the wrong and a glass of whisky all round settled things satisfactorily to all concerned.

The ground which the 16th occupied near Zonnebeke almost defies description. It had been fought over for years and every yard of it was churned up by shell-fire. The area ordinarily was marshy.

ZONNEBEKE!
No pen can describe the above ground—typical of area in which the battles for Paschendaele were fought in October and November, 1917.

Now, with every shell hole full of stagnant water, barbed wire plentifully strewn around, broken vehicles and guns, dead horses and dead men, it was a forbidding waste indeed. It was almost impossible for any attack to be launched by either side, so difficult was it for men to move. As one 16th officer, who went out in charge of a patrol, reported: "In some places men could move 100 yards in 10 minutes; in others 10 yards in 100 minutes!"

On October 23, to the accompaniment of heavy shell fire, the 16th was relieved by the 7th Battalion and the diggers in small parties wandered back to the Canal dugouts. A comic interlude occurred when Captain Lynas picked up his trench gear, which he usually carried in a sand-bag, and trudged slowly through the mud to the rear. After proceeding three kilometres and reaching the Menin Road, Lynas complained that his bag seemed very heavy and Lieut. Ketterer offered to give him a spell. As soon as the latter officer received it he became suspicious and investigated, whereon much to everyone's amusement, except the victim of the joke, it was found that he was carrying two good sized bricks instead of his revolver, field glasses and shaving outfit!

A move by 'bus was made the next day to Devonshire Camp near Reninghelst. The casualties sustained by the battalion from October 13 to 22 were 66 killed and wounded.

On October 27 the battalion marched to Brandhoek where it entrained for Wizernes. At the latter place it embussed for Lisbourg where the men were billeted at midnight. All ranks then settled down for a restful period in which only light training was indulged in. On November 3 each battalion sent a representative platoon to a divisional parade at Beaumetz, where General Sir Wm. Birdwood presented the following ribbons and decorations:—

Military Cross (ribbon):

    Capt. C. Ahearn,
    Lieut. H. J. Bradley,
    2nd Lt. J. B. Minchin.

Croix de Guerre (medal):

    2nd Lt. L. D. McCarthy.

D.C.M. (medal):

    2nd Lt. D. B. Crisp,
    4030 Corp. J. E. Ffoulkes, "B" Coy.

Bar to M.M. (clasp):

    3894 Temp-Corp. J. Elliott, "B" Coy.,
    2699 Sgt. W. R. Rogers, "A" Coy.,
    317 Sgt. A. L. McKinnon, "B" Coy.

Military Medal:

    234 Pte. W. T. Affleck, Headquarters.
    3415 Corp. A. T. H. Bloom, Scouts,
    5473 Sgt. W. E. Spratley, "B" Coy.

LIEUT. J. B. MINCHIN, D.S.O., M.C.

THE OLD SIXTEENTH.

Military Medal (ribbon):

  1807(a) Pte. F. J. Robbins, "D" Coy.
   618 Corp. W. W. Tillbrook, "D" Coy.,
   775 „ J. Gooney, "A" Coy.,
  4904 Sgt. W. A. Schiff, "A" Coy.,
  5436 Pte. V. C. Sparrow, "A" Coy.,
  6276 „ W. E. Inglis, "D" Coy.,
  4052 „ E. Mullen, "A" Coy.,
  2913 Sgt. W. Murray, "C" Coy.,
  3918 Temp-Corp. J. Helsin, "B" Coy.,
  7041 Pte. A. J. Lee, "A" Coy.,
  2465 Driver A. E. Cowley, Transport,
  6946 Temp-Sgt. G. W. Bradshaw, "B" Coy.,
  5162 Pte. W. O'Sullivan, "D" Coy.,
  3894 Temp-Corp. J. Elliott, "B" Coy.,
  6223 L/Corp. A. J. Bonser, "D" Coy.,
  5160 Pte. C. Nineham, "B" Coy.,
  1656 „ T. W. R. Scott, Scouts,
   743 Corp. McQuade, Headquarters,
  2202 L/Corp. W. Dinnie, Signallers,
  3510 Pte. A. Loffman, "A" Coy.,
  1303 „ W. McGuinness, "D." Coy.,
  5469 „ L. White, "C" Coy.,
  6131 „ A. Ochiltree, "A" Coy.,
  6249 „ A. Dance, "C" Coy.,
   157 Sgt. H. P. Wilson, "A" Coy.

On November 14 the 16th played the 4th Field Ambulance football and had the satisfaction of scoring another win. Then the rest period came to an end and on the 17th the 16th marched to Crequey, and billeting one night in each place it successively passed through Beaurainville, Douries, Estrees-les-Crecy, Neuilly L'Hôpital and Chepy to Escarbotin where it remained until December 5. On the march from Douries to Crecy an amusing incident occurred. The Brigadier, General Brand, was very particular about the care and cleanliness of all battalion transport. On this particular morning the drivers thought they would chance a close inspection by "The Brig," who had, unknown to all transport sections, decided to make the occasion one on which he would scrutinise the limbers on the march. Stationing himself near Crecy he awaited the arrival of the 16th transport, which was moving independently of the battalion on another road. A member of the billeting party on a cycle returning to the previous night's billets at Douries passed the transport officer, who inquired as to the whereabouts of General Brand. The cyclist informed him that he was about a mile along the road near Crecy and that he had "roared up" the — Battalion transport for having dirty limbers. "Which side of the road is he on?" asked the officer. "The right-hand side" came the answer. "Transport, halt!—dismount—get out your cleaning gear and go for your life on the right-hand side of your limbers and harness." A quarter of an hour's hard rubbing made the vehicles presentable. Off the transport went and, passing "the Brig.," that officer expressed himself as quite pleased with the outfit. Many months afterwards the circumstances were explained to him and he said then that he had often wondered why the 16th Battalion limbers on that day compared more than favourably with the other units. On December 1, an association football match played between the 16th and the 4th Machine Gun Company was won by the 16th, the members of which were beginning to pride themselves on the prowess of its footballers in both Australian rules and the Soccer game.

December 5 saw another shift down south when the battalion marched to Wourcourt and entrained for Peronne. Here the 4th Division was to be corps reserve in case the Germans made another attempt to break through. Arriving there next day it marched to Moislains, and the men were billeted in huts. The weather through all this period had been generally wet and the advance guard and outpost schemes practised at Moislains were not very enjoyable on that account. On December 10 another Association football match with the 4th Company Australian Engineers was won by the 16th. On the 11th a freezing day was experienced and the conscription referendum vote was taken the same day. On the 15th the battalion played the 15th Battalion at Association football and won again. The next day it played the 48th Battalion two matches, Australian rules and Association. Honours were easy, as the 16th won the Association and lost the Australian rules. The next day, with 4 inches of snow on the ground, the men were set to work to build parapets three feet high around the huts and tents in order to protect the occupants from splinters during air-raids, which were fairly frequent at this time. The roads were very slippery on account of the frost, and wheeled transport was well advised to move cautiously on some of the grades near the camp. On December 20, the battalion marched to Templeux-la-fosse, and on the second night a severe attack by enemy bombing 'planes occurred, fortunately without inflicting any casualties. An Association football match on December 24 between the 16th and 14th Battalions resulted in a draw with 3 goals each. Christmas Day dawned with seasonable weather. There were no parades and a real good spread was provided all ranks—with beer and wine available on purchase. The remaining days of 1917 were spent at this camp. The main job was training in open-order work. The lessons from the Cambrai battle were being practised, particularly the new method of defence in depth, the non-compliance with, or ignorance of which was responsible for the Germans' break-through at Gouzencourt. A few working parties filled in time. To these, of course, the digger had been long accustomed.

During the last few months of the year concert parties had been organised in each brigade and about once a week each battalion while in billets was given an entertainment. These shows proved very welcome breaks in the monotony of periods behind the line—particularly in those wrecked areas which housed no French civilians.

CHAPTER 26.—FLANDERS AGAIN.

The new year opened with snow on the ground and a biting frost which made the blood tingle. The 16th band played the old year out and the new one in and a smart bout of snowballing introduced the diggers to 1918 under somewhat festive conditions. Road work and training was the routine until January 10, and as organised games were part of the syllabus of training, they helped to pass pleasantly what would otherwise have been a monotonous period. The 16th Soccer team played the 13th Battalion on the 2nd and won by one goal to nil, and the 4th Field Ambulance on the 5th, winning by 3 goals to nil. Inter-company and inter-platoon football matches were also indulged in regularly and the result was a rather high standard of physical fitness. Except for isolated air raids and the dropping of bombs close to the camp there was very little to indicate that there was a war on.

However, the German attacks at Cambrai having ceased, this period of comparative inactivity came to an end on January 10, when the battalion marched to Peronne and entrained once more for the northern sector. Arriving at Bailleul at 1 o'clock on the 11th, the men marched to De Zon camp near La Clytte. The first job was the cleaning up of the camp site and the next the erection of splinter proof protective walls around the huts in case of air raids. Specialist training was the programme up to the 18th, interrupted by an inspection by General Sir Wm. Birdwood on the 15th. The 3rd ("Eggs-a-Cook") Division was in the same area and on January 16th the officers of the Western Australian unit in that division, the 44th, entertained the officers of the 16th at tea. On the 19th, the 16th prepared to move into the front line and the next day marched to Kilmarnock Siding (light railway) and proceeded by train to Spoil Bank, near Ypres, where Headquarters, "A," "B," and "D" Companies were accommodated in the tunnel system at the Bluff and "C" Company in the Canal dugouts. The role of the unit was that of forward support battalion.

The officers with the 16th at this time were:

Headquarters:
    Lt.-Col. R. Harwood, D.S.O., In Command.
    Capt. F. Wadge, M.C., Adjutant.
    Lieut. J. D. Howell, Intelligence Officer.
    „ V. Ketterer, Salvage Officer.
    „ J. E. Piercey, Works Officer.
    „ J. Bitmead, Maintenance Officer.
    „ W. Harvey, Signalling Officer.

"A" Company:
    Capt. H. C. Parker.
    2nd Lt. W. F. Broadhurst
      ,,   H. A. Devenish.
      ,,   F. J. Aberle.

"B" Company:
    Capt. H. A. F. Wilkinson.
    Lieut. A. T. Towers.
    2nd Lt. W. Donald.
      ,,   L. G. Bruer.

"C" Company:
    Capt. H. J. Cooke, M.C.
    Lieut. H. F. Klopper.
      ,,   W. Jorgensen.
    2nd Lt. N. L. Terry.

"D" Company:
    Capt. D. S. Aarons, M.C.
    Lieut. H. R. Hillman.
      ,,   D. B. Crisp.
    2nd Lt. A. B. C. Dowling.

The main operations of the battalion up to January 29 were working and carrying parties. The carrying parties had strenuous jobs as the men had to man-handle all sorts of cumbersome materials up to the front line over ground impassable for wheeled transport or even horses or mules. Some of the items which made up the loads were angle-irons and pickets, hurdles, "A" frames (for revetting trenches), sheets of corrugated iron, rolls of malthoid, duckboards, pick heads, shovels, screw pickets, rolls of barbed wire, camouflage screens, rations and hot food containers. Five miles carrying these awkward loads (plus the rifle, ammunition, gas helmet and steel hat which were always an integral part of the digger in France) was quite enough to convince those on whom the job fell, that the Great War was indeed a war of endurance! A story is told of a 16th man in a working party who was struggling over rough ground, with two sheets of galvanised iron and three duck-boards on his back, from the Engineers' dump to the front line. A bystander inquired "Where are you going?" "At the ——— knees," came the reply like a flash, "Where the h—— do you think?"

Stringent precautions were being taken against trench feet, which had been responsible for a large percentage of the army's winter evacuations of men to hospital. This was a distressing complaint, caused by long periods of wet feet, and the cold, which was intense at this time. Whale oil was issued and platoon commanders were instructed to hold a foot inspection daily, during which the feet were rubbed briskly with whale oil and a clean change of socks was provided every second day. Arrangements were also made to return the dirty socks to the Quartermaster in rear, whose responsibility it was to have them washed, dried and returned to the battalion in the line.

Enemy shell-fire was comparatively quiet during this period and nothing of incident occurred. On January 25 two companies were sent to Siege Farm, near Kemmel, where the men had a bath and were issued with a clean change of underclothing. On the 26th three officers and 90 other ranks joined up as reinforcements, and a few days later 124 other ranks who arrived were allotted thirty each to the four companies, then in the front line system.

On January 29 the 16th took over the front line from the 13th Battalion. "D" Company occupied the outpost line, "A" Company support line and "B" and "C" Companies were in reserve. The sector was quiet, with very little artillery fire and machine gun outbursts only at intervals. The aeroplanes of both sides were active but there was little opposition to the work of the 16th in improving its trenches. On the 31st "A" Company took over the outpost line from "D" Company, which moved back to supports. It was noticeable at this period that eighty per cent. of the shells sent over by the enemy were "duds."

The health of the men was satisfactory, except for the usual winter ailments—coughs, colds and foot troubles. This result was helped considerably by the fairly constant receipt of comforts. In a report to brigade headquarters the C/O of the 16th expressed thanks to the Victoria League, Perth, W.A., and the League of Loyal Women of South Australia for the numerous parcels of comforts, particularly socks, that had helped to better the condition of the men.

During the next week nothing happened excepting shells and the inter-company reliefs—giving each a turn in the various positions. On February 5, the 47th Battalion relieved and the 16th moved back to Spoil Bank and, per medium of the light railway, to Kilmarnock Siding, from whence it marched to De Zon Camp.

For a fortnight, with the weather cold, wet and dirty, the programme was work and more work. A reserve line was being built and the 16th was conveyed every day by light railway to this position where the men worked hard building strong points, wiring etc., in the reserve line for the expected German offensive. On one of these trips two of the trucks jumped the rails and a serious accident was narrowly averted. Three men only were injured.

On February 19 orders were received once again to take over the support line and the next day the battalion relieved the 47th Battalion, moving by motor lorries to Voormezelle-St. Eloi and marching to the Canal and Gasper's Cliffs dugouts. The order of dress on this move was "Fighting order, over sheep skin vests, haversacks on back, waterproof sheets folded under flap of haversack, greatcoat and blanket to be rolled and held together by supporting strap and fastened under the haversack, mess tin hanging under the blanket, water bottles filled, sandbags to be worn in lieu of putties."

An enemy attack was expected on this front and the digging and wiring of strong points were energetically proceeded with. At night on the 27th the 16th moved to a position immediately in rear of the supports to the front line. However, nothing happened. The weather at this time was very wet and conditions most uncomfortable. Scabies was also prevalent and the constant itching of this annoying complaint did not tend to lighten the burden of those who were afflicted by it.

The casualties during the month of February were 2 other ranks killed; 1 O.R. wounded, 34 O.R. sick, 1 officer, 9 O.R. gassed. The strength of the battalion was 30 officers, 791 O.R. On the 28th the 9th Battalion relieved and motor 'buses took the 16th to Neuve Eglise where Aldershot Camp was occupied.

The 16th remained here for about eight weeks. Owing to the long period of work in forward areas and front line systems and the fact that during the previous month large drafts of reinforcements had been received, the morale of the battalion was not quite up to the standard of the "Old Sixteenth." The new men had had no opportunity of becoming imbued with the battalion spirit but the period of intensive training now entered upon at Neuve Eglise, with plenty of organised games, and physical training and sports, soon remedied this state of affairs. It was the "Old Sixteenth" indeed which marched out of Aldershot Camp on March 25 *en route* for the Somme where the Australians were to draw a line across the enemy's onward march to Paris.

Lewis gun, musketry and drill were specialised in during this period and the men showed a creditab'e keenness in their work. About a week before leaving Aldershot Camp the commander of an A.I.F. artillery brigade approached the C.O. 16th Battalion for about 40 Lewis gunners to instruct his men. For a week an intensive course was followed in the battery lines. The artillery commander thanked the 16th for the valuable instruction the men had imparted. Little did he know that the knowledge so gained was to be responsible for saving the guns when the Germans broke through a month or so later on the Portuguese front. The enemy reached the battery positions on that occasion but the Lewis gunners were brought into action and the situation was restored. At games the 16th beat the 4th Field Ambulance in Australian rules football by 48 points, on the 21st beat the 14th and on the 23rd beat the 4th Machine Gun Company. At Soccer the 16th played a draw with the 15th, but beat them two days later, so that it can be claimed during this month the battalion representatives worthily upheld the good name of the unit on the football field. A platoon competition within the battalion, embracing drill, shooting, and turnout was won by No. 7 Platoon under Lieut. W. Donald. The strength on March 23 was 36 officers, 792 other ranks. It is interesting to record here that on March 15, Major H. W. Murray, V.C., D.S.O., D.C.M., of the 13th Battalion, was appointed to command the 4th Divisional Machine Gun Battalion with the rank of Lieut.-Colonel.

On March 10 the Corps Commander, Gen. Sir Wm. Birdwood, presented the following decorations to members of the battalion.

Lieut.-Col. E. A. Drake-Brockman, D.S.O. (ribbon.)
341 Sgt. S. McGrath "A" Coy. Military Medal (ribbon).
2815 „ H. Pitman, "D" „ „ „ „
3540 L/C. J. Oxenham, "B" „ „ „ „
2389 Sgt. E. England. "A" Coy., Bar to Military Medal.
3894 Corp. J. Elliot, "B" Coy., Military Medal and bar.
2913 Sgt. W. Murray, H.Qrs., Military Medal.
6276 „ W. E. Inglis, "D" Coy., „ „
157 „ H. P. Wilson, "A" Coy., „ „
743 Corp. C. McQuade, H.Qrs. „ „
2202 „ W. Dinnie, „ „ „
1807 (a) Corp. F. J. Robbins, "D" Coy., Military Medal.
775 „ J. Gooney, "A" Coy., „ „
6223 L/C A. J. Bonser, "D" Coy., „ „
6249 Pte. A. Dance, "C" Coy., „ „
4052 „ E. Mullen, "C" Coy., „ „
7041 „ A. Lee, "A" Coy., „ „
3510 „ P. Loffman, H.Qrs. „ „
2465 Driver A. E. Cowling, Transport, „ „
1303 Pte. W. D. McGuinness, "D" Coy., „ „
5162 „ W. O'Sullivan, "D" Coy., „ „
5436 „ V. C. Sparrow, "D" Coy., „ „
6131 „ A. Ochiltree, "A" Coy., „ „
618 Corp. W. W. Tilbrook, "D" Coy., „ „

CHAPTER 27—"BACKS TO THE WALL!"

On March 25, because of the continued pressure of the Germans on the retiring 5th Army, the 16th moved by 'bus down south. The route was *via* Steenwerck, Doulieu, Neuf Berquin, Merville, St. Venant, Lillers, Dernes, St. Pol, Maiseres, Avesnes, Bavincourt, and the main Doullens-Arras road to Saulty (about 13 miles S.W. of Arras), where the men were billeted in huts for the night.

The next day orders were received to form a defensive line near Squastre. The battalion moved off and was in position by 2 p.m. The 12th Australian Brigade was on the left, but the right flank of the 16th was in the air. The roads were badly blocked with civilians and broken remnants of the 5th Army moving to the rear, and it was a matter of extreme difficulty to move forward against this disorganised traffic. At 3.15 p.m., in response to fresh orders, the 16th shifted to a rendezvous near a windmill on the Bienvillers-Fonquevellers road. Arriving there, after a short rest, it was ordered to move at 9 p.m. and occupy a line near Hebuterne. By 10 p.m. the 16th was in its allotted position. There was no opposition except indirect machine gun fire.

The 12th Brigade was then withdrawn to resume its march with the 4th Division to the south. The 4th Brigade meanwhile had concentrated near Fonquevillers, the temporary headquarters of the 62nd (British) Division, to which it was now to be attached. Wild rumours as to German armoured cars breaking through at Hebuterne (these turned out to be French tractors being salved by the peasants) and conflicting reports concerning the whereabouts of the leading elements of the enemy, whose onward and victorious offensive had begun on March 21, gave the Brigadier much cause for anxiety. Reliable information from exhausted remnants of units which had been fighting against overwhelming odds since that day was unattainable. General Brand decided to do a little personal reconnaissance. After a survey of the situation, in which he penetrated to the market square in Hebuterne, he returned to the brigade and gave all ranks the "dinkum oil." Having seen the refugees and the tired parties of British troops, survivors of a dreadful ordeal, going the opposite way: having heard the wild rumours of armoured cars and false reports of hostile patrols, "the Brig's." statement of the situation was welcome to all ranks. The seriousness of the position was not discounted. Turning to the battalion commanders he said, "Give your men a hot meal; then be in your allotted positions by 10 p.m. The

New Zealanders are coming in on the right." Hearing Lewis gun and rifle fire in Hebuterne after dark many doubted whether General Brand had been as far as he claimed. It later transpired that the enemy had likewise decided to occupy Hebuterne and the important high ground to the south of it, under cover of darkness. In reaching their allotted positions before dawn the 4th Brigade opportunely filled the gap between the 4th and 5th Army Corps. There was still no rest for the tired troops, however, for at 3.45 a.m. (27th) the 16th Battalion was ordered to move forward and occupy a new line. This was accomplished before daybreak, when it was found that the New Zealand Rifle Brigade was in touch on the right. The 16th dispositions were three companies in front line and one at battalion headquarters. Enemy activity at this time was slight. The men were started on digging themselves in, and an artillery S.O.S. line was arranged.

At 11.30 a.m. the enemy was observed massing for an attack 1,000 yards in front of the 16th's line. The artillery was notified and a prompt response dispersed the German formations. There was generally much enemy movement in front and he gave every indication that he intended to continue his hitherto uninterrupted advance as soon as his dispositions were in order.

During the next night the 16th moved further forward and established an outpost line with "B" Company in occupation. It rained heavily during this operation and was very cold. The movement was carried out under heavy machine gun fire which killed three and wounded 13.

In the early hours of the morning of the 28th an officer's patrol went out from the outposts and found that the enemy's post at a quarry in front had been evacuated by him during the night. The line was at once pushed forward to take in the crest of the ridge, which gave splendid observation for several miles and denied to the enemy many good machine gun positions. It was found that one of the posts established by "B" Company the night before was less than 20 yards from a strong enemy post. It was very hard for the 16th men to understand why the enemy gave up the advantages of such a position without a stiff fight. As it was it cost the battalion one killed and one wounded to occupy this commanding ground.

The next day (the 29th) enemy artillery became heavy and his machine guns and snipers more active. "A" Company made an attempt during the morning to bomb the enemy out of a system of trenches on its front but this was not successful. His stretcher bearers were allowed to rescue several German wounded under cover of the Red Cross flag. Throughout the day and night artillery fire, though not heavy, was persistent. The rain had made conditions very wet and muddy and the new trenches were already in a very sloppy condition.

March 31 was a quiet day and the battalion extended its front by taking over portion of the line to the left. The casualties for the four days had been one officer and 29 other ranks killed and wounded. Orders were received that under no circumstances whatever was there to be a withdrawal. The situation demanded that the holding of Hebuterne was all important to the 4th Corps, and the 16th, with every other battalion then in the line, had its back to the wall!

A local operation along the battalion front was decided upon on April 1, details of which were left to the two company commanders concerned, the object being to advance the line about 250 yards. At 1.30 p.m. two parties from "B" Company and "D" Company respectively began to bomb their way along saps leading out of the front trench. The enemy was encountered in great strength at the junction of a road and trench and severe fighting took place. The attack was pushed with such vigour that the German garrison was overcome, 71 prisoners taken, 4 machine guns captured, and one British Lewis gun recaptured. At a low estimate 100 dead Germans were found in the road and saps of the newly gained position. This success put the diggers of the 16th in high spirits and did them more good at this stage than anything else could have done. Their casualties were four killed and five wounded.

The next day, April 2, was quiet and the line was extended further to the right. On the 3rd, to further improve the front, "C" Company, on the right of the battalion sector, pushed a bombing party down a sap leading into the enemy line. This party worked into his front trench and along it to where it junctioned with a quarry. Snipers encountered were shot by Lewis gunners with the bombing party and the whole length of trench was captured. It was very shallow but during the night was deepened and garrisoned and a post established at the quarry. At 10.30 a.m. on the same day a fighting patrol from "D" Company proceeded down the sunken road running from the left of the battalion sector. This party engaged the enemy at the junction of two sunken roads and routed them after a brisk but strenuous struggle. There were no prisoners taken but about 50 dead Germans were lying there when the 16th patrol finally got full possession.

During the night another patrol from "D" Company left the line near the quarry and moved forward silently for 500 yards. The party captured a machine gun and brought it back, but suffered no casualties. The next day was very wet and the muddy trenches made conditions uncomfortable. Artillery and machine gun fire were normal and only a few men were wounded. On the 5th, from 6 o'clock in the morning the enemy put down a violent and sustained bombardment of high explosive shell and gas on the 16th's front line. At 9.30 the barrage lifted and the Germans attacked strongly in waves. This was soon broken by Lewis gun and rifle fire. A second attack launched at 10.30 a.m. met with a like result.

CAPT. W. J. LYNAS, D.S.O., M.C. AND 2 BARS.

It was estimated that 2,000 Germans were engaged in these attacks, and their casualties were very heavy. The 16th lost nine killed and 28 wounded.

The only incident of note on April 6 was when four parties of the enemy were seen marching in file to their front line and, word being sent to the artillery, the groups were scattered. Another attack was expected, but nothing eventuated. During the night the 16th proceeded with the wiring of the front line.

After a quiet day on the 7th and 8th the battalion was relieved by the 13th Royal Fusiliers on April 9 and withdrew to Rossignol Farm, where it camped in tents. The next day a very welcome change of clothing was issued and equipment and arms were given a much needed cleaning. All ranks were well satisfied with their performances of the past two weeks, during which in no uncertain manner they had stood in the path of a hitherto victorious and triumphant foe and stoutly barred his onward progress. Indeed, not only had they stopped the German advance in their sector, they had taken the initiative and forced him to give up some of the ground he had won.

On April 11 Major-General Maclagan, G.O.C. 4th Aust. Division, visited the battalion and walked around among the men. He stated that he hoped soon to have his famous 4th Brigade back with him again. Later in the day, Major-General Williams, the G.O.C. 37th Division, to which the 4th Brigade was now attached, visited headquarters and congratulated the 16th on its fortnight's work in the line.

In this connection the following congratulatory message was received from the G.O.C. 4th Army Corps:—

"April 7, 1918.

"To the 4th Australian Infantry Brigade (through the 37th Division).

"The Corps Commander desires to thank all ranks of the 4th Australian Brigade for their gallant behaviour in the defence of Hebuterne against all attacks during the past 14 days. Without relief and without complaint they have held their positions, and in many cases have advanced and improved their line.

"Heavy attacks on the brigade on the 1st and 5th April were repulsed with severe losses to the enemy.

"Skilful enterprises carried out on the initiation of local commanders have resulted in the capture of several enemy posts with a gain to us of 80 prisoners and eight machine guns, besides inflicting heavy losses on the enemy.

"The Corps Commander considers this a very fine performance which reflects great credit on all ranks of the brigade.

"(Sgd.) R. G. PARKIN, Brig.-General,
"General Staff IV Corps."

THE OLD SIXTEENTH.

The following extracts from "With the 5th Army in March, 1918," show that the operations of the 4th Brigade at this momentous period were of immense importance to the safety of the Western Front:—

"Next day, March 26, was a very grave one north of Albert. A gap existed in this area between the 4th and 5th Corps and German infantry pressed through the gap and worked their way forward till they occupied Colincamps (two miles south of Hebuterne) with machine guns threatening to outflank the whole Ancre line by a south-west drive accompanied by a thrust west and north-west" (page 193).

"Early in the afternoon the New Zealand Division retook Colincamps while the 4th Australian Brigade filled the gap between Hebuterne and Bucquoy" (page 268).

"Australians are naturally proud that it (the gap) was mended by one of their brigades at a time when further delay would have been far and away too hazardous" (page 274).

"Von Bulow's onset, after all day fighting, was defeated by the Guards Division and the 35th Division; by the 42nd Division and by the 62nd Division, aided by the 4th Australian Brigade; whose combined efforts beat off onsets against Bucquoy and Hebuterne by the 3rd Prussian Guards and 5th Bavarians" (page 197).

April 12 saw a resumption of training for a few hours, but the next day the 16th relieved the 14th Battalion and one company of 2nd Auckland Battalion in the front line of Hebuterne sector. The trenches were still muddy, but enemy activity was not very great. On the 15th, in order to secure identification, a small daylight patrol from "A" Company, consisting of 3 N.C.O's., left the front line and worked along a communication trench leading out into No Man's Land. They located an enemy machine gun post and returned with the report. Reinforced by an officer and six men they went back and under cover of a shower of bombs they rushed the post, killing one German and capturing five and the machine guns. The patrol's casualty was one wounded.

The rest of the tour in the line was uneventful. A few losses were sustained each day or night by machine gun or shell fire, but the period was generally very quiet. On the night of April 20 the 15th Battalion relieved and the 16th moved back to Rossignol Farm. A few days were spent at this place and on the 24th the battalion moved by 'buses to Rainneville and marched to billets at Cardonette, where it came once more under the control of the 4th Division. The latter's role at this time was Corps supports.

April 25, the third anniversary of Anzac Day, was passed over on this occasion without any ceremony, and the next day orders were received to move to the line again.

The 27th saw the battalion on the move to Querrieu, and the next day, in heavy rain, it went forward as support to the right sub-sector of the 4th Infantry Brigade sector. There it remained until May 4, working on improving accommodation and digging a defensive line called Villiers Switch. Generally speaking, the weather was fine. The casualites for April were 15 other ranks killed and one officer 63 other ranks wounded; 20 other ranks sick.

On May 4 the 16th took over the front line from the 13th Battalion at Villers Bretonneux. "A" and "B" Companies were disposed in the front line with "C" and "D" in support. There was much movement behind the enemy lines, but otherwise the situation was quiet. As usual the 16th patrols were active in No Man's Land during the nights of their occupation of this sector. The companies worked hard to connect up the various posts and in digging communication trenches.

Villers Bretonneux was an important tactical position situated on high ground overlooking all the country between it and Amiens. Owing to the constant shell fire to which it had been subjected by the Germans since its capture it was placed out of bounds to all troops—who were in trenches in front, flanks, and rear. This did not prevent souveniring by enthusiastic diggers, Tommies and Zouaves, especially as it was known that there were great quantities of "vin-blanc" and champagne in its cellars. Owing to the danger of drunkenness, orders were given to a fatigue party to stave in barrels and destroy bottles. This to the troops, of course, was sacrilege, and there was much competition among "souvenir kings" for receptacles in which to carry some of the precious liquid back to their cobbers in camp or trenches. Among other things souvenired from this town was a piano, and with wine and music one unit in L'Abbe Wood was having a pretty good war when a German shell put the piano out of action and wrote "Finis" to the night's merriment. One officer found a motor car, repaired it, and then was mortified when he received orders to hand it over to the staff. Most of the men changed their dirty underclothing for ladies' undies, singlets and stockings from a factory in which were discovered great stores of those articles.

Lest the digger should be unduly blamed for his souveniring propensities, let it be understood that army orders were always impressing on all ranks the necessity of salvaging the debris, such as rifles, equipment, etc., of the battlefield. Possibly it was this urging which caused the digger to become an inveterate hunter for anything he could find. However, not many battalions, even in the A.I.F., could lay claim to the honour of salvaging a complete and little-damaged aeroplane. The 16th made that unusual claim under the following circumstances: A French aeroplane with an observer and pilot was forced down through engine trouble and landed among some wire entanglements in No Man's Land. The enemy at once commenced to shell it and this forced the two occupants to clear for shelter "at the toot" to the 16th's trenches. At dusk an officer and 12 men armed with wire cutters crawled out to the plane and were immediately welcomed by a salvo of shells. They sheltered until the storm died and then cut the barbed wire that was holding it and man-handled it back across the front line. There they handed it over to the transport section, who carted it to headquarters in L'Abbe Wood, where the Australian Flying Corps took possession next day.

A "BRIDGE" ACROSS THE SOMME, 1918.

On "D" Company's front much annoyance was caused by a German "flare king" and a machine gun crew in a strong point in the railway embankment. This "flare king's" duty seemed to be to fire a flare every minute, thus lighting up No Man's Land and subjecting ration and working parties to the fire of the machine gun. Captain Lynas endured it for a couple of nights and then decided he would clean the post up. He asked for and received half a dozen phosphorus bombs (fearsome things) to be used as rifle grenades. After dark he crawled to within 50 yards of the position and fired his bombs, which exploded with deadly effect right in the German post. There were no more flares fired from it during the 16th's stay in the line, but when Lynas was pointing out the position of the post to the relieving company commander a bullet passed between them, showing that the Germans were still on the alert.

174   THE OLD SIXTEENTH.

The 48th Battalion moved in on May 9 and the 16th marched back to the Blangy area. An unpleasant occurrence during the relief was the action of an artillery battery firing about 50 shells intended for a German front line post, but which landed in and around the 16th's trenches. This sort of thing "put the wind up" the diggers more than anything did which came from the front.

The companies were distributed on relief along the Blangy Line immediately in front of that village. Two days were spent resting and the third saw a visit to the baths and a clean change of underclothes for all ranks. On the 13th the battalion relieved the 14th Battalion in the support area, with headquarters in L'Abbe Wood, near Villers Bretonneux. There it remained until the 18th with nothing eventful except hard digging for the "diggers." Both air forces were showing a renewal of activity at this time. On the

BILLETS—"SOMEWHERE IN FRANCE," 1918.

18th the battalion relieved the 13th in the front line, with "D" and "C" Companies in support. At this stage 30 per cent. of the officers were down with influenza. The 16th was only two days in the line on this occasion and on May 20 was relieved by the 44th Battalion and moved back to its old position in the Blangy Line.

All ranks were now feeling the need of a short rest after their long spell of line work and fatigues. The sunny weather with trenches in fields of growing crops and the good natural conditions were much appreciated after the hardships of the preceding winter. On May

22 the 39th Battalion took over the Blangy Line and the 16th moved back to Cardonette. The march back was very trying owing to the intense heat and the fact that the men were out of condition due to their long spell in the forward area. However, the next day a bath and a change improved matters on the part of those who were inclined to grouse.

At Cardonette the 16th was billeted alongside the church in tumbledown houses, sheds and stables. Soon after its arrival, when the men were in the bathing and shaving stage, No. 8 Platoon was lying or sitting in various stages of undress; some playing cards, others writing home, and many trying to catch the largest of those insects which throughout the war seemed to have a partiality to the seams of soldiers' underclothes, a voice was heard outside, and the platoon diagnosed it with dismay as belonging to "Massa" Johnson, one of the company's sergeants. His visit boded ill for No. 8 Platoon, for "B" Company was duty company for the day, and No. 8 could see its vision of rest rudely dissipated. "Massa" put his head inside the door of the billet and was greeted with "What the 'ell do you want?" from one weary digger, while another told him to go away and lose himself. "Massa" grinned. "Is Day here?" he asked. "I've got a good job and I want him for my second wave. We've got to take over the divisional baths here and run them. We'll probably get the Military Medal for it, too."

When "Massa" and Day arrived at the baths the Divisional Laundry Sergeant was anxious to hand over. Pointing, he said, "There's your supplies; socks, towels, underpants, etc.; give a clean change to every man, or what he wants, but get his dirty clothes in exchange. I'll see you to-night and give you more clean clothes in exchange for the dirties. Sign here; so long," and away he went on the lorry.

As this was one of the domestic duties of a division, perhaps it will be well to explain that in the baths there were a number of bales of clean washed and new underwear. These were checked with the laundry sergeant's tally and stacked alongside a big window with a wide ledge opening into the bathroom. Day was appointed receiver of dirty clothes and issuer of a corresponding amount of clean wear in exchange.

The 4th Brigade units in the vicinity were all booked up to send 30 men every 20 minutes for a bath and a change. The baths were equipped with a small upright boiler which ran a hot shower from three pipes, each about 12 feet long. With everything ready, the first 30 men were allowed in and the door was locked. The men undressed, enjoyed the bath, dried themselves and came to the window for their change. They were supposed to hand in the equivalent dirty clothing for that they received clean.

It was the 4th Brigade's first time out after a long spell in and around Villers Bretonneux, and the diggers, in prowling about that smashed-up town for a month searching in their spare time for vin blanc and souvenirs, had, as mentioned before, helped themselves to the stores of woollen and silken underwear which was lying about in every shop. Their own underclothes being the worse for wear and needing washing badly, it was natural that the diggers should shed their own military issues and don the fancy, if unserviceable, clothing.

This first batch of bathers had been well and truly in Villers Bretonneux. The first man had two pairs of ladies' salmon-coloured stockings, a blue and yellow fancy golfing coat, a lady's chemise and knickers. The second had two pairs of green silk stockings and two pink undervests, all very unclean after a long period in the line. Day called "Massa" across, and he laughed and said, "No, only military issues changed." Then bedlam broke loose in that bathroom. Finally, as the men were commencing to freeze after their hot bath, it was decided to exchange new military issues for the fancy stuff.

The bathing went on swimmingly. The silk and woollen underwear soon made a gorgeous heap of colours, and the pile during the day grew alarmingly. "Massa" went away during the morning to ponder over things, and when he came back he looked worried, and said, "Watch me and that Laundry Sgt. fight the best of 20 rounds for the championship of Muddy Picardy this evening." He went out again and drowned some of his sorrows in an estaminet, for later in the afternoon he reappeared at the baths giving a rather good exhibition of a polka—two steps forward, two sideways, and one backwards. During the afternoon the bathing proceeded merrily. "Massa" smoked cigarettes, looked at the colour scheme growing, and laughed.

At 4 p.m. the Laundry Sgt. arrived and bustled in at the front door. He stood and looked. When he saw the gorgeous heap of coloured finery he turned the colour of dirty fat, swallowed his Adam's apple, and aged ten years. At the moment "Massa" was absent. On being informed, the Laundry Sgt. told Day to "Go and get him at the toot." There was a terrific row when "Massa" returned; the Laundry Sgt. told him he would be charged with all shortages and the war would need to last another 20 years before his pay-book would again be in credit. "Massa" asked him, "What else could I do? They had nothing else to give me in exchange, and by the look and smell of them, those ladies' undies certainly wanted changing."

After the first shock "Massa" stood manfully up to the onslaughts of the Laundry Sgt. It was necessary that he should. He had been in charge of the divisional baths for one day and was reckoned to be 300 flannels, 600 underpants, and a million socks short in his accounts. Several officers were drawn into the argument, and a merry squabble proceeded apace. When Sergeant "Massa" Johnson was allowed to depart he was told, "The issue is still in doubt." So far as he is concerned it still is, for he heard no more about it.

Training was again commenced. On the 26th General Sir Wm. Birdwood presented a further batch of medals and ribbons, and on the 29th the battalion paraded to inspect the new British armoured car. This was done in order to familiarise all ranks with them so that at some later date they would not be mistaken for hostile cars.

On May 31 two shells of large calibre fell in billets occupied by the 14th Battalion in Allonville and killed 18 men and wounded 68. The casualties of the 16th for the month were 3 other ranks killed, 28 other ranks wounded, 6 officers, 28 other ranks, sick. During the day the 16th took over the brigade reserve position from the 60th Battalion and in the evening moved up and relieved the 56th Battalion in the front line at Hamel.

CHAPTER 28.—HAMEL.

The month of June opened with fine weather, during which the 16th was busy improving the trenches. The position held was on the ridge overlooking the remains of the town of Hamel (in enemy hands), and a gully separated the 16th's line from Vaire Wood. Three companies occupied the line with one in support. The air activity of both sides was a feature at this time. Otherwise, however, things were comparatively quiet and arrangements were made for men from support and reserve companies to go down to the Somme in small parties for a swim. The ground in the vicinity had been sown with wheat before the German offensive in March and the crops were at this time about three feet high. On the 10th a 16th patrol was fired on by a machine gun and Lieut. Harlow was wounded. These patrols supplied the only thrills of the diggers during this tour of the line, for here, as elsewhere, the command of No Man's Land rested with the 16th. A good deal of sniping was done by both sides and the 16th diggers reported many hits of Germans in their trenches and in the wheat crops which grew in the enemy's line.

On June 14 it was decided to raid the enemy in order to secure identification. The stunt was well rehearsed and, according to plan, two parties, each of 30 strong, No. 1 from 14 Platoon and No. 2 from 16 Platoon, with co-operation by No. 3 Party (15 Platoon), were to make entry into the German trenches. 2nd. Lieut. Taylor had charge of No. 1 Party, Lieut. A. Dowling No. 2, and Sgt. O'Neil No. 3. Lieut. Piercy was officer in charge of the wire cutting operations, for which purpose Bangalore torpedoes were being used. The O.C. "D" Coy., Capt. W. J. Lynas, M.C., was O.C. Raid and his headquarters was to be on the forming up tape about 70 yards from the enemy's wire. Plenty of bombs were taken by the raiding parties. An artillery barrage was to accompany the assault and it was to lift off the front line for ten minutes, in which time the raiders had to enter the enemy line and complete their various tasks.

The night was cloudless and the moon made forming up a dangerous operation, but nevertheless the assembly in No Man's Land was accomplished with only a few casualties and these caused by some short shooting in the Australian barrage. By means of the Bangalore torpedoes placed in position in face of bombs thrown by the occupants of the trenches, two gaps were successfully blown in the enemy wire and the raiders rushed through the gaps and gained entry to the German trench. No. 1 Party bombed up the southern side of a pear-shaped trench and No. 2 along north. The officer and the two sergeants with No. 2 Party were wounded just as they were entering the trench, but the men, who knew what was to be done, carried on. A considerable number of Germans surrendered, but could not be persuaded to leave the trench and were shot. Their losses were considerable, especially in the sunken road running south-east, where the raiders estimated they killed fifty of the enemy. At Zero plus 9 minutes the O.C. Raid gave the order for withdrawal, which was carried out in an orderly manner. All the wounded were brought back, together with 5 prisoners and 3 light machine guns. During the withdrawal, No. 1 Party covered the retirement of No. 2 and No. 3 Party covered that of No. 1 in successive stages, until it was completed successfully. The 16th casualties in this brilliant operation were 1 officer and 15 men wounded.

The battalion remained in this sector until the 26th. During the last fortnight, the enemy's attitude was alert, though not offensive. Artillery and trench mortars were active, but the fire was well dispersed. Both sides were working hard improving and wiring their defences. The health of the 16th was good except for boils and blood troubles, due to a lack of green vegetables in the men's diet. A mild form of influenza or trench fever caused many men to go into hospital.

The next few days were spent resting in the Aubigny system of defence. In places wheat crops, four feet high, surrounded these trenches. In alternate parties on June 28 and 29, the battalion was taken in motor lorries to Vaux to view a tank demonstration and become acquainted with the possibilities of the new model which was to co-operate with the 16th in its next attack. It compared favourably with its predecessor used at Bullecourt and the officers and crews seemed very keen to regain the confidence of the infantry in their next engagement together.

On July 1, "G" and "H" Companies of the 131st Regiment, 33rd Division, American Army, were allotted to the 16th. The intention was that they should be used with the 16th for instructional purposes and to gain experience in an attack on the village and defences of Hamel. Naturally, the 16th diggers were delighted at this addition to their fighting (and digging) strength. The personnel of the two units became very friendly, as the Americans looked forward eagerly to taking part in their first "stunt" with the Australians, whose fighting qualities had been held up to them by their own commanders as an example to be followed. However, after orders had been issued which allotted the Americans to the various roles they were to play in the coming attack, at the last minute they were all withdrawn. This was annoying to all concerned. To the brigade and battalion staffs it necessitated a hurried modification of the orders already issued and this, almost on the eve of the operation, could easily have proved fatal to the success of the action.

When the messenger arrived with the order to the officers in charge of the Americans to march back to their own unit, they were dumbfounded. When they communicated its contents to their men, the latter were inclined to disobey the command. A violent discussion took place among them and then they came over and sat down among the 16th, who were then making their final dispositions. The officer in command of the Americans gave the 16th his men's best wishes and wished the battalion good luck. While he was speaking, the restraint with which his men held themselves was noticeable, and it could be seen that they were cut to the heart at the change of circumstances. What their feelings would be next morning, when they heard the barrage thundering down, can be left to the imagination. Some Americans did take part with other units.

It may be mentioned here that the battalion orderly room prior to an engagement was always a hive of industry, but unlooked-for complications, such as the one just referred to, caused a great deal of extra work and worry to its harassed staff. Under ordinary circumstances there was plenty to do, but a stunt caused extraordinary activity. The promulgation and carrying out of brigade orders, supplements, appendices, addenda to orders already issued, instructions re battle material, intelligence summaries from division, corps and army, orders for individuals and parties for special duty, entailed an enormous amount of work.

In the forthcoming operation, the 4th Division, assisted by the 11th and 6th Brigades, were to attack and capture Hamel, Vaire and Hamel Woods, and the spur beyond. The 16th was to deal with Vaire and Hamel Woods and mop them up. This task completed, it was to occupy the old front line, as reserve battalion to the 4th Brigade. During the night of July 2, an extraordinary number of guns were moved into position and concealed. All night long an unending stream of transport with ammunition and fighting material passed along the roads to dumps concealed as near as possible to the front line. Tanks by the dozen were sheltered in the woods and orchard near Aubigny. The enemy seemed to suspect that "something was doing," for he shelled and bombed the back areas with considerable vigour and from reports from the line, the front was beginning to become "lively." One half of each company of the battalion was sent forward to the front line, the other half remaining at Aubigny, on the night of July 2.

The next night the Aubigny troops rejoined their respective companies in the front line. The men carried 150 rounds of ammunition in their web equipment with two bandoliers of 50 rounds each slung over their shoulders; 3 Mills bombs each, 3 small egg bombs and a proportion of phosphorous bombs. Extra magazines were also carried for the use of the Lewis gunners. By midnight the jumping off tape had been laid and the assembly on it began of the assaulting troops.

The German front line garrison was active and his "flare kings" necessitated careful movement in No Man's Land. His "golden shawl" was also in evidence. This was something in the nature of a parachute bomb, dropped by an aeroplane in rear of the German front line. A few hundred feet from the ground it would burst and from the nucleus of a dark red flash, a shower of golden red sparks, gathering in size and number, would spread themselves out and travel ever so slowly to the ground. A weird glow would spread outwards and downwards, and light the surrounding country almost like day. The Germans had flares of all colours and descriptions and when they exhibited the full range in one night, as they sometimes did, a picture of fascinating and appalling grandeur was presented to the watchful audiences in both front line systems of trenches.

Aeroplanes were cruising overhead bombing the enemy's front line in order to drown the noise of the tanks moving up. This had been the procedure of the aeroplanes for about a fortnight, so that their action on this occasion was not suspicious. The usual morning harassing fire by the Australian artillery was put over with a few gas and smoke shells included. The tanks were thus brought right up to the assembly position without the enemy being aware that anything unusual was happening. It seemed, however, to the diggers of the 16th, lying on the tape waiting for the barrage, that every German in France must be able to hear the clanging and grinding of these fearsome engines of war as they made their way on to the line of assembly.

A single splitting report from an eighteen pounder close up, a few more isolated cracks; then a far-away roar of the heavies. A huge ear-splitting crash and then an inferno of noise as the barrage came down in front. The time was exactly 3.10 a.m. and the barrage was really splendid. It fell like a curtain on the enemy's line. Unfortunately, it just missed Pear Trench and the occupants of this put up a stiff resistance to its capture. The men crept as near as possible to the barrage and when it lifted, after 4 minutes on the enemy's front line, they followed it closely. Officers with watches controlled the pace, but the men were well schooled and needed little instruction. The greatest need was for the officers to restrain impetuous men from rushing into the creeping barrage in their anxiety to get to close quarters. There was only a feeble artillery reply by the enemy and in most cases the advancing infantry caught his machine gunners before they could man their guns after the barrage had passed. The tanks did splendid work. Hopping off with the infantry, they cruised up and down close to, and sometimes in the barrage, machine-gunning strong points, dispersing groups of the enemy, and generally preparing the way very effectively for the men behind them. To the Germans they must have appeared deadly monsters, wheeling to right and

SGT. H. AXFORD AND CORPORAL T. L. AXFORD, V.C., M.M.

left over trenches and shell holes, and spitting fire from half-a-dozen different points. The dash and the skill with which the tanks were handled on this occasion removed from the minds of the 16th the dislike and distrust which they had borne towards them since the Bullecourt disaster.

The 16th captured the enemy's front line, with many prisoners, without much trouble, excepting at Pear Trench. Many gallant episodes occurred. Private Richardson carried a bag of bombs and used every one in the advance. Every time a machine gun opened he would charge it like a war horse and put it out of action with a well-placed bomb. When the German front line was seen through the smoke, the method was to throw bombs and after a short pause to allow for the burst, to rush it with the bayonet. In the big communication trench in Vaire Wood many prisoners were taken. One party of about a dozen which surrendered was led by a German who laughed when one of the diggers said to him, "Finis le Guerre." "Yes," he replied, "my —— oath." He said he learned the English language on the Boulder mine in Western Australia, and had been called back to the Fatherland early in 1914.

At Pear Trench, where the Germans fought stoutly, Private T. L. Axford's bravery and initiative were responsible for its final capture. When the barrage lifted his platoon was able to reach the trench through gaps in the enemy's wire. The adjoining platoon being delayed by uncut wire, an enemy machine gun came into action and inflicted many casualties, the company commander being among the wounded. Axford at once dashed to the flank, threw his bombs among the machine gun crew, jumped into the trench and charged with his bayonet. Unaided, he killed ten of the enemy and took six prisoners. He threw the machine guns over the parapet and called out to the delayed platoon to come on. He then rejoined his own platoon and did splendid work with it throughout the remainder of the action. For his gallant efforts Axford was awarded the Victoria Cross.

By 6 a.m., the 16th's task was completed. Vaire and Hamel Woods had been cleared of the enemy and all dug-outs and trenches in them had been mopped up. The battalion then returned to the old front line. The casualties were 2 officers and 11 other ranks killed and 3 officers and 62 other ranks wounded. Many of these were incurred by that bugbear of attacking infantry—the shortfiring gun in the battery or brigade of artillery. There does not appear to have been any means of overcoming this difficulty, but certainly the digger in every Australian battalion dreaded more the unexpected short shell from the rear than he did those he knew would come from the front. The aeroplanes performed splendidly. They co-operated with the artillery by giving it the position of the foremost infantry and helped the latter considerably by delivering boxes of ammunition attached to parachutes to the forward positions.

In reserve the battalion occupied itself with clearing up the debris and the backwash of the stunt. On the night of the 6th, it relieved the 13th Battalion in the newly captured trenches, with "A" and "B" Companies in front, "C" in support and "D" Company in reserve. Things were fairly quiet as regards artillery, which was spasmodic. The next night several posts were constructed in front to improve the field of fire. Enemy snipers were very keen, and the least movement above ground brought a well aimed bullet. On the afternoon of the 8th, the enemy raided one of the forward posts dug the night before. Under cover of rifle grenades and pine-apple bombs, he rushed the post and killed and wounded several of the men in garrison. The remainder abandoned the position for shell holes in rear, but re-occupied it again that night when it was found that 7 men had been killed, 6 wounded and two were missing.

On July 9 Lt.-Col. E. A. Drake-Brockman took temporary command of the 4th Brigade. The trenches were heavily "strafed" in the early morning, but this was followed by a period of quietness. On the 11th, the 39th Battalion took over the line and the 16th moved ahead to Bussy-les-Daours. The next day it shifted to dug-outs near Querrieu. Enemy bombing at night on the back areas was heavy and consistent at this time.

Here the 16th remained until August 1. During this period light training was the order, with games and physical training to get the men fit. Various parties of men were sent to a rest camp, established at Eu, on the coast, while others were sent for a month's leave to adjacent villages, where resided real live civilians to whom the 16th had been strangers for five months or more. Cricket matches were played against the 13th Battalion (won by the 16th by 15 runs in the last few minutes) and the 15th Battalion (won by the 16th by 12 runs).

On July 20 brigade sports were held in the Querrieu area. It was a glorious day and the whole programme went with a swing. The aquatic matches were held in the morning and the athletic events in the afternoon. Generals Sir Wm. Birdwood and Sir John Monash were present, and it was the former's last appearance as commander of the Australian Corps. The ground presented a festive appearance, as there were several side shows, including a circus provided by the 7th A.A.S.C., a fortune teller from the Trench Mortar Battery and many men in fancy costumes, whose actions were extremely funny. In addition, various bookmakers shouted the odds and a 15th Battalion captain ran a totalisator. The four battalion bands of the brigade with the assistance of the band of the 132nd U.S. Infantry Regiment dispensed appropriate music during the afternoon.

In the evening a concert party from 108th U.S. Engineers entertained a very large gathering in front of the Querrieu Chateau. It was a very amusing and enjoyable performance. In the opinion of the diggers, this day represented one of the most successful days of entertainment in the history of the battalion.

This was followed on the next day by a presentation of medals and ribbons by Lieut.-General Sir John Monash. The 22nd saw a race meeting organised at Allonville. The weather was ideal and the events interesting, but unfortunately, the outing was marred by a regrettable accident, in which two officers were killed. During the progress of this meeting an enemy plane came over and fired an observation balloon, near to the sports ground.

On the 26th gas helmets were tested by passing all ranks wearing the masks through the gas chamber at Cardonette. The next day rain fell all day. At night the sky cleared and when the moon was high and bright enemy planes became very active. After midnight numerous planes seemed to hover over the vicinity of the camp for about an hour and a-half, dropping scores of bombs, one of which dropped within a few feet of a tent in which many "A" Company N.C.O's. were sleeping. Three were killed and 12 seriously wounded. The enemy's objective was not the camp, but the Amiens-Albert road, about 200 yards from the site, on which there was considerable traffic.

CHAPTER 29—THE BREAK THROUGH.

On August 1 the 16th marched to Tronville Wood, where it rested until night and then relieved the 111th Battalion, 3rd Zouave Regiment, taking over the role of reserve battalion to the brigade in the reserve line stretching from the junction in Blangy and L'Abbe Woods to the vicinity of the village of Gentelles. The handling over of the trenches was accomplished with the aid of interpreters. Two bombs were dropped during the relief and five Zouaves were wounded. Next day it was seen that the whole area was under observation by the enemy. The British planes were very active and seemed to have superiority of the air, but even so, one of the enemy's planes came over and shot down four observation balloons in flames to the right of the 16th. During the night of August 4, when the enemy artillery was more active than usual, the battalion was relieved in this position by the 21st Battalion of the 2nd Canadian Division and moved to a bivouac among the trees lining the Somme between Hamelet and Vair-sous-Corbie. The next day Lt.-Col. Drake-Brockman resumed command of the battalion. During the day one officer (Lieut. Klopper) and 10 other ranks were rendered casualties through gas shells. During the night the men dug in to escape this fire.

Particulars of the forthcoming stunt were now promulgated. It was to be carried out on a big scale with the Canadian Corps on the right, the Australian Corps in the centre, and the 3rd (British) Corps on the left. The first phase, so far as the 3rd and 4th Divisions were concerned, planned that the 9th Brigade on the right and 11th Brigade on the left, under cover of an intense artillery barrage and assisted by tanks, should capture and consolidate the enemy position on the Green Line. Phase 2 was to consist of the 12th Brigade on the right and the 4th Brigade on the left passing through the Green Line and capturing and consolidating the Red Line. In Phase 3 one battalion each of the 12th and 4th Brigades were to exploit the successes of the troops operating in Phases 1 and 2, and they were to pass through the troops on the Red Line and capture and consolidate the Blue Line.

With regard to the 4th Brigade, Phase 2 was to be carried out by the 13th Battalion on right, 14th Battalion centre, and the 15th Battalion on left, the latter to also mop up Cerisy village. Phase 3 was to be carried out by the 16th Battalion.

The night of August 7 was fine and clear. Zero hour was fixed at 4.20 a.m. on the 8th. At dusk on the 7th the 16th moved from its trenches along the Somme to the first assembly position allotted to it during the attack.

The morning was very still until Zero hour, when the barrage came down with a crash. An hour or so afterwards the large number of prisoners coming back testified to the success of Phase 1 and the 3rd Division. Then reports came through that the Green Line was captured. There was a thick fog obscuring the view when the 16th moved off which made the maintenance of direction and co-operation between units very difficult, but afforded good cover for the troops. The battalion advanced steadily during the early stages in lines of platoons in fours, passing to the left of the village of Hamel, on to Forbes Wood, and then to the left of Kate Wood. The second forming-up position, just behind the Green Line, was reached on time, and the 16th waited for the hour, 8.20 a.m., set down for it to move beyond that first objective.

At 8.20 a.m. to the tick the 4th Brigade passed over the Green Line. Thus early it was obvious that the attack had fared badly north of the Somme in front of the 3rd (British) Corps, for enemy guns on the outskirts of Malard Wood were enfilading the Green Line and the troops advancing through it. The 16th moved through the 44th Battalion near Kate Wood and soon afterwards the 4th Divisional Artillery engaged in a duel over the open sights with the guns at Malard Wood and had the satisfaction of blowing them all out by direct hits.

However, despite the serious position of the left flank, the advance of the Australians went on. On time the 13th, 14th, and 15th Battalions reached their objective, the Red Line, and commenced to consolidate. By this time nearly all the tanks which had been allotted to assist the 16th in Phase 3, and which were carrying the bulk of its Vickers and Lewis guns, had been put out of action by direct hits from enemy field guns. Nevertheless, at the allotted time, the 16th pushed on out into the "blue" with the remainder of its Lewis and Vickers guns, and against a heavy fire from the left flank it succeeded in entering and capturing the Blue Line. The enemy on the high ground north of the river near Chipilly caused much trouble and severe casualties resulted from the fire from this quarter. In this final movement the 16th had to swing around on the left from an imaginary line stretching from the south bank of the Somme to the south side of Morgan Wood and then advance 2,500 yards on a front of 2,500 yards. This move was to conform to the course of the River Somme, which at this point formed a letter U. It was up the right-hand side of this letter U that the battalion had to advance and finally dig in on a line which linked up with the old Amiens Defence Line. By the time this operation was carried out the 16th was too weakened, numerically, effectively to man this long frontage of 2,500 yards, and a message to that effect brought the 13th Battalion up on the right, where it relieved the 16th of half the sector. Up to this stage the 16th had lost 32 killed and 76 wounded.

Such was the depth of the advance that the whole of the enemy organisation on the Australian and Canadian sectors was destroyed and he could therefore deliver no effective counter attack in the immediate future. His offensive efforts were confined to the bombing of roads by aircraft at night and machine gunning and bombing the trenches by day.

North of the river, however, the situation was not so satisfactory. After bitter fighting on August 9 the British troops, reinforced by Americans, captured Chipilly Spur and relieved the tension on the Australian left flank. During the night the 16th advanced its line another 800 yards to the outskirts of Mericourt where they improved their position and met with little opposition. Strong patrols were immediately sent forward and they found the high ground behind Mericourt and also St. Germain Wood strongly held by machine guns.

The next day conditions were splendid for aerial work. The whole day the enemy aeroplanes were aggressive and swooped over the lines low, dropping bombs on the trenches and machine gunning the men in them. In Morcourt, one of the captured villages, where there was considerable traffic, his planes flew low just over the main street and caused considerable confusion. Enemy artillery also became increasingly active, denoting that he had brought considerable reinforcements of that arm to this sector of the front, while considerable enemy movement was noticeable in Mericourt. On August 10 the 16th was relieved by the 43rd Battalion and marched to a gully north of the Somme, near the battered cemetery of Sailly Laurette. August 12 was a bright, warm day, and the stream of traffic carrying munitions and foodstuffs up to the forward area passed along a road adjacent to the 16th's bivouac, which was under a continual cloud of dust. Parties of the men took turns during the day to have a much enjoyed swim in the Somme, and four N.C.O's and men proceeded to corps headquarters to take part in a special parade of Australians before His Majesty the King. A brigade canteen which established itself close to the 16th was soon sold out of a goodly stock of refreshments, including some good quality beer. During the night the enemy heavily bombed the road alongside the 16th camp.

The rest was not for long, and August 13 saw the 16th move south across the Somme to a bivouac position near Guillaucourt. Here the heavy streams of traffic caused the air to be heavy with dust, but the only incident of note was the intense night bombing by aeroplanes. On the night of the 15th the battalion relieved the

12th Battalion in the reserve line. The trenches were old and very wide, and several casualties were sustained by an enemy bombardment of gas and H.E. Rear battalion headquarters was established in the cellar of a building which was struck by a big shell on the afternoon of August 16. The shell exploded in the cellar and the building collapsed on top of it. All the records of the battalion, including the War Diary, were more or less damaged—some completely destroyed. The typewriter and tables were blown to pieces, and two N.C.O's and three men were buried. A relief party worked strenuously to remove the debris and soon rescued one man. Immediately afterwards a further section of the building collapsed on top of the cellar and the next two men got out were dead. A fourth man was unconscious but revived, and the fifth body was not recovered until the next day.

CHAPTER 30—"THE SUPER V.C."

By methods of peaceful penetration the front line had been advanced about 500 yards without much opposition and it was decided that a further advance should be made to occupy the old front line system of 1916. Lieut.-Col. E. A. Drake-Brockman again took over the 4th Brigade, leaving Major Ross Harwood in command of the 16th.

On August 20 the 16th relieved the 14th Battalion in the front line on the left of the brigade frontage. The opposing guns were not bothering much at this time about the infantry and were engaged in an artillery duel, during the course of which each was using every effort to locate and blow out of action the other's guns. Needless to say the infantry appreciated their tactics!

The strength of the 16th had dwindled considerably owing to the casualties incurred in the recent strenuous operations, but on August 23 it again engaged in offensive action against the enemy. On this occasion the Germans departed from their recent tactics of surrendering when close fighting became imminent and for a long time a section of the battalion fought a lively engagement with a foe who resisted stoutly. The diggers revelled in the hand to hand fighting and by noticeable instances of individual gallantry they eventually triumphed. The battalion's task was to advance over 700 yards of ground thickly criss-crossed with enemy trenches and establish a new line along Courtline Trench. The 13th Battalion was to carry out a similar task on the right and the 16th Lancashire Fusiliers had to advance about the same depth on the left.

The advance was commenced at 4.45 a.m., accompanied by a splendid barrage, which, however was placed to fall on the trench system to the rear of Courtline Trench and was not played at all on the ground to be won. Two companies, "C" and "D," which had been holding the line, were allotted the forward position in the attack, with "A" Company in support and "B" Company in reserve. The battalion objectives were captured without much resistance, but in connecting up with the battalions on the flanks, particularly on the left, violent opposition was encountered, the enemy fighting stubbornly with machine guns and bombs. The whole of this fighting devolved upon "D" Company, which was commanded by Lieut. L. D. McCarthy. With one platoon of ten men, McCarthy bombed along Courtline Trench and Foch Alley—a communication trench leading into Courtline Trench—with the

LIEUT. L. D. McCARTHY, V.C., (F.).

intention of connecting up with the Lancashire Fusiliers. It soon became evident to this party that the Fusiliers had not won all —if any—of the ground allotted to them. The enemy still had the trench strongly garrisoned and he indicated that he intended to put up a fight. For about two hours the attack in this quarter see-sawed between victory and defeat. A particularly violent encounter was waged at the junction of Foch Alley and Courtline Trench. There the enemy was in a strong position, with plenty of men and three machine guns. When close enough to assault this stronghold, McCarthy had only two men available to carry on the assault, but his fighting Irish blood was up. Accompanied by his runner he crawled over the top and moving quickly from shell hole to shell hole soon reached a spot from where he placed the three machine guns out of action in as many minutes. The first was only a few feet away and McCarthy shot its gunner dead with his revolver. The second he bombed into silence and the crew of the third he despatched with bombs and revolver shots. By this time McCarthy was working alone, his runner having been wounded. He continued to make progress along Courtline Trench, picking up German bombs as he went. Coming suddenly upon the garrison of another section he shot one officer (the company commander) dead and wounded another with his revolver. He then proceeded to bomb the remainder of the garrison, but directly the Germans became aware that their officer had fallen, they "kameraded."

The closing episode of this brilliant piece of single-handed fighting, which owed its success to the amazing audacity of Lieut. McCarthy, was extraordinary. The prisoners closed in on him from all sides, wrenched from his hands the bombs with which he was attacking them, and patted him on the back! In twenty minutes he had killed 20 Germans, taken 50 prisoners and had captured a fair proportion of the trench which was the objective of an attack by a battalion of the Lancashire Fusiliers. But for his wonderful gallantry and resourcefulness it is more than probable that the 4th Brigade's flank would have been seriously menaced if its position had not been rendered untenable.

Lieut. McCarthy then called up scouts and placed them along saps running into the enemy line as far as Wurtemburg Trench. Afterwards "A" Company was sent up to reinforce the garrison and with the assistance of Captain Aarons the position was strongly organised. It was handed over to the Lancashire Fusiliers at noon. In the meantime "C" Company had linked up with the 13th Battalion on the right.

During the day enemy preparations for a counter attack were successfully dealt with by the artillery. The new position was subjected to much artillery fire, including gas shells, during the day. Patrols sent out in the late evening failed to observe any unwonted activity on the part of the enemy.

Towards midnight the 16th was relieved by portion of the 15th Lancashire Fusiliers and after moving to the rear, was met by 'buses and transported *via* Amiens to billets in the village of Coisy. For this extraordinary day's work Lieut. McCarthy was awarded the Victoria Cross. In commenting on it at the time the London Press was highly eulogistic, and dubbed McCarthy the "Super V.C."

CHAPTER 31.—THE LAST FIGHT.

At Coisy the 16th rested until September 8. Light training was entered upon but it was more or less a holiday period for men who had had an arduous time. On August 29 a guard of honour of one captain, two subalterns and 100 other ranks, with the regimental band, was furnished to army headquarters at Bertangles. Capt. W. J. Lynas, D.S.O., M.C., was the officer commanding and the guard in the smartness of its turnout would have done credit to a peace time regiment of British Guards.

On September 8 the battalion marched from Coisy to an embussing point and was picked up by 'buses and transported to the vicinity of Biaches. There it went into bivouac on the southern bank of the Somme near Pèronne. On the 10th, with its transport following, it marched in heavy rain to a bivouac in old trenches south of Cartigny. Two days later it moved to Beaumetz, and from there on September 16 marched to the front line and relieved the 49th Battalion.

The 16th in this last operation was commanded by Major W. Lynas, D.S.O., M.C., who had landed on Gallipoli as a private. The company commanders were Captain H. Wilson, "A" Coy.; Lieut. H. Bradley, M.C., D.C.M., "B" Coy.; Capt. J. Kerr, M.C., "C" Coy.; and Lieut. L. D. McCarthy, V.C., "D" Coy. The "front line" consisted of two pot holes or out-posts about 40 feet long and 4 to 6 feet deep, with about 200 yards between the posts, and the nearest German strong points only 60 yards way. The frontage of the battalion was 400 yards and the two outposts were occupied by "D" Company. These outposts were supposed to be secret and it was ordered that there should be no movement whatever from them during daylight. All communications, rations, water, etc., had to be brought up after dusk. This lying low was a very tedious duty, but at nightfall the whole front presented a scene of activity with carrying parties from the rear, and patrols along the front and to the flanks. "A," "B," and "C" Companies and battalion headquarters were in a sunken road about 150 yards from the outposts.

During the afternoon of September 17 an incident took place, which caused the 16th to think that all the secrecy of its movements and its well laid plans had gone for nought. About four o'clock an Australian officer—afterwards known to be Lt.-Col. R. Marsden, C/O of the 5th Machine Gun Battalion—was seen to leave the support line between the 13th and 16th Battalions and walk towards the enemy's front line. As he passed between the outposts he did not come near enough for the garrisons to attract his attention. On reaching the German trenches he was a much surprised man when a German officer jumped up and called on him to surrender, which, seeing that half a dozen Germans were covering him with their rifles, he did. As Marsden was carrying on his person the orders for the morrow's attack, together with the barrage maps issued to unit commanders, the news, when telephoned through by Captain Lynas, was very disturbing to the higher command.

The great Hindenburg system had been constructed by the Germans to conserve man-power. It was a stupendous creation of their military engineers, and every trench and machine-gun position had been sited to give the defenders the maximum advantage. In front of the Australians the St. Quentin Canal, south of Bullecourt, in a deep cutting with sides 50 feet high, was incorporated in the German scheme, and deep communication trenches led from the canal to the trenches. In the cutting were tier upon tier of comfortable living quarters in which support and reserve troops could live in safety and defy the heaviest bombardments. They could be taken by underground passages or deep trenches to any point in the locality where their presence was needed. The machine-gun positions were built of concrete, and cunningly hidden, with tunnelled trenches leading to roomy dug-outs in which the crews could shelter in safety from the heaviest barrage. Barbed wire was extensively used. In three tremendous belts it barred the approach to the main Hindenburg Line. Such quantities were used that to effectively clear a way for infantry would have needed an intensive barrage for weeks. The supply of tanks was limited as these effective wire-crushers had suffered heavy casualties during the eventful months of August and September. This shortage was a source of great anxiety to the higher command, and an attempt to meet the difficulty in the coming attack was made by doubling the machine guns and manufacturing dummy tanks. These were used with success. The first step in the breaking of the Hindenburg Line was to capture the German outposts, which consisted of an extensive organisation of trenches and defended localities well in front of the main line. The task allotted to the 16th was the capture and mopping up of the village of Le Verguier after which it was to move forward and occupy and consolidate the Brown—or reserve —Line. The early hours of September 18 saw a dull, wet morning with the 16th formed up on tapes waiting for Zero hour.

At 5.20 a.m. the artillery and machine gun barrage fell accurately on the German line of outposts. The tanks which were to co-operate could not get up in time to take part owing to the slippery nature of the ground. Nevertheless the advance went well. The 16th found the capture of Le Verguier to be a difficult task as the enemy's strong points were scattered and well concealed in masses of old brick and masonry, and the fog from the smoke shells rendered their detection extremely hard. In spite of this the mopping-up was done well, the village eventually yielding 450 prisoners, 60 machine guns, a few .77 field guns and much ammunition and miscellaneous stores.

Later the 13th and 15th Battalions took the Red Line and finally the 14th completed the task of the 4th Brigade by capturing the Blue Line.

In the last fight, as usual, the diggers followed the barrage closely, but their old enemy, the short firing gun, was in action and caused a few of the casualties received. When the other battalions went through the 16th was immediately put on the work of salvaging which occupied its time until the 21st when it was relieved by the South Staffordshires and moved back to Tincourt, where it bivouaced in trenches. The casualties in this action were not heavy: 3 men killed and 2 officers and 20 men wounded. It was a great victory, and a fitting finale to the fighting career of the "Old Sixteenth." The 4th Division, out of 3,000 fighting men, lost 500 casualties and captured 2,543 German prisoners.

CHAPTER 32—THE ARMISTICE.

On September 22 the 16th moved across the railway line to make room for the incoming Americans, and the next day marched *via* Pèronne to Biaches where it bivouaced in old dug-outs. To assist the 27th American Division in its first important engagement, on September 27, General Brand and 80 selected officers and N.C.O's. from the 4th Division were detailed for duty for a week prior to and during that attack. Of the 80, 11 were selected from the 16th Battalion. On the 24th 'buses conveyed the men to Picquigny, where they were reorganised. Training and recreation were the two principal items on the military programme, and the fact that Picquigny was inhabited by civilians was appreciated by men who had a longing for some other companionship than their own.

The first portion of November was wet. A divisional boxing tournament at Bovelles proved of great interest to all ranks. On November 1 the whole of the 4th Brigade, at the invitation of the people of Picquigny, marched with the children and townspeople to the British cemetery, where the children placed flowers on the graves and sang the British and French National Anthems. Beautiful addresses were made by the schoolmaster and the Curê of the parish. A translation of the former's speech was read to the troops by Chaplain H. H. Harper, of the 16th. The officer in charge of the French Mission also spoke, after which the battalion marched back to the square, where the National Anthem and Marseillaise were played.

On the 9th orders were received for a forward move again, but it was postponed for a few days.

In the meantime, on the 11th, news of the signing of the armistice was received. There was great excitement in the town, and the bands of the brigade played in the square at 11 a.m. in honour of the great and welcome event. Flags and bunting soon appeared on the houses, the village bells rang out the good tidings, and much rejoicing among soldiers and civilians was expressed.

On the 13th the 16th marched 15 kilometres to Saleux, where, with the remainder of the 4th Brigade, it entrained, reaching Epehy after a long day's journey. There it camped in tents close to the station. The next day it entrained at Templeaux-le-Gerard and proceeded to Brancourt, marching from there to billets in Fresnoy-le-Grand.

On November 16, in glorious, sunny weather, church service of a special thanksgiving nature was held to commemorate the cessation of hostilities. This service was conducted by Padre H. H.

Harper. The next day the first snow of the winter fell and was followed by light rain. To prepare the men for the expected long march to the Rhine the battalion now carried out route marches daily.

On the 23rd the 16th marched to St. Souplet and billeted for the night. This village was considerably damaged and traces of gas from its last bombardment were still noticeable.

The battalion marched out on the 24th to Prisches area and rested at Beaurepaire the next day. The weather was wet and miserable, but the billets were good. It was an old German rest area with a bunk for every man. On the 26th a move was made to Sains-du-Nord, where the men were comfortably billeted in a factory—a former German hospital. Sains was a fine town with many factories and châteaux. The country in the vicinity was very picturesque. Apple orchards abounded, but the people seemed poor and their farms were destitute of stock.

This was the end of the 16th Battalion's wanderings as a unit. For the rest of its existence all ranks were mainly concerned with the problem of getting back to Australia. On November 29 the brigadier, Brigadier-General Drake-Brockman, outlined the scheme in hand for demobilisation in an address to the battalion in which he touched on the following points:—

1. The possibility of the 4th Brigade taking part in the Army of Occupation. At present it looked as though the Australians would relieve the Canadians on the Rhine in two months' time.

2. The length of time—probably more than 12 months—before the A.I.F. could be transhipped to Australia.

3. The intention of the Allies to carry on as though a state of war still existed.

4. The chances of the enemy faithfully carrying out the terms of the armistice.

5. The drawback, apart from the difficulties, of landing 200,000 men in Australia in a short period of time.

6. The formation in England of a governing body of four (included in which was Sir John Monash) to promote facilities for the education and training of A.I.F. personnel so that they might be able to apply such knowledge on return to Australia.

7. The desirability of all men with wives in England (7,000 at present in the A.I.F.) taking advantage of the Government's offer to tranship them to Australia within three months.

Following on this educational classes were established, the aim being to prepare the way for the A.I.F. scheme. Instructors were obtained and classes formed in English, mathematics, book-keeping, French, shorthand, typewriting, electrical engineering, carpentering, tailoring, signwriting, geography, and history. French was very popular, and so also was the class on the internal combustion engine. These classes were carried on throughout the demobilisation period.

A letter of appreciation of the work of the Australians in France from the citizens of Monceau-les-cups was presented to the brigadier by representative citizens, and suitably acknowledged. In many of the villages through which the 16th had passed during this advance the inhabitants testified to the inhuman treatment to which they had been subjected by the Germans during the past four years. In the letter referred to the writer touched on this subject when he said: "I beg to have the honour of saluting our deliverers through you. We have been suffering so much since the beginning of the war that the sight of your gallant troops has been to us the glorious sight of the new arising of the Sun of Liberty."

A few weeks more and the 16th had gradually lost its identity as a unit of the A.I.F. Its members were scattered and many were homeward bound on various transports. All were looking forward to their demobilisation—to the day which would see them free citizens of Australia. Not that they regretted the voluntary act which had bound them in the chains of military discipline—the need was there and they then renounced their personal freedom willingly. But now the war was over every man was obsessed with the desire to return to civilian life. As the means of transport were made available, so men were allotted to the various ships. The return to Australia of 200,000 men was a gigantic job, beset with innumerable difficulties. Thanks to the organising genius of Sir John Monash, this stupendous task was practically completed within twelve months of the armistice with a minimum of friction and delay.

And so the men of the Old Sixteenth returned to Australia; to comforts and modes of living to which they long been strangers. Their problem was to regain their places in the civilian community; to readjust their ideas to the humdrum routine of peace. In the office and workshop they took their places; on the land they started the task of building homes and farms for themselves and their children.

In this respect the State of Western Australia owes much to the post-war efforts of its soldiers, who as manfully resumed their civic responsibilities as they had those which were previously theirs in the A.I.F. There were exceptions, of course. Some men came back broken in body and mind by the stresses they had undergone. They have found civilian life a hard struggle. To them the community owes a duty, and it is the returned soldiers generally who must keep the sympathetic performance of that duty ever to the fore. Certainly the call for comradeship and help is just as evident in peace as it was in war.

In that spirit of comradeship let us leave The Old Sixteenth. Wherever they are, the diggers' thoughts must often be with old times, old places, and old friends. The vicissitudes of the old battalion, the trials and tribulations of its members, are things of the past; but it is certain that the wonderful spirit of the Old Sixteenth will never die. The 16th Battalion is more than a memory. It lives still and its spirit will go marching on to the end of Time. The blood which reddened the soil of Gallipoli and Flanders will also flow in the veins of future generations, and the men who fell certainly bequeathed some of their unquenchable spirit to those who follow them; to future Australians, who, should another testing time arise, will carry on the splendid traditions of The Old Sixteenth.

APPENDIX 1.

16TH BATTALION PRISONERS OF WAR FUND.

Shortly after April 11, 1917 (the day of the attack on the Hindenburg Line near Bullecourt), when nine officers and over 300 other ranks of the battalion fell into German hands as prisoners of war, it was suggested that a fund be opened to enable a regular supply of foodstuffs etc., to be sent to those men. Lt.-Col. E. A. Drake-Brockman, on a battalion parade, put the matter before all ranks and it was unanimously decided that such a fund be started forthwith. Minimum contributions were fixed as follow:—Every pay day, which was every second Wednesday, officers 10 francs, sergeants 3, corporals 2, and others 1 franc. It was further decided that all moneys be paid through the Divisional Paymaster to the Australian branch of the British Red Cross Society—this society to administer the fund.

As a result of this worthy action many letters of appreciation were forwarded to the battalion by the recipients of the parcels, and the men of the 16th who were prisoners of war thought highly of the fact that, in their time of trouble, they were still remembered by their old battalion.

The payments to the fund are set out hereunder:—

	£	s.	d.
23rd June, 1917	84	16	6
20th July, 1917	72	15	3
1st August, 1917	37	13	6
14th August, 1917	34	1	4
29th August, 1917	40	16	6
12th September, 1917	40	7	1
29th September, 1917	27	0	5
16th October, 1917	27	18	9
24th October, 1917	24	5	7
7th November, 1917	29	18	0
21st November, 1917	20	19	5
8th December, 1917	33	19	10
20th December, 1917	29	3	9
2nd January, 1918	38	4	1
16th January, 1918	31	7	7
19th February, 1918	56	16	0
11th March, 1918	37	15	4
16th March, 1918	43	14	10
10th April, 1918	36	13	4
25th April, 1918	43	19	7
23rd May, 1918	87	16	8
20th June, 1918	66	6	3
17th July, 1918	45	15	11
22nd July, 1918	32	10	1
31st July, 1918	29	7	5
18th August, 1918	10	9	8
28th August, 1918	24	9	10
31st August, 1918	26	13	10
10th September, 1918	23	6	9
25th September, 1918	26	10	2
8th October, 1918	26	14	4
28th October, 1918	25	6	4
21st November, 1918	26	9	6
Total	£1,244	3	5

After all prisoners of war had been repatriated there was a credit balance of £55 1s. 9d. in the hands of the Australian branch of the British Red Cross Society. The then commanding officer, Lt.-Col. E. J. Parks, authorised the secretary of the Prisoners of War Department to expend such portion of that amount as was required to liquidate individual prisoners' personal debts to the Red Cross Society and the remaining balance was then to be absorbed into the general funds of the society (Australian branch) as a donation from the officers and other ranks of the 16th Battalion.

APPENDIX 2.

DECORATIONS WON BY MEMBERS OF THE 16th BATTALION.

V.C. (Victoria Cross):
- No. 3970, Private M. O'Meara. Pozieres, August, 1916.
- No. 3399, L/Corp. T. L. Axford, M.M. Hamel, June 4, 1918.
- Lieut. L. D. McCarthy (F). Near Madame Wood, August 23, 1918.

C.B. (Companion of the Order of the Bath):
- Lieut.-Col. H. Pope. Gallipoli, 1915.
- Lieut.-Col. E. A. Drake-Brockman, C.M.G., D.S.O. (F).

C.M.G. (Companion of the Order of St. Michael and St. George):
- Lieut.-Col. E. A. Drake-Brockman, C.B., D.S.O. (F).

D.S.O. (Distinguished Service Order):
- Major P. Black, D.C.M. (F).
- Lieut.-Col. E. A. Drake-Brockman, C.B., C.M.G. (F)
- Major E. L. Margolin.
- Captain R. Harwood.
- " R. S. Somerville, M.C.
- " C. Ahearn, M.C.
- " W. J. D. Lynas, M.C.
- Lieut. J. B. Minchin, M.C.
- Major W. O. Mansbridge. Gallipoli.
- Lieut.-Col. E. J. Parks, M.C.
- Major L. E. Tilney, V.D.

M.C. and two bars (Military Cross):
- Capt. W. J. D. Lynas, D.S.O.

M.C. and bar:
- Captain F. Wadge.
- " D. S. Aarons.
- Lieut. W. Burrows.
- " J. E. Piercy.

THE OLD SIXTEENTH. 203

M.C.:
    Lieut. H. J. Cook.
    Captain D. M. Steele (Med. Officer).
    Lieut. F. B. Wilton.
    Captain A. W. Potts.
        ,, R. S. Somerville, D.S.O.
    2nd Lt. J. P. Courtney.
    Lieut. J. S. Kerr.
    Captain E. J. Parks, D.S.O.
    2nd Lt. J. B. Minchin, D.S.O.
    Lieut. H. J. Bradley, D.C.M.
    Captain C. Ahearn, D.S.O.
    Captain S. U. Timewell.
    2nd Lt. J. K. Robin.
    Lieut. J. G. F. Senior.
    Captain (Hon. Major) H. A. F. Wilkinson.
    Lieut. H. F. Klopper.
    Captain H. Smith.
    Lieut. H. A. Devenish.
      ,, V. Ketterer.
      ,, W. Donald.
      ,, L. Tweedie.
    Captain A. Martin.
    Lieut. F. A. Moseley.
      ,, J. D. Howell.
      ,, W. Harvey.

D.C.M. and bar. (Distinguished Conduct Medal):
    No. 1915, C.Q.M.S. C. C. Garrett.

D.C.M.:
    Major (then L/Corp. P. Black, D.S.O. (F), Gallipoli.
    Lt.-Col. (then Private) H. Murray, V.C., C.M.G., D.S.O. (F), Gallipoli.
    Corp. J. Cosson.
    No. 2467. Sgt. G. C. Dow.
      ,, 140. Sgt. H. J. Bradley.
      ,, 1468. Corp. A. Fraser.
      ,, 2226. Sgt. F. R. Holland.
      ,, 1742 (a). Corp. E. L. C. Hodge.
      ,, 1130. Sgt. J. Bitmead.
      ,, 2105. Sgt. R. G. Bridges.
      ,, 2631. L/Corp. D. B. Crisp.
      ,, 1984. Sgt. L. Boully.
      ,, 4030. Corp. J. E. Ffoulkes.
      ,, 1784. Sgt. G. D. McLean.
      ,, 1463. Corp. C. Cowain.
      ,, 2310. Sgt. H. C. Thompson.
      ,, 1701. R.S.M. J. H. P. Leunig.
      ,, 2751. Sgt. W. J. Prescott.
      ,, 2389. Sgt. E. England, M.M.
      ,, 1391. C.S.M. H. McCabe.
      ,, 6707. L/Corp. W. Nelson.
      ,, 2699. C.S.M. W. R. Rogers, M.M.
      ,, 1112. Sgt. G. Yeates.
      ,, 2193. Sgt. W. Murray, M.M.
      ,, 1807 (a). Sgt. F. J. Robbins, M.M.
      ,, 125. C.S.M. D. C. Phillips.
      ,, 6840. Pte. A. P. Lawrence.
      ,, 7437. C.S.M. H. A. Stubbs.
      ,, —— Sgt. S. Hooper.

M.M. AND BAR. (MILITARY MEDAL.)

2699, Sgt. W. Rogers, D.C.M.
3894, L/Corp. J. Elliot.
317, Serg. A. J. McKinnon.
2389, Pte. E. England, D.C.M.
3461, Pte. P. F. Fox.
2815, Sgt. H. Pitman.
1400, L/Corp. A. Breen.

1934, L/Corp. R. Peters.
8337, Pte. M. Bercovitch.
380, Sgt. H. W. Hutchings.
7027, Pte. G. V. Jaeschke.
3540, Sgt. J. Oxenham.
6072, Corp. G. F. Payne.

MILITARY MEDAL.

Gallipoli.

241, Corp. L. L. Briand.
1353, Pte. E. J. Muller.

689, Sgt. W. Allen.

France.

1822, Sgt. H. A. H. Iffla.
3413, Pte. S. Barrow.
3446, Pte. F. Drew.
350, Pte. L. H. White.
2797, Pte. H. A. Gottlieb.
2635, Pte. H. Schmidt.
34, L/Corp. W. G. Cadwallader.
1400, L/Corp. A. Breen.
534, Pte. P. H. Williams.
3848, Pte. H. Arundel.
2696, Pte. B. Roberts.
3839, Sgt. C. H. Turner.
1595, Pte. E. Buswell.
4808, Corp. A. P. Farmer.
1783, Corp. B. C. Bolton.
7085, Pte. A. D. Watson.
5357, L/Sgt. H. H. Dinsdale.
2468, Corp. W. B. Currie.
2195, Pte. F. J. Rowe.
3474, Corp. F. W. Hart.
44(a), Pte. F. J. Dean.
3892, Pte. A. R. Eastburn.
2724, Pte. A. A. Roberts.
4947, L/Corp. H. H. Roots.
294, Pte. L. Ricci.
5409(a), Pte. M. Payne.
1416, Pte. E. Hayes.
6061, L/Corp. W. L. Menzies.
750, Corp. W. Barker.
1383, Pte. R. Taylor.
500, Pte. J. R. H. S. Turner.
4960, Pte. J. Walsh.
3545, Corp. A. A. Reid.
5473, Pte. W. N. Spratley.
3037, Pte. L. I. Reszkowski.
5737, Pte. P. W. Larrett.
431, Pte. N. L. Terry.
3415, L/Corp. A. T. H. Bloom.
1656, Pte. T. Scott.

3570, Pte. P. Loffman.
5162, Pte. W. O'Sullivan.
6249, Pte. A. Dance.
6946, L/Corp. G. W. Bradshaw.
6131, Pte. A. Ochiltree.
1699(a), Pte. E. Crowe.
2465, Pte. A. Cowling.
1807(a), L/Corp. F. J. Robins.
5469, Pte. L. White.
3540, L/Corp. J. Oxenham.
380, Sgt. H. W. Hutching.
4052, Pte. E. Mullen.
743, Corp. C. McQuade.
2006, Sgt. R. W. Hoskin.
5436, Pte. V. C. Sparrow.
6276, Sgt. W. E. Inglis.
2521, L/Corp. G. E. Rushby.
6248, Sgt. L. Oliver.
4904, L/Corp. W. A. Schiff.
3894, L/Corp. J. Elliott.
2202, L/Corp. W. Dinnie.
157, Sgt. H. P. Wilson.
2913, Sgt. W. Murray.
2699, Sgt. W. R. Rogers.
136, Sgt. G. Richards.
317, L/Corp. L. McKinnon.
5205, Pte. C. W. Thorn.
7232, Pte. G. E. Furness.
3162, Sgt. V. T. Tandy.
5202, Pte. M. Smith.
2781, Corp. R. L. Bennett.
7720, Pte. J. Craik.
6740, L/Corp. H. J. Corpe.
1133, Sgt. G. Brackenbridge.
2819, Pte. A. B. Phillips.
6249, L/Corp. C. B. Worthington.
6085, L/Corp. J. Robinson.
78, Sgt. G. Martin.
341, Sgt. S. McGrath.

THE OLD SIXTEENTH.

4046, Corp. W. H. Plummer.
1042, Pte. W. J. Halliday.
5736, Pte. J. Keating.
1934, Pte. R. Peters.
1494, Sgt. J. Lumbus
2815, Sgt. H. Pitman.
775, Corp. J. Gooney.
5160, Pte. C. Nineham.
618, Corp. W. W. Tillbrook.
6223 L/Corp. A. J. Bonzer.
6384, L/Corp. A. Swindlehurst.
2041, Pte. A. Lee.
1303, Pte. W. McGuinness.
3918, Pte. J. Helsin.
2073, Corp. G. E. Smith.
209, Sgt. A. Mackie.
3399, L/Corp. T. L. Axford.
5394, Sgt. G. R. Manners.
7564, L/Corp. J. A. Johnston.
1977, Sgt. J. Butler.
6218, Sgt. P. Packham.
7314, Pte. R. S. Trigwell.
3502, Pte. Y. Kingdon.
6585, Pte. W. H. Carter.
1790(a), Pte. J. H. Northey.
3006, Corp. R. W. J. Clark.
2680, Corp. R. H. Basham.
1776(a), Pte. A. Morgan.
1387, Pte. H. G. Hudson.
16158, Pte. A. Gepp.
7790, Pte. J. R. Norrish.
7811, Pte. H. H. Richardson.
7129, Pte. E. O. Rodier
7205, Pte. F. J. Allison.
2905, L/Corp. A. F. Laurie.
7082, Pte. W. H. Taylor.
6233, L/Corp. Bleakley.
1074, S/Sgt. J. J. O'Neill.
1783, Corp. B. C. Bolton

749, Sgt. M. McGrath.
207, Sgt. G. Mace.
1943, Pte. L. Thornby.
1684, Pte. T. C. Caldwell.
5337, Pte. M. Bercovitch.
768, Pte. F. G. Jeffrey.
3854, Pte. P. E. Bergstrom.
3427, Pte. W. F. Chalmers
234, Pte. W. J. Afflick.
650, L/Corp. G. Ball.
1794, Sgt. H. L. Choules.
212, Corp. T. Morton.
2778, Pte. H. L. Beaumont.
595, Sgt. A. Hensman.
3521, Pte. W. McGillivray.
3532, Pte. T. J. McMillan.
494, Corp. P. W. O'Shea.
139, Corp. G. Sharp.
2053, L/Corp. J. Williamson.
2107, L/Sgt. A. Towers.
3139, L/Corp. A. L. Matthews.
5445, Pte. G. J. B. Thompson.
6972, Corp. G. E. Payne.
7017, Pte. V. Hagen.
8045, Pte. G. Elder.
4007, Sgt. R. Sweetman.
6949, Sgt. W. Marshall.
2176, Pte. C. L. Buckanarra
2678, Pte. H. K. Lyon.
5159, Pte. W. A. Nelson.
5336, Corp. C. P. Boulton.
6996, Pte. A. C. Forster.
2624, Sgt. W. Stockton
3435, Corp. B. Cusack.
1801(a), Corp. N. V. Pitkin.
5376, L/Corp. W. E. Lilleyman.
7951, Pte. N. Brockman.
2718, Driver A. H. Urjeh.
2049, Pte. J. Twyford.

M.S.M. (MERITORIOUS SERVICE MEDAL).

W.O. (II.) L. Tweedie, M.C.
1104, R.Q.M.S. W. Turner.
1050, Sgt. J. W. Ingham.

228, C.Q.M.S. P. Grant.
2253, S/Sgt. H. Smith.

FOREIGN DECORATIONS.

Order of Danilo, 4th Class (Montenegro).—Lieut.-Col. E. A. Drake-Brockman, C.B., C.M.G., D.S.O.
Croix de Guerre (avec palm) (France).—Lieut. L. D. McCarthy, V.C.
Croix de Guerre (avec palm) (France).—Major P. Black, D.S.O., D.C.M.
Croix de Guerre (Belgium).—No. 5427, Pte A. H. Shervill.
Croix de Guerre (Belgium).—No. 2670, Pte. S. A. Jones.
Croix de Guerre, Etoile d'Argent (France).—Capt. F. Wadge, M.C.
Medal Militaire (French).—R.S.M. J. Tandy, M.M.

MENTIONED IN DESPATCHES.

Gallipoli.

Lieut. A. E. Carse.
Sgt. G. Demel.
L/Corp. P. Black (twice).
Major L. E. Tilney, D.S O.
Lt.--Col. H. Pope, C.B.
Major W. O. Mansbridge, D.S.O. (twice).
L/Corp. H. D. Davies.
Sgt. T. Carr.
Capt. L. D. Heming.
Pte. C. Howland.
Pte. G. V. Brown.
Pte. A. B. Foster.
Pte. R. A. Annear.
Sgt. F. R. Howard.
L/Corp. F. H. Benporath.
Corp. V. Ketterer.
Major E. L. Margolin, D.S.O
C.S.M. O. Jilley.
L/Corp. F. Townsend

France.

Lieut.-Col. E. A. Drake-Brockman, C.B., C.M.G., D.S.O. F. (4 times).
Major R. Harwood, D.S.O. (twice).
Major E. J. Parkes, D.S.O., M.C. (twice).
Major P. Black, D.S.O., D.C.M., F. (once).
Capt. S. U. Timewell, M.C. (twice).
Major E. A. Wilton, D.S.O. (twice).
Capt. R. S. Sommerville, D.S.O., M.C. (once).
Capt. F. Wadge, M.C. (once).
Lieut. F. F. Woods (once).
Capt. C. Ahearn, D.S.O., M.C. (once).
Lieut. R. Minchin, D.S.O., M.C. (once).
Capt. W. J. Lynas, D.S.O., M.C. (once).
1490, C.S.M. V. Ketterer, M.C. (once).
 350, Sgt. J. B. Minchin (once).
 300, C.S.M. S. B. Smith (once).
  78, Sgt. G. H. Martin (once).
3233, C.Q.M.S. H. Blee (once).

APPENDIX 3.

CASUALTIES IN 16TH BATTALION, 1914-18.

Theatre of War.	Killed in Action.		Died of Wounds.		Died of Disease.		Died of Gas. Poisg.		Died of other Causes.		Total Deaths.		Wounded in Action.		Gassed.		Prisoners of War.		Total Battle Casualties.	
	O.	O.R.	O.	O.R.	O.	O.R.	O.	O.R.	O.	O.R.	O.	O.R.	O.	O.R.	O.	O.R.	O.	O.R.	Officers.	Other Ranks.
M.E.F. ...	16	337	2	94	...	9	...	...	...	1	18	441	16	352	...	...	2	5	36	798
E.E.F. ...	...	...	...	...	...	...	...	...	...	...	...	...	...	...	...	...	...	...	...	...
B.E.F. ...	16	472	3	121	2	13	...	...	2	7	23	613	50	1,507	...	30	11	399	84	2,549
U.K. ...	...	...	...	...	1	31	...	...	1	1	2	32	...	...	...	...	...	...	2	32
Totals ...	32	809	5	215	3	53	...	...	3	9	43	1,086	66	1,859	...	30	13	404	122	3,379

APPENDIX 1.

A.I.F. INFANTRY CASUALTIES.

"Thanks are due to Colonel Collett for these tables, which have been compiled by him from official records, and give in detail the losses of the infantry in the four theatres of war in which the A.I.F. was engaged."

TOTAL CASUALTIES, A.I.F., 1914-18.

Theatre.	Infantry.		Other Arms.		Total.	
	Officers.	O. Ranks.	Officers.	O. Ranks.	Officers.	O. Ranks.
M.E.F.	476	15,217	531	9,887	1,007	25,104
E.E.F.		2	416	4,442	416	4,444
B.E.F.	5,854	140,808	1,915	32,514	7,769	173,322
U.K.	29	1,343	78	849	107	2,192
Total	6,359	157,370	2,940	47,692	9,299	205,062

CASUALTIES IN THE INFANTRY, 1914-18.

The letters M.E.F. indicate " Mediterranean Expeditionary Force " ; E.E.F. " Egyptian Expeditionary Force " ; and B.E.F. " British Expeditionary Force."

1st DIVISION.

Theatre.	Battalion— 1		2		3		4		5		6		7	
	O.	O.R.	O.	O.R.	O.	O.R.	O.	O.R.	O.	O.R.	O.	O.R.	O.	O.R.
M.E.F.	23	694	36	706	29	696	20	730	21	600	32	704	23	730
B.E.F.	137	2,650	102	2,580	105	2,752	112	2,660	100	2,254	101	2,235	113	2,237
U.K.		31	1	35		36		30	1	26		20	2	25
Total	160	3,375	139	3,321	134	3,484	132	3,420	122	2,880	133	2,950	138	2,992
Total Deaths	1,165		1,200		1,311		1,203		971		1,066		1,047	

Theatre.	8		9		10		11		12		Totals.	
	O.	O.R.	O.	O.R.	O.	O.R.	O.	O.R.	O.	O.R.	O.	O.R.
M.E.F.	21	536	16	630	16	485	21	657	12	593	270	7,761
B.E.F.	121	2,594	130	2,716	131	2,558	109	2,731	130	2,797	1,391	30,769
U.K.		24		33		34		21	1	64	5	379
Total	142	3,154	146	3,379	147	3,077	130	3,409	143	3,454	1,666	38,909
Total Deaths	877		1,094		1,015		1,115		1,136		13,200	

2ND DIVISION.

Battalion—

Theatre.	17		18		19		20		21		22		23	
	O.	O.R.	O.	O.R.	O.	O.R.	O.	O.R.	O.	O.R.	O.	O.R.	O.	O.R.
M.E.F.	11	458	10	434	7	306	7	216	8	313	6	322	9	372
E.E.F.	...	...	...	...	...	...	...	...	...	...	...	1	...	...
B.E.F.	117	2,728	127	2,959	115	2,884	126	2,789	124	2,901	135	2,791	93	2,659
U.K.	1	15		15	2	19	1	15		34		21		41
Total	129	3,201	137	3,408	124	3,209	134	3,020	132	3,248	141	3,135	102	3,072
Total Deaths	845		1,030		836		848		872		855		827	

Theatre.	24		25		26		27		28		Totals.	
	O.	O.R.	O.	O.R.	O.	O.R.	O.	O.R.	O.	O.R.	O.	O.R.
M.E.F.	12	371	11	387	3	277	2	349	3	317	89	4,122
E.E.F.		1	...	...	...	...	...	...	...	...	...	2
B.E.F.	104	2,900	133	3,339	131	2,964	103	2,563	136	2,793	1,444	34,270
U.K.	1	32	3	17		29		25	2	33	10	296
Total	117	3,304	147	3,743	134	3,270	105	2,937	141	3,143	1,543	38,690
Total Deaths	911		1,929		906		787		1,021		10,797	

3RD DIVISION.

Battalion—

Theatre.	33		34		35		36		37		38		39	
	O.	O.R.	O.	O.R.	O.	O.R.	O.	O.R.	O.	O.R.	O.	O.R.	O.	O.R.
B.E.F.	118	2,386	87	2,144	88	2,144	67	1,609	80	1,876	83	1,884	88	1,680
U.K.		21	1	11		7		13		22	1	15	1	20
Total	118	2,407	88	2,155	88	2,151	67	1,622	80	1,898	84	1,899	89	1,700
Total Deaths	451		482		551		429		483		499		406	

Theatre.	40		41		42		43		44		Totals.	
	O.	O.R.	O.	O.R.	O.	O.R.	O.	O.R.	O.	O.R.	O.	O.R.
B.E.F.	67	2,098	84	1,926	91	2,020	65	1,646	80	1,692	998	23,105
U.K.	1	19		21		17	2	17		15	6	198
Totals	68	2,117	84	1,947	91	2,037	67	1,663	80	1,707	1,004	23,303
Total Deaths	466		454		459		406		433		5,519	

210 THE OLD SIXTEENTH.

4TH DIVISION.

Battalion—

Theatre.	13		14		15		16		45		46		47	
	O.	O.R.	O.	O.R.	O.	O.R.	O.	O.R.	O.	O.R.	O.	O.R.	O.	O.R.
M.E.F.	24	761	22	715	35	1,060	36	798	...	...	...	...	...	...
B.E.F.	138	2,556	104	2,586	111	2,443	84	2,549	88	2,323	83	2,473	83	2,291
U.K.	1	32	1	17	1	32	2	32		15		16		11
Total	163	3,349	127	3,318	147	3,535	122	3,379	88	2,338	83	2,489	83	2,302
Total Deaths	1,091		916		1,195		1,129		688		590		661	

Theatre.	48		49		50		51		52		Totals.	
	O.	O.R.	O.	O.R.	O.	O.R.	O.	O.R.	O.	O.R.	O.	O.R.
M.E.F.	...	...	...	...	...	...	...	...	...	...	117	3,334
B.E.F.	99	2,577	77	2,141	83	2,283	83	2,477	62	2,033	1,095	28,732
U.K.		14	1	18		17	1	17	1	12	8	233
Total	99	2,591	78	2,159	83	2,300	84	2,494	63	2,045	1,220	32,299
Total Deaths	843		770		720		889		651		10,143	

5TH DIVISION.

Battalion—

Theatre.	29		30		31		32		53		54		55	
	O.	O.R.	O.	O.R.	O.	O.R.	O.	O.R.	O.	O.R.	O.	O.R.	O.	O.R.
B.E.F.	86	1,817	55	1,609	77	2,050	70	2,082	83	2,265	83	2,169	71	1,860
U.K.		22		25		30		31		19		10		15
Total	86	1,839	55	1,634	77	2,080	70	2,113	83	2,284	83	2,179	71	1,875
Total Deaths	485		458		575		613		647		544		517	

Theatre.	56		57		58		59		60		Totals.	
	O.	O.R.	O.	O.R.	O.	O.R.	O.	O.R.	O.	O.R.	O.	O.R.
B.E.F.	83	2,064	60	1,687	78	2,075	96	2,316	84	1,938	926	23,932
U.K.		19		16		19		12		19	...	237
Total	83	2,083	60	1,703	78	2,094	96	2,328	84	1,957	926	24,169
Total Deaths	529		505		615		795		701		6,984	

APPENDIX 5.
OFFICER CASUALTIES.
Gallipoli—

Killed in action—
 Capt. F. B. Carter
  „ J. Miller
  „ Townshend
  „ Chabrel
  „ Hemming
 Lieut. Curlewis
  „ Southern
  „ Geddes
  „ Kretchmar
  „ Durston
  „ Mountain
  „ Bruns
  „ Kerr
  „ K. L. Anderson
  „ Burton
  „ A. E. Carse
  „ Brashaw
  „ Thyer

Wounded in action—
  No record.

France.

Killed in action—

Major P. Black, D.S.O., D.C.M. F.; Bullecourt, April 11, 1917.
Capt. V. Tucker; Bullecourt, April 11, 1917.
Lieut. J. K. Robin, M.C.; Gueudecourt, February 1, 1917.
Lieut. C. D. Brown; Polygon Wood, September 26, 1917.
Lieut. G. Hough; Flers, November 6, 1916.
Lieut. D. Freeman; Polygon Wood, September 26, 1917.
Lieut. H. B. Arundel, M.M.; Polygon Wood, September 26, 1917.
Lieut. V. F. Doran; Messines, June 12, 1917.
Lieut. S. B. Smith (whilst P.O.W., Germany); July 31, 1917.
Lieut. L. Boully, D.C.M.; Gapaard, August 6, 1917.
Lieut. L. Halifax; Pozieres, August 8, 1916.
Lieut. L. D. Glowery; Bullecourt, April 11, 1917.
Lieut. L. A. Stephenson; Mouquet Farm, August 30, 1916.
Lieut. J. E. Johnston; Mouquet Farm, August 30, 1916.
Lieut. J. Hutton; Mouquet Farm, August 30, 1916.
Lieut. E. H. Moors; Morlancourt, August 8, 1918.
Lieut. W. R. Rogers, D.C.M., M.M.; Morlancourt, August 9, 1918.
Capt. F. F. Woods; Hamel, July 4, 1918.
2nd Lt. H. E. Blee, M.M.; Hamel, July 4, 1918.
2nd Lt. G. D. Orchard; Le Verguier, D.O.W., October 15, 1918.

Accidentally killed—

 Capt. A. McLeod; Cosock, Scotland, December 5, 1916.

Died of illness—

 Lieut. C. C. Garratt, D.C.M.
 Lieut. J. H. D. Leunig, D.C.M.

Wounded in action—
   Major P. Black, D.S.O., D.C.M. F.; Gallipoli (twice), Mouquet Farm, August 30, 1916.
   Capt. R. Harwood, D.S.O.; Mouquet Farm, August 30, 1916.
   Capt. A. McLeod; Mouquet Farm, August 30, 1916.
   Capt. R. S. Sommerville, D.S.O., M.C.; Bullecourt, April 11, 1917.
   Capt. H. J. Cook, M.C.; Flers, December 3, 1916.
   Capt. F. Wadge, M.C. F.; Mouquet Farm, August 30, 1916.
   Capt. D. S. Aarons, M.C.; Zonnebeke, October 21, 1917.
   Lieut. H. Smith, M.C.; Pozieres, August 6, 1916.
   Lieut. V. B. Wilton, M.C.; Mouquet Farm, August 30, 1916.
   Lieut. L. J. Goldie; Gapaard, August 4, 1917.
   Lieut. G. A. Whiting; Pozieres, August 11, 1916.
   Lieut. C. D. Brown; Spoil Bank, October 3, 1916.
   Lieut. F. W. Morgan; Polygon Wood, September 26, 1917.
   Lieut. L. J. Clark, Flers, December 6, 1916.
   Lieut. W. Jorgensen; Bullecourt, April 11, 1917.
   Lieut. L. D. McCarthy, V.C. F.; Bullecourt, April 11, 1917.
   Lieut. H. W. Leake; Bullecourt, April 11, 1917.
   Lieut. J. Kerr, M.C.; Bullecourt, April 11, 1917.
   Lieut. H. A. H. Iffla, M.M.; Bullecourt, April 11, 1917.
   Lieut. C. J. Long; Polygon Wood, September 26, 1917.
   Lieut. H. M. Sweeney; Polygon Wood, September 26, 1917.
   Lieut. F. I. Webster; Polygon Wood, September 26, 1917.
   Lieut. A. C. Muir; Hebuterne, March 29, 1918.
   Lieut. H. W. Leake; Hebuterne, April 4, 1918.
   Lieut. A. W. H. Harlow;. Hamelet, June 10, 1918.
   Lieut. J. G. F. Senior, M.C.; Villers Bretonneux, April 29, 1918.
   Capt. C. Ahearn, D.S.O., M.C.; Cerisy, August 8, 1918.
   Capt. H. J. Cook, M.C.; Cerisy, August 8, 1918.
   Capt. A. W. Potts, M.C.; Vaire Wood, July 6, 1918.
   Capt. W. J. Lynas, D.S.O., M.C.; Vaire Wood, July 4, 1918.
   Lieut. A. T. Towers, M.M.; Hamelet, June 23, 1918.
   Lieut. L. J. Clark; Le Verquier, September 19, 1918.
   Lieut. J. E. Piercey, M.C.; Cerisy, August 8, 1918.
   Lieut. J. Kerr, M.C.; Vaire Wood, July 4, 1918.
   Lieut. W. R. Peacock; Hamelet, June 22, 1918.
   Lieut. W. F. Broadhurst; Vaire Wood, July 4, 1918.
   Lieut. H. A. Devenish, M.C.; Cerisy, August 8, 1918.
   Lieut. A. B. C. Dowling; Raid Pear Trench, June 15, 1918.
   Lieut. R. C. Hooper; Hamelet, August 5, 1918.
   Lieut. H. V. Woods; Villers Bretonneux, May 3, 1918.
   Lieut. B. C. L. Piesse; Cerisy, August 8, 1918.
   Lieut. E. Day; Vaire Wood, July 4, 1918.
   Lieut. G. D. Orchard; Le Verguier, September 18, 1918.
   Lieut. F. V. Sparrow; Cerisy, August 8, 1918.

APPENDIX 6.
OFFICERS CAPTURED BY THE ENEMY.
   Capt. R. T. A. Macdonald; Gallipoli, April 25, 1915.
   Lieut. W. E. Elston; Gallipoli, April 25, 1915.
   Capt. H. S. Hummerston (wounded); Bullecourt, April 11, 1917.
   Lieut. J. P. Courtney, M.C. (wounded); Bullecourt, April 11, 1917.
   Lieut. G. D. McLean, D.C.M. (wounded); Bullecourt, April 11, 1917.
   Lieut. J. H. Watson (wounded); Bullecourt, April 11, 1917.
   Lieut. K. L. Johnson (wounded); Bullecourt, April 11, 1917.
   Lieut. M. Walton; Bullecourt, April 11, 1917.
   Lieut. F. M. Culverwell; Bullecourt, April 11, 1917.
   Lieut. S. B. Smith (wounded, since died), Bullecourt, April 11, 1917.
   Capt. R. H. O. Cumming (wounded); Bullecourt, April 11, 1917.

APPENDIX 7.

ENGAGEMENTS IN WHICH THE 16th BATTALION TOOK PART.

	Killed and Wounded.	
Gallipoli.	Officers.	Other Ranks.
The Landing. April 25, 1915	12	338
Bloody Angle. May 2, 1915	8	330
Turkish Attacks. May 18, 1915	2	50
Hill 971. August 6, 1915	4	114
France.		
Pozieres. August 8-12, 1916	3	403
Mouquet Farm. August 30-31, 1916	9	222
Guedecourt. February 5, 1917	1	50
Bullecourt. April 11, 1917	17	623
Messines. June 7, 1917	1	20
Polygon Wood. September 26, 1917	7	177
Hebuterne. March 25, 1918	2	122
Hamel. July 4, 1918	5	73
August 8, 1918	7	98
Le Verguier, September 17, 1918	2	30

APPENDIX 8.

OFFICERS WHO WERE PROMOTED FROM RANKS.

Major P. Black, D.S.O., D.C.M. F.; Gallipoli.
Capt. H. C. Parker; Gallipoli.
Capt. C. McLeod; Gallipoli.
Capt. C. Ahearn, D.S.O., M.C.; Gallipoli.
Capt. H. S. Hummerston; Gallipoli.
Capt. J. McPherson; Gallipoli.
Capt. H. J. Cook, M.C.; Gallipoli.
Capt. A. W. Potts, M.C.; Gallipoli.
Capt. W. J. Lynas, D.S.O., M.C.; Gallipoli.
Capt. F. F. Woods; Egypt.
Lieut. H. Smith, M.C.; Egypt.
Hon. Capt. S. U. Timewell, M.C.; France.
Lieut. L. I. Goldie; Egypt.
Lieut. G. A. Whiting; Egypt.
Lieut. J. Hutton; Egypt.
Lieut. J. E. Johnston; Egypt.
Lieut. W. Burrows, M.C.; France.
Lieut. M. Walton; France.
Lieut. G. Hough; France.
Lieut. F. W. Morgan; France.
Lieut. H. J. Bradley, M.C., D.C.M.; France.
Lieut. J. P. Courtney, M.C.; France.
Lieut. H. B. Arundel, M.M.; France.
Lieut. G. D. McLean, D.C.M.; France.
Lieut. A. T. Towers, M.M.; France.
Lieut. W. Jorgensen; France.
Lieut. V. F. Doran; France.
Lieut. V. Ketterer, M.C.; France.

Appendix 8—continued.

Officers who were Promoted from Ranks—continued.

Lieut. S. B. Smith; France.
Lieut. L. D. McCarthy, V.C. F.; France.
Lieut. H. W. Leake; France.
Lieut. A. W. H. Harlow; France.
Lieut. L. Boully, D.C.M.; France.
Lieut. D. B. Crisp, D.C.M.; France.
Lieut. H. R. C. Grieve; France.
Lieut. W. R. Peacock; France.
Lieut. L. Tweedie, M.C.; France.
Capt. P. R. Paull; Gallipoli.
Lieut. W. F. Broadhurst; France.
Lieut. L. G. Bruer; France.
Lieut. H. T. Crouch; Gallipoli.
Lieut. H. A. Devenish, M.C.; France.
Lieut. J. D. Howell, M.C.; France.
Lieut. W. Harvey, M.C.; France.
Lieut. H. A. F. Iffla, M.M.; France.
Lieut. H. F. Klopper, M.C.; France.
Lieut. J. B. Minchin, D.S.O., M.C.; France.
Lieut. N. L. Terry, M.M.; France.
Lieut. H. M. Sweeney; France.
Lieut. L. J. Halifax; France.
Lieut. J. Bitmead, D.C.M.; France.
Lieut. R. H. O. Cummings; Gallipoli.
Lieut. C. C. Garratt, D.C.M.; France.
Lieut. W. Taylor; France.
Lieut. A. Heesman, M.M.; France.
Lieut. W. E. Inglis, M.M.; France.
Lieut. J. H. P. Leunig, D.C.M.; France.
Lieut. G. D. Orchard; France.
Lieut. F. Packham, M.M.; France.
Lieut. J. H. Wiseman; Egypt.
Lieut. W. McCabe, D.C.M.; France.
Lieut. E. England, D.C.M., M.M.; France.
Lieut. H. Pitman, M.M.; France.
Lieut. T. W. Corbett; France.
Lieut. H. D. Forbes; France.
Lieut. S. Hooper, D.C.M.; France.
Lieut. J. A. Johnston, M.M.; France.
Lieut. J. J. McMahon; France.

APPENDIX 9.

ATHLETIC AND OTHER CUPS WON BY THE 16th BATTALION

4th Brigade Sports Cup—January, 1917.
Anzac Day Cup—April, 1917.
Transport Cup—April, 1917.
Australian Football Cup—Season 1916-17.
Australian Football Cup—Season 1918.
4th Brigade Sports Cup—January, 1918.

THE OLD SIXTEENTH.

AUSTRALIAN IMPERIAL FORCE.

NOMINAL ROLL.

16th INFANTRY BATTALION.

(Embarked at Melbourne on Troopship A40, "Ceramic," 22nd December, 1914.)

Head-Quarters.
Pope, Harold, Lt.-Colonel.
Tilney, Leslie Edward, Major.
McDonald, Ronald Tracy Alexander, Captain (Adjt.)
Gorman, Thomas, Hon. Lt. (Qr.-mr.)
Harwood, Ross, Lieutenant (Transport Officer).
Wilton, Eric Arundel, Lieutenant (Signalling Officer).

Officer-Machine Gun Section.
Carse, Arthur Edward, 2nd Lieut.

Attached.
McGregor, Stanley, Captain (Medical Officer).

"A" Company.
Mansbridge, William Owen, Major.
Elston, William Ernest, Lieutenant.
Kretchmar, Edmund Herman, 2nd Lieut.
71, Jenkins, John, Pte.
116, O'Dell, Martin, Pte.
149, Cramond, Angus Glass, Pte.
161, Leake, Harry Wybom, Pte.
164, McDonald, Peter, Pte.
177, Bell, George Hanson, Pte.
178, Bolton, Tom Harold Lewis, Bugler.
179, Burgess, William Henry, Pte.
180, Coombs, Edward James, Pte.
181, Donald, John Gordon, Pte.
185, Flynn, John, Pte.
192, Luke, Edward John, Pte.
193, Mason, Jeffrey, Pte.
194, Morris, Edward George, Pte.
195, Makins, Gerald Ernest, Pte.
196, Oxford, Bernard Fred., Sgt.
197, Porter, Charles Leary, Pte.
198, Rowe, John Herbert, Pte.

"A" Company—continued.
199, Strahan, William Henry, Sgt.
200, Beechey, Harold Reeve, Pte.
201, Bloom, Louis Robert, Pte.
202, Bracey, Joshua Alfred, Pte.
204, Fulcher, Henry James, Pte.
206, Macdonald, Angus, Pte.
280, McKenzie, Atholl Ivo, Pte.
209, Mackie, Andrew, Pte.
210, Mitchison, Matthew, Pte.
212, Morton, Thomas, Pte.
213, Newell, Bernard Henry, Pte.
214, Orr, Hugh McLatchie, L/Cpl.
215, Parker, John, Pte.
216, Peacock, William Robert, Pte.
218, Pirani, Carl Simeon, Pte.
219, Scrimgrour, James, Pte.
220, Sutherland, Oswald Gladstone, Pte.
221, Tansley, Arthur, Cpl.
222, Tegerdine, William James, Cpl.
223, Tibbs, John Anthony, Pte.
228, Grant, Peter, Pte.
231, Nawell, Charles Henry, Cpl.
233, Wiltshire, Edgar Albert, Pte.
312, Davies, William Howard, Pte.
341, McGrath, Samuel, L/Cpl.
342, Griffiths, Stanley Gordon, Pte.
343, Pimm, Frederick, Pte.
345, Broad, Thomas Leslie Cecil, Pte.
346, Parker, Howard Charles, Sgt.
347, Smith, Harry, Pte.
348, Boyes, William Edward, Pte.
350, Meehan, Michael, Pte.
353, Wright, Thomas, Pte.
357, Skinner, John Russell, L/Cpl.
358, Minchin, Basil James, Pte.
359, Sullivan, Arthur Gilbert, Pte.
360, Sperber, William, Pte.
361, McKenzie, James Patterson, L/Cpl.

16th INFANTRY BATTALION—NOMINAL ROLL—continued.

"A" Company—continued.

- 364, Browning, William, Pte.
- 365, Murphy, Richard, Pte.
- 370, Baker, Alexander John, Pte.
- 371, McInerney, John Francis, Pte.
- 372, Knight, Peter, Pte.
- 377, Kenny, Patrick John, Pte.
- 378, Fielder, Frederick William, Pte.
- 380, Hutchings, William Harry, Pte.
- 381, Vernon, George John, Pte.
- 444, Taylor, John, Pte.
- 460, Sedgwick, Charles William, Pte.
- 488, Hurley, Robert, Pte.
- 513, Carr, Thomas John, Pte.
- 514, Window, Allan, Pte.
- 515, Godden, William John, Pte.
- 516, Joyce, Edward William, Pte.
- 517, Patrick, Walter John Wardrop, Pte.
- 518, Dowson, Michael, Pte.
- 520, O'Connor, Philip Everett, Pte.
- 521, Lugar, Albert William, Pte.
- 522, Griffiths, William, Pte.
- 523, Cook, Thomas John, Pte.
- 525, Smith, Samuel, Pte.
- 528, Moreton, Godfrey Francis Gilles, Colour-Sergeant.
- 529, Hadfield, Ralph Begbie, Pte.
- 530, Flanagan, Michael, Pte.
- 531, Short, James, Pte.
- 537, King, George, Pte.
- 541, Crouch, Henry Thomas, Sgt.
- 557, Boundy, Albert Henry, Pte.
- 558, Brown, Roy Rees Broughton, Pte.
- 560, Hogg, John, Cpl.
- 562, McNally, Sylvester Lawrence, Pte.
- 563, Norris, Walter Herbert, Pte.
- 564, Reid, Thomas, Pte.
- 565, Tindal, William Lewis, Pte.
- 566, Lewis, Archie Gordon, Pte.
- 567, Choat, Percy Roy, Pte.
- 603, Bicket, Robert, Pte.
- 642, Braithwaite, Leslie Francis, Pte.
- 643, Dolley, Stanley Hugh Gaspard, Pte.
- 647, Colgate, John Robert, Pte.
- 648, Frampton, Walter John, L/Sgt.
- 664, Russell, Charles Colin, Pte.
- 667, Ivison, John, Pte.
- 670, Underwood, Reginald, Pte.
- 671, Murray, John Henry, Pte.
- 672, Watson, Sydney, Pte.
- 673, Thompson, John Alfred, Pte.
- 674, Fink, Gordon, Pte.

"A" Company—continued.

- 678, Halliday, Percy Francis, Pte.
- 700, Parker, Francis Joseph, Pte.
- 701, Lowe, Edward, Pte.
- 715, Thomas, Allan Leslie, Pte.
- 729, Pavitt, George, Pte.
- 730, Newick, William, Pte.
- 731, Batty, William Kingsley, Pte.
- 732, Sands, William Joseph, Pte.
- 733, Jones, James Hugh, Pte.
- 734, O'Hare, Michael, Pte.
- 735, Cornelius, William Edward, Pte.
- 736, Smith, Albert, Pte.
- 737, Davis, William, Pte.
- 738, Edwards, Charles, Cpl.
- 743, McQuade, Charles, Pte.
- 745, Luetchford, Donovan Frank, Pte.
- 751, Heiler, Robert, Pte.
- Chabrel, Edwin Gilbert, Pte.

"B" Company.

- Margolin, Eliazar Lazar, Captain.
- Southern, Harold Alfred, Lieutenant.
- Geddes, Cyril Arthur, Lieutenant.
- 1, Cannell, Reginald Ramsey, Cpl.
- 29, Sparrow, Frederick William, Pte.
- 42, Stark, Alexander Kennedy, Sgt.
- 49, Ahearne, Charles, Pte.
- 50, Atkins, Arthur Charles, Pte.
- 51, Bates, Wilfred Froud, Pte.
- 52, Burrows, William, Pte.
- 53, Bennett, William, Pte.
- 54, Clyde, Frederick, Pte.
- 61, Calderwood, Neil, Sgt.
- 63, Downey, Ernest Francis, Pte.
- 64, Gleeson, John Bernard, Pte.
- 65, George, Russell Conan, Pte.
- 66, Hall, John Richard, Pte.
- 73, Hodges, Alfred John, Pte.
- 75, Hitchcock, Thomas Alfred, Pte.
- 76, Ibbotson, Leslie Montagu, Pte.
- 77, Mack, William, Pte.
- 78, Martin, George Henry, Pte.
- 83, Pennells, Charles Percy, Pte.
- 86, Townshend, Ernest Richard, Pte.
- 87, Schofield, Thomas Edward, Pte.
- 88, Phease, Reginald Arthur, Pte.
- 89, Andrews, Ernest Lancelot, Sgt.
- 96, Bagiean, Alexander, Pte.
- 97, Benns, Philip Christopher, Pte.
- 98, Carroll, Robert, Pte.

16th INFANTRY BATTALION—NOMINAL ROLL—*continued.*

"B" Company—*continued.*

- 99, Clark, John Carlton, Pte.
- 106, Hollis, Gordon, Cpl.
- 107, Howcroft, Robert, Pte.
- 108, Kirk, James, Pte.
- 109, Mahoney, Lawrence, Pte.
- 110, McKenna, Patrick, Pte.
- 111, Pretty, Frederick Victor, Pte.
- 119, Radosevich, George, Pte.
- 120, Reid, William Edward, Pte.
- 121, Scott, Frederick William, Pte.
- 123, Smith, Harvey, L/Cpl.
- 129, Waddell, Harry Bryson, Pte.
- 131, Young, George, Pte.
- 134, Jilly, Oscar, Colour-Sergeant.
- 142, Brown, Robert Melbourne, Pte.
- 143, Brockman, Frederick Locke, Pte.
- 144, Capps, Arthur, Cpl.
- 151, Hall, Thomas James, Pte.
- 152, Hundley, Walter, L/Sgt.
- 153, Iggleden, Henry Ernest, Pte.
- 160, Lewis, Alexander, Pte.
- 162, Lee, George, Pte.
- 163, Martin, George, Pte.
- 174, Peel, James, Pte.
- 176, Watts, Harold, Pte.
- 183, Walker, George, Pte.
- 184, Wooltorton, Harold Samuel, Pte.
- 187, Hogan, John Patrick, Pte.
- 240, Burnett, Allan, Arm. Cpl.
- 241, Briand, Leon Jean Louise, Pte.
- 306, Webb, James, Pte.
- 314, Clarke, Harry Charles, Pte.
- 321, Orchard, Geoffrey Duncan, O.R. Sgt.
- 324, Roberts, Edward, Pte.
- 383, Sweeney, Henry Mitchell, Pte.
- 384, Edwards, Alfred Outtrim, Pte.
- 385, Bell, Edward James, Pte.
- 386, Plunkett, George, Pte.
- 387, Carter, William, Pte.
- 391, Munro, Walter Hill, Pte.
- 394, Salter, Robert Melville, Pte.
- 395, Massey, Francis Ernest, Pte.
- 396, Habblett, Harold, Pte.
- 397, Deadman, Percival, Pte.
- 401, Munn, Altan Shepherd, Cpl.
- 427, Prior, Richard John, Pte.
- 431, Terry, Norman Leonard, Pte.
- 453, Faulds, Malcolm, Pte.
- 454, Moulton, Richard Ralph, Pte.
- 457, Bird, William, Pte.
- 462, Carter, William Percy John, Pte.
- 468, Wilson, William, Pte.
- 474, Webster, Harry, Pte.
- 484, Parsons, William, Pte.

"B" Company—*continued.*

- 489, Dolla, Carl, Pte.
- 490, Forbes, Alexander, Pte.
- 494, O'Shea, Patrick William, Pte.
- 511, Dawson, Martin Russell McDonald, Pte.
- 538, Court, William John, Pte.
- 545, Thomas, Daniel, Pte.
- 547, Hair, Edward Albert, Pte.
- 549, Jackson, James, Pte.
- 552, Nairn, Archibald, Pte.
- 553, Young, Harold Jesse, Pte.
- 596, Smith, James, Sergeant-Cook.
- 605, Smith, Frank Charles, Sgt.
- 607, Moody, Frederick, Pte.
- 608, Farrell, Thomas Ince, Pte.
- 609, Sheridan, Keith, Pte.
- 611, Beattie, Andrew, Pte.
- 613, Scott, David, Pte.
- 614, Meacock, Frederick Fisher, Pte.
- 621, Bruce, John Henry, Pte.
- 622, Collins, Frank Harcourt, Pte.
- 623, Gibbons, Clarence Gordon, Pte.
- 624, Hartley, John, Pte.
- 625, Holdsworth, Ernest Brook, Pte.
- 626, Hornsby, Roderick, Pte.
- 627, Jones, William, Pte.
- 629, Lovelock, James, Pte.
- 630, Police, William, Pte.
- 631, Smart, Henry, Pte.
- 633, White, Robert, Pte.
- 636, Murray, Hugh, Sgt.
- 639, Kent, Arthur, Pte.
- 675, Gray, Charles Thomas, Pte.
- 676, Smith, Sidney Leslie, Pte.
- 677, Hummerston, Horace Stanley, Pte.
- 681, Jackson, Enoch, Pte.
- 682, Riordan, Michael Alas Hoare Patrick, Sgt.
- 684, Brennan, Ernest George, Sigr.
- 708, Tunewell, Steve Upton, Sgt.-Cook.
- 709, Laming, Charles William, Cpl.
- 720, Applequist, Frank, Pte.
- 721, Stuchbury, Cyril, Pte.
- 740, Nicholls, Henry Stephen, Pte.
- 748, Bateman, William Thomas, Pte.
- 1104, Turner, William, Pte.
- Williams, Robert Stephen, Q.M.S.
- Emmett, Verner Alan, R.S.M.

"C" Company.

- Townshend, Samuel Edward, Captain.
- Durston, Henry Norman, Lieutenant.
- Blyth, Robert Balmain, 2nd Lieut.

16th INFANTRY BATTALION—NOMINAL ROLL—continued.

"C" Company—continued.

- 8, Atkinson, Albert, Pte.
- 9, Bell, Edgar Watson, Pte.
- 12, Bush, Henry William, Colour-Sergeant.
- 19, Bleakley, James, Pte.
- 20, Barker, Jack, Pte.
- 22, Clegg, Herbert Wallace, Pte.
- 24, Courtney, John Patrick, Pte.
- 25, Cordingley, Harold Austin, Pte.
- 31, Carlsen, Sage, Pte.
- 32, Crompton, William Merry, Pte.
- 34, Cadwallader, William George, Pte.
- 36, Dunstan, William Joseph, Pte.
- 43, Donaldson, Robert Henry, Pte.
- 45, Davies, Frank, Pte.
- 46, Daniels, Harry, Pte.
- 48, Edwards, William, Sgt.
- 55, Fairbeard, Charles Henry, Pte.
- 58, Fereday, Daniel, Pte.
- 59, Gipp, George, Pte.
- 60, Gill, Albert, Pte.
- 67, Hannigan, John, Pte.
- 68, Hall, William Douglas, Pte.
- 69, Hume, James, Pte.
- 70, Henley, Henry, Pte.
- 72, Kelly, Norman Harold, Pte.
- 79, Kaye, Wilfred, Pte.
- 80, Kelman, James, Pte.
- 81, Lewis, Walter Kenneth, Pte.
- 82, Lenegan, Clifford, Cpl.
- 83, Litton, Frederick, Pte.
- 84, Monaghan, Patrick, Pte.
- 90, Marshall, Victor Henry, Pte.
- 91, Mead, Jack, Pte.
- 92, Michael, William, Pte.
- 93, Moorehouse, Ernest William, Pte.
- 100, Harrison, Philip Harry, Pte.
- 102, Matthews, Eric Lancelot, Pte.
- 104, Marks, William Ernest, Cpl.
- 105, Mackesey, Lawrence, Bugler.
- 112, McDonald, John Ronald, Pte.
- 113, McCarry, William Francis Stevenson, Pte.
- 114, Orr, Wallace, Pte.
- 117, O'Mara, Patrick John, Pte.
- 125, Phillips, Douglas Charles, Pte.
- 126, Pearce, Leslie Trewelyn, Pte.
- 128, Robertson, George, Pte.
- 136, Richards, Gilbert, Pte.
- 137, Singleton, John, Pte.
- 138, Shaw, William Robert, Pte.
- 139, Sharpe, George, Pte.
- 140, Bradley, Henry Joseph, Pte.
- 141, Briers, Patrick Norman, Pte.
- 146, Smith, Edward, Pte.
- 147, Stewart, Herbert John, Pte.

"C" Company—continued.

- 148, Sullivan, Thomas, Sgt.
- 154, Scott, John Sydney, Pte.
- 155, Toon, Herbert Choice, Pte.
- 156, Volukavitz, Kazinar, Pte.
- 157, Wilson, Horace Patrick, Pte.
- 158, Williams, Thomas, Pte.
- 159, White, Thomas Wood, Pte.
- 166, Wylde, Herbert William, Pte.
- 167, Wheeler, Rex, Pte.
- 168, Wheeler, Ralph, Pte.
- 169, Winch, Albert Charles, Pte.
- 175, Smith, William, Pte.
- 182, Fitzpatrick, Henry Francis, Pte.
- 207, Mace, George, Pte.
- 229, Lear, Albert Frederick, Pte.
- 323, Power, Bertie, Pte.
- 331, Hatcher, Frank John, Pte.
- 344, Paull, Peter Raphael, Sgt.
- 393, Kent, William Cyril, Pte.
- 405, McWhinney, George, Pte.
- 407, Ogden, Errol Charles, Pte.
- 408, Rawlinson, Frederick, Pte.
- 409, Jones, William, Pte.
- 410, Hitch, Albert George John, Pte.
- 411, Dovey, Reginald Walker, Pte.
- 412, Cepkonski, Charles, Pte.
- 413, Liddington, George William, Driver, transport.
- 414, White, John Wesley, Pte.
- 415, Sudlow, Geoffry Charles, Pte.
- 417, Wallis, Leslie, Pte.
- 419, Walton, Michael, Cpl.
- 420, Chamberlain, Harold, Pte.
- 422, McCarthy, Lawrence, Pte.
- 425, Sweeney, Arthur Brier, Sgt.
- 442, Ashby, David, Pte.
- 480, Adams, John, Pte.
- 504, Eccles, Archibald, Pte.
- 505, Pagelson, Alfred Percy, Bugler
- 507, Lushington, Reginald Francis, Pte.
- 533, Thorpe, James, Transport dvr.
- 534, Holland Reginald Wilfred, Transport driver.
- 543, Gilbert, George Alexander, Pte.
- 556, Hawkins, Harold Oliver, Pte.
- 610, Morgan, Frederick William, Pte.
- 615, Gale, George, Pte.
- 620, May, Robert, Pte.
- 634, Silas, Ellis, Pte.
- 638, Slade, Harold George, Pte.
- 640, Cook, Hugh John, Sgt.
- 683, Lynes, William James Dalton, Pte.
- 706, Hall, John William, Pte.
- 708, Hough, George, Cpl.

THE OLD SIXTEENTH.

16th INFANTRY BATTALION—NOMINAL ROLL—*continued*.

"C" Company—*continued*.

710, Ivison, James, Pte.
711, McFarlane, Thomas, Pte.
712, Inglis, Andrew, Pte.
714, Sampson, William, Pte.
741, Richardson, Reginald Horace, Pte.
746, Wallace, Charles, Pte.
747, Shaw, Archibald Owen, Pte.
749, McGrath, Michael, Pte.
750, Barker, William, Pte.
755, Larkin, Hewey, Pte.
756, Lailey, John Charles, Driver.
757, Jones, Harry, Pte.
758, Evans, Sydney Charles Harwood, Pte.
759, Amos, Clarence Ewtan, Pte.
760, Archer, Edward, Pte.
761, Williams, David Victor John, Pte.
762, Rose, Frank, Pte.

"D" Company.

Carter, Francis Bird, Captain.
Curlewis, Gordon Levason, Lt.
Mountain, Arthur Henry Tarres, Lt.
101, Platt, James William, Pte.
145, Carse, Arthur Ronald Mackintosh, Pte.
170, Black, Percy, L/Cpl.
234, Affleck, William Thomas, Pte.
235, Airy, Reginald, Driver.
236, Adams, Spencer Hamp, Sgt.
238, Aldred, Herbert Wright, Pte.
243, Barnes, Robinson, Colour-Sgt.
244, Clark, William Alexander, Pte.
247, Clark, William John, Cpl.
248, Collins, John, Pte.
250, Comery, Francis Edward, Pte.
251, Crowley, John, Pte.
252, Dixon, Alexander, Pte.
253, Davenport, John Allen, Pte.
255, Elliott, Douglas Robert, Pte.
257, Eastham, William, Pte.
259, Foster, Walter Fred, Pte.
261, Garwood, Claude, Pte.
262, Graham, Thomas Watson, Pte.
264, Gray, Mervyn William, Pte.
266, Goss, Gerald Harry, Cpl.
267, Hainsworth, Frederick William, Pte.
268, Hojem, Lauritz, Pte.
269, Hall, Phillip, Pte.
271, Harvey, Ernest, Sgt.
272, Innes, James Alexander, Pte.
273, Job, Percival John, Pte.

"D" Company—*continued*.

274, Jensen, Karl Alfred, Pte.
277, Kettle, Edwin Francis, Pte.
279, Loughton, William, Pte.
280, Mouton, Walter Beaumont, Pte.
281, Maunder, Frank, Pte.
282, Miller, James Edgar, Pte.
283, Muir, Rollo, Pte.
284, Maddocks, Alfred, Pte.
286, Mack, William Alfred, Pte.
287, Nelson, William, Bugler.
288, Parrott, Lionel Eric, Pte.
289, Plater, George Baldwin, Pte.
290, Plummer, Edward, Pte.
291, Pullen, William Arthur, Pte.
293, Rennie, John, Cpl.
294, Ricci, Louis, Pte.
295, Rieusset, William Francis, Pte.
297, Skinner, Robert, Pte.
298, Sly, Arthur, Pte.
299, Sheridan, Patrick Daniel, Pte.
300, Smith, Stanley Brown, Pte.
302, Thompson, Thomas, Pte.
303, Thomlinson, George William, Pte.
304, Tyrrell, Fred., Pte.
305, Watson, Frank Wentworth, Cpl.
307, Waugh, William Edward, L/Cpl.
308, Webb, Francis Russell, Pte.
315, Murray, Henry William, Pte.
318, Maxwell, David, Pte.
319, McMillan, Jack, Pte.
320, Noble, Thomas Arthur, Pte.
325, Smalls, Michael, Pte.
326, Davies, William James, Pte.
327, Smith, Percy Henderson, Pte.
328, McDonald, Richard, Pte.
330, Hatcher, Clifford, Pte.
332, Vince, William Frederick John, Sgt.
334, Bell, Willoughby George, L/Cpl.
335, Furlong, Alfred Herbert, Pte.
337, Cumming, Redmond Harry Owen, L/Cpl.
338, Higgins, Patrick, Pte.
339, Sykes, Herbert James, L/Cpl.
340, Sykes, Reginald, Pte.
352, Thorne, Henry, Pte.
366, McLeod, Albert, Pte.
367, Campbell, Henry Alexander, Pte.
375, Grieveson, Peter, Cpl.
418, Tree, Arthur Riverley, Pte.
433, Ives, Leonard, Pte.
447, Dorrington, Herbert William, Pte.

THE OLD SIXTEENTH.

16th INFANTRY BATTALION—NOMINAL ROLL—continued.

"D" Company—continued.

458, Baker, Roy, Pte.
472, Annakin, Randolph, Pte.
475, Kelley, Charles Henry, Pte.
485, Melican, Thomas Pembroke, Pte.
500, Turner, John Reginald Hartley, Pte.
502, Thomas, Albert Whiteway, Pte.
503, Hicks, Frederick, Pte.
535, Webb, Edwin, Pte.
539, Lawrence, Henry, Pte.
544, Merrick, Norman William, Pte.
550, Kitchener, Frederick George, Pte.
568, Ashton, John, Pte.
571, Richond, Percy James, Pte.
617, O'Brien, Patrick, Pte.
619, Fawkes, Richard Thomas, Pte.
637, Rowley, William Ronald Leslie, Pte.
645, Burton, Harry, Driver.
650, Ball, George, Pte.
651, Boddy, Herbert, Driver.
652, Clues, Hubert Clement, Pte.
653, Cumming, Eric, Pte.
654, Dunkley, Arthur, Pte.
656, Hart, William, Pte.
657, Hiscox, Alfred John, Pte.
659, Mullane, William Edward, Pte.
660, Mumby, Thomas, Pte.
661, Peat, Leonard Hugh, Pte.
662, McLoskey, Clarence Lewis, Pte.
663, Ford, Arthur, Cpl.
688, Troy, Martin John, Pte.
689, Allan, William, L/Cpl.
690, Denholm, John Hughes, Pte.
691, Chase, Richard Henry, Pte.
692, James, Ernest John, Pte.
693, Gidney, Horatio, Pte.
694, Smith, William Thomas, Pte.
695, Rowe, George Thornton, Pte.
696, Manns, Thomas Henley, Pte.
697, Cloutt, John Beversham, Pte.
704, Demel, George Blake, Sgt.
705, George Harold, Pte.
724, Jack, John, Pte.
725, Matson, Thomas, Pte.
726, Lee, Alfred Patrick Henry, Pte.
727, Peter, Robert, Pte.
728, Stevens, George, Pte.
763, Naughton, Joseph Edward, Pte.
764, Robertson, Percy William, Pte.
765, Ryan, Henry John James, Pte.

"E" Company.

Miller, James, Captain.
2, Bradshaw, Alfred Edward, Pte.
3, Burton, Stephen Matthews, Pte.
4, Corbett, Walter James, Pte.
5, Curlewis, George Campbell, Cpl.
6, Curlewis, Selwyn Lord, L/Cpl.
14, Duncan, George William, Pte.
16, Foster, Alfred Bertie, Pte.
17, Foster, Frederick Bernard, Pte.
18, Giles, William Herbert, Pte.
26, Jonas, Charles, Pte.
27, Menzies, David, L/Cpl.
28, Murphy, Henry Blaney, Pte.
30, Smith, Richard, Pte.
38, Torrence, Robert, Pte.
39, Treasure, Leo, Pte.
40, Wells, William Henry John, Driver.
41, Wilkinson, Clarence William Anstruther, Pte.
74, Henry, William Thomas, Pte.
101, Hemmings, Benjamin, L/Cpl.
130, Muncaster, Edward Ferdinand, Driver.
165, McCallum, Arthur Edward, Pte.
190, Lamb, Joseph, Pte.
205, Butler, Albert Walker, Pte.
211, Moore, George Douglas, L/Cpl.
217, Phillips, John Gibbons, L/Cpl.
227, Breen, John, L/Cpl.
232, Roney, Charles George William, Driver.
313, Culling, John William, Pte.
317, McKinnon, Alexander John, Driver.
322, Pyke, Henry Bertram, Cpl.
349, Hill, Frederick James, Pte.
351, Rowe, Ernest Edward, Pte.
354, Leeder, Henry George, Pte.
362, Pantall, Leonard, Pte.
363, Ralph, Henry Thomas, Pte.
374, Karnaghan, James George, Pte.
379, Morgan, Edgar Eynon, Pte.
389, Haskett, Thomas Edward, Pte.
390, Silvester, William, Driver.
392, Silvester, Frank, Private.
399, White, Walter Thomas, Pte.
400, Whittington, Aubrey Jesse, Pte.
402, Branley, Arthur Joseph Lavery, Pte.
432, Gerhard, Carl, Sgt.
434, Head, Edward, Pte.
436, Howard, Frank Rodney, Pte.
437, Lindell, Ernest, Pte.
439, Wildash, John, Pte.
440, Tier, Arthur, Pte.

16th INFANTRY BATTALION—NOMINAL ROLL—continued.

"E" Company—continued.

441, Geary, John Govett, Driver.
443, Mortimer, Harry Robert, Pte.
445, Matthews, John, L/Cpl.
449, Cox, Ernest Sydney, Pte.
450, Thompson, George William, Driver.
451, Tweedie, Wallace Arthur, Pte.
452, Tweedie, Leslie, Pte.
455, Smith, Herbert, Sgt.
456, Woods, Albert John, Pte.
464, Sandstrom, Swen Addvin, Cpl.
466, Cork, George Albert, Pte.
469, Noble, Thomas Alfred, Pte.
470, McSullea, William John, Pte.
471, Atkinson, Leonard Hugh, Drv.
473, Thorpe, John, Pte.
476, Malin, Lloyd Herbert, Pte.
477, Hewson, William George, Pte.
479, Jordan, Frederick, Pte.
483, Marriott, Alfred, Pte.
486, Saul, James, Pte.
487, Carless, George William, Pte.
492, Young, Oliver Charles, Bugler.
496, Smith, Henry, Pte.
497, Reynolds, William, Pte.
498, Taylor, Thomas, Pte.
499, Prue, William Webster, Pte.
512, Brooks, William Edward, Pte.
532, Delacour, Lawrence Louis, L/Sgt.
548, Jackson, Albert George, Pte.
546, Evans, John David, Signaller.
551, McPherson, James, Sgt.
569, Arniott, Patrick August, Pte.
570, Barton, Horace Albert, Pte.
572, Coward, Thomas Roy, Pte.
575, Frappell, Jack, Pte.
576, Geggie, William Mark, Pte.
578, Parnell, Rex, Pte.
579, Pitchford, William, Pte.
581, Sorenson, Peter, Pte.
582, Woolmington, William James, Pte.
586, Noon, Henry Dodson, Pte.
588, Hollingdale, Harry Edgar, Pte.
589, Cousins, William John, Pte.
590, Bolton, Henry, Pte.
591, Eames, Edward, Pte.
592, Fraser, William Henry, Pte.
593, Seager, Howard Cecil, Pte.
594, Kite, Frederick George, Pte.
595, Heasman, Albert, Pte.
597, Saunders, Thomas, Pte.
598, O'Grady, John, Pte.
599, Megaw, James, Pte.
600, Parker, Frederick John, Pte.
601, Bradley, George Stewart, Pte
602, Carlson, George Benjamin, Pte

"E" Company—continued.

612, Collins, William Ernest, Colour-Sgt.
635, Morrissey, William, Driver.
649, Stenson, Walter, Driver.
665, McDonald, John, Pte.
666, Nestor, Robert John, Bugler.
685, Ellis, Harry, Cpl.
686, Jewell, Charles Alfred, Driver.
687, Gardiner, Amos Jesse, Driver.
699, Murray, John Joseph, Pte.
703, Philp, David, Cpl.
716, Moor, Charles Basil, Pte.
717, Moor, Frank Cruyet, Pte.
718, Macpherson, David Campbell, Pte.
719, Howard, Cecil John, Pte.
722, Bartlett, Edgar Ashby, Pte.
723, Huffam, Lawrence, Driver.
739, Bugden, Stanley, Pte.
763, Johns, William Albert, Pte.
Knight, Edwin Theodore, Lt.

"F" Company.

Baker, Edgar Kendall, Major.
Heming, Leslie Duncan, Lieut.
Kerr, William Buchanan, 2nd Lieut.
1000, Aikman, Robert Andrew, Pte.
1001, Alldritt, Arthur, Pte.
1002, Archer, Colin, Pte.
1003, Bailey, Arthur, Pte.
1004, Barden, John, Cpl.
1005, Baynes, John Joseph, Pte.
1006, Beck, Augustus Harold, Pte.
1008, Boehm, Theodore Ewald Gerhard, Pte.
1009, Bray, Percival Beaumont, Pte.
1010, Broadbent, Victor, Pte.
1011, Bruer, Lionel Gregory, Pte.
1012, Bullock, Alfred Herbert, L/Cpl.
1015, Carter, John Edward, Pte.
1016, Chadwick, Alfred, Pte.
1017, Charlton, Alfred Williams, Pte.
1018, Clark, Augustian Francis, Pte.
1019, Clark, William Albert, Pte. (Signaller).
1020, Clayton, Frederick, Pte.
1021, Cook, Lance Edward, Pte.
1023, Cowie, James, Pte.
1024, Craig, William Henry, Pte.
1025, Crawford, Ronald, Pte.
1026, Crook, William Charles, Pte.
1027, Crowther, Kenneth Singleton, Pte.
1028, Curnow, William, Pte.
1029, Cutts, Lawrence Henry, L/Cpl.

16th INFANTRY BATTALION—NOMINAL ROLL—continued.

"F" Company—continued.

1030, Daly, Gordon, Pte.
1031, Davis, George, Pte.
1032, Davis, Harry Herbert, Pte.
1033, Dugan, Ernest Sydney, Pte.
1034, Eden, Alfred, Pte.
1035, Edge, Arthur, Colour-Sgt.
1036, Franklin, James Leonard, Pte.
1037, George, Theodore Frederick, Pte.
1038, Gladstonbury, Sefton Ridley, Pte.
1039, Goldie, Edward, Pte.
1040, Greenham, William Frederick, Sgt.
1041, Hallam, Ainsley, Pte.
1042, Halliday, William John, Pte.
1043, Hart, Leonard Charles, Pte.
1044, Hartnett, Joseph George, Dvr.
1045, Harris, Willie, Pte.
1046, Horsman, Henry Alfred, Pte.
1047, Howie, Alexander Stuart, Pte.
1049, Ind, Milton Howard, Pte.
1050, Ingham, John William, Pte.
1051, James, Edward John Gordon, Pte.
1052, Jennings, Hubert Roy, Pte.
1053, Jolley, Leslie Garnet, Pte.
1054, Joyner, Colin Elder, L/Sgt.
1055, Kalpaktchieff, John Nicholas, Pte.
1056, Kenny, Reginald Thomas, Pte.
1057, Larking, Martin, Pte.
1058, Lodge, Gerald, Pte.
1060, MacGowan, Bernard Robert Shields, Pte.
1063, McInnes, Roy Randell, Pte.
1064, McMurray, Leopold James, Cpl.
1065, McRae, John Archibald, Sgt.
1066, Miller, Arthur, Pte.
1067, Miller, Donovan James, Pte.
1068, Mitchell, Henry Albert Clifford, Sgt.
1069, Munks, Melville Bert, Pte.
1070, Munden, Frank Charles, Pte.
1071, Munks, Charles William Alfred, Pte.
1072, Olds, Joseph, Pte.
1073, O'Leary, David Patrick, Pte.
1074, O'Neil, John James, Pte.
1075, Oswald, Howard, Pte.
1076, Page, William James, Pte.
1080, Pope, Albert Henry, Pte.
1082, Priest, Richard Thomas Hewitt, Pte.
1083, Robertson, James, Pte.
1084, Reed, Stuart George, Signaller.
1085, Richards, Francis Percival, Pte.
1086, Rogan, Selwyn James, Pte.

"F" Company—continued.

1087, Sage, Arthur, Pte.
1088, Scattergood, Harold Thomas, Pte.
1089, Shepley, Thomas Alan, Cpl.
1090, Shurwen, Harold, Pte.
1091, Simmonds, Ernest Henry, Pte.
1092, Simons, Benjamin Quartermain, Pte.
1093, Simpson, Arthur Ernest, Pte.
1094, Simpson, Arthur Francis, Pte.
1095, Simpson, John, Pte.
1096, Solomon, Albert, Cpl.
1097, Stopani, William Leslie, Cpl.
1098, Stow, Donald Jefferson, Pte.
1099, Talbot, George Edward, L/Cpl.
1100, Till, James Victor, Pte.
1101, Tonkin, Frederick, Pte.
1102, Trevaskis, Thomas Henry, Pte.
1103, Trowbridge, Frank, Pte.
1106, Walsh, James, Pte.
1107, Webbing, Darby, Pte.
1108, Whelan, Joseph Harold, Pte.
1109, Williams, Albert Thomas, Pte.
1110, Woods, Robert, Pte.
1111, Woodhead, Robert George, Pte.
1113, Young, Ernest Walter, Pte.
1114, Young, George, Pte.
1115, Burdett, John, Bugler.
1350, Roberts, Alexander Francis Dawe, Cpl.
1351, Day, Essington, Pte.
1352, Morrison, Harold George, Pte.
1353, Miller, Edward John, Driver.
1354, Marshall, Albert Clarence, Pte.
1358, Glover, William Allen, Pte.
1359, Kennedy, Francis John, Pte.
1360, Hopkins, Horatio Reginald, Pte.
1371, Starkey, Arthur, Pte.
1372, Cooper, Frank Enoe, Pte.
1374, Austin, Charlie, Pte.
1375, Cameron, Samuel, Pte.
Moore, John, Pte.

"G" Company.

Gladman, Frank Barnes, Lieutenant.
Langsford, John Kingsley, Lieut.
Burton, Harry James, Lieut.
1117, Asher, Francis Alexander, Pte.
1118, Akehurst, Charles, Pte.
1119, Alderson, Lancelot Reginald, Sgt.
1120, Arnold, John Peter, L/Cpl.
1122, Bowditch, Reginald John, Sgt.
1123, Bavistock, Harold, Pte.

THE OLD SIXTEENTH 223

16th INFANTRY BATTALION—NOMINAL ROLL—*continued*.

"G" Company—*continued*.
1124, Brusnahan, Patrick John, Pte.
1125, Branford, James Alfred, Pte.
1126, Bates, Henry Leo, Pte.
1127, Blows, Joseph, Sgt.
1128, Birtles, Earnest, Cpl.
1129, Blight, James Henry, Pte.
1130, Bitmead, John, Pte.
1131, Bulling, Edgar Stephen, Pte.
1132, Blatchford, William George, Pte.
1133, Brackenridge, George, Driver.
1134, Bland, George, Signaller.
1135, Carter, Frederick George Walters, Pte.
1138, Cooper, Percy Harold, Pte.
1139, Connell, James, Pte.
1140, Cooper, Jack, Pte.
1141, Craigie, Leslie Thomas, Cpl.
1142, Collins, Leo. Paul, Pte.
1143, Cameron, Norman Seymour, Pte.
1144, Cornwall, Clifford Gordon, Pte.
1145, Casey, Michael, Pte.
1146, Cole, Charles William, Pte.
1147, Crook, Ernest Lloyd, Pte.
1148, Croger, James Augustus, Pte.
1149, Delinecorte, Francis Henry William, Pioneer.
1150, Davies, Henry Durham, Pte.
1151, Draper, William, Pte.
1153, Dunlop, John Edgar, Pte.
1154, Davis, John, Pte.
1155, Day, Sylvester Sydney, L/Cpl.
1156, Dudley, Clarence Merchison, Pte.
1157, Earl, George, Pte.
1158, Earl, James, S/B.
1159, Erikson, John Werner, Pte.
1160, Evans, Thomas Harry Skermer, Bugler.
1161, Field, Arthur, Pte.
1162, Fuller, James Albert, Pte.
1164, Francis, Paul Maslie, Pte.
1165, Giles, Dudley Frederic Lionel, Pte.
1166, Gilbert, William, Pte.
1167, Gibson, James Raymond, Pte.
1168, Hammond, Arthur Charles, Pte.
1169, Harvey, Lionel William, Pte.
1170, Henning, Benno Oscar, Pte.
1171, Hapgood, George Edward, Pte.
1172, Harris, Walter Charles, Pte.
1173, Higgins, Frank, Pte.
1174, Hobbs, William Oliver, Pte.
1175, Hughes, Robert, Pte.
1176, Hann, Sterling Charles, Pte.
1178, Hutchison, John, Pte.
1179, Hogben, Richard Hubert, Sgt.

"G" Company—*continued*.
1181, Johncock, John Austin Tyrrell, Pte.
1182, Jenetzky, William Ernest, Pte.
1183, Jenkins, Philip, Pte.
1184, Johnston, Harold John, Cpl.
1185, Kyloh, Percy William, Pte.
1186, Kennedy, William, Pte.
1187, Luck, Frederick William Benjamin, Pte.
1188, Liddy, James, Pte.
1192, McClusky, Henry, Pte.
1193, McMaster, John Charles, Pte.
1194, McGough, Thomas John, Pte.
1195, Munroe, Frank, Colour-Sgt.
1196, McDonald, Alexander Stirling, Pte.
1197, Matt, Charles Ernest, Pte.
1198, Matt, William George, Pte.
1200, O'Gorman, Anselin, Pte.
1201, Peters, Edward, Pte.
1202, Peters, Roy, Pte.
1203, Phillips, William, Pte.
1204, Roper, Harry Ernest, L/Cpl.
1205, Robertson, Percy, Pte.
1206, Ross, Charles Vangelion, Pte.
1207, Randell, Roy Barrier, Pte.
1208, Russell, Vivian Arthur, Pte.
1209, Rowe, Rowland, Pte.
1210, Reppe, Charles, Pte.
1211, Robinson, Harold Glen, Pte.
1212, Stoerkel, Charles William, Sig.
1213, Saunders, Herbert William, Pte.
1214, Simpson, William, Pte.
1215, Stanyer, John Edward, Pte.
1216, Saint, Arnold Michael, L/Cpl.
1217, Sprague, James, Pte.
1219, Snow, William Arthur, Pte.
1220, Townsend, Fred, Pte.
1221, Turner, Harry Victor, Pte.
1222, Tilby, Henry Herbert, Pte.
1223, Usher, Jack Wilfred, Pte.
1224, Winter, John Charles, Pte.
1225, Williams, David John, Pte.
1226, Wylie, Roy, Pte.
1227, Whitehead, Robert, Pte.
1230, Williams, Bertie, L/Cpl.
1231, Young, William, Pte.
1333, Taylor, Frederick George, Pay Cpl.
1357, Wright, Alfred, Pte.
1361, O'Neil, Charles, Pte.
1362, Watts, Norman Roy, Pte.
1363, Berry, Bryan Peirce, Pte.
1364, Bennett, Hollis Berty, Driver.
1376, Mack, George Frederick, Pte.
1377, Jones, James Henry, Pte.
1378, Coulthard, Thomas, Pte.
1369, Coverlid, James, Pte.

16th INFANTRY BATTALION—NOMINAL ROLL—*continued.*

"G" Company—*continued.*
1380, Paton, James Hart, Pte.
1381, Frost, Stuart Clifton, Pte.
1382, Healey, Harry Percival, Pte.
Park, James, Pte.

"H" Company.
Brittain, Herbert Pascoe Howard, Captain.
Bruns, Ernest Otto Alfred, Lieut.
Imlay, Alexander Peter, 2nd Lieut.
1112, Yeates, George, Pte.
1232, Allen, Archibald Robert, Pte.
1233, Allen, Henry Robert, Pte.
1234, Amey, Percy Harold, Pte.
1235, Atkins, Frederick Allen, L/Sgt.
1236, Attrill, James Benjamin, Pte.
1237, Bartley, Maurice, Pte.
1238, Barton, John Joseph, Pte.
1239, Bilney, Harry, Pte.
1240, Bozzett, Ernest Walter, Cpl.
1242, Brown, Clarence, Pte.
1243, Brown, William John, Pte.
1245, Byard, Douglas Austin, Pte.
1246, Byrt, Eugene Clarence, Pte.
1247, Calf, Henry Somerton, Pte.
1248, Calvert, Reuben, Pte.
1249, Christopher, Charles Leslie, Pte.
1250, Collins, Thomas Patrick, Pte.
1251, Cootes, William Edward, Pte.
1252, Cousens, Bertie Ernest, Pte.
1253, Cousens, Norman, Pte.
1254, Cranston, Alexander Charles, Pte.
1255, Daniel, Herbert Johnson, Pte.
1256, Devine, Henry, Pte.
1257, Detmar, Arthur August Chas., Driver.
1259, Donnelly, Patrick, Pte.
1260, Drabsh, Heinrich, Driver.
1261, Elliston, William Arnold, Pte.
1262, Elphick, Arthur Thomas, Pte.
1263, Elso, Leslie Charles Thos., Cpl.
1264, Fechner, Herman Alfred, Pte.
1265, Finch, Reginald Hales, Bugler.
1266, Fletcher, Joseph, Pte.
1267, Foster, George, Pte.
1268, Francis James, Pte.
1269, Fraser, Robert, Colour-Sgt.
1271, Fruther, Herbert Leslie, Pte.
1272, Furse, Edward James, Pte.
1273, Gabel, Benhardt Alfred, Pte.
1274, Gaghen, Christmas Harold, Pte.
1275, Gosden, Robert Patterson, Pte.
1276, Gilfoyle, Joseph Patrick, Pte.
1277, Harris, Edgar, Pte.
1278, Hembury, Albert, Pte.
1279, Hill, Francis Gordon, Pte.
1280, Hill, Stanley George, Pte.

"H" Company—*continued.*
1281, Hill, Thomas Henry, Pte.
1283, Hope, William, Sgt.
1284, Hughes, Thomas, Pte.
1285, Humphries, Frederick, Cpl.
1286, Inkster, John McRae, Pte.
1288, Jones, Thomas Walter, Pte.
1299, Kidman, George, Pte.
1290, Kingston, Allen Charles Waters, Pte.
1291, Klopp, Arthur, Pte.
1292, Kohler, William Joseph, Pte.
1293, Krummel, Oscar Otto, Pte.
1294, Lambert, William, Pte.
1295, Law, Stephen, Pte.
1296, Lawrie, Robert Hall, Pte.
1297, Leech, Alfred, Pte.
1298, Lewis, Charles Robert, Pte.
1299, Malcolm, Ernest John, Pte.
1300, Malone, Edward, Sgt.
1301, Marshall, Thomas Edgar, Pte.
1302, McDonald, Douglas, Pte.
1303, McGuinnes, William, Pte.
1304, McLeod, Frederick, L/Cpl.
1305, McLeod, Norman, L/Cpl.
1307, Milton, William Henry, Pte.
1308, Murphy, Bernard, Pte.
1309, Must, Frederick John James, Pte.
1310, Paley, Charles Gordon, Pte.
1311, Noon, Leslie Edward, Pte.
1312, Norton, William, L/Cpl.
1313, O'Brien, Peter, Pte.
1314, O'Leary, John, Pte.
1315, O'Toole, John James, Pte.
1316, Painter, Frederick John, Pte.
1317, Palmer, Ernest George, Pte.
1318, Pilane, Alfred, Pte.
1319, Polden, William, Pte.
1320, Prentice, Victor, Pte.
1321, Richmond, Wm. Henry, Pte.
1322, Robertson, David, Pte.
1323, Rodgers, Thomas, Pte.
1324, Row, Richard, Pte.
1325, Ryan, John Paul, Pte.
1326, Sandery, Edwin John, Pte.
1327, Skinner, Herbert, Pte.
1328, Sloan, Sydney Roy, Pte.
1329, Slocombe, Robert James, Pte.
1331, Smith, Harold Ryan, Pte.
1332, Stephenson, Roy Kennings, Pte.
1334, Thorp, Harold, Pte.
1335, Toombs, Allen Victor Cyril, Pte.
1336, Wallace, John, Pte.
1337, Waller, Charles Steven, Pte.
1338, Waters, Frank Albert, Pte.
1339, Watson, Spurgeon Marshall, Pte.

THE OLD SIXTEENTH.

16th INFANTRY BATTALION—NOMINAL ROLL—*continued.*

"H" Company—*continued.*

1340, Watts, Stephen Henry, Pte.
1341, Welsh, Richard Samuel, Pte.
1342, White, Albert Bowden, Pte.
1343, Whiting, George Alfred, Sgt.
1344, Williams, Leonard, Pte.
1346, Winkworth, Albert George Nolan, Pte.
1347, Woods, Frederick Frank, Cpl.
1348, Noon, Harold England, Pte.

"H" Company—*continued.*

1349, Stuart, William George Raymond, Sgt.
1365, Cathro, Frank, Pte.
1366, Forde, Roy Alexander, Pte.
1367, Kempster, Cyril James Stephen, Pte.
1368, Kemerick, William, Pte.
1369, Shorney, Arthur Burton, Pte.
1370, Taylor, Newman Wain, Pte.

1st Reinforcements.

(Embarked at Melbourne, Victoria, on H.M.A.T. A35, "Berrima," 22nd December, 1914.)

Anderson, Kiernan Leopold, 2nd Lieut.
755, Goldie, Louis Isaac, Colour-Sgt.
756, Upton, Harold Percy, Sgt.
757, McLachlan, Adam, Sgt.
759, Brown, John, Pte.
760, Nichols, Thomas John, Cpl.
761, Taylor, Robert Harold, Pte.
762, Angus, James Laurence, Pte.
763, Anderson, Alfred Albert, Pte.
764, Barr, Robert Wright, Pte.
765, Ball, Frank, Pte.
766, Bradford, Arthur Jesse George, Pte.
767, Bryan, James, Pte.
768, Bishop, Samuel Richard, Pte.
769, Barry, Ernest Francis, Pte.
770, Crews, Cecil Arthur, Pte.
771, Cousins, Gerald Napier Gordon, Pte.
772, Dorter, Philip, Pte.
773, Ellis, Charles, Pte.
774, Emery, Herbert John, Pte.
775, Gooney, James, Pte.
776, Hawes, Robert, L/Cpl.
777, Hanson, Ernest John, L/Cpl.
778, Miller, John Moffat, Pte.
779, Hutton, Alexander, Pte.
780, Hubbert, Thomas Richard, Pte.
781, Jenkins, Tom, Pte.
782, Jackson, Joseph Walter, Pte.
783, Kewley, Robert Edward, Pte.
784, Kerss, Alexander, Pte.
785, Kiely, William James, Pte.
786, Laugher, James Edward, Pte.
787, Loughman, James, Pte.
788, Howard, Norman Edward, Pte.
789, Manuell, Alexander Victor, Pte.
790, Pearson, Chas. William, Pte.
791, Parker, James, Pte.
792, Rice, Alfred Ernest, Pte.
793, Reid, George, Pte.
794, Ross, Ernest, Pte.
795, Tate, Ernest James, Pte.
796, Thomas, Joseph, Pte.
797, Veitch, William, Pte.
798, Williams, Henry Wallis, Pte.
799, Young, Cyrus Carson, Pte.
800, Harvey, Arthur John, Pte.
801, Lewis, John Clarence, Pte.
805, Down, Cecil Vernon, Cpl.
Brown, Alexander, Pte.
1385, Glazbrook, James William, Pte.
1386, Harvey, Lowan Forman, Pte.
1387, Hudson, Herbert Graythorne, Pte.
1388, Marshall, Lancelot Dale, Pte.
1389, Maley, Arthur William, Pte.
1390, Milton, Lloyd, Pte.
1391, McCabe, Hugh, Pte.
1392, Opie, Victor Allan, Pte.
1393, Paterson, William Robert Harold, Pte.
1394, Turner, Martin William, Pte.
1395, Williams, James, Pte.
1396, Addison, James, Pte.
1397, Becker, William Henry, Pte.
1398, Betton, Thomas, Pte.
1399, Burns, Joseph, Pte.
1400, Breen, Alexander, Pte.
1401, Bisset, Norman Sinclair, Pte.
1402, Blair, Reginald, Pte.
1403, Cowell, Harry Stephen, Pte.
1404, Clarke, Phillip, Pte.
1405, Collison, Ralph Victor, Pte.
1406, Curry, Alexander, Pte.
1407, Durham, Joseph Henry, Pte.
1408, Dooley, Michael, Pte.
1409, Fyfe, Hugh Brown, Pte.
1410, Forsyth, Jack Joseph, Pte.
1411, Gibbs, Stephen Leslie, Pte.
1412, George, Edwin, Pte
1413, Hill, William, Pte.
1414, Higgins, Fredrick, Pte.

16th INFANTRY BATTALION—NOMINAL ROLL—*continued*.

1st Reinforcements—continued.

1415, Holmes, Alfred Thomas, Pte.
1416, Hayes, Leslie, Pte.
1417, Holliday, John William, Pte.
1418, Hyrons, John, Pte.
1419, Maquire, John, Pte.
1420, Moody, Fred., Pte.
1421, Martini, William Henry, Pte.
1422, Morgan, Alfred, Pte.
1423, McDonald, Norman, Pte.
1424, Newsome, William, Pte.
1425, Newsome, Harry, Pte.
1426, Stephen, Frederick Arthur, Pte.
1427, Spang, Harold Howard, Pte.
1428, Thomas, Harold Ernest, Pte.
1429, Willmott, Albert Edward, Pte.
1430, Windsor, John, Pte.
1431, Webb, William Christopher, Pte.
1432, Watson, John, Pte.
1433, Ward, Hugh, Pte.
1434, Wells, Edgar, Pte.
1435, Guley, Chester, Pte.
1436, Harley, Thomas William Pratt, Cpl.
1437, Conrad, Herbert Selmar, Pte.
1438, Walker, Daniel, Pte.
1439, Harrison, Ernest Edward, Pte.
1440, Grimison, Norman Harold, Pte.
1441, Stratton, Alexander Francis, Pte.
1442, Shaw, George Aloysius, Pte.
Hower, Fred., Pte.
Jeffrey, Francis James Vickers, Pte.
Paton, James Hart, Pte.

2nd Reinforcements.

(Embarked at Melbourne, Victoria, on H.M.A.T. A46, "Clan McGillivray," 2nd February, 1915.)

1301, Atkinson, Vincent, Pte.
1302, Ball, Harold Keith, Pte.
1303, Ballantyne, David, Cpl.
1304, Banwell, William John, Pte.
1305, Bartlett, Clarence Leslie, Pte.
1306, Battye, Morter Wilkinson, Pte.
1307, Benfield, Roy William, Pte.
1308, Bishop, Lindon Reginald, Pte.
1309, Bowley, Sidney Ernest Victor, Pte.
1310, Brown, Frederick, Pte.
1311, Carmody, Matthew, Pte.
1312, Codling, Roy Nathaniel, Pte.
1314, Cornford, John Martin Ward, Pte.
1315, Cox, Josias Sinm, Pte.
1316, Dodd, Howard George, Pte.
1317, Gobell, James, Pte.
1318, Goodman, Arthur, Pte.
1319, Henderson, George, Pte.
1321, Heyer, Frederick William, Pte.
1323, Jarvis, Harold Arthur, Pte.
1324, Lewis, Harry William, Sgt.
1325, Lyons, John, Pte.
1326, McMurray, Edward James, Pte.
1327, Marshall, Thomas Edward, Pte.
1328, Marstin, Archibald, Pte.
1329, Mullins, John, Pte.
1330, Norton, Charles, Pte.
1331, Nourse, Frank Edward, Pte.
1332, Nourse, Louis Percy, Pte.
1333, Oxer, Arthur Lucas, Pte.
1334, Pike, Arthur William, Pte.
1335, Powell, Edward Archie, Pte.
1336, Shannon, Richard, Pte.
1337, Sinclair, James, Pte.
1338, Sporle, Thomas Henry, Pte.
1339, Sullivan, George Henry, Pte.
1341, Walker, James, Pte.
1342, Weeden, Edward Theodore, Pte.
1343, Williams, Percival Ernest, Pte.
1344, Wilson, George Arnold, Pte.
1345, Marsh, John Charles, Pte.
1346, Keep, Richard Sidney, Pte.
1347, Sandercock, William Edward, Pte.
1348, Connolly, Mortimer Augustine, Pte.
1350, Buse, Alfred, Pte.
1351, Dowling, Alfred James, Pte.
1403, Birrell, Rupert, Pte.
1404, Middleton, Harold Norman, Pte.
1405, Rombouts, Jacobus Johonnes, Pte.
1406, Viant, William Evans, Pte.
1407, Matthews, John Crust, Pte.

16th INFANTRY BATTALION—NOMINAL ROLL—continued.

2nd Reinforcements—continued.

(Embarked at Fremantle, Western Australia, on H.M.A.T. A50, "Itonus," 22nd February, 1915.)

Brashaw, Joseph Arthur, Lt.
1451, Ainsworth, Jack, Pte.
1452, Berry, Wilfred Henry, Pte.
1453, Bacon, Lester Sydney, Pte.
1454, Battison, Robert, Pte.
1455, Blake, John, Pte.
1456, Burks, Charles Percy, Pte.
1457, Blinman, Harold Loldie, Pte.
1458, Brashaw, Leslie, Cpl.
1459, Burnell, George Edward, Pte.
1460, Chapple, James Henry, Pte.
1461, Christie, Andrew, Pte.
1462, Corbett, Thomas William, Pte.
1463, Cowain, Charles, Pte.
1464, Chandler, Roy, Pte.
1465, Drew, Vernon, Pte.
1466, Emery, John James, Pte.
1467, Fay, John, Pte.
1468, Fraser, Arthur, Pte.
1469, Fathers, Eugene Alfred, Pte.
1470, Farrell, Ernest, Pte.
1471, Gibson, Thomas George, Pte.
1472, Godfrey, Leslie James, Pte.
1473, Ganfield, Richard John, Pte.
1474, Gardiner, Alfred Walter, Pte.
1475, Graham, Samuel, Pte.
1476, Gallagher, Archie, Pte.
1477, Healy, Martin John, Pte.
1478, Haimes, William Henry, Pte.
1479, Hames, Charles, Pte.
1480, Hammond, Wallis, Pte.
1481, Harris, Joseph Thomas, Pte.
1482, Heston, John, Pte.
1483, Harrison, Herbert, Pte.
1484, Irwin, Reginald, Pte.
1485, Irving, Harry, Pte.
1486, Jell, Charles, Pte.
1487, Johnston, Sydney Tasman, Pte.
1489, Kilminster, Errol Rutter, Pte.
1490, Ketterer, Victor, Pte.
1492, Luke, William Arthur Jenkins, Pte.
1493, Leeden, William Henry, Pte.
1494, Lumbus, James, Pte.
1496, McKenzie, James Henry, Pte.
1497, Morrell, Harold Joseph Frederick, Pte.
1498, Matthews, William, Pte.
1499, O'Sullivan, John, Pte.
1500, McConnochie, Francis Patrick, Pte.
1501, Matthewson, Robert, Pte.
1502, Moor, Edward, Pte.
1503, Mansfield, Alexander Jas., Pte.
1504, Morris, Morgan, Pte.
1505, O'Neill, George, Pte.
1506, O'Reilly, Bernard, Pte.
1507, Ozanne, Eugene Charles Arthur, Sgt.
1508, Potts, William, Pte.
1509, Pink, Thomas George, Pte.
1510, Painter, Albert William, Pte.
1511, Pasco, Merlin Owen, Pte.
1512, Phillips, Horace, Pte.
1513, Pollard, Arthur Albert, Pte.
1514, Parkinson, Valentine Christopher, Pte.
1515, Robinson, Alexander, Pte.
1516, Ryder, Robert Herbert, Pte.
1518, Robottom, Richard, Pte.
1519, Shannon, John Johnstone, Pte.
1520, Sanguay, Herbert, Pte.
1521, Sabberton, Ernest Edward, Pte.
1522, Segrott, Gordon Bertram, Pte.
1523, Southern, Arthur Richard, Pte.
1524, Shortland, Herbert Leslie, Cpl.
1525, Thyer, Walter Harvey, Cpl.
1526, Taylor, Charles, Pte.
1527, Taylor, Fredk. Thomas, Pte.
1528, Taylor, Ralph Walter, Pte.
1529, Thomas, Bert Joseph, Pte.
1530, Vincent, John, Pte.
1531, Wallis, William Thomas, Pte.
1532, Woodall, Sydney, Pte.
1533, Watson, Frederick, Pte.
1534, Williams, Percy James, Pte.
1535, Wainey, John, Pte.
1536, Wilson, Samuel Benjamin, Pte.
1538, Sullivan, Joseph Daniel, Pte.
1539, Stamp, Reginald, Pte.
1541, Hughes, Alfred Thomas, Pte.
1542, Dunn, Daniel, Pte.
1543, Beddall, Charles Albert, Pte.
1545, Lenton, Charles Joseph, Pte.
1546, Evans, Geoffrey Cartarch, Pte.
1547, Brown, Alexander, Pte.
1548, Goldstein, Leon, Pte.
1549, Carter, Harold Reginald, Pte.
1550, Yeldon, Richard Charles, Pte.
1551, Byrne, Thomas Edward, Pte.
1552, Jones, Laidley Edwin Elbert, Pte.
1553, Keegan, Horace Paul, Pte.
1554, O'Connor, Timothy, Pte.
1555, Wheeler, Roy, Pte.

THE OLD SIXTEENTH.

16th INFANTRY BATTALION—NOMINAL ROLL –continued.

3rd Reinforcements.

(Embarked at Melbourne, Victoria, on H.M.A.T. A54, "Runic," 19th February, 1915.)

1352, Bullen, Frank Ritchie, Sgt.
1353, Bugg, Percy, Pte.
1357, Carey, Frank Cyril, Pte.
1358, Clarke, Douglas Harold, Pte.
1359, Cockington, Jasper, Pte.
1361, Edmondstone, Alfred Reginald, Pte.
1362, Freeman, Herbert Henry, Pte.
1363, Ferrier, James, Pte.
1364, Gully, William Alfred, Pte.
1365, Inglebret, William Henry, Pte.
1366, Jeffs, William, Pte.
1367, Jenkinson, Joseph, Pte.
1368, James, Percival Clarence Rover, Pte.
1369, Kerntke, Archibald Carl, Pte.
1370, McCabe, Ruben Ernest, Pte.
1371, McEvoy, Harold James, Pte.
1372, Napier, Arthur James, Pte.
1373, Newman, Sydney Clare, Pte.
1374, Pollard, Henry Alfred, Pte.
1376, Pidgeon, Thomas Sidney, Pte.
1377, Patten, Charles, Pte.
1378, Roach, William, Pte.
1379, Richardson, Sylvester Fredk., Pte.
1380, Rowland, Frederick, Pte.
1381, Tulloch, William, Pte.
1382, Trembath, William Lawrence, Pte.
1383, Taylor, Rowland, Pte.
1384, Taylor, George, Pte.
1385, Warren, Urban Guy, Cpl.
1386, Simpson, William James, Pte.
1387, Scott, John, Pte.
1388, Schumacher, Fred, Pte.
1389, Seabrook, George Henry, Pte.
1390, Stewart, Clarence Arthur, Pte.
1391, Wicker, Arthur, Pte.
1392, Wilson, Lloyd, Pte.
1393, Williamson, Adam Gordon, Pte.
1394, Williams, Evan Thomas, Pte.
1395, White, Frank Ornba, Pte.
1396, Willoughby, Joseph George, Pte.
1398, Zinkner, Fredk. William John, Pte.
1399, Alexander, Frank, Bugler.
1400, Jarrett, Stanley, Pte.
1401, Briggs, Albert Harold Wilden, Pte.
1402, Spratt, James Charles, Pte.
1408, Reardon, Cornelius Valentine.
1409, Barnett, James Arthur, Pte.
1410, Payne, Charles, Pte.
1412, Villespastour, Alphonse Arnold, Pte.
1414, Barker, Harold George, Pte.
1484, Baxter, Matthew Roland, Pte.
1576, King, Harry William, Sgt.

(Embarked at Fremantle, Western Australia, on H.M.A.T. A50, "Itonus," 22nd February, 1915.)

Taylor, Theodore Vallancey, 2nd Lt.
1576, King, Harry William, Sgt.
1577, Bolton, Percy Roy, Cpl.
1578, Benporath, Clement Wilder, Cpl.
1580, Anderson, Henry George, Pte.
1581, Axford, Harry Arnold, Pte.
1582, Barnes, Percival George, Pte.
1583, Behr, Willem Brordus Peterus, Pte.
1584, Barrett, Sydney, Pte.
1585, Benbow, Harry, Pte.
1586, Bennett, Clarence Gilbert, Pte.
1587, Bennett, James Francis, Pte.
1588, Berry, Robert Alfred, Pte.
1589, Beckett, Albert Edward, Pte.
1590, Branson, William, Pte.
1591, Brett, James, Pte.
1592, Brown, Leslie St. John, Pte.
1593, Brown, Marshall Leonard, Pte.
1594, Bunworth, Joseph F., Pte.
1595, Buswell, Elliott, Pte.
1596, Blunt, Harry Edward, Pte.
1598, Buckley, Sylvester, Pte.
1599, Burgess, Alan Listor, Pte.
1600, Carr, Albert, Pte.
1601, Close, Fredk. Laurence, Pte.
1602, Currie, Vincent John, Pte.
1603, Clark, Charles Albert, Pte.
1604, Dixon, Harry Fredk. A., Pte.
1605, Dunn, James Roy, Pte.
1606, Ellis, Arthur, Pte.
1607, England, John, Pte.
1608, Fry, Stanley, Pte.
1609, Gordon, John, Pte.
1610, Graham, Robert W. D., Pte.
1611, Gray, Leslie James, Pte.

THE OLD SIXTEENTH.

16th INFANTRY BATTALION—NOMINAL ROLL—*continued*.

3rd Reinforcements—continued.

1612, Gravestock, John, Pte.
1613, Hak, Frederick, Pte.
1613A, Williams, T. J., Pte.
1616, Hall, Sydney Chilcott, Pte.
1617, Healey, George, Pte.
1618, Hinson, John William, Pte.
1619, Hudgins, Robert, Pte.
1620, Bennett, Howard Raymond, Pte.
1621, Howe, Robert Charles, Pte.
1622, Jackman, Lewis, Pte.
1623, Johnson, Fredk. Henry, Pte.
1624, Jose, William Graham, Pte.
1626, Knight, John Robert, Pte.
1627, Laidlaw, James, Pte.
1628, Law, William, Pte.
1629, Longson, Abraham Page, Pte.
1630, Lyons, Richard, Pte.
1632, Lindsay, Harry David, Pte.
1634, MacIntosh, Clifford Gordon A., Pte.
1635, Maddock, R. Thomas, Pte.
1637, Marchant, William Clarence, Pte.
1639, McLean, John, Pte.
1640, Menhennett, Percy G., Pte.
1641, Mitchell, Robert Spencer, Pte.
1642, Mulgrave, Andrew, Pte.
1643, Munro, Frederick, Pte.
1644, Morris, Anthony, Pte.
1645, Mahlit, Rudolf, Pte.
1647, Parsons, Percy James, Pte.
1648, Partridge, Thomas D., Pte.
1651, Robertson, Alex., Pte.
1653, Sage, Arthur, Pte.

1654, Sansom, William A., Pte.
1655, Savage, John C., Pte.
1656, Scott, Thomas R. W., Pte.
1657, Shepherdson, Herbert M., Pte.
1658, Shipp, Peter W., Pte.
1659, Skinner, Charles, Pte.
1660, Stapleton, Alfred E., Pte.
1661, Sutherland, Alex., Pte.
1662, Skinner, Ernest C., Pte.
1663, Stevens, Percy Arthur, Pte.
1664, Taylor, William, Pte.
1665, Teede, Alan R., Pte.
1666, Turnbull, William A., Pte.
1667, Tonkin, Robert Richard, Pte.
1668, Voyer, Robert B., Pte.
1669, Ward, Henry H., Pte.
1670, Warnecke, Albert Hugh, Pte.
1671, Webb, Alfred, Pte.
1672, Weston, George C., Pte.
1673, Wood, Albert Henry, Pte.
1674, Loane, George, Cpl.
1675, Batchelor, John, Pte.
1676, Evans, Lewis, Pte.
1677, Lanigan, John, Pte.
1678, Mullane, John James Christopher, Pte.
1679, Mehew, Reuben, Pte.
1680, Touzel, John Charles, Pte.
1681, Todd, James Austin, Pte.
1682, Snowdon, Thomas, Pte.
1683, Townsend, Fred. James, Pte.
1684, Caldwell, Thomas Campbell, Pte.
1685, Jacobs, Herbert, Pte.
Mann, George Edwards, Pte.

4th Reinforcements.

(Embarked at Adelaide, South Australia, on H.M.A.T. A17, "Port Lincoln," 1st April, 1915.

135, Rhodes, Thomas Victor, Pte.
1375, Plummer, John Thomas, Pte.
1701, Leunig, James Henry, A/Sgt.
1702, Pearson, James Ford, A/Cpl.
1703, Aitchison, Leslie Henry, L/Cpl.
1704, Noel, Martin Edward, L/Cpl.
1706, Arnesen, Leslie John, Pte.
1707, Amolin, John, Pte.
1708, Bennett, Roy Douglas, Pte.
1709, Campion, Willie Edmond, Pte.
1710, Charnock, James, Pte.
1711, Clayton, William, Pte.
1712, Dyer, Frank, Pte.
1713, Dyer, Charles, Pte.

1714, Edwards, Percy, Pte.
1715, Ey, Archibald Leslie Phillip, Pte.
1716, Foden, Arthur, Pte.
1717, Francis, Augusta Herbert, Pte.
1718, Fulton, Sydney Albert, Pte.
1719, Fish, Samuel, Pte.
1720, Gray, Archibald Harold, Pte.
1721, Giles, Frank, Pte.
1722, Gillard, William Gordon, Pte.
1723, Gardner, James Henry, Pte.
1724, Good, John Ridge, Pte.
1725, Green, Clifford Gladstone Cyril, Pte.

THE OLD SIXTEENTH.

16th INFANTRY BATTALION—NOMINAL ROLL—*continued.*

4th Reinforcements—continued.

1726, Hansen, Walter William, Pte.
1727, Hann, Bennetts, Pte.
1728, Hefron, Alfred Edward, Pte.
1729, Jennings, Percy Arthur, Pte.
1730, Leunig, George, Pte.
1731, Murdoch, John Hector, Pte.
1732, Murdoch, Hector Ernest, Pte.
1733, Mani, Walter, Pte.
1734, Nelson, John James, Pte.
1736, Potter, Francis Joseph, Pte.
1737, Parlich, Henry John, Pte.
1738, Piercy, George, Pte.
1739, Rogers, Herbert, Pte.
1740, Solomon, Laurence, Pte.
1741, Simpson, Malcolm Henry, Pte.
1743, Scanlon, Thomas Joseph, Pte.
1744, Short, Arthur Gawler, Pte.
1745, Tubel, Robert, Pte.
1746, Todd, Harold, Pte.
1747, Tucker, Charles, Pte.
1748, Tucker, John Phillip Hill, Pte.
1749, Taylor, Richard Batchelor, Pte.
1750, Whiting, Charles, Pte.
1751, Walton, William Pollock, Pte.
1752, Chaplin, John Robert, Pte.
1753, Langford, Arthur, Pte.
1754, Marshall, Albert Clarence, Pte.

(Embarked at Fremantle, Western Australia, on H.M.A.T. A8, "Argyllshire," 19th April, 1915.)

Hutton, Alan Robert, 2nd Lt.
1775, Abrahams, Ernest Tasman, A/Cpl.
1777, Angelo, Clennell Collingwood, Pte.
1778, Attwood, Charles Neville, Pte.
1779, Austin, John, Pte.
1780, Barlow, Joseph, Pte.
1781, Black, Water Frederick, Pte.
1782, Boggs, John, Pte.
1783, Bolton, Bert Cyril, Pte.
1784, Borthwick, William, Pte.
1785, Brady, Dennis, Pte.
1786, Brooke, Alfred, Pte.
1787, Browne, George Vernon, Pte.
1789, Cadzow, William, Pte.
1790, Touzel, Clifford Norman, Pte.
1790, Candler, John, Pte.
1791, Carter, Reginald John, Pte.
1792, Carroll, Joseph John, Pte.
1793, Catlin, William Chas., Pte.
1794, Choules, Henry Leslie, Pte.
1796, Collins, William James, Pte.
1797, Connaughton, Thomas, Pte.
1799, Cowell, John, Pte,
1800, Cunnane, James, Pte.
1801, Cuthbertson, Whitfield, Pte.
1802, Dawson, George Fife, Pte.
1803, Dunstall, Charles Guy, Pte.
1805, Fereday, John, Pte.
1806, Foster, William Robert, Pte.
1807, Gillett, John Joseph, Pte.
1808, Glasson, Ezra, Pte.
1809, Goad, Cecil James, Pte.
1811, Hall, Harry Wilson, Pte.
1813, Harris, William Charles, Pte.
1817, Hill, Ashworth, Pte.
1818, Hiliary, Montague Harry, Cpl.
1819, Holroyd, Ernest Wright, Pte.
1820, Holt, William Edward, Pte.
1821, Hunter, Bernard Douglas, Pte.
1822, Iffla, Harold Athelston Hereward, Pte.
1824, Jones, Alfred Chas., Pte.
1827, Kelly, Rupert Joseph, Pte.
1830, King, Charles Leslie, Pte.
1832, Lewis, Horace, Pte.
1833, Lockton, John, Pte.
1834, Lovat, William Johnson, Pte.
1835, Mason, Fredk. Francis, Pte.
1836, Matson, Glanville, Pte.
1837, Measures, Joseph, Pte.
1838, Middleton, George, Pte.
1839, Mills, Joseph Stephenson, Pte.
1840, Millar, Arthur, Pte.
1841, Minchum, Walter Wilton, Pte.
1842, Morris, Arthur, Pte.
1845, McPhee, William, Pte.
1846, Newby, Frederick, Pte.
1847, Nicholls, Percival Leonard, Pte.
1848, Norris, Daniel, Pte.
1849, Ormsby, Robert, Pte.
1850, Pearse, Arthur Gordon, Pte.
1851, Pollard, Frederick, Pte.
1852, Pollard, Vivian, Pte.
1853, Potts, Arnold William, A/Sgt.
1854, Prestage, George, Pte.
1855, Read, Arthur Florance, Pte.
1857, Salamon, Daniel Joseph, Pte.
1858, Shanahan, William, Pte.
1859, Simpson, John Crawford, Pte.
1860, Single, Wentworth, Pte.
1861, Sparks, Robert, Pte.
1862, Spouse, Stanley Garfield, Pte.

THE OLD SIXTEENTH.

16th INFANTRY BATTALION—NOMINAL ROLL—continued.

4th Reinforcements—continued.

1863, Stubbs, Sidney, Pte.
1864, Strangman, Mark, Pte.
1865, Symes, Percy, Pte.
1867, Timms, Henry John, Pte.
1868, Todd, Charles Samuel, Pte.
1869, Tudor, Jesse, Pte.
1870, Ventris, Ernest Herbert, Pte.
1872, Wells, Albert John, Pte.
1873, Wilson, Alfred Gordon, Pte.
1874, Wise, Charles Knightly, Pte
1875, Wrighton, Percy, Pte.
1876, Stares, Henry Percival, Pte.
1878, Evans, Alfred Lionel, Pte.
1879, Martin, Henry, Pte.
1881, Corker, William, Pte.

1882, Horsey, Alfred Edwin, Pte.
1883, Wishart, Henry Ernest, Pte.
1884, Anderson, Reginald, Pte.
1885, Brodie, Donald, Pte.
1886, Collins, Joseph, Pte.
1887, Howland, Charles, Pte.
1888, Prater, William, Pte.
1889, Parkin, Alfred, Pte.
1890, Rason, Ernest, Pte.
1891, Wells, Sydney James, Pte.
1892, Newling, Clarence Harold, Pte.
1893, Turnbull, Harold, Pte.
1894, Winter, Noel Stephen, Pte.
1895, Wood, Arthur William, Pte.

5th Reinforcements.

(Embarked at Adelaide, South Australia, on H.M.A.T. A20, "Hororata," 20th April, 1915.)

1901, Ashworth, Ernest, Pte
1902, Bawden, Arthur Osborne, Pte.
1903, Bennett, William John, Pte.
1904, Bermingham, Walter Jas., Pte.
1905, Boulden, Arthur Edward, Pte.
1906, Bourke, Fred Arnold, Pte.
1907, Burnett, Frederick, Pte.
1908, Burns, John, Pte.
1909, Byrne, Clarry, Pte.
1910, Chadwick, Thomas, Pte.
1911, Dunkley, Errol Edward, Pte.
1912, Davies, Charles John, Pte.
1913, Duthie, Rudley Ernest, Pte.
1914, French, Charles Gordon, Pte.
1915, Garratt, Charles Clement, Sgt.
1916, Galles, Paul Frederick, Pte.
1917, Giles, Robert Ernest Harland, Pte.
1918, Gregory, Samuel, Pte.
1919, Gathercole, Wm. Robson, Pte.
1920, Harris, Edgar Claude, Pte.
1921, Hawkesworth, Fred., Pte.
1922, Johnson, William, Pte.
1923, King, Thos. Arthur, Pte.
1924, Knott, James Henry, Pte.
1925, Lewis, Ernest Vivian, Pte.
1926, Lillis, John, Pte.
1928, Lloyd, Job, Pte.
1929, McIntyre, James, Pte.

1930, McKenzie, Archd. Frank, Pte.
1931, Morgan, Percival, Pte.
1932, Parmiter, Charles, Pte.
1933, Parmiter, Philip Albert, Pte.
1934, Peters, Robert, Pte.
1935, Richards, James Cuthbert, Pte.
1936, Robertson, John, Pte.
1937, Rudolph, Karl, Pte.
1938, Speck, John Charles, Pte.
1939, Stradling, John Burden, Pte.
1940, St. Clair, Donald, Pte.
1941, Taylor, Ern James, Pte.
1942, Theodore, William Henry, Pte.
1943, Thornby, Lovell, Pte.
1944, Utting, Arthur Edward, Pte.
1945, Vickery, Leslie Joseph, Pte.
1946, Walsh, Alexander John, Pte.
1947, Hooker, Claude, A/Cpl.
1948, King, Anthony Timothy, A/Cpl.
1949, Taylor, Henry, Pte.
1950, Wood, William Edward, Pte.
1951, Marshall, William, Pte.
1952, Muggleton, Walter, Pte.
1977, Butler, Jack, Pte.
1979, Baldwin, Amos, Pte.
1980, Bailiff, James, Pte.
1981, Baldwin, William, Pte.

THE OLD SIXTEENTH.

16th INFANTRY BATTALION—NOMINAL ROLL—*continued.*

5th Reinforcements—continued.

(Embarked at Fremantle, Western Australia, on H.M.A.T. A20, "Hororata," 26th April, 1915.)

Hamersley, Harold Allan, 2nd Lt.
1982, Bounsell, William, Pte.
1983, Beverley, Thomas Caine, Pte.
1984, Boully, Leslie, Pte.
1985, Campbell, Frederick Thomas, Pte.
1986, Crichton, George Baxter, Pte.
1987, Carwardine, Clarence, Pte.
1988, Carter, John James, Pte.
1989, Donovan, Michael, Pte.
1990, Dillistone, William Jacob, Pte.
1991, Davey, William Ernest, Pte.
1992, Delaporte, Arnold, Pte.
1993, Dewing, Edward John, Pte.
1994, Evans, William Ewart, Pte.
1995, Elverd, William Augustus, Pte.
1996, Elsworth, James, Pte.
1997, Ferstat, Aaron, Pte.
1998, Gilbert, Arthur James, Pte.
1999, Groessler, Frank Bernard, Pte.
8000, Gurry, Richard, Pte.
8001, Gallagher, Thomas William, Pte.
8003, Hughes, George, Pte.
8004, Hunter, William, Pte.
8005, Horne, George Athol, Pte.
8006, Hoskin, William Richard, Pte.
8007, Jones, Bryn Awfon, A/Cpl.
2008, Jones, Richard James, Pte.
2009, Joyce, John Edward, Pte.
2010, Kitschke, Roy Arthur, Pte.
2011, Knight, William John, Pte.
2012, Kyle, Harry Bruce, Pte.
2013, Kelso, Samuel John, Pte.
2014, Lack, Alfred James, Pte.
2015, Lawson, Irvine, Pte.
2016, Lawson, James, Pte.
2019, Marshall, Harold, Pte.
2020, Morrow, George Meredith, Pte.
2021, Morris, Alfred Ernest, Pte.
2022, Miller, Samuel, Pte.
2024, Martin, Henry Robert, Pte.
2025, Moody, Robert Alexander, Pte.
2026, McPhee, Archibald, Pte.
2028, Newton, Isaac Rudolph, Pte.
2029, O'Donoghue, John Stephen, Pte.
2030, Oldfield, Sydney John, Pte.
2031, Parker, Harry, Pte.
2032, Peebles, Peter Connacher, Pte.
2033, Pope, William, Pte.
2034, Porteous, Ernest, Pte.
2035, Price, Alfred James, Pte.
2036, Ryan, Edmond, Pte.
2037, Seaborn, Harry, A/Cpl.
2038, Simpson, Ernest Warne, Pte.
2039, Slater, Alfred Arthur, A/Sgt.
2040, Strachan, William Tough, Pte.
2041, Spencer, Harold, Pte.
2042, Sellers, Hubert, Pte.
2044, Tucker, Henry, Pte.
2045, Townson, Frank, A/Cpl.
2046, Thomas, William, Pte.
2048, Turner, Percy Thomas, Pte.
2049, Twyford, John, Pte.
2051, Williams, John Francis, Pte.
2052, Watkins, Arthur, Pte.
2053, Williamson, John, Pte.
2054, Ward, William Richard, Pte.
2055, Williams, Wilfred, Pte.
2056, Walter, Arthur, Pte.
2057, Walter, George, Pte.
2058, Weatherall, Samuel, Pte.
2059, Wheeler, Harold, Pte.
2060, Wheeler, Herbert, Pte.
2061, Wilson, William, Pte.
2063, Wordsworth, John, Pte.
2064, Yates, Albert Victor, Pte.
2065, Annear, Robert Loton, Pte.
2067, Hoddy, Lionel Peter, Pte.
2068, Sibley, Clarence, Pte.
2069, Fowler, Herbert Leopold Arthur, Pte.
2070, Sharpe, Frank Edward, Pte.
2071, Steeds, Roger Dutton, Pte.
2072, Hughes, John Roy, Pte.
2073, Smith, George Edward, Pte.
2074, Stalker, John, Pte.
2076, Shackleton, Ernest, Pte.
2078, Radway, Joshua, Pte.
2082, Diffen, Joseph, Pte.
2083, Murphy, John Joseph, Pte.
2084, Groves, George Albert Percy, Pte.
2085, Whittingham, Harry, Pte.
2086, Morris, Thomas, Pte.
2087, Jorgensen, Walter, Sgt.
2088, Lee, Gerald St. Clair, Sgt.
2089, Mann, Andrew, Pte.
2090, Thomas, Henry, Cpl.
2136, Rankine, Leonard John,

THE OLD SIXTEENTH. 233

16th INFANTRY BATTALION—NOMINAL ROLL—*continued.*

6th Reinforcements.

(Embarked at Adelaide, South Australia, on H.M.A.T. A30, "Borda," 23rd June, 1915.)

2101, Admore, Albert Hugh, Pte.
2103, Baldock, Thomas Alfred Bee, Pte.
2104, Best, George Harold, Pte.
2105, Bridges, Roy Gilbert, Pte.
2106, Carr, William George, Pte.
2107, Court, Robert Stephen, Pte.
2109, Davis, John, Pte.
2110, Dewar, Henry Gordon, A/Cpl.
2111, Eckersley, Ernest George, Pte.
2112, Erickson, Ernest Reuben, Pte.
2113, Finnerty, Herbert Gerald, Pte.
2115, Ford, Leslie James, Pte.
2117, Garland, Leslie, Pte.
2119, Gillen, Henry, Pte.
2120, Harris, James Edward, Pte.
2121, Harrison, Arthur, Pte.
2122, Haines, Henry George, Pte.
2123, Holton, Edward Gordon, Pte.
2124, Howard, John, Pte.
2125, Johnson, John Edward, A/Cpl.
2127, Kuchenmeister, Carl Adolph, Pte.
2128, Madigan, John, Pte.
2129, May, Ernest Stanislaus, Pte.
2130, May, Percival Edmund, Pte.
2132, Mogg, Benjamin Silvenius, Pte.
2133, McSweeney, Edmund, Pte.
2134, O'Brien, John Joseph, Pte.
2135, Osborn, George, Pte.
2136, Rankine, Leonard John, Pte.
2138, Senior, Francis Arthur, Pte.
2140, Todd, Emanuel James Joseph, Pte.
2142, Webster, Joseph, Pte.
2143, White, Sterling Clement, Pte.
2144, Wiles, Henry John, Pte.
2145, Zbierski, Alexander, Pte.
2147, George, Francis, Pte.
2148, Llewellyn, Ernest, Pte.
2149, Gilbert, John Gordon, Pte.
2151, Harris, Ivor, Pte.
2152, Pengelley, John Young, Pte.
2153, Hallam, Edgar Lealand, Pte.
2154, Ditchburn, William Arthur, A/Sgt.
2156, Lovick, Robert Lewis, Pte.
2157, Thomas, George, Pte.
2158, Smith, William Alfred, Pte.
2159, Jones, Randall Rowland, Pte.
2160, Best, Frederick George, Pte.
2594, Wilkey, Charles, Pte.
2595, Nowland, Thomas Henry, Pte.
2596, Clarke, Alfred Carrington, Pte.

(Embarked at Fremantle, Western Australia, on H.M.A.T. A62, "Wandilla," 25th June, 1915.)

Evans, George Freeman, Lt.
2161, McMahon, Edward, Pte.
2176, Buckenara, Clarence Louis, A/Sgt.
2177, Clarke, Norman Nesbit, A/Sgt.
2178, Wright, Thomas Robert, A/Cpl.
2180, Andrews, Henry, Pte.
2184, Jolly, Arthur, Pte.
2185, Beattie, Samuel, Pte.
2187, Bickerton, William, Pte.
2188, Boyle, Vivian, Pte.
2191, Byrne, James Joseph, Pte.
2192, Carra, David Charles, A/Cpl.
2193, Chisholm, John, Pte.
2194, Clarke, William, Pte.
2195, Clifton, Roy Kimberley, Pte.
2196, Piper, Edgar Albert, Pte.
2198, Cordes, Frederick, Pte.
2199, Crichton, Joseph Michael Smith, Pte.
2201, Daniels, William Vivian, Pte.
2202, Dinnie, William, Pte.
2203, Doyle, James, Pte.
2204, Dunne, Bernard Joseph, Pte.
2205, Egglestone, Charles William, Pte.
2206, Enright, Edward, Pte.
2207, Ensor, Eugene Thomas, Pte.
2208, Eyden, Leslie William, Pte.
2209, Farrell, William Ephraim, Pte.
2212, Fiddler, Robert, Pte.
2213, Fisher, Edward Theophilus, Pte.
2215, Francis, John Richard, Pte.
2219, Greenhill, Samuel Clifton Warren, Pte.
2221, Harford, Francis Xavier, Pte.
2223, Higgins, Eric, Pte.
2224, Hoffman, Wolfe, Pte.
2225, Holbrook, Herbert, Pte.
2226, Holland, Edwin Richard, Pte.
2228, Howell, John Denison, A/Cpl.
2233, Kelly, Thomas James, Pte.
2235, McCabe, John, Pte.

16th INFANTRY BATTALION—NOMINAL ROLL —continued.

6th Reinforcements—continued.

2236, Lunt, William, Pte.
2238, Marshall, Reginald Herbert, Pte.
2239, Mattinson, James Webb, Pte.
2240, Meakins, Edward James, Pte.
2242, More, Arthur, Pte.
2247, O'Brien, Richard, Pte.
2248, O'Connor, John, Pte.
2249, Otly, William Henry, Pte.
2250, Philips, Reginald Thomas, Pte.
2251, Roberts, Harold, Pte.
2253, Smith, Harry, Pte.
2256, Strickland, John, Pte.
2257, Stritch, Charles Vincent, Pte.
2261, Taylor, Herbert Stewart, Pte.
2262, Thompson, James, Pte.
2263, Thorn, Norman, Pte.
2264, Thorn, Robert, A/Cpl.
2265, Thumwood, Arthur Henry, Pte.
2266, Torpey, Sylvester, Pte.
2267, Trainor, John, Pte
2268, Virgo, William, Pte.
2270, Wallis, Sydney Arthur, Pte.
2271, Watts, Albert John, Pte.
2273, Whitehead, Frederick, Pte.
2274, Whittle, Albert Botwood, Pte.
2275, Whyte, William George, Pte.
2278, Woolston, Archibald Cyril, Pte.
2280, Williams, Henry Hubert, A/St.
2281, Aarons, Maurice Lewis, Pte.
2282, Austin, Basil Wake, Pte.
2283, Braddock, Charles Thomas, Pte.
2284, Vincent, Lucius George, Pte.
2287, Bacon, Arthur, Pte.
2288, Baldwin, Arthur Wilfred, Pte.
2289, Boyd, William, Pte.
2290, Downey, Elijah Haynes, Pte.
2291, Firns, George Weston Pte.
2292, Gill, Arthur Clarence, Pte.
2293, Gould, John, Pte.
2294, Hay, James, Pte.
2295, Man, Herman Emil, Pte.
2296, McCreery, George, Pte.
2297, McEllister, Edmond Langford, Pte.
2298, Garth, Frank, Pte.
2299, McNab, John, Pte.
2301, Norman, Charles Henry, Pte.
2302, Osmond, John James Thomas Henry, Pte.
2303, Park, John Jack, Pte.
2304, Reader, Frank, Pte.
2305, Rowe, Stephen, Pte.
2306, Yorke, Bernard, Pte.
2307, Wheeler, Hewitt Oliver, Pte.
2308, Jones, David, Pte.
2309, Lind, Ernest William, Pte.
2310, Thompson, Henry Charles, Pte.
2311, Iles, Albert Henry, Pte.
2312, Swindells, Eli, Pte.
2313, Carter, Mervyn William Earle, Pte.
2314, Hulton, James McAdam, Pte.
2315, Cleaver, Percy, Pte.
2316, Boylan, Tomas, Pte.
2369, Thomas, John Roy, Pte.
2374, Waterman, Frank Hubert, Pte.
2593, Thomas, Horatio Sidney C., Pte.

7th Reinforcements.

(Embarked at Fremantle, Western Australia, on H.M.A.T. A51, "Chilka," 18th June, 1915.)

Jeffrey, Lionel, Lieut.
1947, Hooker, Claude, Pte.
2157, Beresford, Edgar John Andrew, Pte.
2165, Donaldson, David, Pte.
2218, Green, George Spencer, Pte.
2246, Norris, John Henry, Pte.
2389, England, Ernest, Pte.
2391, Fogarty, Joseph Ambrose, Pte.
2408, Martin, Arthur, Pte.
2435, Anderson, John Arthur, Pte.
2436, Angel, Victor Herbert, Pte.
2438, Brennan, John Augusta, Pte.
2439, Boyes, Cabel Samuel, Pte.
2440, Barrett, Leslie Roy, Pte.
2441, Bradshaw, William John, Pte.
2442, Bolander, Theodore, Pte.
2443, Burns, Ernest Edward, Pte.
2444, Brown, Edward Frederick, Pte.
2445, Baker, Bob Heard, Pte.
2446, Bowers, Arthur, Pte.
2447, Boyd, John, Pte.
2448, Bull, George William, Pte.
2454, Cosson, John George, Pte.
2455, Cook, Alfred Charles, Pte.
2456, Connor, Frank, Pte.
2457, Cooke, Arnold Victor, Pte.
2458, Clark, James Pringle, Pte.
2460, Clune, Francis, Pte.
2461, Craddock, Percival, Pte.

THE OLD SIXTEENTH.

16th INFANTRY BATTALION—NOMINAL ROLL—*continued*.

7th Reinforcements—continued.

2462, Collins, Edward Francis, Pte.
2463, Collier, Albert, Pte.
2464, Coulter, Wilfred, Pte.
2465, Cowling, Albert Ernest, Pte.
2466, Deeble, William, Pte.
2467, Dow, George Conway, Pte.
2468, Dixon, George William, Pte.
2469, Delaney, Michael, Pte.
2470, Doran, Victor Frederick, Pte.
2471, Drew, Oscar Desmond, Pte.
2472, Davies, Thomas Owen, Pte.
2474, Davern, John, Pte.
2475, Goodchild, Stanley, Pte.
2477, Gidney, John Harold, Pte.
2478, Halliday, Robert Michael, Pte.
2479, Hutton, John, Pte.
2480, Harvey, James, Pte.
2482, Hammond, John, Pte.
2483, Hopkins, Robert Bramwell, Pte.
2484, Hernan, Thomas William Joseph, Pte.
2486, Harrison, Edward, Pte.
2488, Jenkins, Harry Togamah, Pte.
2489, Hocking, Ernest Charles, Pte.
2490, James, Trevor, Pte.
2491, Jacob, Llewellyn Frank, Pte.
2492, Kell, James, Pte.
2494, Kipping, Ralph Ezekiah, Pte.
2495, Kevan, Edward Harold, Pte.
2496, Keyte, Francis Garrett, Pte.
2497, Kidgell, Eric Gawthorne, Pte.
2499, Kelly, Roy, Pte.
2500, Lawson, Alexander Vernon, Pte.
2501, Lowther, Harry, Pte.

2504, McPherson, Alexander, Pte.
2505, McEntee, Charles Walter, Pte.
2508, Muir, William Hope, Pte.
2511, Nugent, Richard, Pte.
2512, O'Rourke, Samuel, Pte.
2513, O'Reilly, John, Pte.
2514, Malone, Joseph John, Pte.
2515, Paddon, Charles Henry, Pte.
2518, Richardson, Charles John, Pte.
2520, Rimoldi, Luigi Frederick, Pte.
2521, Rushby, George Edward, Pte.
2523, Sherar, James Henry, Pte.
2524, Stockton, William Norman, Pte.
2526, Smith, James Augustus, Pte.
2528, Steedman, William Thomas, Pte.
2529, Stradling, Harry, Pte.
2530, Senior, Reason Hugh, Pte.
2531, Satinover, Jacob, Pte.
2532, Simons, Charles William, Pte.
2533, Tipping, William, Pte.
2534, Warren, John Henry, Pte.
2537, Walker, John, Pte.
2538, Young, Robert Charles, Pte.
2540, Pentilla, Christopher Sydney, Pte.
2541, Galt, William, Pte.
2542, Hughes, David Morris, Pte.
2543, Horrocks, James Owen, Pte.
2544, Lacey, Frederick, Pte.
2545, Hinton, John, Pte.
2546, Wilson, Thomas Henry, Pte.
2547, Williams, William Arthur, Pte.
2554, Marshall, Reginal Herbert, Pte.
2819, Brewer, Frederick, Pte.

(Embarked at Adelaide, South Australia, on H.M.A.T. A61, "Kanowna," 24th June, 1915.)

Parks, Edward Joseph, Lieut.
2326, Appleton, William Squires, Pte.
2327, Baldwin, Barrington Grace, Pte.
2328, Breen, Leslie James, Pte.
2330, Campbell, Horace Lyall, Pte.
2331, Coffey, Edward Daley, Pte.
2332, Colebatch, Hector Edwin, Pte.
2333, Collett, Malcolm Ross, Pte.
2335, Collins, Thomas Edwin, Pte.
2336, Cook, George, Pte.
2338, Chamberlain, Joseph, Pte.
2339, Dolan, Murray, Pte.
2340, Dutton, Sydney John, Pte.
2342, Evans, Leonard, Pte.
2343, Foster, Charles Edward, Pte.

2344, Goddard, Reginald, Pte.
2345, Gray, James Clyde, Pte.
2347, Hughes, John, Pte.
2348, Ivy, Allen Gordon, Pte.
2350, Kilmartin, Francis Thomas Joseph, Pte.
2351, Long, Harold, Pte.
2352, McKim, William John, Pte.
2353, McNeill, Thomas Borthwick, Pte.
2354, Herbert, John, Pte
2355, Mundy, Andrew, Pte.
2356, Mundy, James Wallace, Pte.
2357, Mutton, Albert, Pte.
2358, Nichol, John Reginald Clifford, Pte.

16th INFANTRY BATTALION—NOMINAL ROLL —continued.

7th Reinforcements—continued.

2359, Parsons, Harry Alec., Pte.
2360, Pepall, Claude, Pte.
2361, Puikkula, Otto, Pte.
2362, Powell, Frederick William, Pte.
2363, Quigley, Alick, Pte.
2364, Roberson, William Henry, Pte.
2365, Schmidt, Harold Edward, Pte.
2366, Sharp, Henry, Pte.
2367, Steward, Lawrence Napier, Pte.
2368, Stone, John, Pte.
2370, Tomley, Ernest William, Pte.
2371, Twining, Percy, Pte.
2372, Tyler, Arthur Henry, Pte

2373, Wahlstead, Thomas, Pte.
2375, Waters, Maurice Henry, Pte.
2376, Weaver, Reuben, Pte.
2377, Williams, Arthur Henry, Pte.
2378, Lightfoot, Lancelot Douglas, Pte.
2379, Beck, Cyril Hurst, Pte.
2380, Chivers, Charles James, Pte.
2381, McNeill, Alexander John, Pte.
2573, Mouser, James Clement, Pte.
2574, Palagrens, Pascal, Pte.
2592, Thayne, Douglas Murray, Pte.
2593, Munro, William, Pte.

8th Reinforcements.

(Embarked at Fremantle, Western Australia, on H.M.A.T. A68, "Anchises," 2nd September, 1915.)

Morris, Robin, 2nd Lt.
2626, Dalziell, George Christopher, Pte.
2627, Orkney, Harry Spencer, Pte.
2628, Bull, William, Pte.
2629, Twining, David Austral, Pte.
2630, McLeod, Duncan Albert, Pte.
2631, West, Hedley Charles, Pte.
2632, Klopper, Henry Ferdinand, Pte.
2633, Acton, Frank Robert, Pte.
2634, Alger, Frederick, Pte.
2635, Anderson, William Joseph, Pte.
2636, Archibald Matthew, Pte.
2637, Armstrong, Frank, Pte.
2638, Bray, Alexander Stuart, Pte.
2639, Bruce, Albert Edward, Pte.
2640, Butler, Hurtle James Rowe, Pte.
2641, Carter, Geoffrey Grant, Pte.
2642, Carter, Thomas Broughton, Pte.
2643, Clayton, Frederick Charles, Pte.
2644, Clisby, Charles Henry, Pte.
2645, Compassi, Victor Thomas Emanuel, Pte.
2646, Cook, Nelson Henry, Pte.
2647, Crawford, Stanley Arthur, Pte.
2648, Currie, William Bernard, Pte.
2649, Dadley, Oliver, Pte.
2650, Dalgleigh, James McLean, Pte.
2651, Davies, Leslie Francis, Pte
2652, Day, Charles, Pte.
2653, Duffy, Michael, Pte.
2654, Edgar, Wallace, Pte.

2655, Ehrlich, Victor Adam, Pte.
2656, Elliott, Frederick Charles, Pte.
2657, Emery, Cyril, Pte.
2658, Fox, Frank Leslie, Pte.
2659, Gabrielson, Harold Bull, Pte.
2660, Gee, Frederick William, Pte.
2661, Gibson, Keith Edwin, Pte.
2662, Grainger, Thos. Alexander, Pte.
2663, Hager, Henry William, Pte.
2664, Hendry, Douglas Anderson, Pte.
2665, Holloway, Ernest Charles, Pte.
2667, Howlett, John William, Pte.
2668, Ick, Henry Edwin, Pte.
2669, Jones, Frederick, Pte.
2670, Jones, Sydney Arthur, Pte.
1671, Kellow, Francis Joseph, Pte.
2673, Lenton, Thomas Samuel, Pte.
2674, Lewis, David, Pte.
2675, Lindt, Augus, Pte.
2676, Lockhart, Ernest Edward Pte.
2677, Lukies, John Edgar Duncan, Pte.
2678, Lyon, Herbert Keith, Pte.
2760, Marshall, William John, Pte.
2680, Martin, Harvey Milverton, Pte.
2681, Meikle, Peter, Pte.
2682, Meller, Joseph James, Pte.
2683, Moore, Newton, Pte.
2684, Morgan, Leopold George, Pte.
2685, Moxham, John, Pte.
2686, Murphy, Matthew, Pte.
2687, McGorrery, Fredk. Stanley, Pte.
2688, McPhee, Edward Duncan, Pte.
2689, Nock, Frank Arthur, Pte.

THE OLD SIXTEENTH.

16th INFANTRY BATTALION—NOMINAL ROLL—*continued*.

8th Reinforcements—continued.

2690, Pekin, John, Pte.
2691, Preston, Frederick Henry, Pte.
2692, Purdy, Thomas, Pte.
2693, Radford, Walter Francis, Pte.
2694, Rafferty, Robert Scott, Pte.
2695, Randle, John, Pte.
2696, Roberts, Benjamin, Pte.
2698, Rogers, John Edmond, Pte.
2699, Rogers, William Richard, Pte.
2700, Sanders, Walter, Pte.
2701, Scott, James Alfred, Pte.
2702, Sharp, Charles Steven, Pte.
2703, Sharpe, Samuel Charles, Pte.
2704, Shenfield, Harry, Pte.
2705, Simpson, James, Pte.
2706, Sinden, Frederick Ernest, Pte.
2707, Smith, Arthur Chaloner, Pte.
2708, Smith, Herbert Clarence Sinclair, Pte.
2709, Smith, Howard William Bowyear, Pte.
2710, Spry, William Henry, Pte.
2711, Thompson, Thruman Cromwell, Pte.
2712, Toy, William Edward, Pte.
2713, Truran, William Howard, Pte.
2714, Wadeson, Samuel Jackson, Pte.
2715, Watson, Herbert Henry, Pte.
2716, Weight, Harold Stuart, Pte.
2717, Wilson, George Henry, Pte.
2718, Wych, Augustus Hugh, Pte.
2719, Wynne, William, Pte.
2720, Alcorn, Ebenezer Cyril, Pte.
2721, Cupid, Frederick Charles, Pte.
2722, Scott, David, Pte.
2723, Jones, Samuel James, Pte.
2724, Roberts, Albert Amos, Pte.
2725, Watson, William, Pte.
2726, Peake, Jack Inns, Pte.
2727, Harding, Samuel George.

(Embarked at Adelaide, South Australia, on R.M.S. "Morea."
26th August, 1915.)

Tucker, Virgil, 2nd Lt.
2346, Howard, Ambrose Leo, Pte.
2551, Anderson, David Johannes Gottfried, Pte.
2553, Burrows, Alfred William, Pte.
2554, Carruthers, Joseph Herbert, Pte.
2559, Farley, Thomas Francis, Pte.
2561, Grant, Lewis, Pte.
2562, Hanrahan, Michael Francis, Pte.
2563, Klemich, Alwin Oscar, Pte.
2571, MacKenzie, Edward, Pte.
2572, Maraun, Frederick Henning, Pte.
2575, Petersen, Franc, Pte.
2576, Rittberger, Leslie John, Pte.
2579, Rowey, Francis Arthur, Pte.
2581, Skinner, Roderick James, Pte.
2582, Sparshott, Percival Henry, Pte.
2583, Staker, Hedley Alfred Lawrence, Pte.
2586, Savage, Alfred Austin, Pte.
2587, Siggs, William Harold, Pte.
2590, Starr, Ernest Charles, Pte.
2591, Stevens, William Henry, Pte.
2594, Trudgen, Hedley Augustus, Pte.
2597, White, Frederick George, Pte.
2598, Whittle, John, Pte.
2599, Winkler, Charles Herman, Pte.
2602, Warr, Joseph Thomas, Pte.
2603, Woite, Gustav Ronald, Pte.
2605, Winter, Ernest Clifton, Pte.
2607, Shinn, James William, Pte.
2608, Bradford, Cyril Frederick, Pte.
2609, Clark, Clarence, Pte.
2610, Drever, Frederick Niell, Pte.
2611, Emery, Hurtle William, Pte.
2612, Grant, Frederick Kenneth, Pte.
2613, Johnson, Alfred Michael, Pte.
2614, Neaylon, Roy Eric Norman, Pte.
2615, Quinn, Charles Edward Leslie, Pte.
2616, Schultz, Leonard Roy Edmund, Pte.
2617, Bawden, Samuel Joseph, Pte.
2619, Edgewood, James, Pte.
2620, Freckleton, Frank, Pte.
2621, Hill, John, Pte.
2622, May, Leslie Charles, Pte.
2623, Parsons, James, Pte.
2624, Storry, Ernest, Pte.
2627, West, Frank Anthony, Pte.
2628, Moore, Thomas, Pte.
2629, Strano, Angelo, Pte.
2630, Sagar, Eric Noel, Pte.
2631, Crisp, Douglas Bertram, Pte.
2632, Garland, Hugh Gordon, Pte.
2633, Hoare, Stanley Ivanhoe, Pte.
2634, Schmoock, Robert Wilson, Pte.

16th INFANTRY BATTALION—NOMINAL ROLL—continued.

9th Reinforcements.

(Embarked at Adelaide, South Australia, on H.M.A.T. A15, "Star of England," 21st September, 1915.)

Hartley, William Garfield, Lt.
309, White, Thomas John William, Pte.
2604, Way, Marshall Western Moore, Pte.
2776, Armbrusher, Charles Augustus, Pte.
2777, Arthur, Conrad Oswald, Pte.
2778, Beaumont, Harold Lionell, Pte.
2779, Barker, Leslie Clarence, Pte.
2780, Bird, Henry Robert Willie, Pte.
2781, Bennett, Roy Lindsay, Pte.
2782, Beaufoot, James Cornelius, Pte.
2783, Bampton, George William Duncan, Pte.
2784, Bowker, John Martin, Pte.
2785, Bulgin, Alfred Spencer, Pte.
2786, Clemow, Albert George, Pte.
2787, Clemow, Edward Victor, Pte.
2788, Croston, William Harold Payne, Pte.
2789, Cox, James Percy, Pte.
2790, Cronin, Daniel Timothy, Pte.
2791, Cameron, Donald Nicholas, Pte.
2792, Cole, Henry, Pte.
2793, Donovan, William Cornelius, Pte.
2794, Dowleans, Albert Mirabean, Pte.
2795, Elkan, Ferdinand, Pte.
2796, Fitzgerald, Thomas Vincent, Pte.
2797, Gottlieb, Harold Alfred, Pte.
2798, Hall, Harold Albert, Pte.
2799, Hills, William Edward, Pte.
2800, Hart, Charles Wilfred, Pte.
2801, Herewane, Leigh Elijah, Pte.
2802, Kennedy, Roy, Pte.
2803, Knight, George Johnston, Pte.
2804, Lawson, Bernard, Pte.
2805, Murphy, Claude, Pte.
2807, McMahon, John Joseph, Pte.
2808, Medlen, Charles, Pte.
2809, Marshall, Alan George, Pte.
2810, McFarlane, William John, Pte.
2811, O'Neill, John Patrick, Pte.
2812, O'Kely, Richard Nicholson, Pte.
2813, Palmer, Edward, Pte
2815, Pitman, Harold, Pte
2816, Pool, Jack, Pte.
2817, Paterson, Harold Walter, Pte.
2818, Patten, George Frederick, Pte.
2819, Phillips, Arthur Bradshaw, Pte.
2820, Self, Reginald, Pte.
2821, Schrader, Carl Laneustein, Pte.
2822, Walters, Percy George Immanuel, Pte.
2823, Whitfield, Walter, Pte.
2825, Webster, George, Pte.
2226, O'Neill, Francis Michael, Pte.
2827, Roeszler, Arthur William, Pte.
2828, Ware, Charles Clifford, Pte.
3065, Hutchins, William Harold, Pte.

(Embarked at Fremantle, Western Australia, on H.M.A.T. A20, "Hororata," 5th October, 1915.)

Bardwell, Bernard Everett, Lt.
2851, Doig, David MacNair, Pte.
2852, Ottaway, Bertram Hope, Pte.
2854, Schryver, Harold Sydney, Pte.
2855, Monck-Mason, Thos George, Pte.
2857, Challen, Leslie George Reginald, Pte.
2858, Alcorn, Charles Henry, Pte.
2859, Alnwick, Harry, Pte.
2860, Anderson, George Albert, Pte.
2861, Blab, Garnet, Pte.
2862, Black, Archibald, Pte.
2863, Blencowe, Sydney Fenner, Pte.
2864, Bonney, John Edwin, Pte.
2865, Bray, Albert, Pte.
2866, Brice, Arthur, Pte.
2867, Butcher, Thomas Edward, Pte.
2868, Cameron-Smith, Roy, Pte.
2869, Campbell, Thomas, Pte.
2870, Casey, Jeremiah Joseph, Pte.
2871, Cates, George, Pte.
2872, Chatley, Ernest William, Pte.
2873, Clark, Arthur Dudley, Pte.
2874, Crocker, James Arnold, Pte.
2875, Crombie, David, Pte.
2876, Crothers, Albert, Pte.
2877, Davies, David Henry, Pte.
2878, De Lany, Leslie Stephens, Pte.
2879, Dier, John Frederick, Pte.

THE OLD SIXTEENTH.

16th INFANTRY BATTALION—NOMINAL ROLL—*continued.*

9th Reinforcements—continued.

2880, Doyle, Sidney Campbell, Pte.
2881, Elsbury, Cyril, Pte.
2882, Elshaw, John William Barker, Pte.
2883, Fairhead, Allen Leopold Pte.
2884, Flint, George, Pte.
2885, Forbes, John, Pte.
2886, Gillvoyte, Hubert Joseph, Pte.
2887, Gilsenan, Leslie Richard, Pte.
2888, Goodall, Arthur Sinclair, Pte.
2889, Gray, James, Pte.
2890, Green, Arthur Wilson, Pte.
2891, Greenham, Arthur Engle, Pte.
2892, Griffiths, Charles Frederick, Pte.
2893, Grono, Percival Charles, Pte.
2894, Hamre, Samuel Joseph, Pte.
2895, Hayes, James, Pte.
2896, Head, John, Pte.
2897, Heron, Thomas George, Pte.
2898, Hunt, Herbert John, Pte.
2899, Hutton, David Lionel, Pte.
2900, James, Waldo Albert, Pte.
2902, Jones, William, Pte.
2903, Kelly, William Roy, Pte.
2904, Kramer, Leslie, Pte.
2905, Lawrie, Aron Frank, Pte.
2906, Lawrie, John, Pte.
2907, Logan, William, Pte.
2908, Marshall, Joseph, Pte.
2909, Middleton, Wallace, Pte.
2910, Mitchell, Roy Francis, Pte.
2911, Moore, John William Beverhoudt, Pte.
2912, Moyse, Samuel Ellis, Pte.
2913, Murray, William, Pte.
2914, McDonnell, John, Pte.
2915, McLeod, James Robinson, Pte.
2916, Nesbitt, Richard William Thomas, Pte.
2917, Nielsen, Hans Kristian August, Pte.
2918, O'Brien, Michael Patrick, Pte.
2919, Phillips, Samuel Gilbert, Pte.
2920, Price, Harold Thomas, Pte.
2921, Purvis, John Clifford, Pte.
2922, Rawlings, Charles, Pte.
2923, Reading, Alfred Ernest Sydney, Pte.
2924, Reid, William, Pte.
2925, Ricketts, William Charles, Pte.
2926, Russell, John Felix, Pte.
2927, Sampford, Charles Raymond, Pte.
2928, Sampford, William Miles, Pte.
2929, Skinner, John, Pte.
2930, Smith, John, Pte.
2931, Smith, Arthur Joseph, Pte.
2932, Smith, Ronald Blundell, Pte.
2933, Symonds, John Edward, Pte.
2934, Sherlock, Rupert Gardiner, Pte.
2935, Tainsh, Frederick James, Pte.
2936, Thomas, James Louis, Pte.
2937, Turner, Bertie, Pte.
2938, Walker, Alexander, Pte.
2939, Wall, George Thomas, Pte.
2940, White, Henry, Pte.
2941, Whiteley, James Murray, Pte.
2942, Whitford, Richard, Pte.
2943, Wills, Ernest John, Pte.
2944, Williams, Edward, Pte.
2945, Williams, Kenneth Langi, Pte.
2946, Wilson, William John, Pte.
2947, Wirta, Tobias Oscar Richard, Pte.
2948, Witts, Albert Henry, Pte.
2949, Ducie, Henry, Pte.
2950, Cameron, Robert, Pte.
2951, Barrett, John Edward, Pte.

10th Reinforcements.

(Embarked at Adelaide, South Australia, on H.M.A.T. A70, "Ballarat," 14th September, 1915.)

Somerville, Robert Smith, 2nd Lieut.
1712, Dyer, Frank Gordon, Pte.
1716, Foden, Arthur, Pte.
3001, Beecken, Herman Ernest, Pte.
3003, Bedford, Thomas, Pte.
3004, Beaumont, Sidney Newport, Pte.
3005, Bishop, Arthur, Pte.
3006, Clark, Roy William John, Pte.
3009, Gill, Percy Roy, Pte.
3010, Hughes, Percival James, Pte.
3011, Haines, Herbert John, Pte.
3012, Hutton, Ernest Norman, Pte.
3014, Lotton, Victor, Pte.
3015, Mercer, Stanley Archer, Pte.
3016, Mudie, David James, Pte.
3019, McMurray, Leonard Wm., Pte.
3020, Nolan, Alexander Patrick, Pte.
3021, Nankivell, Edgar Lyle, Pte.
3023, Opie, Jack Bennet, Pte.

16th INFANTRY BATTALION—NOMINAL ROLL –continued.

10th Reinforcements --continued.

3026, Olsen, Richard Henry, Pte.
3028, Ould, Richard Harold, Pte.
3029, Painter, William Albert, Pte.
3030, Plummer, Albert Kelso, Pte.
3031, Peterson, George Olaf, Pte.
3032, Pearson, Fredk. Lancelot, Pte.
3033, Pearce, Frederick Charles, Pte.
3034, Pickering, Gordon, Pte.
3035, Rose, Clarence Hallbroook, Pte.
3036, Rowe, Clarence Richard, Pte.
3037, Rzeszkowski, Leonard Ignatius, Pte.
3038, Rosson, Alfred Thomas, Pte.
3039, Tilbrook, George Edward, Pte.
3040, Talbot, Henry Arthur, Pte.
3041, Willing, Sydney Livingston, Pte.
3043, Sowton, Claude Colin Bruce, Pte.
3044, Emmins, Arthur Oliver, Pte.
3045, Charles, Francis Allen, Pte.
3046, Deslandes, Cecil Melville, Pte.
3047, McGinness, Charles, Pte.
3048, Chapple, Douglas Leonard, Pte.
3049, Ashby, Albert Victor, Pte.
3050, Hobbs, Ernest George, Pte.
3051, Johnson, Alfred, Pte.
3055, Watkins, Harold Stuart, Pte.
3056, Taylor, Charles John, Pte.
3057, Strong, Andrew Jerome, Pte.
3058, Palmer, Arthur John Thomas, Pte.
3059, Nottage, Reuben Nichol, Pte.
3060, McLean, Eric Ernest, Pte.
3061, Park, James Henry, Pte.
3062, Pile, Alfred Edward, Pte.
3063, Cooper, John Charles, Pte.
McMaster, Samuel Crawford, Pte.

(Embarked at Fremantle, Western Australia, on H.M.A.T. A32, "Themistocles," 13th October, 1915.)

Hilary, Wilfrid, 2nd Lieut.
3076, Walter, William Guy Ardagh, Pte.
3077, Slee, Frank Dilloway, Pte.
3078, Clarke, Fred, Pte.
3079, Foster, Robert Samuel, Pte.
3080, Ogden, Errol Charles, Pte.
3081, Jones, Henry Fletcher, Pte.
3082, Brodie, John Thomas, Pte.
3083, Attle, Clement Frederick, Pte.
3084, Banks, William Henry, Pte.
3085, Buckley, Harold, Pte.
3086, Brotherwood, William John, Pte.
3087, Bole, Henry Thomas, Pte.
3088, Banfield, George William, Pte.
3089, Brown, Henry, Pte.
3090, Bate, Francis Joseph, Pte.
3091, Brown, Harold Clare, Pte.
3092, Cook, Alfred Reginald, Pte.
3093, Cook, Leslie Robert, Pte.
3094, Connolly, Thomas, Pte.
3095, Cameron, Donald, Pte.
3096, Chester, Frank Herbert, Pte.
3097, Cook, Walter Theodore, Pte.
3098, Coughlan, John Joseph, Pte.
3099, Cole, Arthur Herbert, Pte.
3100, Cooper, Charles, Pte.
3101, Devon, John, Pte.
3102, Dimond, Charles Leslie, Pte.
3103, Egan, Horace John William, Pte.
3104, Edwards, Reginald Gordon, Pte.
3105, Farrington, Louis, Pte.
3106, Fisher, Osborne, Pte.
3107, Fleet, Edward, Pte.
3108, Freeman, Frederick, Pte.
3109, Glass, Andrew, Pte.
3110, Gregson, William, Pte.
3111, Grant, Robert, Pte.
3112, Gee, William James, Pte.
3113, Hamburger, William, Pte.
3114, Hannan, Leonard Vernon, Pte.
3115, Hay, William Walter Shaw, Pte.
3116, Howells, Samuel Walter, Pte.
3117, Howson, Robert Richard, Pte.
3118, Hopkins, Frank Raymond, Pte.
3119, Howlett, Percy, Pte.
3120, Herbert, Thomas Fredk., Pte.
3121, Houston, Bertram William, Pte.
3122, Jackson, Vidal Fitzgerald, Pte.
3123, John, Hugh Davies, Pte.
3124, Joy, Carl Lindsay, Pte.
3125, Jones, Frederick Henry, Pte.
3126, Kirkham, Charles Richard, Pte.
3127, King, Frederick, Pte.
3128, Kamman, George, Pte
3129, Linton, William, Pte.
3130, Litton, Edgar Ernest, Pte.
3131, Maschitti, Antoni, Pte.
3132, Mearns, Lewis Roy, Pte.
3133, McGlinn, Thomas Henry, Pte.
3134, McKenzie, Hugh Newcomen, Pte.

THE OLD SIXTEENTH. 241

16th INFANTRY BATTALION—NOMINAL ROLL—continued.

10th Reinforcements—continued.

3135, McKenzie, Stephen Nowell, Pte.
3136, Montague, Albert Henry, Pte.
3137, McNee, Robert, Pte.
3138, McHugh, William, Pte.
3139, Matthews, Arthur Leslie, Pte.
3140, Matthews, James William, Pte.
3141, Martin, Alfred Arthur, Pte.
3142, Matheson, Henry Thomas, Pte.
3144, Michie, John, Pte.
3145, Munro, Donald Gordon, Pte.
3146, McLean, Robert George, Pte.
3147, Moore, Thomas Vincent, Pte.
3148, Newmarch, Oliver, Pte.
3149, Nicol, Leonard James, Pte.
3150, Nicholls, Charles Joseph, Pte.
*3151, Owens, Patrick Henry, Pte.
3152, O'Connor, Owen Edward, Pte.
3153, Patterson, Samuel James, Pte.
3154, Peacock, Alfred, Pte.
3155, Phillips, Reginald David, Pte.
3156, Rowe, Phillip George, Pte.
3157, Ritchie, Ernest Avenal, Pte.
3158, Sorensen, David Theodore, Pte.
3159, Shearer, William Edward, Pte.
3160, Saunders, Clifford Leake, Pte.
3161, Seal, George Cosmos, Pte.
3162, Tandy, John Thomas, Pte.
3163, Thacker, Sidney, Pte.
3164, Taylor, Albert Gordon, Pte.
3165, Taylor, William Joseph, Pte.
3166, Toomath, Frank Sewart, Pte.
3167, Underwood, Hugh Llewellyn Endra, Pte.
3168, Wilkins, Henry, Pte.
3169, Westbury, John Lloyd Arthur, Pte.
3170, Walton, Leslie Gordon, Pte.
3171, Wood, Herbert, Pte.
3172, Woodings, John Harrison, Pte.
3173, Young, Kenneth, Pte.
3174, Chamberlain, Gordon Charles, Pte.

11th Reinforcements.

(Embarked at Adelaide, South Australia, on H.M.A.T. A24, "Benalla," 27th October, 1915.)

Robin, James Keeling, Lt.
3226, Amber, William John, Pte.
3227, Anderson, Herbert George, Pte.
3228, Burn, Robert William, Pte.
3229, Bateman, John Alfred, Pte.
3230, Bermingham, Francis, Pte.
3231, Black, Archie Norman Grant, Pte.
3232, Blaskett, William George, Pte.
3233, Blee, Horace Edgar, Pte.
3234, Boockmeyer, Christian Gordon, Pte.
3235, Brown, Clement Herbert, Pte.
3236, Brown, Joseph Patrick, Pte.
3237, Burgess, John Atkins, Pte.
3238, Cahill, Lawrence Victor, Pte.
3239, Carr, James Aaron, Pte.
3141, Cherry, Frederick Graham, Pte.
3243, Cocks, Frederick James, Pte.
3244, Clunes, Daniel, Pte.
3245, Collins, James Gillet, Pte.
3246, Cornish, Alfred Herbert, Pte.
3247, Cruzer, Rudolph Otto Paul, Pte.
3248, Daw, Richard, Pte.
3249, Dawson, George Edgar, Pte.
3250, Dearden, Frank, Pte.
3252, Dennis, Arthur, Pte.
3253, Dennis, George Robert, Pte.
3255, Dengarde, Phillip Francis, Pte.
3256, Earle, Frederick Harvey, Pte.
3257, Lee, John, Pte.
3259, Farnden, Albert John, Pte.
3260, Feirclough, Royal Frank, Pte.
3261, Fisher, Francis Henry John, Pte.
3262, Ferriss, James, Pte.
3264, Franke, Albert Frederick, Pte.
3265, Gambrell, Roy Lancelot, Pte.
3266, Gilding, Richard, Pte.
3267, Golley, Maurice Parminter, Pte.
3268, Gregurke, Clarence Ivan, Pte.
3269, Griffiths, George Henry, Pte.
3271, Harrison, Henry Herbert, Pte.
3272, Harvey, Herbert William, Pte.
3273, Hicks, Wilmot Leslie, Pte.
3274, Holl, Clarence Victor, Pte.
3275, Hill, Martin Pascoe, Pte.
3276, Jeffs, Charles Gordon, Pte.
3277, Lambert, Arthur Stanley, Pte.
3278, Lapthorne, Thomas Frank, Pte.
3279, Larking, Edgar Victor Claude, Pte.
3280, Manser, George, Pte.

THE OLD SIXTEENTH.

16th INFANTRY BATTALION—NOMINAL ROLL—*continued.*

11th Reinforcements—continued.

3281, Matson, Daniel, Pte.
3283, Martin, Sydney Herbert, Pte.
3284, May, Stanley Gordon, Pte.
3285, Mead, William Edward, Pte.
3286, Miller, Roy, Pte.
3288, McDonald, Henry, Pte.
3289, McCann, Joseph, Pte.
3290, McInerney, Thomas Harold, Pte.
3291, McRay, Sydney George, Pte.
3293, Nash, Edwin Albury, Pte.
3294, Neice, Percy, Pte.
3295, O'Leary, Dennis John, Pte.
3296, Olliver, Augustus Roy, Pte.
3298, Phillips, William Edmund, Pte.
3299, Plumpton, Charles William, Pte.
3300, Price, Thomas Albert, Pte.
3301, Rickard, James Joseph, Pte.
3302, Richards, Richard Morris, Pte.
3303, Rogers, Charles Sydney, Pte.
3304, Sando, Leslie William, Pte.
3305, Scott, John Walter, Pte.
3306, Shannon, John Francis, Pte.
3307, Shannon, John George, Pte.
3308, Shepherdson, Joseph Henry, Pte.
3310, Schultze, Emil Herman, Pte.
3311, Simpson, Frank Lawrence, Pte.
3312, Smith, Edward John, Pte.
3313, Smith, Lancelot Beck, Pte.
3314, Smith, Merton Goode, Pte.
3316, Stewart, William, Pte.
3317, Taylor, George Frederick, Pte.
3318, Wuttke, Arthur Paul, Pte.
3319, Vardon, Frederick Henry, Pte.
3320, Von Einem, Frederick Albert, Pte.
3321, Ward, James Vincent, Pte.
3322, Watts, John, Pte.
3323, Walkley, William Roger, Pte.
3324, Williams, John Davies, Pte.
3325, Wallace, George Charles, Pte.
3326, Walker, Roy, Pte.
3327, Whitaker, Tom Worthley, Pte.
3328, Wright, William Henry, Pte.
3329, Yeo, Lindley Walter, Pte.
3330, Young, Alexander Livingstone, Pte.
3331, Angus, John Stanley Douglas, Pte.
3332, Clarken, Thomas Michael, Pte.
3334, Foreman, George Thomas Raymond, Pte.
3335, Martin, Daniel Leopold, Pte.
3336, Moffatt, George, Pte.
3337, Murray, George Horace, Pte.
3338, Pearson, Charlie, Pte.
3339, Robbins, Leslie Thomas Francis, Pte.
3340, Thompson, Walter Frederick, Pte.
3341, Spear, Trevellyn Wilberforce, Pte.
Liddle, Thomas Draver, Pte.
Tozer, Charles Henry, Pte.

(Embarked at Fremantle, Western Australia, on H.M.A.T. A24, "Benalla," 1st November, 1915.)

Wilson, Harry, 2nd Lt.
Brearley, Montague Sharp, 2nd Lt.
3381, Gray, David, Pte.
3382, Cooper, James Wesley Brittain, Pte.
3383, Revell, William Henry, Pte.
3384, Fairley, Thomas Clarence, Pte.
3385, Robinson, Ernest William, Pte.
3386, Grinlington, Dudley, Pte.
3387, Campbell, Bruce, Pte.
3388, Kelly, Hubert O'Donovan, Pte.
3389, Bliss, Herbert Richard Henry, Pte.
3390, Phillipson, Clarence Lancelot, Pte.
3391, Pimm, William Rule, Pte.
3392, Gilmour, Robert Hugh, Pte.
3393, Cutmore, James, Pte.
3395, Ralston, Charles William, Pte.
3396, Andrews, Harold Edward, Pte.
3397, Archer, David, Pte.
3398, Allender, Thomas Francis, Pte.
3399, Axford, Thomas Leslie, Pte.
3400, Austin, Sydney, Pte.
3401, Andrews, Arthur Dudley, Pte.
3402, Abbott, Albert Ernest, Pte.
3403, Bentley, Edgar, Pte.
3404, Bach, Ted, Pte.
3405, Benson, John, Pte.
3406, Bishop, Jesse Gerald, Pte.

THE OLD SIXTEENTH.

16th INFANTRY BATTALION—NOMINAL ROLL—continued.

11th Reinforcements—continued.

3407, Binning, Walter Priestly, Pte.
3408, Borrell, Harry, Pte.
3409, Brennan, John, Pte.
3410, Bain, Archibald, Pte.
3411, Beresford, Wallace William, Pte.
3412, Beardsworth, John, Pte.
3413, Barrow, Samuel James, Pte.
3414, Byrne, Andrew, Pte.
3415, Bloom, Alma Thick Holmes, Pte.
3416, Buckingham, Hugh, Pte.
3417, Henry, Charles Edwin, Pte.
3418, Buist, Herbert Pte.
3419, Bell, Frederick Arthur, Pte.
3420, Bent, Thomas Edward, Pte.
3421, Barry, James, Pte.
3422, Brownrigg, Norman, Pte.
3423, Bailey, Alexander Gregory, Pte.
3424, Carter, William, Pte.
3425, Casey, George, Pte.
3426, Cassidy, Robert James, Pte.
3427, Chalmers, William Fraser, Pte.
3428, Chapple, Charles James Stacey, Pte.
3429, Corkery, Patrick, Pte.
3430, Cooper, Joseph, Pte.
3431, Coffey, Aloysius Francis, Pte.
3432, Cumming, Langley, Pte.
3433, Cusack, Bernard, Pte.
3434, Calvo, Charles, Pte.
3435, Cooper, Bertie Frederick, Pte.
3436, Curven, James George, Pte.
3437, Corkhill, Maurice, Pte.
3438, Corlett, Frederick James, Pte.
3439, Devereux, William George, Pte.
3440, Day, Charles Thomas, Pte.
3441, Dee, Henry Thomas, Pte
3442, Dee, Joseph, Pte.
3443, Deverell, Francis Alfred Daniel, Pte.
3444, Denyer, Henry Dennies, Pte.
3445, Drew, Thomas Henry, Pte.
3446, Drew, Frederick, Pte.
3447, Doherty, Michael, Pte.
3448, Diggles, James, Pte.
3449, Doig, William Cleve Robinson Alexander, Pte.
3450, Doyle, Henry Wright, Pte.
3451, Duce, Eric, Pte.
3452, Dunbar, James, Pte.
3453, Donovan, Percy, Pte.
3454, Douglas, Stanley Alison, Pte.
3455, Duckham, William John, Pte.
3456, Ecclestone, William Basil, Pte.
3457, Edwards, Henry, Pte.
3458, Edmunds, George William, Pte.
3459, Emery, Frederick Washington, Pte.
3460, Fletcher, Joseph, Pte.
3461, Fox, Frederick Francis, Pte.
3462, Fox, George Alfred, Pte.
3463, Fannon, Thomas, Pte.
3464, Gibbins, Leonard Broadmeadow, Pte.
3465, Glance, Albert, Pte.
3466, Gmiener, Eric Percival, Pte.
3467, Goudie, William, Pte.
3468, Gray, William, Pte.
3469, Greenhalgh, James, Pte.
3470, Grieve, Leslie Charles, Pte.
3471, Golding, James, Pte.
3472, Griffiths, Ernest Norman, Pte.
3473, Geldard, Lancelot Ingle, Pte.
3474, Hart, Frederick William, Pte.
3475, Henry, David, Pte.
3476, Hide, Cecil, Pte.
3477, Hicks, Arthur, Pte.
3478, Holland, Claude Harold, Pte.
3479, Hopkinson, Henry, Pte.
3480, Horne, Robert Somerville, Pte.
3481, Hodson, Arthur, Pte.
3482, Helm, Charles Ernest, Pte.
3483, Harrison, Leonard Harry, Pte.
3484, Harper, Arthur Lewis, Pte.
3485, Hall, Edgar, Pte.
3486, Hancock, John, Pte.
3487, Harvey, James, Pte.
3488, Higgins, John Thomas, Pte.
3489, Hickman, Neville William, Pte
3490, Hart, William, Pte.
3491, Hunter, David, Pte.
3492, Hurst, Robert Raymond, Pte.
3493, Henry, Thomas Darling, Pte.
3494, Jarvis, Jack, Pte.
3495, Jenkin, William Hurford, Pte.
3496, Johnston, Leslie, Pte.
3497, Jenkins, Henry William, Pte.
3498, James, Gomer Lewis, Pte.
3499, Kinna, Frederick William, Pte.
3500, Kendrick, Roy John, Pte.
3501, Kelly, Cyril Harvey, Pte.
3502, Knudson, Yul, Pte.
3503, Kippist, Percy Harold, Pte.
3504, Kroeber, Waldemar Franz Von, Pte.
3505, Longbottom, David Henry, Pte.
3506, Lettington, William, Pte.

16th INFANTRY BATTALION—NOMINAL ROLL—*continued.*

11th Reinforcements—continued.

3507, Lange, Gustav August William, Pte.
3508, Lester, Thomas David, Pte.
3509, Littlejohn, John, Pte.
3510, Lofman, Philip, Pte.
3511, Luckey, Harry, Pte.
3512, Lee, William, Pte.
3513, Lathwell, George Earnest, Pte.
3514, Ledger, Albert John, Pte.
3515, Manton, Arthur King, Pte.
3516, Maloney, Edward, Pte.
3517, Maddocks, Cyril Braden, Pte.
3518, Marsh, Thomas Cecil, Pte.
3519, McCullock, Thomas Albert, Pte.
3520, McDonald, John Allen, Pte.
3521, McGilvray, William, Pte.
3522, McEwen, Charles Henry, Pte.
3523, McLeish, Joseph, Pte.
3524, Midgley, Charles Herbert, Pte.
3525, Miles, John James, Pte.
3526, Monk, Edward, Pte.
3527, Mathewy, Charles, Pte.
3528, McGilvray, Robert, Pte.
3529, McCallum, George, Pte.
3530, Merchant, Joseph, Pte.
3531, McDonald, Hugh John, Pte.
3532, McMillan, Thomas James, Pte.
3533, Matheson, Angus John, Pte.
3534, Morris, John Robert, Pte.
3535, McDonald, John Thomas, Pte.
3536, Murray, Leslie Alan, Pte.
3537, Nicholls, John William, Pte.
3538, Nankiville, Norman Henry, Pte.
3539, O'Donnell, Arthur, Pte.
3540, Oxenham, Joseph, Pte.
3541, Palmer, Charles, Pte.
3542, Partlon, Christopher Joseph, Pte.
3543, Priest, Thomas Elrad, Pte.
3544, Riordan, David, Pte.
3545, Reed, Albert Agar, Pte.
3546, Robinson, Edward William Pte.
3547, Stewart, James Leslie, Pte.
3548, Samson, David, Pte.
3550, Shea, John Patrick, Pte.
3551, Smith, Edward George, Pte.
3552, Stevens, James, Pte.
3553, Smythe, Leslie, Pte.
3554, Sullivan, Daniel, Pte.
3555, Shanhun, Alfred, Pte.
3556, Smith, Dave, Pte.
3557, Smith, Walter Percy, Pte.
3558, Sweeting, George Palmer, Pte.
3559, Symonds, Jack Therman, Pte.
3560, Stephens, Eric John, Pte.
3561, Tubb, Thomas Samuel, Pte.
3562, Trigwell, Leonard Frank, Pte.
3563, Tempest, George Henry, Pte.
3564, Thorp, Robert James, Pte.
3565, Taft, Frederick Thomas, Pte.
3566, Tremlett, Frederick, Pte.
3567, Taylor, Sydney Joseph, Pte.
3568, Williams, John Vivian, Pte.
3569, Wetherall, Norman, Pte.
3570, Weatherall, Norman, Pte.
3571, Walker, Alexander Enoch, Pte.
3572, Wilks, Matthew Harold, Pte.
3573, Williams, Walter Wynne, Pte.
3574, Wilson, Leslie James, Pte.
3575, Wood, Edward James Cecil, Pte.
3576, Youd, George Richard, Pte.
3577, McLean, Walter Alex., Pte.
3578, Macfarlan, Cuthbert, Pte.

12th Reinforcements.

(Embarked at Adelaide, South Australia, on R.M.S. "Malwa," 2nd December, 1915.)

Dyke, George Connock, 2nd Lt.
3162, Jackson, Thomas Douglas, Pte.
3676, Abraham, William, Pte.
3677, Badenoch, Arthur Gilbert, Pte.
3678, Balchin, William Henry, Pte.
3679, Barker, Archibald Ray, Pte.
3680, Barker, Richard Thomas, Pte.
3681, Benson, Arthur Ernest, Pte.
3682, Bingley, Joseph Arthur, Pte.
3683, Brown, Charles Tasman, Pte.
3684, Brown, Lionel Samuel, Pte.
3685, Burnett, Hurtle John, Pte.
3686, Clarke, Stanley Victor, Pte.
3687, Coulls, George Vernon, Pte.
3688, Coulls, William Albert, Pte.
3689, Davoren, Hugh James, Pte.
3690, Dixon, Albert Stanley, Pte.
3691, Dunbar, Irwin, Pte.
3692, Everatt, James Henry, Pte.
3693, Fisher, David Henry, Pte.
3694, Fisher, John, Pte.
3695, Feely, Edward James, Pte.
3696, Freak, William Clem, Pte.
3697, Garie, John Albert, Pte.
3698, Gillespie, Clive, Pte.
3699, Greer, Lawrence Allen, Pte.

THE OLD SIXTEENTH.

16th INFANTRY BATTALION—NOMINAL ROLL—*continued.*

12th Reinforcements —continued.

3700, Grigg, Isaac, Pte.
3701, Harnett, Daniel Aloysius, Pte.
3702, Hayes, Edward Patrick, Pte.
3703, Herbert, William John, Pte.
3704, Holden, Arnold William, Pte.
3705, Innes, James Robert, Pte.
3706, Jeffery, Alfred William, Pte.
3707, Jones, Roy Norish, Pte.
3708, Johnson, Norman Eustron, Pte.
3709, Kay, James Francis, Pte.
3710, Kelly, Frederick William, Pte.
3711, Kelly, Lionel Edwin, Pte.
3712, Knnaley, Steven Ernest, Pte.
3713, Keays, Alfred Charles, Pte.
3714, Kidner, Frederick George, Pte.
3715, King, Bert, Pte.
3716, Klemettila, August, Pte.
3717, Langley, Clarence Roy, Pte.
3718, Lindner, Leslie William, Pte.
3719, Lindsay, Donald Elder, Pte.
3720, Lindsay, Walter Clarence Leslie, Pte.
3721, Loader, Harold Gordon, Pte.
3722, Loader, Reginald William, Pte.
3724, Masters, Roy, Pte.
3725, Matthews, John Francis. Pte.
3725a, Mackereth, William Harold Luxton Percy, Pte.
3726, Matten, John, Pte.
3727, Marshall, Frederick Stanley, Pte.
3728, Menhennett, Henry Morcom, Pte.
3729, Miatke, Frederick Alick, Pte.
3730, Morris, William Joseph, Pte.
3731, Moxham, Frederick, Pte.
3732, McAuliffe, Edward Daniel, Pte.
3733, McCarthy, Jeremiah Joseph, Pte.
3734, McCormack, John, Pte.
3735, McDonnell, John, Pte.
3736, McKenna, Thomas James, Pte.
3737, McKenzie, Fred, Pte.
3738, McMahon, James, Pte.

3739, Norton, Arthur Stuart, Pte.
3740, Noy, Ernest Henry, Pte.
3741, Oatey, John Maitland, Pte.
3742, Opperman, Martin Otto, Pte.
3743, O'Sullivan, John Joseph, Pte.
3744, Parish, Murdoch Morrison, Pte.
3745, Pascoe, Rickardo Wiltshire, Pte.
3746, Peters, Arthur, Pte.
3747, Playford, Frank, Pte.
3748, Poole, Benjamin Clement Garfield, Pte.
3749, Rabechi, Henry, Pte.
3750, Ralph, Sylvester Leopold, Pte.
3751, Rochow, Frederick August, Pte.
3752, Rees, Harry, Pte.
3753, Rogers, Alfred Vincent, Pte.
3754, Rhymer, Edwin, Pte.
3755, Scaresbrook, John, Pte.
3756, Schocroft, Charles Sidney, Pte.
3757, Scott, Raymond Victor, Pte.
3758, Sitters, Henry Tolchard, Pte.
3759, Smiley, William George, Pte.
3760, Smythe, Harold, Pte.
3761, Smyth, John, Pte.
3762, Smyth, Matthew Aloysious, Pte
3763, Stephenson, Keith Hessell, Pte.
3765, Taylor, Rees Llewellyn, Pte.
3766, Vincent, William Charles, Pte.
3767, Walker, Frederick Horace, Pte.
3768, Washington, Lavington Ainsley, Pte.
3769, Way, James Frederick, Pte.
3770a, Webster, Cyril Robert, Pte.
3771, White, Victor Sales, Pte.
3772, Whiteford, James William, Pte.
3774, Whittle, Harry Cleggett, Pte.
3775, Willard, Frederick, Pte.
3776, Williams, Leonard Leopold, Pte.
3777, Woods, Malcolm Edward, Pte.
3778, Yates, Wilbert Hallam, Pte.
3780, Elphick, Alfred William, Pte.
3781, Kearey, Richard George, Pte.

(Embarked at Fremantle, Western Australia, on H.M.A.T. A31, "Ajana," 22nd December, 1915.)

Wadge, Frank, 2nd Lieut.
Stephenson, Leonard Armstrong, 2nd Lieut.
1394, Turner, Martin William, Pte.
3831, Carrick, Edward Angus, Pte.
3833, McAdam, William Claude, Pte.
3834, Gunner, Harold, Pte.
3835, Caine, Patrick Henry, Pte.

3836, Wadge, Herbert, Pte.
3837, Higgins, Georgie, Pte.
3838, Mawby, Arthur Henry, Pte.
3839, Turner, Charles Herbert, Pte.
3840, Osborn, Georgie, Pte.
3841, Hiscock, Charles Frank, Pte.
3842, Stewart, John, Pte.
3843, Paterson, George Bell, Pte.

16th INFANTRY BATTALION—NOMINAL ROLL—*continued.*

12th Reinforcements—continued.

3844, Synnot, George Houston, Pte.
3845, Carter, Martin, Pte.
3848, Arundel, Henry, Pte.
3849, Ashcroft, Robert, Pte.
3850, Banfield, Harrie Iliffe, Pte.
3851, Barry, William Francis, Pte.
3852, Bass, Albert James, Pte.
3854, Bergstrom, Petrus Efiam, Pte.
3855, Biggs, William Leonard, Pte.
3856, Bishop, Walter James, Pte.
3858, Bray, Thomas Henry, Pte.
3859, Brockman, Charles, Pte.
3860, Broom, Wallace, Pte.
3861, Buckley, Albert Augustine, Pte
3862, Burgess, John, Pte.
3863, Burn, Ralph, Pte.
3865, Caldwell, James, Pte.
3866, Cameron, William, Pte.
3867, Chivers, Charles, Pte.
3868, Clements, John David, Pte.
3869, Colbourne, Frank, Pte.
3870, Collins, Frank, Pte.
3871, Comiskey, Henry, Pte.
3872, Cook, Augustus, Pte.
3873, Cooper, Charles William, Pte.
3875, Cox, Henry, Pte.
3876, Craig, George Henry, Pte.
3879, Cunningham, Thomas, Pte.
3880, Damon, Ted, Pte.
3881, Davies, Robert Fyfe, Pte.
3882, Davis, Alfred, Pte.
3884, Desmond, Frank, Pte.
3885, Devereux, John, Pte.
3886, Dickerson, Charles Rowland, Pte.
3887, Dixon, Edwin, Pte.
3889, Doherty, Joseph, Pte.
3890, Douglas, John, Pte.
3891, Dunlop, William, Pte.
3892, Eastburn, Arthur Robinson, Pte.
3893, Eastland, Frank, Pte.
3894, Elliot, James, Pte.
3895, Emery, Joseph, Pte.
3896, Fanning, James St. Witten, Pte.
3897, Farrell, Charles Edward, Pte.
3898, Fawcett, William Lot, Pte.
3899, Fisher, Charles, Pte.
3900, Francis, William Harry, Pte.
3901, Fraser, Robert Irving, Pte.
3902, Fuller, Harry, Pte.
3904, Gaden, Robert George, Pte.
3905, Gailey, William Desney Alexander, Pte.
3906, Goddard, George William, Pte.
3907, Goninon, Harry, Pte.
3908, Goodier, Frederick, Pte.
3911, Greensitt, Herbert, Pte.
3912, Greenway, Herbert Charles, Pte.
3915, Harwood, Matthew, Pte.
3916, Hayward, Arthur, Pte.
3917, Heal, George William Alex., Pte.
3918, Helsin, John, Pte.
3921, Hollings, Fred., Pte.
3922, Hopkins, James Francis, Pte.
3923, Hough, Geoffrey Malcolm, Pte.
3924, Hudson, Harold Percy, Pte.
3925, Hyman, Joseph, Pte.
3926, Ireland, Arthur George, Pte.
3927, Isbister, George Thomas, Pte.
3928, Jahn Conrad Albert Alford, Pte.
3929, James, William Joseph Wearne, Pte.
3930, Jones, Thomas John, Pte.
3032, Kean, James, Pte.
3933, Keenan, Thomas, Pte.
3935, Keogh, Thomas, Pte.
3936, King, William, Pte.
3938, Lacy, Alfred, Pte.
3940, Larsen, Cecil George, Pte.
3941, Lee, Ernest, Pte.
3942, Lloyd, James Stewart, Pte.
3943, Logan, William Edwin, Pte.
3945, Martin, Charles, jun., Pte.
3946, Martin, Thomas William, Pte.
3947, Matthews, William Francis, Pte.
3948, May, Thomas William Herey, Pte.
3949, Meakins, Harry Hayden, Pte.
3950, Menagh, John Wilson, Pte.
3951, Midolo, Clifton, Pte.
3952, Minn, Robert Charles, Pte.
3954, Mooney, George Thomas, Pte.
3955, Moore, Felix, Pte.
3956, Moore, Frederick Marshall, Pte.
3957, Morgan, Joseph Forrest, Pte.
3958, Mumford, Frederick Arthur, Pte.
3960, McDougall, Thomas Wilson, Pte.
3961, McGehey, William, Pte.
3962, McKay, Gordon Leslie, Pte.
3963, McWilliams, John, Pte.
3964, Neal, Edward, Pte.
3965, Newton, Frederick Robert, Pte.
3966, Nisbett, Edward James, Pte.
3967, Nordstrom, Albert, Pte.

THE OLD SIXTEENTH.

16th INFANTRY BATTALION—NOMINAL ROLL—continued.

12th Reinforcements—continued.

3968, Nulsen, Albert Francis, Pte.
3969, Overington, Herbert Leonard, Pte.
3970, O'Meara, Martin, Pte.
3971, O'Sullivan, Joseph Francis, Pte.
3972, Pacey, Cecil, Pte.
3973, Palmer, Lawrence Turner, Pte.
3974, Parker, George Robert, Pte.
3976, Pontago, Peter, Pte.
3977, Poole, Horace George, Pte.
3978, Porter, Robert, Pte.
3979, Potter, William Lyne, Pte.
3980, Power, Henry Horace, Pte.
3981, Preston, Joseph Robert, Pte.
3982, Randell, Sidney, Pte.
3983, Rea, William Alexander, Pte.
3984, Reardon, Thomas, Pte.
3985, Richards, Albert Leonard, Pte.
3986, Rickards, William Walter, Pte.
3987, Robinson, Cecil William, Pte.
3989, Rowland, Charles Johnston, Pte.
3990, Russell, George Amos, Pte.
3991, Samson, Charles Frank, Pte.
3992, Saunders, Arthur Gordon, Pte.
3993, Scott, George, Pte.
3994, Sinclair, Gerald Arthur, Pte.
3995, Skurrie, Frederick Arthur, Pte.
3996, Sloper, Walter, Pte.
3997, Smethurst, James Henry, Pte.
3998, Smith, Charles, Pte.
4000, Smout, Thomas Frederick, Pte.
4001, Standen, Frederick Samuel, Pte.
4002, Stevens, William Dobson, Pte.
4003, Strang, Robert, Pte.
4004, Sturtridge, Guy, Pte.
4006, Sutherland, Matthew Dickson, Pte.
4007, Sweetnam, Robert, Pte.
4008, Taylor, Gerald Patrick, Pte.
4009, Taylor, James Gaul, Pte.
4010, Taylor, Joseph, Pte.
4011, Thomas, John Nicholas, Pte.
4014, Torrie, George, Pte.
4016, Truran, Basil Claude, Pte.
4017, Vernede, Charles William Ewart, Pte.
4018, Vinicombe, Edward Wm., Pte.
4019, Waddell, David Dickson, Pte.
4021, Wallace, William, Pte.
4022, Waterman, William Cromwell Outrid, Pte.
4024, Whitting, William Archelaus, Pte.
4025, Williams, Samuel, Pte.
4026, Wither, John Vivian, Pte.
4027, Wright, Allan Stuart, Pte.
4028, Wright, Raymond Hamilton, Pte.
4029, Anderson, Ernest, Pte.
4030, Ffoulkes, John Edwin, Pte.
4031, Grant, William Alexander, Pte.
4032, Huntley, Herbert, Pte.
4033, Sheridan, Edward, Pte.
4034, Wood, Hubert, James, Pte.
4035, Goode, Wilfred Leslie, Pte.
4037, Briggs, John Albert, Pte.
4038, Drake, Clements John, Pte.
4039, Francis, Joseph, Pte.
4040, Harrison, Thomas Frank, Pte.
4041, Lynch, Joseph Patrick, Pte.
4043, Maxfield, George Edgar, Pte.
4045, Perry, Robert Hamilton, Pte.
4046, Plummer, William Henry, Pte.
4047, Preston, Hugh James, Pte.
4048, Willis, Joseph Daniel, Pte.
4049, Rootsey, Henry Albert, Pte.
4050, Ferguson, Alen, Pte.
4051, Kirby, Fred, Pte.
4052, Mullen, Edward, Pte.
4054, Lafferty, John, Pte.
4055, Hall, Edward, Pte.
4056, Ivory, William, Pte.
4057, Jenkins, Edward, Pte.
4058, McKay, Alexander Patrick, Pte.
4059, Roberts, Sam, Pte.
4060, Ryan, Bernard, Pte.
4061, Murrahy, Michael, Pte.
4013, Tollis, Walter Reuben, Pte.

13th Reinforcements.

(Embarked at Adelaide, South Australia, on H.M.A.T. A30, "Borda," 11th January, 1916.)

Moyes, Alban George, 2nd Lt.
4126, Alley, Thomas William, Pte.
4127, Baker, Edward Ross, Pte.
4128, Bald, Albert Harold, Pte.
4129, Barnfather, Ernest James, Pte.

16th INFANTRY BATTALION—NOMINAL ROLL—*continued.*

13th Reinforcements—continued.

4130, Best, Richard Sydney, Pte.
4131, Birt, Harry Williams, Pte.
4132, Bradey, Alfred James, Pte.
4133, Bradley, Alfred Lionel, Pte.
4134, Buckley, Thomas, Pte.
4135, Campbell, Philip Henry, Pte.
4136, Carnie, Robert Davidson, Pte.
4137, Carslaw, John, Pte.
4138, Chasteauneuf, William George, Pte.
4139, Clemens, Edward, Pte.
4140, Coulson, George, Pte.
4141, Coulson, Joseph, Pte.
4142, Dodd, Thomas James Harold, Pte.
4143, Emms, Frederick William, Pte.
4144, Finey, Hastwell, Pte.
4145, Galbraith, David John, Pte.
4146, Gelston, Arthur John, Pte.
4147, Glover, Henry, Pte.
4148, Gobell, James, Pte.
4149, Hammond, Percival, Pte.
4150, Harris, Rowland, Pte.
4151, Hendy, Albert Stanley, Pte.
4152, Hill, William Hugh, Pte.
4153, Holyoak, William Alfred, Pte.
4154, Inns, Wilfred Cole, Pte.
4155, Keelty, William Francis, Pte.
4156, Kelly, Harry, Pte.
4157, Kerry, Samuel, Pte.
4158, Kitchin, William, Pte.
4159, Knuckey, William Hector, Pte.
4160, Lamb, John William, Pte.
4161, Lane, John Clifton, Pte.
4162, Lane, William Henry, Pte.
4163, Love, Sydney Earl, Pte.
4164, Loxton, Thomas Samuel, Pte.
4165, Maddison, Lionel Foster, Pte.
4166, Maddock, Charles Frederick, Pte.
4168, Marshall, Hector Ernest Eugene, Pte.
4169, Mason, Claud William, Pte.
4170, Maynard, Walter Budd, Pte.
4171, McArthur, Colin Neil, Pte.
4172, McCartney, Stanley John, Pte.
4173, McDonald, John, Pte.
4174, McKail, Ronald George, Pte.
4175, McKellar, William John, Pte.
4176, Nalty, Thomas Newsome, Pte.
4177, O'Dean, Marcus, Pte.
4178, Pankhurst, Gordon, Pte.
4179, Pedder, Frank John, Pte.
4180, Rogers, Sydney William, Pte.
4181, Russell, William Paterson, Pte.
4182, Savery, Arthur, Pte.
4183, Scantlebury, Harry Ernest, Pte.
4184, Schwark, Alfred August, Pte.
4185, Shepley, Percy Phillip, Pte.
4186, Smith, Robert Harold, Pte.
4187, Sexton, William Francis, Pte.
4188, South, Jack Northmore, Pte.
4189, Stephen, Frederick Lawrence, Pte.
4190, Sugars, George Robert, Pte.
4191, Symons, Stanley Richard, Pte.
4192, Vince, Alfred Eli, Pte.
4193, Wallace, Harold, Pte.
4194, Warrenton, Charles, Pte.
4195, Waters, Victor Clarence, Pte.
4196, Woods, Bertram Lawrence, Pte.
4197, Young, Thomas, Pte.
4198, George, Henry Lionel, Pte.

(Embarked at Fremantle, Western Australia, on H.M.A.T. A54, "Runic," 29th January, 1916.)

Kerr, John Strachan, Lieut.
2247, O'Brien, Richard, Pte.
4239, Reynolds, Percy, Pte.
4240, Wilcox, William Francis, Pte.
4241, Bussell, Alfred Joseph, Pte.
4242, Pemble, William Henry Claude, Pte.
4244, Mason, Oliver James, Pte.
4245, McKie, John, Pte.
4246, Adamson, John, Pte.
4247, Archer, Harry, Pte.
4248, Bovell, William Allan, Pte.
4250, Blackwood, Walter, Pte.
4251, Best, Sidney Thomas, Pte.
4252, Brown, George, Pte.
4253, Bingham, Ernest, Pte.
4254, Bingham, Stephen, Pte.
4255, Bell, Hilton Charles, Pte.
4256, Conroy, John William, Pte.
4257, Condron, Thomas, Pte.
4258, Connor, Michael, Pte.
4259, Casey, Albert Richard Booth, Pte.
4260, Cummins, Arthur, Pte.
4261, Cook, James Augustus, Pte.
4263, Chadwick, Eli, Pte.
4264, Conway, George, Pte.
4265, Daly, James Patrick, Pte.
4266, Datchens, Joseph, Pte.
4267, Eppey, Harry, Pte.

THE OLD SIXTEENTH.

16th INFANTRY BATTALION—NOMINAL ROLL—*continued.*

13th Reinforcements—continued.

4268, Ellis, Frederick, Pte.
4269, Evans, Arthur Clarence, Pte.
4270, Field, Lawrence Ridley, Pte.
4271, Ferguson, William, Pte.
4272, Fisher, Walter Stanley, Pte.
4273, Fraser, Albert Duncan, Pte.
4274, Fraser, Robert, Pte.
4275, Fulwood, William Dawson, Pte.
4276, Gibson, Jack Hayden, Pte.
4277, Guthrie, Frank, Pte.
4278, Gray, Edward, Pte.
4279, Gillard, Charles, Pte.
4280, Goodman, Francis Joseph, Pte.
4281, Hannagan, Andrew Joseph, Pte.
4282, Handley, Basil James, Pte.
4284, Hoult, Herbert, Pte.
4285, Halliday, Frank, Pte.
4286, Hayman, Spencer John, Pte.
4288, Hallam, James, Pte.
4289, Hann, Edward John, Pte.
4293, Hughes, John Arthur, Pte.
4294, Hurlston, Arthur, Pte.
4295, Henry, Hollis, Pte.
4296, Jones, Harry Waters, Pte.
4297, Jones, Wilfred Dray, Pte.
4299, Kealy, James Stephen, Pte.
4300, Kershaw, Harold Herbert, Pte.
4301, Langdon, Wallace York, Pte.
4303, Laws, Arthur, Pte.
4305, Mills, John, Pte.
4307, Murphy, Sydney Arthur, Pte.
4308, Mannix, James William, Pte.
4309, Mellowship, Edward Clarence, Pte.
4310, Manning, Oliver Arthur, Pte.
4311, Mudge, Harold George, Pte.
4312, McArthur, Bernard Duncan, Pte.
4313, McColl, William Gregor, Pte.
4314, McDermid, Robert James, Pte.
4315, McKenzie, Frank, Pte.
4316, McParlan, Frank, Pte.
4317, Nettleton, William, Pte.
4318, Nixon, Stanley William, Pte.
4319, Parncutt, Arthur, Pte.
4320, Power, William Henry, Pte.
4321, Preedy, Eric John, Pte.
4323, Pritchard, Wallace Douglas, Pte.
4324, Quinn, Michael Andrew, Pte.
4325, Quan, Walter, Pte.
4326, Queen, Wilfred Walker, Pte.
4327, Roe, Albert Alfred, Pte.
4328, Randell, Herbert Samuel, Pte.
4329, Russell, Robert Joseph, Pte.
4330, Russell, William Alban, Pte.
4331, Reilly, William John, Pte.
4332, Rowe, Francis Thomas, Pte.
4333, Smillie, Lauchlan, Pte.
4336, Schryver, Lester, Pte.
4338, Staniland, Leonard, Pte.
4339, Schofield, Thomas Frederick, Pte.
4341, Sheppard, John, Pte.
4342, Thomson, Joseph, Pte.
4343, Tognini, Charles, Pte.
4345, Taylor, George Frederick, Pte.
4346, Thompson, Arthur, Pte.
4347, Ticklie, Albert Thomas, Pte.
4348, Tilbee, George Stephen, Pte.
4349, Thomson, Joseph Duncan, Pte.
4350, Vaughan, Joseph, Pte.
4351, Vaughan, William George, Pte.
4352, Valli, Baptiste, Pte.
4353, Wearne, Leslie Arnold, Pte.
4354, Wilding, William Opie, Pte.
4356, Wolfe, Walter, Pte.
4357, Watson, Archibald Cameron, Pte.
4358, Wilson, Arthur Gilbert, Pte.
4359, Woodhams, Frederick William, Pte.
4360, Watters, Bertie Glanvell, Pte.
4361, Wilkinson, Walter James, Pte
4362, Walker, Robert, Pte.
4363, Young, Gordon Leslie, Pte.
4364, Young, Alexander Greig, Pte.
4365, Arnold, Clarence, Pte.
4366, Acton, Arthur Thomas, Pte.
4367, Dawson, Alexander John, Pte
4368, Ford, Alfred Percy, Pte.
4370, Gorman, Frank, Pte.
4371, Kennedy, Matthew Bernard, Pte.
4372, Morrissey, Michael Roy, Pte.
4373, Mann, Louis, Pte.
4374, Rogers, Lawrence James, Pte.
4376, Edwards, Jack Leslie, Pte.
4377, Nenke, Stanley Berthold, Pte.
4378, Maschmedt, Lawrence Phillip, Pte.
4379, Hemming, John James, Pte.
4380, Linnane, Martin, Pte.
4381, Keirle, Albert, Pte.
4382, Deehan, William Clement, Pte.
4383, Smith, William, Pte.
4384, Breuer, James Herman, Pte.
4385, Crone, Harold Felix, Pte.
4386, Killelea, Thomas, Pte.

16th INFANTRY BATTALION—NOMINAL ROLL—*continued.*

14th Reinforcements.

(Embarked at Fremantle, Western Australia, on H.M.A.T. A28, "Miltades," 12th February, 1916.)

Elliot, Thomas Hampton, 2nd Lt.
Glowrey, Lindsay Gordon, 2nd Lt.
Roche, Francis John, 2nd Lt.
Caldwell, William, 2nd Lt.
1499, O'Sullivan, Jack, Pte.
4427, Urch, George, Pte.
4428, Vawdrey, Thomas Faull, Pte.
4429, Wood, David, Pte.
4430, Wood, John Morgan, Pte.
4431, Williams, William, Pte.
4432, Webster, Alexander, Pte.
4433, Whittington, Selby Maurice, Pte.
4434, Watson, Jack, Pte.
4435, Wharton, William Manuel, Pte.
4436, Wilton, Martin Adolphus, Pte.
4437, Wilsdon, Henry, Pte.
4438, Wishart, Clarence Bede, Pte.
4439, Watt, Andrew Kenneth George, Pte.
4440, Fern, Charles Stuart, Pte.
4441, Ferguson, Edward Charles, Pte.
4442, Phillips, James Thompson, Pte.
4443, Pinto, Reuben, Pte.
4444, Hawkins, John Michael, Pte.
4445, Baker, Percy, Pte.
4446, Scott, Richard Patrick, Pte.
4447, Jones, Frederick Arthur, Pte.
4448, Rogers, David Owen, Pte.
4449, Rose, John, Pte.
4450, Grace, Michael James, Pte.
4451, Wachman, Robert, Pte.
4452, Bing, George, Pte.
4536, Waters, William Herbert, Pte.
4537, Thompson, John Wilkinson, Pte.
4538, Muir, Alexander McDonald, Pte.
4539, Welch, Sydney Charles, Pte.
4540, Cox, James, Pte.
4541, Gilbert, Robert William, Pte.
4542, Dale, Cecil Maurice Edmund, Pte.
4543, Brown, Roger Peinlott, Pte.
4544, Mowforth, John Joseph, Pte.
4545, Maggs, Joseph Robert, Pte.
4546, Lower, Henry Benjamin, Pte.
4547, Fallon, Vernon Daniel, Pte.
4548, Hardy, George, Pte.
4549, Plant, William, Pte.
4550, Ibbotson, Reginald Montague, Pte.
4551, Truslove, Arthur George, Pte.
4552, Adcock, Sydney, Pte.
4553, Anderson, David Vincent, Pte.
4554, Atkinson, George, Pte.
4555, Ashmore, Luther, Pte.
4556, Andrews, Francis George, Pte.
4557, Aim, Lewis James, Pte.
4558, Barrow, Frank Rupert, Pte.
4559, Boyle, Victor Leo Gordon, Pte.
4560, Butcher, Charles John James. Pte.
4561, Brennan, Frank Matthews, Pte.
4562, Blomeley, Walter Edgar, Pte.
4563, Branch, Thomas, Pte.
4564, Birt, William, Pte.
4565, Banks, Stanley Algernon Richard, Pte.
4566, Barwell, George, Pte.
4567, Beaton, Ernest, Pte.
4568, Broadhurst, Wm. Florance, Pte.
4567, Bartlett, John, Pte.
4570, Bollard, Hugh Worthington. Pte.
4571, Brooks, Thomas, Pte.
4572, Browning, Henry, Pte.
4573, Brand, James Richard, Pte.
4574, Brooks, Percy Neil, Pte.
4576, Brown, William Joseph, Pte.
4578, Burnard, Harry, Pte.
4579, Cahill, Denis, Pte.
4580, Cockman, Ross Roy, Pte.
4581, Cairns, John Blackwood, Pte.
4582, Campbell, James, Pte.
4582, Corkery, Patrick, Pte.
4585, Clinton, Isiah, Pte.
4586, Clemow, James, Pte.
4588, Cameron, Thomas, Pte.
4589, Cumming, Herbert, Pte.
4590, Carter, Alfred James, Pte.
4591, Costello, John, Pte.
4592, Carr, Albert Francis, Pte.
4594, Dedman, George, Pte.
4595, Davis, Davis James, Pte.
4596, Davis, William Philcox, Pte.
4597, Dobbie, Gordon McKellar, Pte.
4598, Edhouse, James Benjamin Rigby, Pte.

THE OLD SIXTEENTH.

16th INFANTRY BATTALION—NOMINAL ROLL—continued.

14th Reinforcements—continued.

4599, Eldridge, Thomas Albert John, Pte.
4600, Elliott, Wilfred, Pte.
4601, Foster, Harold, Pte.
4603, Glynn, Thomas, Pte.
4604, Farmer, Kenneth, Pte.
4605, Fairburn, George, Pte.
4606, Franklin, George Stanley, Pte.
4607, Gandy, George, Pte.
4608, Gandy, Arthur Henry, Pte.
4609, Gladstone, Frederick Sidney, Pte.
4610, Gilling, Cyril, Pte.
4612, Gordon, James Currie, Pte.
4613, Graham, Andrew John, Pte.
4614, Harvey, Harry Charles, Pte.
4615, Hickey, Bernard, Pte.
4616, Heason, Percy Charles, Pte.
4617, Haldane, Andrew, Pte.
4618, Harper, Frank Edwin, Pte.
4619, Heffernan, Michael, Pte.
4620, Hillier, George Marlland, Pte.
4621, Hyde, Lance Albert, Pte.
4622, Horne, Thomas People, Pte.
4623, Hawke, John, Pte.
4624, Hunt, William, Pte.
4625, Hunter, Gordon, Pte.
4646, Holzberger, Harold Joseph, Pte.
4627, Hill, Herbert Clifton, Pte.
4628, Hancock, Herbert Paull, Pte.
4629, Houghton, William, Pte.
4630, Irvine, John Lennie, Pte.
4631, Jones, George, Pte.
4632, Jecks, Alec Charles, Pte.
4633, Jackson, Alfred James, Pte.
4634, Jackson, Harold Melmouth, Pte.
4636, Jones, John James, Pte.
4637, Johnson, Robert, Pte.
4638, Karhu, Hjalmar, Pte.
4639, Keefe, James, Pte.
4640, Kennedy, John, Pte.
4641, King, Cecil Aubrey, Pte.
4642, King, Alfred Albert, Pte.
4644, Lamond, Emanuel Murdock, Pte.
4645, Lynch, James, Pte.
4646, Lowe, Richard, Pte.
4647, Lackmann, Rupert Oswald, Pte.
4648, Matthews, Edwin, Pte.
4649, Miles, Wilfred John, Pte.
4650, Millar, Alexander Bilshend, Pte.
4651, Morgan, Leonard Frederick Wilkes, Pte.
4652, Minty, Edwin James, Pte.
4653, Mildenhall, Charles, Pte.
4654, Martin, Geoffrey Clarence, Pte.
4655, Mann, Walter, Pte.
4657, Mauchline, William Andrew, Pte.
4658, May, Willie Brian, Pte.
4659, Meadows, Percy, Pte.
4660, Mills, Reginald, Pte.
4661, Menzies, Duncan, Pte.
4662, Menzies, John, Pte.
4663, Mathews, Charles Henry, Pte.
4664, McLelland, John, Pte.
4665, McKenna, Walter William, Pte.
4666, McMahon, Henry, Pte.
4667, McNab, William Drayton, Pte.
4668, McLean, Dugald, Pte.
4671, McLerie, John Alexandra, Pte.
4672, McPherson, Alexander, Pte.
4673, McLeod, Angus, Pte.
4674, McKenna, John Patrick, Pte.
4675, McKenna, James Francis, Pte.
4676, McCavana, Henry, Pte.
4677, McKay, Arthur Alfred, Pte.
4678, McWhirter, Robert Birkett, Pte.
4679, Nicoll, Alexander Hay, Pte.
4680, Neale, Ernest Wilfred, Pte.
4681, O'Sullivan, George Patrick, Pte.
4682, Owen, Robert, Pte.
4683, Onslow, Ernest, Pte.
4684, Oxman, Alfred William, Pte.
4685, O'Brien, John Thomas, Pte.
4686, Patterson, Robert John, Pte.
4687, Pickersgill, William, Pte.
4688, Padley, Jack Williams, Pte.
4689, Pattison, Horace John Dickens, Pte.
4690, Powell, John James, Pte.
4691, Raitt, William, Pte.
4692, Roberts, David George, Pte.
4693, Ross, James Robert, Pte.
4694, Reidy, William Garner Leopold, Pte.
4695, Ryan, Arthur, Pte.
4696, Robertson, Archer George, Pte.
4698, Rogers, James, Pte.
4699, Roberts, William James, Pte.
4700, Reardon, William Alec, Pte.
4701, Sturrock, David Webster, Pte.
4702, Smith, Thomas Wallace, Pte.
4703, Smith, Harry, Pte.
4704, Smith, Albert Edward, Pte.
4705, Smith, Lawrence Sydney, Pte.
4706, Salter, Richard, Pte.
4707, Shedden, Ernest George, Pte.
4708, Scott, William Joseph, Pte.

16th INFANTRY BATTALION—NOMINAL ROLL.—*continued.*

14th Reinforcements—continued.

4709, Seery, Thomas, Pte.
4710, Seymour, William David, Pte.
4711, Standing, Harry, Pte.
4712, Scott, James Hubert, Pte.
4713, Spencer, Forrest, Pte.
4714, Skinner, Robert Tierney, Pte.
7415, Smith, Lawrence Henry, Pte.
4716, Salliss, Henry, Pte.
4718, Simpson, Alexander, Pte.
4719, Tomkinson, Frank, Pte.
4720, Thurley, Harold Henry, Pte.
4721, Tufnell, West Trollope, Pte.
4724, Taylor, Stephen Douglas Steward, Pte.
4725, Tankey, William Alfred, Pte.

15th Reinforcements.

(Embarked at Fremantle, Western Australia, on H.M.A.T. A35, "Ulysses," 1st April, 1916.)

Aarons, Daniel Sidney, 2nd Lt.
Freeman, Douglas, 2nd Lt.
Ryan, Matthew John, 2nd Lt.
Witte, William Claude, 2nd Lt.
303, Thomlinson, George William, Pte.
4727, Barrington, Arthur Victor Royal, Pte.
4728, Jeffery, William, Pte.
4729, Miller, Frederick Edward, Pte.
4730, Strassburg, Rudolph Ernest, Pte.
4731, Webb, Charles, Pte.
4732, Cherry, Arthur Frederick, Pte.
4733, Ferrie, James, Pte.
4734, Harman, James Francis, Pte.
4737, Rosenberg, Julius Myar, Pte.
4738, Thompson, John Leslie, Pte.
4739, Williams, Richard Alfred, Pte.
4740, Smith, Raymond Victor, Pte.
4741, Rodda, Harold Bernard, Pte.
4742, Anderson, Maurice, Pte.
4743, Anderson, James Duncan, Pte.
4744, Allen, Owen Moore, Pte.
4745, Adams, James, Pte.
4746, Adams, William Henry, Pte.
4747, Ainge, Walter Edward, Pte.
4750, Alfieri, Arthur, Pte.
4751, Brown, George Robert, Pte.
4752, Brazier, Abdal, Pte.
4754, Bennetts, Leslie, Pte.
4755, Blake, Arthur Ernest, Pte.
4756, Brown, William Stephens, Pte.
4757, Barber, Sydney Alfred, Pte.
4758, Buswell, George Edward, Pte.
4759, Brackenridge, Douglas, Pte.
4760, Burrows, Frederick Birmingham, Pte.
4764, Bourne, Horace Wilfred, Pte.
4767, Barrett, Thomas George, Pte.
4768, Bramwell, William, Pte.
4769, Barry, John, Pte.
4770, Beveridge, Herbert James, Pte.
4771, Cowan, Thomas, Pte.
4772, Calhoun, William, Pte.
4773, Carey, Lawrence James, Pte.
4774, Crump, Jack, Pte.
4775, Connolly, Frederick William, Pte.
4776, Connaughton, William James, Pte.
4777, Cook, Sidney Robert, Pte.
4778, Collyer, Edward, Pte.
4780, Craig, James Burnet, Pte.
4784, Cusack, Joseph Mark, Pte.
4785, Collins, Lewis Frank, Pte.
4786, Crawley, John, Pte.
4787, Colgan, Charles, Pte.
4788, Cronin, Daniel, Pte.
4790, Crosbie, Stanley James, Pte.
4792, Davis, James Percy, Pte.
4793, Devereux, Andrew Lewis, Pte.
4794, Davies, Harold George, Pte.
4795, Doyle, Murt, Pte.
4796, Dewhurst, Eli, Pte.
4797, Davidson, William, Pte.
4798, Digan, Daniel, Pte.
4801, Davis, Richard John, Pte.
4802, Dobson, Evelyn Garnet, Pte.
4803, Ellement, Victor Ernest, Pte.
4805, Fuhrmann, Herbert, Pte.
4806, Faulkner, Alfred William, Pte.
4807, Ferry, Edward, Pte.
4808, Farmer, Augustus Pegg, Pte.
4809, Falkingham, George, Pte.
4810, Flynn, Thomas Joseph, Pte.
4811, Flanagan, Luke, Pte.
4812, Foggin, George, Pte.
4813, Flanagan, John, Pte.
4814, Flynn, Joseph Patrick, Pte.
4815, Faull, John, Pte.

THE OLD SIXTEENTH.

16th INFANTRY BATTALION—NOMINAL ROLL—*continued.*

15th Reinforcements—continued.

4816, Griffiths, John Paull, Pte.
4817, Glover, Joseph Lawrence, Pte.
4818, Gargett, John Wilfred, Pte.
4819, Geddes, John Roy, Pte.
4820, Gratte, Henry Charles, Pte.
4821, Gurney, Joseph James, Pte.
4824, Horne, John Frederick, Pte.
4826, Harris, Thomas, Pte.
4827, Hynes, Henry, Pte.
4828, Holloway, William John, Pte.
4830, Hooper, Thomas Peairce, Pte.
4831, Hazell, Charles Richard, Pte.
4832, Hemsley, Frank, Pte.
4833, Inman, John William, Pte.
4834, Jones, William, Pte.
4835, Jackson, Percival, Pte.
4836, Jones, Daniel, Pte.
4837, Jones, Arthur Stanley, Pte.
4840, Krakouer, Harman Philip, Pte.
4842, Kirkpatrick, Robert Leigh, Pte.
4843, Kelly, William George, Pte.
4844, Keogh, William, Pte.
4846, Kilby, Robert, Pte.
4848, Laker, Arthur, Pte.
4849, Lee, Edgar Charles, Pte.
4850, Lavington, William Sexton, Pte.
4851, Lawler, Charles, Pte.
4852, Lewis, Frederick William, Pte.
4853, Liddell, William Watson, Pte.
4856, McIntyre, Joseph, Pte.
4857, McColl, Charles Frederick, Pte.
4858, McCreery, Joseph, Pte.
4859, McPherson, Norman, Pte.
4860, McCann, Thomas, Pte.
4861, McNee, William, Pte.
4862, Maxim, Frederick, Pte.
4864, Morton, John, Pte.
4865, Machich, Mark, Pte.
4866, Montgomery, James, Pte.
4867, Malt, George Filtness, Pte.
4868, Maley, Reginald Herbert, Pte.
4872, Mills, James Greenway, Pte.
4873, McGrath, James, Pte.
4874, Monaghan, William Leo, Pte.
4875, Murchie, David, Pte.
4878, Neilson, Peter, Pte.
4881, Norton, William Healy, Pte.
4882, Nelmes, Joseph Henry, Pte.
4884, Petchell, William Henry, Pte.
4885, Pearce, Daniel, Pte.
4886, Piper, Harry James, Pte.
4887, Payne, Sydney Joseph, Pte.
4888, Rice, Alfred Ernest, Pte.
4889, Rogers, Arthur Wilks, Pte.
4890, Rowe, Jack, Pte.
4891, Rennie, Richard Henry, Pte.

4892, Redman, Alexander Henry, Pte.
4893, Rassmussen, Peter Rasmus, Pte.
4894, Spargo, Leslie Vernon, Pte.
4895, Straughair, Robert Thomas, Pte.
4896, Scott, William Jenkin Robert, Pte.
4897, Scott, John, Pte.
4898, Sinclair, James, Pte.
4900, Scrivener, Harry Hubert, Pte.
4901, Stacey, John James, Pte.
4902, Smith, William, Pte.
4903, Stevenson, John, Pte.
4904, Schiff, William Andrew, Pte.
4906, Sadler, Edmund, Pte.
4907, Sutherland, John Fordyce, Pte.
4908, Stevens, Eucla Graham, Pte.
4909, Sullivan, Charles Michael, Pte.
4910, Sutton, William, Pte
4911, Stevenson, William John, Pte.
4913, Thomas, Frederick James, Pte.
4914, Turner, Walter Thomas, Pte.
4915, Thompson, Alfred Joseph, Pte.
4916, Tuckey, Arthur George, Pte.
4918, Trevivian, John, Pte.
4919, Taylor, Ernest, Pte.
4920, Towle, John Herbert, Pte.
4921, Thomas, Albert Victor, Pte.
4922, Tolano, Phil., Pte.
4923, Thomason, Richard, Pte.
4924, Todd, George Dudley Brydges, Pte.
4925, Tippett, William Henry, Pte.
4926, Todd, George, Pte.
4927, Ward, Francis Goodwin, Pte.
4032, Wallace, Alexander, Pte.
4933, Willox, Leonard, Pte.
4934, White, Roy Clifford Francis, Pte.
4935, Willmore, Alfred Edward, Pte.
4936, Walsh, Frederick William, Pte.
4937, Weir, John Bryce, Pte.
4938, Wilshaw, Henry, Pte.
4939, Waywood, Stanley William, Pte.
4940, Webster, James John, Pte.
4941, White, Henry Ernest, Pte.
4942, White, Joseph, Pte.
4943, Whitelaw, William Bloomfield, Pte.
4944, Wimmer, Ernest, Pte.
4946, Young, Frederick Ludwick, Pte.
4947, Roots, Hubert Henry, Pte.

THE OLD SIXTEENTH.

16th INFANTRY BATTALION—NOMINAL ROLL—*continued.*

15th Reinforcements—continued.

4948, Heventon, Thomas, Pte.
4950, Baldry, Frederick Oswald, Pte.
4951, Binks, John, Pte.
4952, Foster, George Henry Harold, Pte.
4954, Hiorns, John Thomas, Pte.
4955, Lennell, Edward Samuel, Pte.
4956, Lawther, Roderick, Pte.
4957, Mavor, James, Pte.
4958, Scullin, Patrick, Pte.
4959, Willington, Spencer William, Pte.
4960, Walsh, James, Pte.
4961, Williams, Frederick Edgar, Pte.
4962, Cassidy, John, Pte.
4964, Wright, Arthur Edwin, Pte.
4965, McInerney, James, Pte.
4966, Crowe, James, Pte.
4967, Dunstan, Edward John, Pte.
4968, Oscar, Enbom Andreas, Pte.
4969, Hodges, Thomas Boucher, Pte.
4971, Rummer, Ross Edward, Pte.
4972, Rose, William Stanley, Pte.
4973, Albert, Arthur, Pte.
4974, Dwyer, Thomas, Pte.
4975, Le Blanc, Jack, Pte.
4976, Hammond, Henry, Pte.

16th Reinforcements.

(Embarked at Fremantle, Western Australia, on H.M.A.T. A9, "Shropshire," 31st March, 1916.)

Ayling, Walter Anthony, 2nd Lt.
Mott, John Eldred, 2nd Lt.
Carter, Lionel Lewin, 2nd Lt.
Mayersbeth, Joseph William, 2nd Lt.
316, Job, Henry Frederick, Pte.
5026, Baines, David, Pte.
5028, Hayes, Edward Sydney, Pte.
5030, Jago, Charles Edwin, Pte.
5031, Minchin, Herbert Keane, Pte.
5032, Carroll, Albert Edward, Pte.
5033, Hammond, Frederick Wilson, Pte.
5034, Hill, Bertram Thomas, Pte.
5035, Kelly, Arthur Charles, Pte.
5036, McGrath, John Joseph, Pte.
5037, Sansum, Arthur Harold, Pte.
5038, Stewart, William, Pte.
5039, Stout, Arthur Edward, Pte.
5040, Johnston, John Foster, Pte.
5041, Read, Joseph Henry, Pte.
5042, Amiott, Herbert, Pte.
5043, Anderson, Herbert, Pte.
5044, Allen, Raymond William, Pte.
5045, Asker, William, Pte.
5046, Annandale, John Williamson, Pte.
5047, Ashworth, Charles Alexander, Pte.
5048, Aird, Archibald John, Pte.
5049, Bennetts, Roy John, Pte.
5050, Barr, Alfred George, Pte.
5051, Bent, Reginald, Pte.
5052, Bailey, Alex. Charles, Pte.
5053, Brown, Frederick Chapman, Pte.
5054, Bohan, Michael Henry, Pte.
5055, Buckthought, Frederick, Pte.
5056, Blount, Edward, Pte.
5057, Broomhall, Bertie William, Pte.
5058, Burke, Robert Bowyer, Pte.
5059, Baker, Samuel Eric, Pte.
5060, Biddle, Vernon Everard, Pte.
5062, Butcher, John Arthur, Pte.
5063, Bole, Harold, Pte.
5063, Botton, George, Pte.
5065, Bell, Clarence Bickford, Pte.
5066, Collard, Frederick, Pte.
5067, Cruickshank, Leonard, Pte.
5068, Clayton, Tasman Mervyn, Pte.
5069, Campbell, George, Pte.
5070, Cade, Henry Sydney, Pte.
5071, Cummings, Roy Leo, Pte.
5072, Cummings, Mark Hughy, Pte.
5073, Cunningham, Thomas Clinton, Pte.
5074, Candish, Arthur, Pte.
5075, Colley, John Henry, Pte.
5076, Cousens, Frank Ernest, Pte.
5077, Cox, Robert, Pte.
5078, Collier, George, Pte.
5079, Duncuff, Albert, Pte.
5080, Doherty, William Thomas, Pte.
5081, Daniel, George Francis, Pte.
5082, Delaney, Thomas Walter, Pte.
5083, Dunderdale, John, Pte.
5084, Dickens, Alick George William, Pte.
5085, Donovan, Christopher, Pte.

THE OLD SIXTEENTH.

16th INFANTRY BATTALION—NOMINAL ROLL—*continued.*

16th Reinforcements—continued.

5086, Eaton, John Heady, Pte.
5087, Edwards, Eric Stanley, Pte.
5088, Ellery, Bertie, Pte.
5090, Faulkner, Lionel Herbert, Pte.
5091, Franks, Cecil Henry Ernest, Pte.
5092, Fennell, John, Pte.
5093, French, James, Pte.
5094, Fingland, William Thomas,
5095, Gardiner, Keith Menzies, Pte.
5096, Goldsmith, James Arthur, Pte.
5097, Green, Fred, Pte.
5099, Gridley, Henry, Pte.
5100, Gard, Thomas James Bastin, Pte.
5101, Griffiths, Tasman Guy, Pte.
5102, Gilman, Oswald, Pte.
5103, Garman, Ernest, Pte.
5104, Gay, Alfred Thomas William, Pte.
5105, Green, William Arthur, Pte.
5106, Gunst, Frederick Samuel, Pte.
5107, Gladstone, Wilfred Victor, Pte.
5108, Gerrard, Robert Stirling, Pte.
5109, Higgs, William Carling, Pte.
5110, Haines, Harry, Pte.
5111, Hickey, John, Pte.
5112, Handmer, William George, Pte.
5113, Hamill, Andrew Clarkson, Pte.
5114, Harris, John Albert, Pte.
5115, Higgins, William Henry, Pte.
5116, Higgins, Michael Walter, Pte.
5117, Inglis, Thomas Orr, Pte.
5118, Ivey, William Alfred, Pte.
5119, James, Arthur, Pte.
5120, Jennings, Charles Thornville, Pte.
5121, Jennings, William Henry, Pte.
5122, Jack, Cyril Roy, Pte.
5123, Jennings, John Edward, Pte.
5124, King, John William, Pte.
5125, Kennedy, John Alfred, Pte.
5126, Kindred, Percy Henry, Pte.
5127, King, Edgar Henry, Pte.
5128, Knight, Percy Hudson, Pte.
5129, Lang, Eric, Pte.
5130, Lloyd, Walter, Pte.
5131, Larkman, Robert Harvey, Pte.
5132, Leavesley, Charles Arthur, Pte.
5133, Lowe, Richard, Pte.
5134, McLean, Norman, Pte.
5135, Motion, George Anderson, Pte.
5136, Millman, Percival, Pte.
5137, McMaster, John Duncan, Pte.
5138, Malcolm, Alexander Chrystal, Pte.
5139, Mort, James Herbert, Pte.
5140, McGregor, Roy Edward, Pte.
5141, McDonald, Robert, Pte.
5142, Munro, Robertson, Pte.
5143, Millington, Walter, Pte.
5144, McKay, James Alexander, Pte.
5145, McManus, William Richard, Pte.
5146, Morris, Stanley Kalter, Pte.
5147, Murdoch, William Stewart, Pte.
5148, McManus, Michael Henry, Pte.
5149, Martin, Daniel, Pte.
5150, Markey, John Patrick, Pte.
5151, Marsh, Harry Percival, Pte.
5152, Morgan, George, Pte.
5153, Mann, Leslie Rupert, Pte.
5154, Moore, John Thomas, Pte.
5155, McLaren, John Henry, Pte.
5156, McIntosh, David, Pte.
5157, Newport, Walter Henry, Pte.
5158, Naylor, Leonard, Pte.
5159, Nelson, William Alfred, Pte.
5160, Ninehan, Arthur Charles, Pte.
5168, Needle, Samuel, Pte.
5162, O'Sullivan, William, Pte.
5163, Parsons, Hamilton, Pte.
5164, Powell, William John, Pte.
5165, Powell, George Samuel, Pte.
5166, Pitts, James John, Pte.
5167, Paine, Stephen, Pte.
5168, Payne, Henry William, Pte.
5169, Perks, Joseph James, Pte.
5170, Pepall, James Harry, Pte.
5171, Parker, John William, Pte.
5172, Quinlan, Alexander, Pte.
5173, Rawlings, Ernest James, Pte.
5174, Rayner, William Albany, Pte.
5175, Reilly, John Thomas, Pte.
5176, Roesmer, Leonard Sanley, Pte.
5177, Read, Leonard Maurice, Pte.
5178, Roebuck, Benjamin, Pte.
5179, Rodgers, Michael John, Pte.
5189, Raper, Victor Angus, Pte.
5181, Raper, Robert John, Pte.
5182, Reynolds, Edward Joseph, Pte.
5183, Robertson, Thomas, Pte
5184, Rye, George, Pte.
5185, Robinson, John Cremorne, Pte.
5186, Raitt, Allan, Pte.
5187, Robinson, Harry Hammett, Pte.
5188, Richards, Ernest Clyde Mitchell, Pte.

16th INFANTRY BATTALION—NOMINAL ROLL—*continued*.

16th Reinforcements—continued.

5190, Skinner, Ernest Lee, Pte.
5191, Suthers, William, Pte.
5192, Smith, Henry William, Pte.
5193, Stroud, Charles Edgar, Pte.
5194, Sowerbutts, George, Pte.
5195, Smith, Richard, Pte.
5196, Shaw, Roland Hugh, Pte.
5198, Stallard, James Archibald, Pte.
5199, Scott, George Powell, Pte.
5200, Shatwell, James Thomas, Pte.
5201, Smith, Arthur Teasdale, Pte.
5202, Smith, Maurice, Pte.
5203, Terlick, Walter David, Pte.
5204, Thomas, George, Pte.
5205, Thorn, Colin Melville, Pte.
5206, Turner, Hobart, Pte.
5207, Torrie, William, Pte.
5208, Tillet, William, Pte.
5210, Underwood, Thomas Andrew, Pte.
5211, Wood, Frederick Charles, Pte.
5212, Williams, Henry Joseph, Pte.
5213, Ward, James, Pte.
5214, Walter, Phillip Henry, Pte.
5215, Williams, John Robert, Pte.
5216, Washer, Harry, Pte.
5217, Willey, Edward Albert, Pte.
5218, Webb, Frederick Alfred Fleming Joyce, Pte.
5219, Wilson, William, Pte.
5220, Watts, Walter, Pte.
5221, Wellman, William Arthur, Pte.
5222, Ward, Claude McClarence, Pte.
5223, Whetten, Allan Read, Pte.
5224, Williams, Walter Charles, Pte.
5225, Warwick, Harold Hugh, Pte.
5226, Morris, William John, Pte.
5227, Lynbery, Alfred, Pte.
5228, Greig, Henry Darcy Simpson, Pte.
5229, Hatton, James William, Pte.
5230, Towie, John Michael, Pte.

17th Reinforcements.

(Embarked at Fremantle, Western Australia, on H.M.A.T. A60, "Aeneas," 17th April, 1916.)

Day, Essington, Lt.
Brown, Charles Dane, Lt.
280, Mouton, Walter Beaumont, Pte.
1850, Pearse, Arthur Gordon, Pte.
2251, Roberts, Harold, Pte.
4475, Kelly, John Hamilton, Pte.
5326, Hyde, Harry, Pte.
5327, Jorgensen, Henry Hansen, Pte.
5328, Crofts, Harold Robert, Pte.
5329, Warren, George, Pte.
5330, Hancock, Maurice George, Pte.
5331, Turner, Herbert Winton, Pte.
5332, Hennerty, Joseph Leonard, Pte.
5333, Butler, Norman Thomas, Pte.
5334, Schmidt, Christian Fredk. Walter, Pte.
5341, Bloor, Herbert, Pte.
5335, Asplin, James Henry, Pte.
5336, Boulton, Charles Perrin, Pte.
5337, Bercovitch, Maurice, Pte.
5338, Bingham, Arthur Edward, Pte.
5339, Bingham, Austin Henry, Pte.
5340, Brady, James Alphonso, Pte.
5342, Bellgrove, George Henry, Pte.
5343, Bryson, John Lindsay, Pte.
5344, Benbow, William George, Pte.
5345, Cobbe, George, Pte.
5346, Coverley, James Walter, Pte.
5347, Cook, George John, Pte.
5348, Coff, Earl James, Pte.
5349, Causer, Benjamin, Pte.
5350, Cross, Gordon Vidgin, Pte.
5351, Christmas, Sydney Elliott, Pte.
5352, Christmass, Alfred James, Pte.
5353, Cross, James Howard, Pte.
5354, Crawford, Stanley Hamilton, Pte.
5355, Downey, Francis Charles, Pte.
5356, Dorney, Walter George, Pte.
5357, Dinsdale, Harold Herbert, Pte.
5358, Eve, Frederick, Pte.
5359, Enright, Thomas, Pte.
5360, Foord, Bertram, Pte.
5361, Finn, James William, Pte.
5362, Genoni, Ernesto, Pte.
5363, Gildea, John Louis, Pte.
5364, Goddard, Harold Thomas, Pte.
5365, Hodder, James Albert, Pte.
5366, Hallengren, Eric Charles, Pte.
5367, Harris, George, Pte.
5368, Jones, George Edwin, Pte.

16th INFANTRY BATTALION—NOMINAL ROLL—*continued.*

17th Reinforcements—continued.

5370, Kelman, William, Pte.
5371, Longbottom, Stephen Mervyn, Pte.
5372, Longbottom, Edward Charles, Pte.
5373, Longbottom, Charles Leslie, Pte.
5374, Lawrenson, William, Pte.
5375, Leonard, Frederick, Pte.
5376, Lilleyman, Walter Herbert Edgar, Pte.
5377, McMahon, John James, Pte.
5378, Mulgrave, Walter Alex., Pte.
5379, McCarthy, Henry Edward, Pte.
5380, Maher, Frederick, Pte.
5381, Makutz, Rudolph, Pte.
5382, Meredith, Frederick Ernest, Pte.
5383, Main, David Alex., Pte.
5384, Morrice, James, Pte.
5386, McCarthy, John William, Pte.
5387, McGaw, Henry James, Pte.
5388, McEwen, Gavin, Pte.
5389, McLean, Angus, Pte.
5390, Mitchell, Ernest Reginald, Pte.
5392, Manners, Thomas James, Pte.
5394, Manners, George Percival Robson, Pte.
5395, Martin, William, Pte.
5396, MacQueen, Archibald Lachlan, Pte.
5397, North, Reginald Henry, Pte.
5398, Noyce, Ernest Clifford, Pte.
5399, Oberhansli, Jacob, Pte.
5400, O'Mahoney, Robert, Pte.
5401, O'Donnell, John, Pte.
5402, Power, James Joseph, Pte.
5403, Press, Basil William Isaac, Pte.
5404, Pearce, John Frederick, Pte.
5405, Pedretti, Peter, Pte.
5406, Page, Charles Herbert, Pte.
5409, Payne, Mark, Pte.
5410, Port, Cecil Percy, Pte.
5411, Pegg, David William, Pte.
5412, Quinlivan, Joseph Patrick, Pte.
5413, Raper, Thomas William, Pte.
5414, Rodger, Anderson Ritchie, Pte.
5415, Rouse, Alfred Arthur, Pte.
5416, Rees, Edward Humphrey, Pte.
5417, Robinson, Alexander, Pte.
5418, Rosser, Sydney Crickton, Pte.
5419, Rowland, Hugh Thomas Alex., Pte.
5420, Robertson, George Johnstone, Pte.
5421, Rickard, Thomas James, Pte.
5422, Ramsay, Robert, Pte.
5423, Samuel, George, Pte.
5424, Spruce, Harold Francis, Pte.
5425, Shanahan, Patrick John, Pte.
5426, Scott, John Patrick, Pte.
5427, Shervill, Alfred Henry, Pte.
5428, Sutton, Arthur Brockman, Pte.
5429, Smith, Henry, Pte.
5430, Sims, Alfred Christopher Daniel, Pte.
5431, Sermon, Selby William, Pte.
5432, Smith, William Edward, Pte.
5433, Smith, William Harold, Pte.
5434, Spencer, Edmund Charles, Pte.
5435, Spencer, John Morpeth, Pte.
5436, Sparrow, Valentine Christopher, Pte.
5437, Smith, Frederick John, Pte.
5438, Symons, James Arthur, Pte.
5439, Smith, John, Pte.
5440, Smith, Richard Donald, Pte.
5441, Tanswell, Sydney Samuel, Pte.
5442, Taylor, Ernest Herbert, Pte.
5443, Thomson, James Lusk Gibson, Pte.
5445, Thompson, George John Bertram, Pte.
5446, Tilley, William Richard, Pte.
5447, Treacey, William, Pte.
5447, McMonagle, William, Pte.
5448, Turner, James Edward, Pte.
5449, Tierney, John, Pte.
5450, Upton, William, Pte.
5451, Ullyott, John Francis, Pte.
5453, Williams, Charles, Pte.
5454, Wrangham, William, Pte.
5455, White, Gordon Wesley, Pte.
5456, Wright, Herbert, Pte.
5457, Ward, Richard Henry, Pte.
5458, West, Robert Pierce, Pte.
5459, Walker, William James, Pte.
5460, Wood, Frank, Pte.
5461, Williams, Harry, Pte.
5462, Ward, David Henry, Pte.
5463, Wisbey, John Edward, Pte.
5464, Wood, Thomas Liston, Pte.
5465, Wintle, Walter, Pte.
5466, Woodley, Herbert Harold, Pte.
5467, Wallis, Harry Edward, Pte.
5468, Watson, Archibald Nicol, Pte.
5469, White, Laurence John, Pte.
5470, Wineberg, Harry, Pte.

16th INFANTRY BATTALION—NOMINAL ROLL—*continued*.

17th Reinforcements—continued.

5471, Zowe, Arthur Percy, Pte.
5472, Inkpen, Gilbert George, Pte.
5473, Spratley, William Nelson, Pte.
5474, Moulden, John, Pte.
5476, O'Connor, Jeremiah, Pte.
5478, Hanton, Arnold Lester Roy, Pte.
5479, James, John Vincent, Pte.
5480, Cooper, William Wallace, Pte.

18th Reinforcements.

(Embarked at Fremantle, Western Australia, on H.M.A.T. A48, "Seang Bee," 18th July, 1916.)

Stutchbury, William Waldo Evelyn, 2nd Lt.
Watson, James Harrold, 2nd Lt.
206, McDonald, Angus, Pte.
427, Prior, Richard John, Pte.
462, Carter, William Percy John, Pte.
1496, McKenzie, James Henry, Pte.
5646, Lucas, Frank, Pte.
5649, Evans, Arthur Stanley, Pte.
5650, Criddle, Herbert Melbourne, Pte.
5651, McLeod, Peter, Pte.
5652, Linton, John Henry, Pte.
5653, Wallington, Milford John, Pte.
5654, Atkinson, Charles Andrew Templeton, Pte.
5655, Macey, Arthur Charles, Pte.
5656, Paine, Thomas, Pte.
5657, Johnson, Alexander Edward, Pte.
5658, Adkins, Arthur, Pte.
5659, Ainger, Percy John, Pte.
5660, Alderson, John, Pte.
5661, Annakin, Richard Edward, Pte.
5662, Anthony, George Henry, Pte.
5663, Armstrong, Thomas, Pte.
5664, Bairstow, Percy Wilfred, Pte.
5665, Baker, David Jones, Pte.
5666, Bates, James, Pte.
5668, Begg, Frederick James, Pte.
5669, Bell, Frederick George, Pte.
5670, Benari, Rowland Louis, Pte.
5671, Bettles, Richard William, Pte.
5672, Bonney, Maurice, Pte.
5673, Bovell, Henry Thomas, Pte.
5674, Bowers, Henry, Pte.
5675, Brimson, James, Pte.
5676, Brown, Frederick William, Pte.
5677, Brownlie, David Herbert, Pte.
5678, Brunskill, Percy, Pte.
5679, Buckley, Walter, Pte.
5680, Bunter, Charles Henry, Pte.
5681, Bunter, John Joseph, Pte.
5682, Burgess, Alexander George, Pte.
5684, Burgess, James Boyd, Pte.
5685, Carter, Percy Houghton, Pte.
5686, Carroll, Sydney Charles, Pte.
5687, Carter, Charles Forbes, Pte.
5688, Carpenter, Arthur, Pte.
5690, Coffey, Leslie, Pte.
5691, Collins, Albert John, Pte.
5692, Comery, Reuben James, Pte.
5693, Coppin, George, Pte.
5694, Coppock, Guy, Pte.
5695, Coombs, Walter George, Pte.
5696, Corbitt, Samuel Thomas, Pte.
5697, Corcoran, Matthew James, Pte.
5698, Cover, Walter Henry, Pte.
5699, Cowley, Charles Seymour, Pte.
5700, Cox, Louis Frederick, Pte.
5701, Crane, Aubrey Henry, Pte.
5702, Crellin, Walter Henry, Pte.
5703, Criddle, Harold, Pte.
5704, Dallimore, Charles John, Pte.
5705, Daykin, Richard Francis, Pte.
5706, Divall, Burban Frederick, Pte.
5707, Dixey, Arthur Daniel, Pte.
5708, Dornan, James Francis, Pte.
5709, Dornan, William Harry, Pte.
5711, Earle, Frederick James, Pte.
5712, Eastcott, Francis Leo, Pte.
5714, Fathers, Ernest George, Pte.
5715, Feast, Arthur Thomas, Pte.
5716, Feltham, Reginald Walter, Pte.
5717, Ford, George John, Pte.
5718, Gibbs, William Henry, Pte.
5719, Gibson, Francis Joseph William, Pte.
5720, Gilbertson, Charles William, Pte.
5721, Gilbride, Alfred, Pte.
5722, Glasson, Thomas, Pte.
5723, Goss, Edmund Dryden, Pte.

THE OLD SIXTEENTH.

16th INFANTRY BATTALION—NOMINAL ROLL—*continued*.

18th Reinforcements—continued.

5724, Gulvin, Reginald Victor, Pte.
5725, Gurney, George Frederick, Pte.
5726, Hannabry, Edmund, Ryan, Pte.
5727, Hardiman, Charles Frederick, Pte.
5728, Hawkes, Frederick Henry, Pte.
5729, Higham, George Edward, Pte.
5730, Hipper, Thomas Clarence, Pte.
5731, Hislop, John Drummond, Pte.
5732, Hodgson, Harold, Pte.
5733, Hutchings, Benjamin George, Pte.
5734, Jahn, Rudolph Victor, Pte.
5735, Keating, James, Pte.
5736, Keirel, Claude Thomas, Pte.
5737, Larratt, Percy Wilfred, Pte.
5738, Langlands, John Donald, Pte.
5739, Makeham, John William, Pte.
5740, Mansell, John William, Pte.
5741, Martin, Ernest, Pte.
5742, Martin, Lionel Charles, Pte.
5743, Matthews, Alfred George, Pte.
5744, Mayo, Thomas, Pte.
5745, Meginess, Michael, Pte.
5746, Meginess, William Simmons Pte.
5747, Meyer, George Ralph, Pte.
5748, Miller, Carl, Pte.
5749, Martin, Thomas Simon, Pte.
5750, Moss, James George, Pte.
5751, Morris, Arthur Stanley, Pte.
5752, Mole, William Edward, Pte.
5753, Moore, Albert James, Pte.
5754, Munyard, Edwin, Pte.
5755, Munyard, Henry Charles, Pte.
5756, McCann, James, Pte.
5757, McCormick, Francis George, Pte.
5758, McDonald, Frank Edward, Pte.
5759, McFarlane, John Francis Ignatius, Pte.
5760, McGrath, Peter, Pte.
5761, McKenzie, Alex. Grant, Pte.

5702, McMinn, Harry Tudor, Pte.
5764, O'Connor, Francis Michael Lawrence, Pte.
5765, O'Flaherty, Henry Lenard, Pte.
5766, Owen, William Sydney, Pte.
5767, Palmer, Arthur Thomas Henry, Pte.
5768, Paolinelli, Peter, Pte.
5769, Parker, William John, Pte.
5770, Payne, Mervyn Daniel, Pte.
5771, Pearce, William Frank, Pte.
5772, Phelan, William George, Pte.
5773, Pinnell, Edward George, Pte.
5774, Price, William Sheriff, Pte.
5775, Rae, James Spencer, Pte.
5776, Ratke, Ernest Huntly, Pte.
5777, Reddin, John, Pte.
5778, Reid, Percy Constantine, Pte.
5779, Robin, Cecil Harry Johnson, Pte.
5780, Rogers, Daniel Joseph Pte.
5871, Rowsell, Clarence Victor, Pte.
5783, Runnalls, Francis Robert, Pte.
5784, Saunders, James Joseph, Pte.
5785, Saw, William Thomas, Pte.
5786, Scaddan, Joseph Wilfred, Pte.
5787, Sleight, Edward Aaron, Pte.
5788, Smith, Walter Pedley, Pte.
5790, Short, John Tregenthen, Pte.
5791, Trotter, Percy George, Pte.
5792, Truelove, Frank Benjamin, Pte.
5793, Webb, Harry Walter, Pte.
5794, Cole, Harry Trevor, Pte.
5795, Elliott, Frederick Thomas, Pte.
5796, Penton, Arthur Cecil, Pte.
5797, Standing, George Henry Theodore, Pte.
5798, Kent, Jack Clifford, Pte.
5799, Cowley, Henry Thomas, Pte.
5800, Alexander, Francis, Pte.

19th Reinforcements.

(Embarked at Fremantle, Western Australia, on H.M.A.T. A28, "Miltiades," 7th August, 1916.)

Harvey, Francis Clayton, 2nd Lt.
Mills, Stanley Joseph 2nd Lt.
5966, Williamson, Roy Malcolm, Pte.
5967, Green, Charles William, Pte.
5968, Peacock, Richard John Wilson, Pte.
5969, Webb, Walter Roy, Pte.
5970, Norman, Harry Benjamin, Pte.
5971, Stehn, Norman Dedrick, Pte.

THE OLD SIXTEENTH.

16th INFANTRY BATTALION—NOMINAL ROLL—*continued*.

19th Reinforcements—continued.

5972, Holey, Henry Hunt, Pte.
5973, Woodbrook, Stanley, Pte.
5974, Stewart, Victor Jonathan Keer, Pte.
5975, Rieger, David James, Pte.
5976, Robertson, Robert Bayley, Pte.
5978, Andrew, Henry Robert, Pte.
5979, Armstrong, Archibald Henry, Pte.
5980, Aubrey, Ernest James, Pte.
5982, Abbott, Reginald Charles, Pte
5983, Blythe, George Albert, Pte.
5984, Barden, George Henry, Pte.
5985, Bain, Alexander Grant, Pte.
5986, Budden, William John, Pte.
5987, Bickle, Thomas Herbert, Pte.
5989, Barlow, William James, Pte.
5990, Bazeley, William, Pte.
5991, Blanchard, Alfonso James, Pte.
5995, Barr, Gilbert Robert, Pte.
5996, Barnecut, Horace Jasper, Pte.
5998, Brealey, Newman James, Pte.
5999, Bright, Charles Hedley Middleton, Pte.
6000, Bates, John Henry, Pte.
6001, Brown, George, Pte.
6002, Cohu, William Francis, Pte.
6003, Carter, Alfred James, Pte.
6004, Currington, Albert Henry, Pte.
6005, Clarke, Arthur Henry, Pte.
6008, Cowley, Edward. Pte.
6009, Cuiss, Andrew John. Pte.
6010, Cooper, Thomas Edward, Pte.
6011, Carter, Sidney Herrick, Pte.
6013, Dalton, James, Pte.
6014, Dusenburg, Albert Adolph, Pte.
6015, Davis, Leslie Edward, Pte.
6016, Forrest, Leo, Pte.
6017, Forrest, Davey Wesley, Pte.
6018, Finn, Mathew Robert, Pte.
6019, Fair, Alexander, Pte.
6020, Fleming, Alec, Pte.
6021, Fowler, Alwin Draper Robert, Pte.
6022, Gent, Robert Lionel, Pte.
6023, Glossop, Frederick Augustus, Pte.
6024, Gibney, Albert Henry, Pte.
6025, Gilsenan, Walter Patrick, Pte.
6027, Hall, Lawrence Alwyn, Pte
6028, Hughan, Peter Morrison, Pte.
6029, Hay, James, Pte.
6030, Higgs, John Alfred, Pte.
6031, Hollingsworth, William, Pte.

6032, Hartwell, Arthur Ernest, Pte.
6034, Harrison, Burn, Pte.
6035, Hills, Charles, Pte.
6036, Holiday, Horace, Pte.
6037, Harris, Edward Tester, Pte.
6038, Hoddell, Thomas, Pte.
6039, Ingham, William John Robertson, Pte.
6041, Judge, James Henry, Pte.
6042, Jacobson, Fritz Johann, Pte.
6043, Johnson, Albert Lars, Pte.
6044, Jones, Walter James, Pte.
6045, Johns, Thomas, Pte.
6046, Jacobs, Victor Newman, Pte.
6047, Jones, Frederick Arthur Bradley, Pte.
6048, Keenan, Claude, Pte.
6049, King, Albert Hogan, Pte.
6051, Kinsella, Edward Charles Moore, Pte.
6052, Lynch, Thomas, Pte.
6053, Lucas, Leonard, Pte.
6054, Larson, Olaf William, Pte.
6055, Leslie, Richard William, Pte.
6057, Main, William Elliott, Pte.
6059, McKernan, Edward Walter Pte.
6060, Moore, Alfred George, Pte.
6061, Menzies, Walter Leslie, Pte.
6066, Miles, Edwin George, Pte.
6067, Martin, Henry Leslie, Pte.
6068, McAlpine, James Henry, Pte.
6069, O'Brien, Joseph David, Pte.
6070, O'Brien, Harry, Pte.
6071, Power, Dudley Bernard, Pte.
6072, Payne, George Edward, Pte.
6073, Parsons, John David. Pte.
6075, Pritchard, Charles Henry, Pte
6076, Pickett, John, Pte.
6077, Parker, Charles, Pte.
6078, Pettit, Stanley Edward, Pte.
6081, Rose, Charlie Clifton, Pte.
6082, Rawle, Alfred, Pte.
6083, Rowe, George Joseph Alick, Pte.
6084, Reeves, Egbert Robert, Pte.
6085, Robinson, John, Pte.
6086, Skipworth, Harry Hedley, Pte.
6087, Smith, Harry, Pte.
6089, Stone, Fredrick Carl, Pte.
6090, Stephen, Henry Charles, Pte
6091, Smith, James, Pte.
6093, Strachan, James, Pte
6094, South, Henry James, Pte.
6095, Sargeant, Cecil Harry, Pte.
6096, Shorten, Alfred, Pte.

THE OLD SIXTEENTH.

16th INFANTRY BATTALION—NOMINAL ROLL—continued.

19th Reinforcements—continued.

6097, Simmonds, Ernest, Pte.
6098, Smith, Arthur Bernard, Pte.
6099, Trestrail, Alfred Bertram, Pte.
6101, Urquhart, John, Pte.
6102, Uphill, Robert George Duncan, Pte.
6103, Veitch, James Edgar, Pte.
6104, Webb, Henry Charles William, Pte.
6105, Whitfield, Robert, Pte.
6106, Weir, Norman John, Pte.
6107, Wallace, John Mitchell William, Pte.
6108, Walker, Edward Henry, Pte.
6109, Wreford, Valentine George, Pte.
6110, Watsons, John, Pte.
6111, Woodland, Cyril Arthur, Pte.
6112, White, William Ewart, Pte.
6113, Pash, Darrell Frederick, Pte.
6114, Williamson, James, Pte.
6118, White, George Thomas, Pte.
6119, Ware, Tommy, Pte.
6121, Watson, William Henry, Pte.
6122, Campbell, Samuel, Pte.
6123, Doney, George, Pte.
6124, Fordham, Charles Edward, Pte.
6125, Guthrie, Ivan, Pte.
6126, Gourley, James, Pte.
6127, Hulkes, Elias James, Pte.
6128, Hinkley, Reuben Hunter, Pte.
6129, Jeffrey, Samuel John, Pte.
6131, Ochiltree, Andrew, Pte.
6132, Pooley, Charles Leonard Lionel, Pte.
6133, Roberts, Alfred, Pte.
6134, Reilly, Cecil, Pte.
6135, Wallin, Edward William, Pte.
6137A, Whyatt, Ambrose Allan, Pte.
6137, Burton, Robert John, Pte.
6138, Burley, William George, Pte.
6139, Cody, William, Pte.
6140, Crowder, Frederick Sinclair, Pte.
6141, Cotten, Lewy, Pte.
6142, Webb, Leslie James, Pte.
6143, Falconer, Peter, Pte.
6144, Kelly, Sydney, Pte.
6144A, Moore, Thomas William, Pte.
6145, Sadleir, John William Crofton, Pte.

20th Reinforcements.

(Embarked at Fremantle, Western Australia, on H.M.A.T. A23, "Suffolk," 13th October, 1916.)

Crouch, Henry Thomas, 2nd Lt.
Moseley, Francis Arnold, 2nd Lt.
241, Briand, Leon Louis Jean, Cpl.
344, West, George, Pte.
349, Hill, Frederick James, Pte.
770, Crews, Cecil Arthur, Pte.
1735, Martin, Albert James, Pte.
1837, Measures, Joseph, Pte.
1915, Sturrock, Frank, Pte
2191, Harvey, James Percy, Pte.
2691, Preston, Frederick Henry, Pte.
3162, Tandy, John Thomas, Pte.
5663, Bennett, Charles Lefroy, Pte.
6211, Absolon, Rowland George, Pte.
6212, Dodds, James Atkinson, Pte.
6213, Latham, Charles George, Pte.
6214, Stewart, George, Pte.
6216, Eastmon, Albert Andrew, Pte.
6217, Ross, Robert Charles, Pte.
6218, Packham, Frank, Pte.
6219, Pond, John Henry, Pte.
6220, Richardson, David, Pte.
6221, Plank, Charles Henry, Pte.
6222, Anderson, Alfred Ernest, Pte.
6223, Bonser, Albert Joseph, Pte.
6224, Cook, Ernest Nelson, Pte.
6225, Hagg, Arthur Edward, Pte.
6226, McCormack, John Robert, Pte.
6227, Kannman, Henry Charles, Pte.
6228, Acres, Reginald, Pte.
6229, Corlett, Walker Bell, Pte.
6230, Anderson, James Murray, Pte.
6231, Aylward, Sidney John, Pte.
6232, Baxter, John Henry, Pte.
6233, Bleakley, James Henry, Pte.
6234, Bleakley, John Thomas, Pte.
6235, Bonser, George Ernest, Pte.
6236, Buckingham, Frank, Pte.
6237, Buckingham, George Henry, Pte.
6238, Buckingham, William Samuel Ezekiel, Pte.
6239, Bufton, William, Pte.
6240, Grimwade, Arthur John, Pte.
6241, Cash, Percy, Pte.
6242, Chandler, Charles Robert, Pte.
6243, Chipper, Michael, Pte.

16th INFANTRY BATTALION—NOMINAL ROLL—continued.

20th Reinforcements—continued.

6244, Crackel, Harry, Pte.
6245, Game, Albert Edward, Pte.
6248, Oliver, Leslie, Pte
6249, Dance, Albert, Pte.
6250, Potts, James Carter, Pte.
6251, Denteith, Thomas, Pte.
6252, Driver, Frederick Gordon, Pte.
6253, Dunstan, Leslie Edward, Pte.
6254, Dunstan, Percy Phillip, Pte.
6255, Dyer, Edward Joseph, Pte.
6257, Egan, Michael Patrick, Pte.
6258, Elliott, William, Pte.
6259, Evans, Harry, Pte.
6260, Fairhead, Leslie Henry, Pte.
6261, Johnstone, William Robert, Pte.
6262, Fisher, Thomas Edwin, Pte.
6263, Floate, Alfred, Pte.
6264, Ford, Frank, Pte.
6265, Forsyth, Samuel, Pte.
6266, Franklin, Thomas, Pte.
6267, Frost, Edward Michael, Pte.
6268, Frost, John Clarence, Pte.
6269, Gare, Joseph Marshall, Pte.
6270, Goodhand, Fred, Pte.
6271, Hamilton, William, Pte.
6272, Hartnup, Bertie, Pte.
6273, Hobson, Edward, Pte.
6274, Holdsworth, Thomas Gilbert, Pte.
6275, Hurt, Alexander, Pte.
6276, Inglis, William Edward, Pte.
6277, James, Harold, Pte.
6278, Johnston, James Sidney, Pte.
6279, Johannesen, Peter Emanuel, Pte.
6280, Kelly, Arthur, Pte.
6281, Kemble, Walter Royston, Pte.
6282, Kemp, Albert Victor, Pte.
6283, Kennard, Vincent Arthur, Pte.
6284, Kerr, James Ernest Daniel, Pte.
6285, Kirby, Nathaniel Albert, Pte.
6286, Lansdown, Hubert, Pte.
6287, James, Horace, Pte.
6288, Lacey, Ernest, Pte.
6289, Lewis, James Walter, Pte.
6291, Lynch, Patrick, Pte.
6292, Maddock, Percival Ernest Allen, Pte.
6293, Maitland, Frederick Orbell, Pte.
6294, Marquis, Clarence George, Pte.
6295, Milburn, William Henry, Pte.
6296, Messer, Charles John, Pte.
6297, Miller, Joseph, Pte.
6298, Mills, Albert, Pte.
6299, Mills, John, Pte.
6300, Morrison, Arthur, Pte.
6303, McCallum, Angus Duncan, Pte.
6304, Maclean, Peter, Pte.
6305, McWhinney, Stanley, Pte.
6306, Nelson, William, Pte.
6308, Norwood, Henry, Pte.
6310, O'Reilly, Peter Joseph, Pte.
6311, O'Sullivan, Percy Cornelius, Pte.
6312, Oyston, Francis McMillan, Pte.
6313, Parker, George William, Pte.
6314, Pellett, Stephen Henry, Pte.
6315, Pickering, Norman, Pte.
6316, Piggin, Percy Turner, Pte.
6317, Pope, Edmund Hall, Pte.
6318, Oatway, William Alfred, Pte.
6319, Pound, George Tristran, Pte.
6322, Read, Frederick Henry, Pte.
6323, Reid, George Kilgour, Pte.
6324, Richards, Hartland Wheare, Pte.
6325, Richardson, Reginald Cyril, Pte.
6326, Russell, Percy Everett, Pte.
6327, Scull, Harvey, Pte.
6328, Seaman, Douglas Ernest, Pte.
6329, Slee, Edgar Josiah Walter, Pte.
6330, Slee, Francis Charles Henry, Pte.
6331, Sloggett, Edmond Charles, Pte.
6332, Sloggett, George Henry, Pte.
6333, Stevenson, Alfred Henry, Pte.
6335, MacDonald, Alexander, Pte.
6336, Sturrock, Andrew Griz Huntley, Pte.
6337, Smith, Reuben Frank, Pte.
6338, Swindlehurst, Arthur, Pte.
6340, Reid, John, Pte.
6341, Thomas, Ernest Charles, Pte.
6342, Thompson, James, Pte.
6343, Thompson, Lionel Francis Seymour, Pte.
6344, Thompson, Stephen James, Pte.
6345, Tondut, Aubrey Francis, Pte.
6346, Tondut, Ferdenand, Pte.
6347, Vokins, John, Pte.
6348, Walker, Adnah, Pte.
6349, Walker, George William, Pte.
6350, Waller, William John, Pte.
6351, Ward, Alfred Willoughby, Pte.
6352, White, Walter, Pte.
6353, Williams, Everard Bradley, Pte.
6354, Williams, Frederick George, Pte.

THE OLD SIXTEENTH.

16th INFANTRY BATTALION—NOMINAL ROLL—*continued.*

20th Reinforcements—continued.

6355, Willmott, William Henry Francis, Pte.
6356, Wray, William Robert, Pte.
6357, Harris, William Hervey, Pte.
6358, Rumble, Horace, Pte.
6358a, Watkins, Thomas George, Pte.
6359, Mose, William Henry, Pte.
6359a, Muir, Wilfred James, Pte.
6360, Dew, Albert George, Pte.

21st Reinforcements.

(Embarked at Fremantle, Western Australia, on H.M.A.T. A23, "Suffolk," 13th October, 1916.)

Long, Christopher John, Lieut.
Hooper, Richard Crooke, 2nd Lieut.
250, Comery, Francis Edward, Pte.
1543, Hawkins, Frank William, Pte.
6456, Bond, Alexander Beckett, Pte.
6457, Thompson, Arthur, Pte.
6458, Gloster, Alexander Burns, Pte.
6459, Clark, William Joseph, Pte.
6460, Davis, Charles Meyer, Pte.
6461, Bagshaw, Alfred Edward, Pte.
6462, Drake, Walter Carlyle, Pte.
6463, Wiseman, Archibald, Pte.
6464, Croker, Carl Louis, Pte.
6465, Bradbury, William, Pte.
6466, McEvoy, Benjamin Arthur, Pte.
6468, Harris, Cromwell, Pte.
6470, Yeo, Willie Elphinstone, Pte.
6471, Armstrong, Francis Aubrey, Pte.
6473, Allen, George William Spencer, Pte.
6475, Brennan, Raymond, Pte.
6476, Board, Alfred James, Pte.
6478, Bentley, Edward Loftus, Pte.
6479, Burnett, Sydney Young, Pte.
6480, Burns, John, Pte.
6481, Buckingham, James Roger, Pte.
6482, Brown, Herbert Oscar, Pte.
6483, Brunton, Andrew, Pte.
6485, Brain, Frank, Pte.
6487, Burrows, Ronald Allen, Pte.
6488, Bloxsome, Charles Enos, Pte.
6489, Charman, Ralph William, Pte.
6490, Chambers, Henry James, Pte.
6491, Cox, Rupert Henry, Pte.
6492, Campbell, William Flemming, Pte.
6493, Clark, Donald Goldie, Pte.
6494, Clark, Alexander, Pte.
6496, Carter, Ernest, Pte.
6497, Dalgleish, George, Pte.
6498, Davidson, Christopher, Pte.
6499, Darcy, Charles Michael, Pte.
6501, Demasson, Hubert Peter, Pte.
6502, Donaldson, David Nelson, Pte.
6503, Ecclestone, John Josiah, Pte.
6504, Evans, Norman James, Pte.
6506, Edwards, Alfred Davies, Pte.
6508, Evans, Ernest, Pte.
6509, Ferguson, Arthur Percival, Pte.
6510, Fulton, Frank, Pte.
6511, Fredrickson, Frans Oscar, Pte.
6512, Fancote, Charles, Pte.
6513, Flynn, John Augustine, Pte.
6514, Greenlees, Daniel, Pte.
6515, Gregory, Charles, Pte.
6516, Goodchild, Paul Franklyn Joseph, Pte.
6517, Grover, Percy Robert, Pte.
6518, Green, Victor Mainwaring, Pte.
6519, Ganson, Horatio, Pte.
6520, Grant, Duncan, Pte.
6521, Gower, Thomas Henry, Pte.
6522, Hobson, James William, Pte.
6523, Hayes, Samuel John, Pte.
6524, Harris, Carl Francis, Pte.
6525, Harrington, William Joseph, Pte.
6526, Higgins, Frederick, Pte.
6527, Harrison, Henry, Pte.
6528, Hehir, Frederick, Pte.
6529, Hughes, James, Pte.
6530, Henderson, Charles Stewart, Pte.
6531, Johnson, Frank William, Pte.
6532, Jackman, Thomas William, Pte.
6533, Jenkin, William Thomas, Pte.
6534, Kern, Edward Henry, Pte.
6535, Kerr, William George, Pte.
6536, Linsey, Robert Joseph, Pte.
6537, Lord, Edward John, Pte.
6538, Lund, Douglas, Pte.
6539, Linnell, Albert Edgar, Pte.
6540, McDowell, William, Pte.
6542, Morrish, George, Pte.
6543, Murphy, John Blancy, Pte.
6544, McGill, Thomas, Pte.
6545, McIlwraith, Bernard Neill, Pte.
6546, MacDonald, Alexander, Pte.
6547, McNamara, John Leo, Pte.

THE OLD SIXTEENTH.

16th INFANTRY BATTALION—NOMINAL ROLL—continued.

21st Reinforcements—continued.

6548, McDougall, James McQueen, Pte.
6549, McKay, Stanley Sibbald, Pte.
6550, Marshall, William, Pte.
6551, McConnell, John, Pte.
6552, Martin, Richard Batley, Pte.
6553, Marsh, Claude Robert, Pte.
6554, McCann, William, Pte.
6555, Meredith, Benjamin Richard, Pte.
6556, Lindley, Cecil, Pte.
6557, McMahon, Joseph John, Pte.
6558, Mottram, Charles Francis, Pte.
6560, Maskiell, Walter Francis, Pte.
6561, Noble, James, Pte.
6562, Orr, Walter, Pte.
6563, Osborne, Frank Oliver, Pte.
6564, Prest, George William, Pte.
6565, Page, Nelson Victor, Pte.
6566, Preistley, Thomas, Pte.
6567, Phillips, Percy Fabian, Pte.
6568, Ruthven, Sydney William, Pte.
6569, Rhodes, John Edmond, Pte.
6570, Rosseiloty, John Burgh, Pte.
6571, Roberts, Thomas John, Pte.
6572, Roberts, James Arthur, Pte.
6573, Riseley, Alfred Ernest, Pte.
6574, Schilling, Robert Julius, Pte.
6575, Strand, Walter, Pte.
6576, Smith, John Thomas, Pte.
6577, Shreeve, Richard, Pte.
6578, Smith, John, Pte.
6579, Sells, James Prideaux, Pte.
6580, Smith, Percy, Pte.
6581, Slight, John Walter, Pte.
6582, Sloss, Thomas William, Pte.
6583, Schultze, Leonard Oscar, Pte.
6584, Simcock, Victor George Lionel, Pte.
6585, Todhunter, Henry, Pte.
6586, Thomas, Joseph, Pte.
6587, Townsend, Francis, Pte.
6588, Troyle, Konrat Jank, Pte.
6589, Taylor, Arthur Ernest, Pte
6590, Uff, Thomas John, Pte.
6592, Vaughan, Arthur Langdon, Pte.
6593, Ward, Charles, Pte.
6594, Williams, William Thomas, Pte.
6595, Wood, Victor Roy Neville, Pte.
6596, Wallbank, Joseph, Pte.
6597, Whittingham, Harry, Pte.
6598, Whitten, James Sibley, Pte.
6599, White, Cecil James, Pte.
6600, Wareing, George, Pte.
6601, Wood, Ernest, Pte.
6602, Young, John Lorenzo, Pte.
6604, McEntee, Angus Norman, Pte.
6605, Dymock, James Alfred, Pte.
6606, Eriksen, Christen, Pte.
6607, Hart, Sidney, Pte.
6616, McNamee, James, Pte.
6619, Morris, John Thomas, Pte.
6620, Symes, Frederick Charles, Pte.
6622, Larwood, Alfred, Pte.
6623, Milton, Albert Tom, Pte.
6624, Drew, William, Pte.
6609, Fripp, William George Giles, Pte.
6610, Cooper, Ernest Garnet, Pte.
6611, Dickenson, Herbert, Pte.
6612, Dunn, Frank Albert, Pte.
6614, Wilson, James Fenwick, Pte.

22nd Reinforcements.

(Embarked at Fremantle, Western Australia, on H.M.A.T. A8, "Argyllshire," 9th November, 1916.)

Lathlain, Frank Byford, 2nd Lt.
Hillman, Herbert Ralph, 2nd Lt.
3160, Petrie, George, Pte.
4145, Knowles, Henry, Pte.
6701, Bales, George Thomas, Pte.
6702, Carson, Wilfred Harold, Pte.
6703, Lechmer, Robert Thomas, Pte.
6704, Loaring, Harold Archie, Pte.
6705, Bay, Albert Mervyn, Pte
6706, Cook, William Thomas, Pte.
6707, Nelson, William August, Pte.
6708, Ottaway, Herbert George, Pte.
6709, Palmer, William Thomas, Pte.
6710, Sara, Edgar Wilfred, Pte.
6711, Smith, Ernest Albert, Pte.
6713, Williams, Francis Gilbert, Pte.
6716, Andrews, Frederick Joseph, Pte.
6717, Armstrong, Leslie, Pte.
6718, Ammon, Thomas, Pte.
6719, Aspinall, George Henry, Pte.
6721, Backman, Evert Isidor, Pte.

THE OLD SIXTEENTH.

16th INFANTRY BATTALION—NOMINAL ROLL—*continued.*

22nd Reinforcements —continued.

6722, Bailey, Robert Prior, Pte.
6723, Baker, William Ernest Charles, Pte.
6724, Birch, Harold Ernest, Pte.
6725, Bowden, Jeremiah, Pte.
6726, Bowen, Charles Herbert, Pte.
6727, Bradshaw, Francis George, Pte
6728, Brown, Thomas, Pte.
6729, Baird, Patrick David, Pte.
6730, Bromberg, Julias Maurice, Pte.
6731, Bloomer, George Christopher, Pte.
6732, Cale, Harold James, Pte.
6733, Cameron, Kenneth, Pte.
6734, Carlyon, John Samson, Pte.
6735, Carson, Vivian Harry, Pte.
6736, Cary, Walter Joseph, Pte.
6737, Castle, Francis Gabriel, Pte.
6738, Clipstone, Stanley Carlyle, Pte.
6739, Cohen, Alexander, Pte.
6740, Corke, Harold Johnstone, Pte.
6741, Criddle, Sydney James, Pte.
6742, Criddle, Horace John, Pte.
6743, Crowder, Robert John, Pte.
6744, Curness, George William, Pte.
6745, Chester, Sydney, Pte
6746, Cross, William Joseph, Pte.
6747, Clark, Bertram, Pte.
6748, Coyle, Albert, Pte.
6749, Daley, James Francis, Pte.
6750, Dods, John Rutherford, Pte.
6751, Dolton, Leslie Arthur, Pte.
6752, Drummond, Arthur Sydney, Pte.
6753, Duerden, William, Pte.
6754, Duff, Thomas, Pte.
6755, Dunbar, Thomas William, Pte.
6756, Eakins, George Cyril, Pte.
6757, Edmonds, John, Pte.
6758, Ellis, Henry, Pte.
6759, Evans, Walter Stanley Edward, Pte.
6760, Ferguson, Hurtle Henry, Pte.
6761, Fitzsimons, William John, Pte.
6762, Flanagan, John Richard, Pte.
6763, Fowles, Frederick William, Pte.
6764, Francis, Charles Leslie Claude, Pte.
6765, Francis, Reginald Conrad, Pte.
6766, Frood, James Bennett, Pte.
6767, Geyer, Charles Henry, Pte.
6768, Gidley, Edward, Pte.
6769, Gracie, Louis, Pte.
6770, Grant, Peter Donaldson, Pte.
6771, Grieve, James, Pte.
6772, Groessler, Eugene Lawrence, Pte.
6773, Hannan, Albert Charles, Pte.
6774, Hayto, Percy Bosworth, Pte.
6775, Hayton, Stanley Clyde, Pte.
6776, Hendry, William George, Pte.
6779, Hill, Frank, Pte.
6780, Hogan, William Edward, Pte.
6782, Jones, Chevilly Thomas, Pte.
6783, Joy, Thomas, Pte.
6784, Kelsall, Joseph, Pte.
6785, Lambert, Harold Stanley, Pte.
6786, Ledsham, Leicester Inis Forbes, Pte.
6787, Lockyer, Philip, Pte.
6788, Little, Richard, Alexander, Pte.
6789, Lowth, Samuel Thomas, Pte.
6790, Lummis, George Henry, Pte.
6791, Malmgren, Oscar Hilding, Pte.
6793, May, Richard Oswald, Pte.
6794, McCardey, Edward Joseph, Pte.
6795, McDonald, Donald, Pte.
6796, Moloney, Thomas, Pte.
6797, Moore, David Vernon, Pte.
6798, Moughton, John Haigh, Pte.
6800, Newby, George Arthur, Pte.
6801, Newman, Alfred Charles, Pte.
6803, Nicholas, John Briscoe, Pte.
6804, Noonan, James Edward, Pte.
6805, Nettleton, George, Pte.
6806, O'Brien, Patrick Joseph, Pte.
6807, Palmer, Ernest Allan, Pte.
6808, Parker, Thomas, Pte.
6809, Parry, George Elwell, Pte.
6810, Parvin, Leonard Rawson, Pte.
6811, Pember, Barnabas Leslie, Pte.
6813, Penter, Henry Alfred, Pte.
6814, Porter, Charles Leary, Pte.
6815, Powell, Isaac Robert, Pte.
6816, Powell, Robert Henry, Pte.
6817, Press, William Stevens, Pte.
6818, Prime, George Henri Garnet, Pte.
6819, Pulley, Frederick James, Pte.
6820, Ramsey, David, Pte.
6821, Rayner, Austin Alfred, Pte.
6822, Roberts, Francis Sydney, Pte.
6823, Russ, Alfred George, Pte.
6824, Sainsbury, Stanley Francis, Pte.
6825, Sergeant, Edward George, Pte.
6826, Shaw, Stanley, Pte.
6827, Simms, William, Pte.
6828, Sinclair, Clarence McIntosh Ringwood, Pte.

16th INFANTRY BATTALION—NOMINAL ROLL—continued.

22nd Reinforcements—continued.

6829, Singleton, Henry, Pte.
6830, Smith, Herbert Edward Buckley, Pte.
6831, Stanley, Thomas, Pte.
6832, Sharpe, Samuel, Pte.
6833, Stephenson, Joseph Whitford, Pte.
6834, Sullivan, Jack, Pte.
6837, Taylor, Andrew, Pte.
6838, Trew, Edward Maurice, Pte.
6839, Vagg, Harold Pte.
6840, Wallace, Charles, Pte.
6841, Wallis, George, Pte.
6842, Ward, William Francis, Pte.
6843, Warren, William Henry, Pte.
6844, Weston, Frank Cecil, Pte.
6845, Wheatley, Thomas Harold, Pte.
6847, Wisher, Stewart Fredrick, Pte.
6848, Withers, Ernest David, Pte.
6849, Worthington, Charles Boldan, Pte.
6851, Walsh, Matthew, Pte.
6852, Bickley, Thomas George, Pte.
6853, Hislop, David Knox, Pte.
6854, Mumme, Charles Edward, Pte.
6855, Timewell, Frank Arthur, Pte.
6856, Butchard, William Edward, Pte.
6857, Cosgrave, David, Pte.
6858, Sealey, George, Pte.
6859, Williams, James Thomas, Pte.
6860, Wishart, William Frederick, Pte.
6861, Stanley, George, Pte.
6862, Bradley, John Ramsden, Pte.
6863, Burns, Charles, Pte.

23rd Reinforcements.

(Embarked at Fremantle, Western Australia, on H.M.A.T. A35, "Berrima," 23rd December, 1916.)

Martin, Allan, 2nd Lt.
Webster, Frank Irwin, 2nd Lt.
R706, Hall, William, Pte.
R1586, Bennett, Clarence Gilbert, Pte.
R2521, Rushby, George Edward, Pte.
6946, Bradshaw, George William, Pte.
6947, Hughes, John Richard, Pte.
6948, Parkin, Joseph Perry, Pte.
6949, Marshall, William, Pte.
6950, Bonnett, Reginald, Pte.
6952, Donald, Thomas Alan, Pte.
6953, Dewar, Alexander, Pte.
6954, Dreyer, Robert De Villiers, Pte.
6955, Tillotson, Arthur Herbert, Pte.
6956, McDowell, Stewart Arthur, Pte.
6957, Alcock, Hamilton, Pte.
6958, Ashton, William, Pte
6959, Andrews, John William, Pte.
6960, Austin, Frederick James, Pte.
6961, Brown, Alfred, Pte.
6962, Bates, John Thomas, Pte.
6963, Berryman, George, Pte.
6964, Burridge, Charles Thomas, Pte.
6965, Burnett, Richard Edward, Pte.
6967, Bedford, Ernest Everett, Pte.
6968, Bevan, Charles, Pte.
6969, Beck, Waldemar, Pte.
6970, Boddy, Jack, Pte.
6972, Carter, Harold John, Pte.
6973, Capell, Charles, Pte.
6974, Chapman, Clarence Wilfred, Pte.
6975, Clelland, William, Pte.
6976, Copeland, Edward, Pte.
6978, Collins, Archibald, Pte.
6979, Carter, Albert John, Pte.
6980, Cranstoun, Jack Cuthbert, Pte.
6981, Clayton-Bridges, Frederick, Pte
6983, Dixon, Edgar William, Pte.
6984, Dick, John Struin Robertson, Pte.
6985, Durrant, George Henry, Pte.
6986, Deveson, Alfred James, Pte.
6987, Evans, William John, Pte.
6988, Elsegood, Roy Reginald, Pte.
6989, Ferguson, Moses Allan, Pte.
6990, Fenwick, Alfred John, Pte.
6993, Frost, Arthur Cecil, Pte.
6994, Frazer, Thomas, Pte.
6995, Forsyth, Joseph Greig, Pte.
6996, Forster, Alexander Coulton, Pte.
6997, Fisher, Reginald Clive, Pte.
6998, Greenwood, Joe, Pte.
7000, Gathercole, John, Pte.
7002, Gray, John, Pte.

16th INFANTRY BATTALION—NOMINAL ROLL—continued.
23rd Reinforcements—continued.

7003, Grant, John William Mortimer, Pte.
7004, Green, Vernon Roy, Pte.
7006, Holmberg, Edward, Pte
7007, Hayson, Edward Lewis, Pte.
7008, Hexamer, Phillip, Pte.
7009, Henningsen, George Henry, Pte.
7010, Hogan, Leo David, Pte.
7011, Hodge, George, Pte.
7012, Hurlston, Bert John, Pte.
7013, Hart, Albert, Pte.
7015, House, Robert John, Pte.
7016, Host, John, Pte.
7017, Hagan, John, Pte.
7018, Hanrahan, Edwin Patrick, Pte.
7020, Harrington, Reginald Humphrey, Pte.
7021, Hodges, Frank, Pte.
7022, Hager, James, Pte.
7024, Hother, Stuart Killick, Pte.
7025, Johnstone, Michael John, Pte.
7026, Jordan, Charles Reginald, Pte.
7027, Jaeschke, Gerald Victor, Pte.
7028, Jones, William Percy, Pte.
7029, Jackson, Joseph, Pte
7030, King, Howard Ernest, Pte.
7032, King, Albert Edward, Pte.
7033, Lucas, Cecil, Pte.
7034, Leonard, Frederick, Pte.
7035, Lauriston, James, Pte.
7036, Lobb, Frederick Charles, Pte.
7037, Lukies, William, Pte.
7038, Laurence, James Duncan, Pte.
7039, Lawrance, George Vincent, Pte.
7040, Lawson, Hans, Pte.
7041, Lee, Arthur Joseph, Pte.
7043, McKenna, George Edward, Pte.
7044, McNess, Charles, Pte.
7046, Mitchell, Alex., Pte.
7048, Masters, Cornelius Edward, Pte.
7049, Murray, William Charles, Pte.
7053, Nolan, Vivian Michael, Pte.
7054, Nelson, Alfred Ernest, Pte.
7055, Nelson, Thomas Henry, Pte
7056, O'Donnell, Martin, Pte.
7057, Purser, James Hartell, Pte.
7058, Pulley, Thomas Henry, Pte.
7059, Peeffer, Richard Charles, Pte.
7060, Patterson, Jack, Pte.
7061, Patterson, Charles James, Pte.
7062, Paxman, Ernest Jason, Pte.
7063, Rose, Herbert, Pte.
7064, Robinson, Arthur, Pte.
7065, Rommeis, Christian Frederick, Pte.
7066, Ranger, Arthur James, Pte.
7069, Ross, Frank, Pte.
7070, Sorensen, Neil Albert Valdeman, Pte.
7071, Stratford, Herbert George, Pte.
7072, Spelman, Arthur Augustus, Pte.
7073, Schicklering, Percy, Pte.
7074, Sawyer, William Frederick, Pte.
7075, Stanley, Robert Leonard, Pte.
7076, Stoer, William Rudolph, Pte.
7078, Sangster, Charles Arthur, Pte.
7080, Thompson, Henry Thomas, Pte.
7081, Thompson, Ralph, Pte.
7082, Taylor, William Henry, Pte.
7083, Tillotson, Charles, Pte.
7084, Uren, Richard Leslie, Pte.
7085, Watson, Arnold David, Pte.
7086, Watts, Edward, Pte.
7087, Wynn, Reginald Charles, Pte.
7088, Walker, George, Pte.
7089, Williams, Alfred Robert, Pte.
7090, Wilson, Robert Affleck, Pte.
7091, Weiss, Joseph, Pte.
7092, Williams, George Clarence, Pte.
7095, Zerk, Alfred Ernest, Pte.
7096, Baseden, Jack, Pte.
7097, Cooke, Wesley John, Pte.
7098, Roberts, Walter Arnold Raymond, Pte.
7099, Wylie, Matthew, Pte.
7100, Bailey, Christopher Stuart, Pte.
7102, Mofflin, Horace Edgar, Pte.
7103, James, Philip Charles, Pte.
7104, Kirk, Percy, Pte.
7107, Manders, Richard Clive, Pte.
7108, Leisk, Edward Hutton, Pte.
7109, Parkinson, Alfred Henry, Pte.
7110, Lewis-Kelly, Harry, Pte.
7111, Eggleston, Tom, Pte.
7112, Holt, Hubert Henry, Pte.
7113, Geale, Philip, Pte.
7114, Barnes, Henry, Pte.
7115, Vallender, Phillip, Pte.
7116, Jones, Francis John, Pte.
7117, Epis, Mattia, Pte.
7118, Roberts, William Henry, Pte.

16th INFANTRY BATTALION—NOMINAL ROLL—*continued.*

23rd Reinforcements—continued.

7119, Rogers, William George Owen, Pte.
7120, Folwell, John, Pte.
7121, Slattery, Joseph Gregory, Pte.

24th Reinforcements.

(Embarked at Fremantle, Western Australia, per H.M.A.T. A28, "Miltiades," 29th January, 1917.)

Paull, Peter Raphael, Captain.
Senior, Joseph George Frederick, 2nd Lieut.
7191, Scott, Alexander Paterson, Pte.
7192, Outridge, Harrie Rutherford, Pte.
7193, Van Raalte, Peter Emanuel, Pte.
7194, Parham, Arthur Frank, Pte.
7195, Hooper, Stanley, Pte.
7196, Prior, Charles, Pte.
7197, Woodward, James, Pte.
7198, McMahon, Peter Thomas, Pte.
7199, Glover, Arthur Milton, Pte.
7200, Neville, Willie, Pte.
7201, Tomlinson, Percy, Pte.
7202, Bromham, Louis Frederick, Pte.
7203, Anderson, Frederick James, Pte.
7204, Atkins, John Robert, Pte.
7205, Allison, Frederick James, Pte.
7206, Burnham, James, Pte.
7207, Bennett, William John, Pte.
7208, Ball, George, Pte.
7210, Baird, Charles Frederick, Pte.
7211, Barrett, Alfred Jack, Pte.
7212, Brickhill, Leonard Bromley, Pte.
7213, Barrass, John James, Pte.
7214, Berger, John, Pte.
7215, Butler, Edwin Elliott, Pte.
7216, Clements, John Thomas, Pte.
7217, Campbell, Donald Clyde, Pte.
7218, Clark, Victor Stanley, Pte.
7221, Connell, William Cross, Pte.
7222, Criddle, Athol Douglas, Pte.
7223, Dawson, Albert Charles Oscar, Pte.
7225, Eley, Charles Henry, Pte.
7226, Elliott, Joseph Mitchell, Pte.
7228, Fariss, Thomas John, Pte.
7229, Fitzgerald, John, Pte.
7230, Follick, Alexander Clifton, Pte.
7231, Flinn, Thomas Sydney, Pte.
7232, Furness, George Elwyn, Pte.
7233, Ferguson, William Kilpatrick, Pte.
7234, Forsyth, Andrew Soutar, Pte.
7235, Gillies, Alexander William, Pte.
7237, Green, John, Pte.
7238, Gorton, Sydney Maurice, Pte.
7239, Gwynne, Charles Edmond, Pte.
7240, Garlick, Clive Lancelot, Pte.
7241, Gamble, Frederick Charles, Pte.
7242, Hough, Colville, Pte.
7245, Halpin, Thomas Stephen, Pte.
7246, Hardy, Henry, Pte.
7247, Hall, George, Pte.
7248, Hughes, Thomas, Pte.
7249, Hehir, Patrick Vincent, Pte.
7250, Holmes, Ernest, Pte.
7251, Holder, Harry, Pte.
7252, Hume, Robert Schofield, Pte.
7253, Huntley, John Addison, Pte.
7254, Hayles, Albert Hansell, Pte.
7255, Henderson, James, Pte.
7256, Jones, Robert, Pte.
7257, Jupp, Percy, Pte.
7258, Joyce, Matthew, Pte.
7259, Knight, Charles Henry, Pte.
7260, Keane, Sydney Gunson, Pte.
7261, Knott, Cecil Harold, Pte.
7262, Kelly, Jervoise William, Pte.
7263, Liedle, Vincent, Pte.
7264, Lenneberg, Frank Benjamin, Pte.
7266, Lawson, Frederick Gustave, Pte.
7267, Mallen, John Mortimer, Pte.
7268, Massey, Edward James, Pte.
7269, Munro, Donald, Pte.
7270, Mitchell, John Henry, Pte.
7271, Melling, William, Pte.
7272, Minchin, Lionel James, Pte.
7273, Meller, Arthur, Pte.
7274, McWhirr, Peter, Pte.
7275, Nicholls, Richard, Pte.
7276, Nelson, Robert Bruce, Pte.
7277, O'Connell, James Adolphus, Pte.
7278, Outen, George Edward, Pte.
7280, O'Keeffe, Maurice, Pte.
7282, Olive, Stanley Lockwood, Pte.

THE OLD SIXTEENTH.

16th INFANTRY BATTALION—NOMINAL ROLL—*continued.*

24th Reinforcements—continued.

7284, Pugh, Frank Reginald Hendy, Pte.
7285, Potter, James George, Pte.
7287, Palmer, John Gregory, Pte.
7289, Roycroft, John Edward, Pte.
7290, Reith, David, Pte.
7291, Rankin, John Neil, Pte.
7292, Rankin, William Harper, Pte.
7293, Ray, William Edward, Pte.
7295, Reycraft, Cecil Layton, Pte.
7296, Reed, Edwin Lawrence, Pte
7297, Sinclair, Frederick William, Pte.
7298, Stanfield, William, Pte.
7300, Sherlock, William George, Pte.
7301, Stone, Walter, Pte.
7302, Suraski, Andrew John, Pte.
7303, Strother, Joseph James, Pte.
7305, Stafford, Martin Joseph, Pte.
7306, Stooke, Walter, Pte.
7307, Smallwood, William, Pte.
7308, Sinclair, Frederick Ringwood, Pte.
7309, Stephens, George Alexander, Pte.
7310, Snook, Stanley Eaton, Pte.
7311, Smith, John Donald, Pte.
7312, Stokes, Cyril Alfred, Pte.
7314, Trigwell, Randal James, Pte.
7315, Tredinnick, Nicholas Moreton, Pte.
7317, Thorpe, Harold, Pte.
7318, Turner, Norman James, Pte.
7319, Turner, Albert Harold, Pte.
7320, Vognsen, Carl, Pte.
7321, Watson, Herbert Charles, Pte.
7322, Wymond, Alnozo Pearse, Pte.
7323, Wymond, Beaumont Stocker, Pte.
7324, Weller, Albert Edward, Pte.
7325, Williams, Edward George, Pte.
7326, Woods, Francis Joseph, Pte.
7327, Waller, Arthur, Pte.
7328, Wulff, Harry William, Pte.
7329, Walker, John, Pte.
7330, Watt, Frederick George, Pte.
7331, Williams, George Loranda, Pte.
7332, Yde, Ernest Allen John, Pte.
7333, Whittington, Ernest William, Pte.
7334, Murray, James Nichol, Pte.
7335, McPherson, Neil McInnes, Pte.
7336, McManus, George, Pte.
7338, Sladden, Clarence Otto, Pte.
7339, Brown, Harold Joseph, Pte.
7340, Cornish, Herbert Ernest, Pte.
7341, Gladstone, Rupert, Pte.
7342, Spice, Herbert Kenneth, Pte.
7343, Weatherall, Samuel, Pte.
7344, Eichler, Charles William Frederick, Pte.
7345, Garnett, Benjamin Francis, Pte.
7346, Chapman, Stanley, Pte.
7347, Downes, Thomas George, Pte.
7348, Downing, William, Pte.
7349, Paul, John Albert, Pte.
7351, Hayden, Alfred, Pte.
7352, Hansen, Ernest, Pte.
7353, Weller, Stanley John, Pte.
7354, Richardson, Cyril Kelly St. John, Pte.
7355, Gladwell, Alfred William, Pte.
7356, Smith, Thomas Alfred, Pte.
7357, Stokes, Ernest Athol, Pte.
7358, Foody, William, Pte.
7359, Potter, William John, Pte.
7360, Lucas, Henry Grattan, Pte.
7361, Smyth, Michael, Pte.

25th Reinforcements.

(Embarked at Fremantle, Western Australia, per H.M.A.T. A30, "Borda," 29th June, 1917.)

Aberle, Frederick John, 2nd Lieut.
Muir, Alan Campbell, 2nd Lt.
409, Jones, William John, Pte.
898, Dickson, Fred, Pte.
1038, Randles, Albert Henry, Pte.
1056, Kenny, Reginald Thomas, Pte.
2419, Warren, Denzel William, Pte.
2896, Westaway, James Gilles, Pte.
2947, Adshead, John Leonard, Pte.
3179, Lawson, James Patrick, Pte
3488, Higgins, John Thomas, Pte.
3527a, Cox, William, Pte.
3527, Campbell, Matthew Samuel Lawson, Pte.
5294, Aitchison, James, Pte.
5755, Thomas, William Francis, Pte.
6540, McCarthy, Michael John, Pte.
6622, Cox, William Edwin, Pte.
6650, Williams, Edwin Daniel, Pte.
6809, Delaney, Charles, Pte.
6814, Gannaway, George, Pte.

16th INFANTRY BATTALION—NOMINAL ROLL—continued.

25th Reinforcements—continued.

6825, Mills, John William, Pte.
6843, Strickland, Thomas Claude, Pte.
7246, Hede, Francis Joseph, Pte.
7436, Roberts, Frank, Sgt.
7437, Stubbs, Henry Arthur, Sgt.
7438, Parker, John Melville, Sgt.
7439, Dugdale, Richard, Pte.
7440, Ford, John Henry, Pte.
7441, Gardiner, Branat Richmond, Pte.
7442, Moore, Donald Ross, Pte.
7443, Hutt, Alfred Edmund, Pte.
7444, Manners, Charles Brown, Pte.
7445, O'Rourke, William Alfred, Pte.
7446, Sleep, Charles, Pte.
7447, Allen, Arthur Edward, Pte.
7449, Nunn, George William, Pte.
7450, Gittins, Alfred, Pte.
7451, Andrews, Edward John, Pte.
7452, Bird, Samuel, Pte.
7453, Bow, Wilfred George, Pte.
7454, Brennan, Charles Edward, Pte.
7455, Bull, Charles Ripley, Pte.
7457, Bartlett, James, Pte.
7458, Fisher, Douglas Tasman, Pte.
7459, Cunnold, John Thomas, Pte.
7460, Clifford, James, Pte.
7461, Collins, Reuben Henry, Pte.
7462, Evans, Charles, Pte.
7463, Chadwick, Charles, Pte.
7464, Bennett, Henry Hosking, Pte.
7465, Howlett, Samuel James, Pte.
7466, Cooper, Wilfred George, Pte.
7467, Dyer, Ira Ernest, Pte.
7468, Elliott, Alfred, Pte.
7471, Fraser, Gordon Colin Campbell, Pte.
7472, Blakey, Leslie Nettleton, Pte.
7473, Fry, Thomas Leonard, Pte.
7474, Fryer-Smith, Richard, Pte.
7475, Gealer, Trophimus George, Pte.
7476, Gill, Frederick William, Pte.
7477, Gill, John James, Pte.
7478, Gillett, Townley, Pte.
7479, Grant, Alexander Dunlop, Pte.
7480, Hall, James, Pte.
7481, Flanagan, John, Pte.
7482, Henry, George Cyril, Pte.
7483, Henry, Leslie Robert, Pte.
7484, Hewitt, Ernest Henry, Pte.
7485, Higgins, Thomas, Pte.
7486, Hill, Donald, Cpl.
7488, Hope, Percy Thomas Lloyd, Pte.
7489, Jones, Evan, Pte.
7490, Jolly, Walter Henry Rogers, Pte.
7491, Johnson, Roy, Pte.
7492, Kelly, Ernest Roger, Pte.
7493, Kelly, Joseph Thomas Patrick, Pte.
7494, Turner, Henry Newtown, Pte.
7495, Keeffe, Charles Isaac, Pte.
7496, Kiely, John, Pte.
7497, Kilpatrick, Samuel Walter Alexander, Pte.
7498, King, George Chapman, Pte.
7499, Kern, Ernest Stanley, Pte.
7500, Lane, Cecil Arthur, Pte.

7501, Wilshusen, James, Pte.
7502, Lintott, Thomas, Pte.
7503, Longmuir, Douglas Charles, Pte.
7504, Laurance, John Wallace, Pte.
7505, Lindsay, George, Pte.
7506, Markillie, Arthur, Pte.
7510, McIntosh, John Francis, Pte.
7513, McNally, Walter, Pte.
7514, McDermott, Clarence Leslie, Pte.
7516, Miller, Alexander Cook, Pte.
7517, Mitchell, Edward Benjamin, Pte.
7518, Neil, Henry McCleland, Pte.
7519, Muller, Ernest, Pte.
7520, McDonald, Alexander, Pte.
7521, Needham, Charles Alfred, Pte.
7523, Nicholson, Otto Nelson, Pte
7524, Jordan, Francis Rupert Stanley, Pte.
7525, Parker, Charles Arthur, Pte.
7526, Owens, George, Pte.
7527, O'Mara, Frederick, Pte.
7528, O'Mara, Joseph, Pte.
7529, Platton, Everet, Pte.
7530, Pomeroy, Laurance Alfred, Pte.
7531, Priest, Emanual, Pte.
7532, Shillington, William Lowry, Pte.
7533, Prince, Ernest Edward, Pte.
7534, Read, Ernest Albert, Pte.
7535, Rees, Richard, Pte.
7536, Reeves, Francis William, Pte.
7537, Robinson, Stanley Fortescue, Pte.
7539, Sage, Frederick Wycliffe, Pte.
7540, Sands, Albert Victor, Pte.
7542, Schultz, John Thomas, Pte.
7545, Spiller, Henry, Pte.

THE OLD SIXTEENTH.

16th INFANTRY BATTALION—NOMINAL ROLL—*continued*.

25th Reinforcements—continued.

7546, Thomas, Hector Frederick George, Pte.
7547, Taaffe, John Edward, Pte.
7548, Tate, George, Pte.
7549, Treasure, Francis Henry, Pte.
7550, Turner, Arthur, Pte.
7551, Way, Henry Victor, Pte.
7552, Weston, Albert Edward, Pte.
7553, Watkins, Douglas Oswald, Pte.
7554, Wheeler, Charles George, Pte.
7555, Wolfe, Richard Travers, Pte.
7556, Wolfe, Frank, Pte.
7560, Workman, John Alexander, Pte.
7561, Childs, Frank, Pte.
7562, McGilvray, Robert, Pte.
7564, Johnston, Jack Albert, Pte.
7566, Walsh, Aloysius Joseph, Pte.
7567, Burns, Stephen, Pte.
7568, Fannon, Patrick, Pte.

7570, Billett, Herbert Edward, Pte.
7572, Hayes, Ernest Ignatius, Pte.
7574, Budge, William David, Pte.
7575, Larwoood, John Thomas, Pte.
7576, O'Neill, William Joseph, Pte.
7577, Reed, George, Pte.
7578, Wiseman, William Alexander, Pte.
7579, Walker, John William, Pte.
7580, Nuttall, William Charles, Pte.
7581, Cleaver, Bertie, Pte.
7582, Hale, Norman Francis Aubrey, Pte.
7583, Smyth, Frank, Pte.
7584, Wood, Clifford, Pte.
7585, George, Thomas, Pte.
7586, Criddle, Lewis Albert, Pte.
7587, Annakin, Cecil Heath, Pte.
7588, Coles, Wilfred James, Pte.

26th Reinforcements.

(Embarked at Sydney, New South Wales, per H.M.A.T. A7. "Medic," 1st August, 1917.)

Moss, Morrie Melville, 2nd Lt. (Hon. Lieut.)
Piesse, Bertram Charles Leslie, 2nd Lieut.
3529, Ninnes, Charley, Pte.
7381, Hodge, John, Pte.
7681, Slater, Harry Osborne, Sgt.
7682, Cockburn, William Alexander, Pte.
7683, Dimond, Wilfred Robert Major, Pte.
7684, Linwood, George Alexander, Pte.
7685, Cooper, William Henry, Sgt.
7687, Taylor, Norman Rayson, Pte.
7688, Horne, Albert Edward, Pte.
7689, Canny, Denis Atkinson, Pte.
7690, Kendall, Richard Ferguson, Pte.
7691, Salmon, Ralph Winter, Pte.
7692, Day, Henry Stuart, Pte.
7693, Bantock, Howard Granville, Pte.
7695, Allan, James, Pte.
7696, Amos, Ernest, Pte.
7697, Arkell, Percy James, Pte.
7698, Arnold, Herbert William, Pte.
7699, Ashford, Allen Fawcett, Pte.
7700, Baker, John Albert Henry, Pte.
7701, Bale, Henry James, Pte.
7702, Barbier, Louis, Pte.

7703, Barrington, John, Pte.
7704, Bateman, Henry George, Pte.
7706, Berich, Tom, Pte.
7707, Bevis, Leonard Clarence, Pte.
7708, Biggerstaff, Ernest, Pte.
7709, Biss, Frederick Genery, Pte.
7710, Black, John Brownlie, Pte.
7711, Bowen, Frederick Ebenezer, Pte.
7713, Bradley, Nicholas Mervyn, Pte.
7715, Carter, John Henry, Pte.
7716, Cathcart, William Rea, Pte.
7717, Clunas, John Clark, Pte.
7718, Collins, Cornelius William, Pte.
7720, Craik, John, Pte.
7721, Darragh, James, Pte.
7722, Day, Clarence James, Pte.
7723, Dedman, Thomas William, Pte.
7725, Dixon, Edward John, Pte.
7726, Dodd, Norman, Pte.
7727, Dornan, Leslie Cyril, Pte.
7728, Dower, Henry Joseph, Pte.
7729, Dunlop, Andrew, Pte.
7730, Ellingworth, Charles Henry, Pte.
7731, Evans, Frederic Herbert, Pte.
7732, Fairgrieve, Negonde Juliein Pierre, Pte.
7733, Firth, James, Pte.
7734, Fleming, Hubert Luke, Pte.
7735, Forbes, Arthur Slade, Pte.

16th INFANTRY BATTALION—NOMINAL ROLL—*continued.*

26th Reinforcements—continued.

7736, Foweraker, Percy Frederick, Pte.
7737, Fraser, Neil Alexander, Pte.
7738, Fryer, Joseph Roy, Pte.
7740, Garmony, Hugh, Pte.
7741, Gellatly, Robert, Pte.
7742, Gershen, Morris, Pte.
7743, Gillespie, Eugene Anthony, Pte.
7744, Glass, James, Pte.
7745, Godfrey, Basil, Pte.
7746, Golding, William Thomas Henry, Pte.
7747, Grady, Arthur William, Pte.
7748, Hale, Arthur, Pte.
7750, Harris, Albert, Pte.
7751, Hayes, William Edward, Pte.
7752, Haynes, Jack May, Pte.
7753, Hill, Thomas Henry, Pte.
7754, Hill, William Hume, Pte.
7755, Holland, William, Pte.
7756, Horne, James, Pte.
7757, Horton, George William, Pte.
7759, Humphries, Cecil Digby, Pte.
7760, James, Oswald, Pte.
7761, Johnson, Herbert Austin, Pte.
7762, Johnson, Joseph, Pte.
7763, Jones, Albert George, Pte.
7764, Kerr, James Henry, Pte.
7765, Keyser, Herbert George, Pte.
7766, Kimber, Ernest Armadale, Pte.
7767, King, William, Pte.
7768, Kinsman, Royden Garnet, Pte.
7769, Knight, Edward, Pte.
7770, Lees, William Henry, Pte.
7771, Longman, Henry Robert, Pte.
7773, McCracken, John, Pte.
7774, McFarlane, Thomas, Pte.
7775, McGregor, Colin Anderson, Pte.
7776, McMath, James Francis, Pte.
7778, McVicar, William Henry Kaye, Pte.
7779, MacPherson, Trevor Charles Aneas, Pte.
7780, Moore, Harold Gilbert, Pte.
7781, Marsh, Roy Edward, Pte.
7782, Martin, Harold Percival, Pte.
7783, Mayes, Edward John, Pte.
7784, Mingkam, Albert, Pte.
7785, Mitchell, David, Pte.
7787, Myales, Frank, Pte.
7789, Nind, Augustus Pitt, Pte.
7790, Norrish, John Richard, Pte.
7792, Ogilvie, Wesley Douglas, Pte.
7793, Olsen, Andrew, Pte.
7794, Page, William Frederick, Pte.
7795, Patience, Frank Nicholas, Pte.
7796, Paull, Charles, Pte.
7797, Pawlson, Leslie Henry, Pte.
7798, Peacock, Bertie Henry, Pte.
7799, Pedley, William, Pte.
7800, Penn, John William Henry, Pte.
7802, Perrie, John, Pte.
7803, Pickles, John Richard, Pte.
7805, Powis, George, Pte.
7806, Price, Albert Victor, Pte.
7807, Proud, James, Pte.
7808, Pusey, Frederick, Pte.
7809, Quinn, James Stanley, Pte.
7811, Richardson, Henry Howard, Pte.
7813, Rosewall, Frederick, Pte.
7814, Rosewarne, Harold, Pte.
7815, Rowe, John Edgar, Pte.
7816, Rumble, Harry, Pte.
7817, Scott, David, Pte.
7818, Sellars, Ralph, Pte.
7819, Shaddick, John Frederick, Pte.
7820, Shade, James George, Pte.
7821, Sinclair, John Hugh, Pte.
7822, Sinnott, Henry Joseph, Pte.
7824, Sparks, Hugo Sidney George, Pte.
7825, Strachan, Alfred Main Turnbull, Pte.
7826, Strang, Walter Ernest, Pte.
7827, Summons, John Frederick Albon, Pte.
7828, Sworn, Robert Cecil, Pte.
7829, Talbot, Walter Henry, Pte.
7830, Taylor, Arthur William, Pte.
7831, Taylor, Clifford Lorne, Pte.
7832, Taylor, Harold, Pte.
7833, Tilley, Edward Samuel George, Pte.
7834, Tostevin, Adolphus Theodore, Pte.
7835, Usher, Richard Henry Fancourt, Pte.
7836, Wallis, Harry, Pte.
7837, Warren, John Campbell Dale, Pte.
7838, Waters, Fred, Pte.
7840, Wells, Frank, Pte.
7842, Whitlock, Frank Cecil, Pte.
7843, Brown, James, Pte.
7844, Williams, James Henry, Pte.
7845, Worthy, Ralph, Pte.
7846, Bush, William, Pte.
7847, Carter, Alfred Walter, Pte.
7848, Elliott, Edward, Pte.
7850, Breeden, Sidney Arthur, Pte.
7851, Wells, Edward, Pte.

THE OLD SIXTEENTH.

16th INFANTRY BATTALION—NOMINAL ROLL—*continued.*

27th Reinforcements.

(Embarked at Fremantle, Western Australia, per S.S. "Canberra," 23rd November, 1917.)

Eggleston, William John, 2nd Lieut.
Davidson, Robert Ednie, 2nd Lieut.
3153, Morris, Henry Charles, Pte.
7926, McBride, Arthur, Company Sgt.-Major (W.O., Class II.)
7928, McLarty, Douglas, Pte.
7929, Wylie, James Hall, Pte.
7930, Philp, Garnet Hawkins, Pte.
7932, Lewis, Denis William, Pte.
7933, Fisher, Leslie Sutherland, Pte.
7934, Cook, Hubert Constant, Pte.
7935, Walker, Andrew Duncan, Pte.
7936, Forbes, Harold Dundee, Pte.
7938, Allen, Hamilton Edward, Pte.
7939, Appleton, Cecil Ernest, Pte.
7940, Ardagh, Walter Keith, Pte.
7942, Ashley, George, Pte.
7943, Barker, Francis William, Pte.
7944, Bandy, Arthur, Pte.
7945, Barnett, Barry, Pte.
7946, Bastian, Vernon Clyde, Pte.
7947, Bathurst, William Henry, Pte.
7948, Billings, John Henry, Pte.
7949, Breeze, Cecil James, Pte.
7950, Briggs, George, Pte.
7951, Brockman, Norman Alton Gordon, Pte.
7952, Browne, Albert, Pte.
7953, Buchanan, Alfred Percival, Pte.
7954, Bufton, Edward James, Pte.
7956, Burnett, Alan Robinson, Pte.
7958, Budd, Percy Denham, Pte.
7960, Cabassi, William John, Pte.
7963, Davies, Evan Morris, Pte.
7964, Cooke, Charles David, Pte.
7965, Daymond, Henry Vincent, Pte.
7966, Davison, George Reginald, Pte.
7967, Dewar, James Weir, Pte.
7968, Dyson, Matthew, Pte.
7971, Dowdell, John Ward, Pte.
7972, Dreyer, Alexander, Pte.
7973, Elston, Waltham Egbert Roy, Pte.
7974, Falls, John Patrick, Pte.
7975, Gallagher, Joseph, Pte.
7976, Garrett, John Henry, Pte.
7977, Gudgeon, Reuben, Pte.
7979, Hitchcock, Herbert Henry, Pte.
7982, Jarrett, William Lakey, Pte.
7983, Jefferies, Edward James, Pte.
7985, Johansen, Alexander, Pte.
7987, Joyce, Leslie Mervyn Vincent, Pte.
7989, Kerr, Basil Theodore, Pte.
7990, Kristiansen, Otto Ludwig, Pte.
7991, Lambert, Percy, Pte.
7992, Lawrence, Marshall, Pte.
7993, Le Boydre, Philip Louis, Pte.
7994, Lee, Laurence, Pte.
7995, Levy, Jacob Alfred, Pte.
7996, Marriott, Walter, Pte.
7997, Marshall, Henry Stuart, Pte.
7998, Martin, William Roy, Pte.
7999, Mathiasen, Carl Frederick, Pte.
8000, McAleavey, Robert, Pte.
8001, McArthur, Alexander, Pte.
8002, McCormick, William, Pte.
8003, McDougal, Charles, Pte.
8005, Molloy, Maximilian, Pte.
8006, Monti, Victor Bartholomew, Pte.
8007, Moseley, Edwin Otis, Pte.
8010, Newton, George Henry, Pte.
8012, Olsen, Henry, Pte.
8014, Parker, John, Pte.
8015, Palmer, Christopher, Pte.
8016, Preedy, Frederick, Pte.
8017, Rigby, Thomas, Pte.
8018, Robertson, John Finlayson, Pte.
8019, Rogers, William, Pte.
8021, Sharples, John, Pte.
8022, Sheldon, Norman Edwin, Pte.
8023, Simpson, James Jessopp Clarke, Pte.
8024, Simpson, Thomas Clarke, Pte.
8025, Smith, Harold Eaton, Pte.
8026, Smith, Thomas, Pte.
8027, Smith, Thomas Edward, Pte.
8028, Spencer, Victor William, Pte.
8029, Tanner, Roland Ivor, Pte.
8030, Taylor, William Henry, Pte.
8031, Thomas, Harry William, Pte.
8032, Tucker, Harry Arthur, Pte.
8033, Vaughan, Arthur Clement, Pte.
8035, Walton, George Albert, Pte.
8036, Wardell-Johnson, Frank, Pte.
8037, Watson, John Leonard, Pte.
8038, Whittle, Keith Haines, Pte.
8039, Whyte, John, Pte.
8041, Williams, Harry, Pte.
8043, White, John, Pte.
8044, Doak, Irwin James, Pte.

16th INFANTRY BATTALION—NOMINAL ROLL—*continued*.

27th **Reinforcements**--continued.

8045, Elder, George, Pte.
8049, Bannister, Charles Norman, Pte.
8050, Bradshaw, Roy, Pte.
8052, Cartledge, Mervyn Reginald, Pte.
8057, Green, Richard Underwood, Pte.
8061, Malcolm, William Douglas, Pte.
8062, Marchant, Neil Thomas, Pte.
8063, MacDonald, Donald Pearce, Pte.
8064, Nyman, Gustav, Pte.
8068, Whitton, Norman McGregor, Pte.
8069, Carlson, Harold Richard, Pte.
8070, Beaver, Joseph George, Pte.
8071, Turner, Aubrey, Pte.
8072, Lewis, Frederick Alfred, Pte.
14281, Woodward, George, Pte.
17035, Martin, Percy Francis, Pte.

www.ingramcontent.com/pod-product-compliance
Lightning Source LLC
Chambersburg PA
CBHW050338230426
43663CB00010B/1912